NCERT SOLUTIONS

With

Links to Video Solutions

Physics

Class XI

NCERT SOLUTIONS

With

Links to Video Solutions

Physics

Class XI

Ashish Arora
Mentor & Founder
PHYSICSGALAXY.COM
World's largest encyclopedia of online video lectures on High School Physics

G K Publications (P) Ltd

CAREER LAUNCHER INFRASTRUCTURE (P) LTD.

Edition 2020

ISBN : **978-93-90187-40-9**

Typeset by : *CLIP DTP Unit*

Administrative and Production Offices

Published by : **CLIP**

A-45, Mohan Cooperative Industrial Area,
Near Mohan Estate Metro Station,
New Delhi - 110044

Marketed by : **G.K. Publications (P) Ltd.**

A-45, Mohan Cooperative Industrial Area,
Near Mohan Estate Metro Station,
New Delhi - 110044

For product information :

Visit ***www.gkpublications.com*** or email to ***gkp@gkpublications.com***

Dedicated to

My Parents, Son, Daughter and

My beloved wife

About The Author

The complexities of Physics have given nightmares to many, but the homegrown genius of Jaipur- Ashish Arora has helped several students to live their dreams by decoding it.

Newton Law of Gravitation and Faraday's Magnetic force of attraction apply perfectly well with this unassuming genius. A Pied Piper of students, his webportal https://www.physicsgalaxy.com, The world's largest encyclopedia of video lectures on high school Physics possesses strong gravitational pull and magnetic attraction for students who want to make it big in life.

Ashish Arora, gifted with rare ability to train masterminds, has mentored over 10,000 IITians in his past 24 years of teaching sojourn including lots of students made it to Top 100 in IITJEE/ JEE(Advance) including AIR-1 and many in Top-10. Apart from that, he has also groomed hundreds of students for cracking International Physics Olympiad. No wonder his student Navneet Loiwal brought laurel to the country by becoming the first Indian to win a Gold medal at the 2000 - International Physics Olympiad in London (UK).

His special ability to simplify the toughest of the Physics theorems and applications rates him as one among the best Physics teachers in the world. With this, Arora simply defies the logic that perfection comes with age. Even at 18 when he started teaching Physics while pursuing engineering, he was as engaging as he is now. Experience, besides graying his hair, has just widened his horizon.

Dedicated to global students of middle and high school level, his website www.physicsgalaxy.com also has teaching sessions dubbed in American accent and subtitles in 87 languages. For students in India preparing for CBSE, JEE & NEET, his online courses and e-Books will be available soon on PHYSICSGALAXY.COM.

Preface

For a science student, Physics is the most important subject, unlike to other subjects it requires logical reasoning and high imagination of brain. Without improving the level of physics it is very difficult to achieve a goal in the present age of competitions. To score better, one does not require hard working at least in physics. It just requires a simple understanding and approach to think a physical situation. Actually physics is the surrounding of our everyday life. If you wish to make the concepts of physics strong, you should try to understand core concepts of physics in practical approach rather than theoretical. Whenever you try to solve a physics problem, first create a hypothetical world in your imagination about the problem and try to think psychologically, what the next step should be, the best answer would be given by your brain psychology.

This book NCERT SOLUTIONS is designed in a totally different and friendly approach to develop the physics concepts psychologically along with the solutions of NCERT Text books in grade 11 and 12. Rather than conventional solution based approach which is expected in CBSE final exams, all the unsolved questions at the end of each chapter of NCERT text book are solved with explanation of concepts used and the solution videos are recorded and uploaded on the physics galaxy web portal for video references. The screenshots of all these videos are compiled systematically in this book for quick reference of every solution.

The handwritten format of the screenshots gives a clear understanding of the application of concepts studied which helps in quick grasping and revision of the solutions. Once the core concept to be used in solving a question is clear to students, it will be a cake walk to write the solution in the stipulated format expected in CBSE final exams.

On each solution of the question, QR CODE is given for the web reference of the video solutions, students can download any QR CODE scanning app on their 'Android' and 'iOS' devices and for any confusion they can open the video solution of the respective question.

In this book of compiled screenshots of the video solutions, I have tried my best to make the solutions error free but owing to the nature of work, inadvertently, there is possibility of errors left untouched. I shall be grateful to the readers, if they point out me regarding errors and oblige me by giving their valuable and constructive suggestions via emails for further improvement of the book.

Ashish Arora
PHYSICSGALAXY.COM
B-80, Model Town, Malviya Nagar, Jaipur-302017
e-mails: ashisharora@physicsgalaxy.com
ashash12345@gmail.com

CBSE Exam Solution Format

In final CBSE exams of class 11 or 12, students are expected to write the solution of a question asked in a specific format which is given below. For any format of solving question in Physics most important thing is the core concept/formula of the solution, while reading a question if students are able to catch the core concept/formula to be applied to solve the question then in the below specified format the solution can be written while solving the question in class 11 final exams or in class 12 board exams.

Answer Copy

Sol :	List the Data/Information given in the question.	→	**Solution Body Part -1**
	Mention the details and clearly write/explain the Concept/Formula using which the situation given in question can be solved. If it is based on some standard laws then always mention how the name of the law.	→	**Solution Body Part -2**
	Relate the concept with the situation of the given question and explain the desired/required things which are asked in question. If it is a numerical then substitute the data in the formula clearly and solve for the final answer.	→	**Solution Body Part -3**

Most important part of solving a question is relating the specific concept/formula with the given situation and solving the question to the final answer. If students are able to judge which concept/formula is to be used in solving a specific question then arranging the solution in the above format is a straight process which can be done in almost no time.

Contents

Chapter 1

Physical World

QR Code of Link to the Video Lectures of Theory of this chapter Physical World at ‘Physics Galaxy’ web portal

QR Code of Link to the NCERT textbook Video Solutions of unsolved exercises at the end of each chapter in sequence of this chapter at ‘Physics Galaxy’ web portal

- **Some of the most profound statements on the nature of science have come from Albert Einstein, one of the greatest scientists of all time. What do you think did Einstein mean when he said : "The most incomprehensible thing about the world is that it is comprehensible"?**

Solⁿ: for a layman.
↓
no knowlege of basic laws of Physics/Science.
↓
All phenomenomans in nature in our surrounding are incomprehensible

Some one who studied basic laws of Science & can explain the logics for happenings in our surroundings
↓
with explanations under specific basic laws & boundaries the world & happenings in our surrounding are comprehensible.

- **"Every great physical theory starts as a heresy and ends as a dogma". Give some examples from the history of science of the validity of this incisive remark.**

Sol.ⁿ heresy → an option against the established theory.

dogma → a well established/accepted theory

Eg₁ → Geocentric theory → It was a belief that Sun, stars, other planets revolve around Earth.
(relative to Earth centre)

Galileo's Heliocentric theory → Sun is at rest & other planets/stars revolve around it.
(relative to Sun Centre)

Eg₂ → Newton's Corpuscular theory of light → light is a stream of shiny particles

Plank's quantum theory → light Consist of quantas (pkts of energy) Called photons.

Video Solution

- "Politics is the art of the possible". Similarly, "Science is the art of the soluble". Explain this beautiful aphorism on the nature and practice of science.

Sol^n:

Politics → impractical promises → possibility of happening is not sure.

Science → All phenomenon in Nature can be explained by some std basic laws.

↓

Soluble.

- **Though India now has a large base in science and technology, which is fast expanding, it is still a long way from realising its potential of becoming a world leader in science. Name some important factors, which in your view have hindered the advancement of science in India.**

Sol^n: There are several factors hindering advancement of Science in India. Some of these are -

1. lack of infrastructure → good research labs, clean rooms, testing labs etc
2. lack of management of Science education
3. large gap between researchers & Industries.
4. Brain Drain.
5. Poverty & good resources & opportunities in career in Science.

Video Solution

- **No physicist has ever "seen" an electron. Yet, all physicists believe in the existence of electrons. An intelligent but superstitious man advances this analogy to argue that 'ghosts' exist even though no one has 'seen' one. How will you refute his argument?**

Sol^n: There is NO Comparison in these two cases -

Electron	Ghosts
↓	↓
Noone has ever seen it	Noone has ever seen it
↓	↓
But there are many cases/experiments in evidence of existence of electron	But there are no valid & acceptable evidences practically found which can prove the existence of ghosts.

- The shells of crabs found around a particular coastal location in Japan seem mostly to resemble the legendary face of a Samurai. Given below are two explanations of this observed fact. Which of these strikes you as a scientific explanation ?

(a) A tragic sea accident several centuries ago drowned a young Samurai. As a tribute to his bravery, nature through its inscrutable ways immortalised his face by imprinting it on the crab shells in that area.

(b) After the sea tragedy, fishermen in that area, in a gesture of honour to their dead hero, let free any crab shell caught by them which accidentally had a shape resembling the face of a Samurai. Consequently, the particular shape of the crab shell survived longer and therefore in course of time the shape was genetically propagated. This is an example of evolution by artificial selection.

[Note : This interesting illustration taken from Carl Sagan's 'The Cosmos' highlights the fact that often strange and inexplicable facts which on the first sight appear 'supernatural' actually turn out to have simple scientific explanations. Try to think out other examples of this kind].

Sol^n: Option (b) is the fact which we can consider as a scientific explanation for this fact.

Video Solution

- **The industrial revolution in England and Western Europe more than two centuries ago was triggered by some key scientific and technological advances. What were these advances ?**

Sol^n: Some of the tech developments in England and Western Europe were –

1. Invention of Steam engine
2. Invention of Safety lamp
3. Invention of electricity
4. Invention of powerloom
5. Invention of Cotton gin.

- **It is often said that the world is witnessing now a second industrial revolution, which will transform the society as radically as did the first. List some key contemporary areas of science and technology, which are responsible for this revolution.**

Sol^n: Areas/Domains of S&T which will transform the society radically are –

(1) uses of laser in IT as laser can transmits many (in thousands) signals simultaneously without losses.

(2) Dev of superconducting material at high (room) temperature is revolutionizing the advancement in field of supercomputers, locomotives & Communication sector.

(3) Development in Biotechnological research.

(4) Satellite communication.

- **Write in about 1000 words a fiction piece based on your speculation on the science and technology of the twenty-second century.**

Sol^n: hint —

(A) Space travel with imaginary scientific gadgets.

(B) A war (virtual) backed up by mobile technology.

(C) A game involving 100 or more people simultaneously and redefining the tech gaming industry.

⋮

- **Attempt to formulate your 'moral' views on the practice of science. Imagine yourself stumbling upon a discovery, which has great academic interest but is certain to have nothing but dangerous consequences for the human society. How, if at all, will you resolve your dilemma ?**

Sol^n: Science Discovery (Good or Bad) → we must make people aware about both the factors.

A discovery which is bad/ has dangerous consequences may be used in some good development of our society.

e.g. Nuclear fission → used to generate electricity
→ used to make Atom bomb.

- **Science, like any knowledge, can be put to good or bad use, depending on the user. Given below are some of the applications of science. Formulate your views on whether the particular application is good, bad or something that cannot be so clearly categorised :**

(a) **Mass vaccination against small pox to curb and finally eradicate this disease from the population. (This has already been successfully done in India)**

(b) **Television for eradication of illiteracy and for mass communication of news and ideas**

(c) **Prenatal sex determination**

(d) **Computers for increase in work efficiency**

(e) **Putting artificial satellites into orbits around the Earth**

(f) **Development of nuclear weapons**

(g) **Development of new and powerful techniques of chemical and biological warfare)**

(h) **Purification of water for drinking**

(i) **Plastic surgery**

(j) **Cloning**

Sol^n: (a) Good (b) Good (c) Bad (d) Good (e) Good (f) Bad

(g) Good or Bad (h) Good (i) Good (j) Good upto some extent for animals & plants but Bad for humans.

- **India has had a long and unbroken tradition of great scholarship — in mathematics, astronomy, linguistics, logic and ethics. Yet, in parallel with this, several superstitious and obscurantistic attitudes and practices flourished in our society and unfortunately continue even today — among many educated people too. How will you use your knowledge of science to develop strategies to counter these attitudes ?**

Sol: This is possible only by spreading awareness and Science education
↓
day to day Science.

The major role will be played by our media → newspaper, internet Radio, TV etc.

By educating our society we can come over it!

- **Though the law gives women equal status in India, many people hold unscientific views on a woman's innate nature, capacity and intelligence, and in practice give them a secondary status and role. Demolish this view using scientific arguments, and by quoting examples of great women in science and other spheres; and persuade yourself and others that, given equal opportunity, women are on par with men.**

Solⁿ: The intellectual characters in a human
↳ Intelligence, quick & proper decision making, hardwork, leadership etc.

it all depends upon human brain & nutrient diet one takes since childhood. it does not depend on gender.

⇒ All woman are at par with all man.

e.g. Kalpana Chawala, Mother Teresa, Madam Curie, Lata Mangeshkar and Margret Thacher etc.

- **"It is more important to have beauty in the equations of physics than to have them agree with experiments". The great British physicist P. A. M. Dirac held this view. Criticize this statement. Look out for some equations and results in this book which strike you as beautiful.**

Sol^n: As a general view point in science, this statement is correct. It is very imp to explain any phenomenon in a simple & straight way.

in many industrial dev also now a days KISS methodology is being adopted at most.
KISS ↓ Keep It Simple & Stupid/Straight

e.g. Newton's II law $F = ma$
Einstein's mass - energy equivalence $E = mc^2$
] simple relations

BUT in many other domains of science it is not correct like in theory of relativity above two relations are not directly applicable.

Video Solution

- Though the statement quoted above may be disputed, most physicists do have a feeling that the great laws of physics are at once simple and beautiful. Some of the notable physicists, besides Dirac, who have articulated this feeling, are : Einstein, Bohr, Heisenberg, Chandrasekhar and Feynman. You are urged to make special efforts to get access to the general books and writings by these and other great masters of physics. (See the Bibliography at the end of this book.) Their writings are truly inspiring !

Sol^n: Assignment for you to search & list up relations like

$F = ma$ ✓ | $E = mc^2$ ✓ | $W = F.s$ × | $\lambda = \frac{h}{mv}$ ✓

$F = ma$ ↓ Newton

$E = mc^2$ ↓ Einstein

$W = F.s$: Simple calculation of energy being transferred.

$\lambda = \frac{h}{mv}$ ↓ De Broglie.

- Textbooks on science may give you a wrong impression that studying science is dry and all too serious and that scientists are absent-minded introverts who never laugh or grin. This image of science and scientists is patently false. Scientists, like any other group of humans, have their share of humorists, and many have led their lives with a great sense of fun and adventure, even as they seriously pursued their scientific work. Two great physicists of this genre are Gamow and Feynman. You will enjoy reading their books listed in the Bibliography.

Sol^n: That's true & other scientists who were also of such kind are

CV Raman

Neils Bohr

APJ Abdul kalam

Eienstien

→ Assignment for you to study about these scientists.

Video Solution

Chapter 2

Units and Measurements

QR Code of Link to the Video Lectures
of Theory of this chapter Units and Measurements
at 'Physics Galaxy' web portal

QR Code of Link to the NCERT textbook Video Solutions
of unsolved exercises at the end of each chapter in sequence
of this chapter at 'Physics Galaxy' web portal

- Fill in the blanks

(a) The volume of a cube of side 1 cm is equal to .... m^3

(b) The surface area of a solid cylinder of radius 2.0 cm and height 10.0 cm is equal to .... $(mm)^2$

(c) A vehicle moving with a speed of 18 km h^{-1} covers .... m in 1s

(d) The relative density of lead is 11.3. Its density is .... g cm^{-3} or .... kg m^{-3}

Sol^n (a) Volume of a cube

$V = a^3 = (1\,cm)^3 = 1\,cm^3$

as $1\,cm = \frac{1}{100}\,m$

$\Rightarrow V = 1\left(\frac{1}{100}m\right)^3$

$= 10^{-6}\,m^3$ Ans

(b) Surface area of a solid cylinder

$S = 2\pi r^2 + 2\pi r h$

$= 2 \times 3.14 \times (2)^2 + 2 \times 3.14 \times 2 \times 10\ cm^2$

also we use $1\,cm = 10\,mm$

$= 15085\ mm^2$

$\simeq 1.5 \times 10^4\ mm^2$ Ans

(c) $v = 18\ \frac{km}{hour}$

we use $1\,km = 1000\,m$

$1\,hr = 3600\,s$

$\Rightarrow v = 18 \times \frac{1000}{3600}\ m/s$

$v = 18 \times 5/18 = 5\ m/s$

distance $s = vt$

$= 5 \times 1$

$= 5\,m$ Ans

(d) rel density $= \frac{d_{body}}{d_{water}}$

$d_{rel} = 11.3 = \frac{d_{lead}}{1\,gm/cm^3}$

$\Rightarrow d_{lead} = 11.3\ gm/cm^3$

we use Ans

$1\,gm = 10^{-3}\,kg$

$1\,cm = 10^{-2}\,m$

$d_{lead} = \frac{11.3 \times 10^{-3}\,kg}{(10^{-2}\,m)^3}$

$= 1.13 \times 10^4\ kg/m^3$ Ans

- **Fill in the blanks by suitable conversion of units**

(a) $1\ \text{kg m}^2\,\text{s}^{-2}$ = ... $\text{g cm}^2\,\text{s}^{-2}$

(b) 1 m = ... *ly*

(c) $3.0\ \text{m s}^{-2}$ = ... km h^{-2}

(d) $G = 6.67 \times 10^{-11}\ \text{N m}^2\,(\text{kg})^{-2}$ = ... $(\text{cm})^3\,\text{s}^{-2}\,\text{g}^{-1}$

Sol: (a)

$1\ \frac{\text{kg m}^2}{\text{s}^2}$

we use 1 Kg = 1000 g

1 m = 100 cm

$\Rightarrow 1\ \frac{\text{kg-m}^2}{\text{s}^2} = 1\ \frac{(10^3\text{g})(10^2\text{cm})^2}{\text{s}^2}$

$= 10^7\ \text{gm-cm}^2/\text{s}^2$ Ans

(b) we use

$1\text{ly} = 9.46 \times 10^{15}\ \text{m}$

$\Rightarrow 1\text{m} = \frac{1}{9.46 \times 10^{15}}\ \text{ly}$

$= 1.057 \times 10^{-16}\ \text{ly}$

Ans

(c) $3.0\ \text{m/s}^2$

we use

1 km = 1000 m

1 h = 3600 s

$\Rightarrow$

$3\ \frac{\text{m}}{\text{s}^2} = 3\ \frac{(10^{-3}\text{km})}{(1/3600\ \text{h})^2}$

$= 3.9 \times 10^4\ \text{km/hr}^2$

Ans

(d) $G = 6.67 \times 10^{-11}\ \frac{\text{Nm}^2}{\text{kg}^2}$

$1\text{N} = 10^5$ dyne (gm-cm/s²)

1 m = 100 cm

1 kg = 1000 g

$\Rightarrow G = 6.67 \times 10^{-11}\ \frac{(10^5\text{d})(10^2\text{cm})^2}{(10^3\text{g})^2}$

$G = 6.67 \times 10^{-8}\ \frac{\text{cm}^3}{\text{s}^2\,\text{g}}$ Ans

Video Solution

- A calorie is a unit of heat or energy and it equals about 4.2 J where 1J = 1 kg m^2 s^{-2}. Suppose we employ a system of units in which the unit of mass equals α kg, the unit of length equals βm, the unit of time is γs. Show that a calorie has a magnitude 4.2 $\alpha^{-1}\beta^{-2}\gamma^2$ in terms of the new units.

Solⁿ: In all system of units we know for any physical quantity we use

magnitude × units = Constant

for two system we can use

$D(u_{energy}) = ML^2T^{-2}$

$m_1u_1 = m_2u_2 \Rightarrow m_2 = m_1\frac{u_1}{u_2} = 4.2 \times \frac{[M_1L_1^2T_1^{-2}]}{[M_2L_2^2T_2^{-2}]}$

↑ magnitude (numerical value)

$= 4.2 \times \frac{kg - m^2 - s^{-2}}{\alpha kg - \beta^2 m^2 - \gamma^{-2} s^{-2}}$

$= 4.2\,\alpha^{-1}\beta^{-2}\gamma^2$ Ans.

hence proved!

- Explain this statement clearly :
  "To call a dimensional quantity 'large' or 'small' is meaningless without specifying a standard for comparison". In view of this, reframe the following statements wherever necessary :

(a) atoms are very small objects

(b) a jet plane moves with great speed

(c) the mass of Jupiter is very large

(d) the air inside this room contains a large number of molecules

(e) a proton is much more massive than an electron

(f) the speed of sound is much smaller than the speed of light

Sol^n: 'Large' or 'Small' are always relative terms & defined in Comparison to some other similar physical quantity → as a standard or a refrence

(a) atoms are v. small — Compared to a pen or an eraser.

(b) Speed of jet plane is large — Compared to speed of car on road.

(c) mass of Jupiter is v. large — Compared mass of moon.

(d) no of molecules in air are large in a room — Compared to no of books in a shelf.

(e) proton is more massive — as compared to electron

(f) speed of sound is v. small — as compared to speed of light

Video Solution

- **A new unit of length is chosen such that the speed of light in vacuum is unity. What is the distance between the Sun and the Earth in terms of the new unit if light takes 8 min and 20 s to cover this distance ?**

Sol^n: speed of light $= 3\times10^8$ m/s

$= 1$ (NL/s)

new unit of length is NL.

$1\ NL = 3\times10^8\ m$.

time taken by light to cover the distance between Sun & Earth is $t = 8\ m, 20\ s$

$= 480\ s + 20\ s = 500\ s$

distance $l = v\times t$

$= 1\frac{NL}{s}\times 500\ s = 500\ NL$ Ans.

- Which of the following is the most precise device for measuring length :

(a) a vernier callipers with 20 divisions on the sliding scale

(b) a screw gauge of pitch 1 mm and 100 divisions on the circular scale

(c) an optical instrument that can measure length to within a wavelength of light ?

Sol^n: The most precise instrument is the one which has lowest value of 'least count'

(least count → min distance / length which can be measure.)

(a) vernier callipers → MSD = 1mm.

as there are 20 div on vernier scale, these we consider coinciding with 19 MSD

$\Rightarrow 1 VSD = \frac{19}{20} MSD$

least count = 1 MSD − 1 VSD $= \left(1 - \frac{19}{20}\right) \times 1mm = \frac{1}{20} m = 0.005 cm.$

(b) least count of screw gauge $= \frac{\text{Pitch length}}{\text{no. of div on circular scale}} = \frac{1}{100} = 0.001 cm.$

(c) for optical instrument, least count $\simeq 4000 - 8000 \mathring{A} \simeq 10^{-7} m \simeq 10^{-5} cm$
$= 0.00001 cm$ lowest value

Video Solution

- A student measures the thickness of a human hair by looking at it through a microscope of magnification 100. He makes 20 observations and finds that the average width of the hair in the field of view of the microscope is 3.5 mm. What is the estimate on the thickness of hair ?

Solⁿ: We define magnification as–

$$\text{magnification} = \frac{\text{observed size}}{\text{Real size}}$$

$$\Rightarrow \text{Real size} = \frac{\text{observed size}}{\text{magnification}} = \frac{3.5\,mm}{100}$$

$$= 0.035\,mm \text{ Ans.}$$

- Answer the following :

(a) You are given a thread and a metre scale. How will you estimate the diameter of the thread ?

(b) A screw gauge has a pitch of 1.0 mm and 200 divisions on the circular scale. Do you think it is possible to increase the accuracy of the screw gauge arbitrarily by increasing the number of divisions on the circular scale ?

(c) The mean diameter of a thin brass rod is to be measured by vernier callipers. Why is a set of 100 measurements of the diameter expected to yield a more reliable estimate than a set of 5 measurements only ?

Sol^n (a)

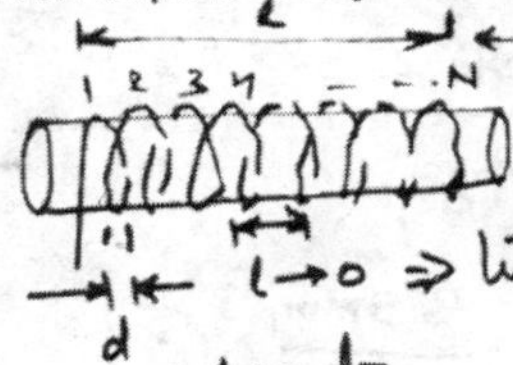

← this length can be measured by scale

$l \to 0 \Rightarrow$ turns are almost touching each other.

thread diameter

for N turns we use $l = Nd \Rightarrow d = \frac{l}{N} = \frac{\text{length of N turns}}{\text{no of turns}}$

(b) least count = $\frac{\text{Pitch}}{\text{no of div on CS}} = \frac{1}{200}$ mm.

if no of divisions on circular Scale are increased then least count will decrease $\Rightarrow$ theoretically accuracy will increase BUT

difficult to read by human eye

Due to errors of proper reading by human eye in case of large divisions accuracy of measurement will go down practically

(c) lot of readings are required for reducing random error in experiments because while experimenting → (probability of +ve random errors = prob of -ve random errors)

- The photograph of a house occupies an area of 1.75 cm^2 on a 35 mm slide. The slide is projected on to a screen, and the area of the house on the screen is 1.55 m^2. What is the linear magnification of the projector-screen arrangement.

Sol^n: Area of object $= 1.75\ cm^2$

Area of projection (image) $= 1.55\ m^2 = 1.55 \times 10^4\ cm^2$

$$\text{area magnification} = \frac{\text{Area of image}}{\text{Area of object}} = \frac{1.55 \times 10^4}{1.75} \simeq 8860$$

$$\text{linear magnification} = \sqrt{\text{area magnification}} = \sqrt{8860} \simeq 94.1 \text{ Ans}$$

Video Solution

- State the number of significant figures in the following :

(a) $0.007\ m^2$ (b) 2.64×10^{24} kg (c) $0.2370\ g\ cm^{-3}$ (d) 6.320 J

(e) $6.032\ N\ m^{-2}$ (f) $0.0006032\ m^2$

Sol^n: (a) $0.007\ m^2$ → SD → 1.

(b) 2.64×10^{24} kg. → SD → 3

(c) $0.2370\ g/cm^3$ → SD → 4

(d) 6.320 J → SD → 4

(e) $6.032\ N/m^2$ → SD → 4

(f) $0.0006032\ m^2$ → SD → 4

We analyzed all SD as per rules we studied in Basic Theory.

Ans.

- The length, breadth and thickness of a rectangular sheet of metal are 4.234 m, 1.005 m, and 2.01 cm respectively. Give the area and volume of the sheet to correct significant figures.

Sol: Area of sheet $A = 2(lb + bt + tl)$

$$= 2(4.234 \times 1.005 + 1.005 \times 0.0201 + 0.0201 \times 4.234)$$

$$= 8.7209478 \text{ m}^2$$

in l, b & t, Thickness $t = 0.0201$ m has 3 significant figures (least among l, b & t)

$$\Rightarrow \quad A = 8.72 \text{ m}^2 \text{ Ans.}$$

Volume of Sheet $V = lbt = 4.234 \times 1.005 \times 0.0201 \text{ m}^3$

$$= 0.0855289 \text{ m}^3$$

$$= 0.0855 \text{ m}^3 \text{ Ans.}$$

Video Solution

- The mass of a box measured by a grocer's balance is 2.300 kg. Two gold pieces of masses 20.15 g and 20.17 g are added to the box. What is

(a) the total mass of the box,

(b) the difference in the masses of the pieces to correct significant figures ?

Sol^n (a) mass of box 2.300 kg.

after adding gold pieces total mass of box

$$m_T = 2.\underline{3}00 + 0.02015 + 0.02017 \text{ kg}$$

$$= 2.\underline{3}4032 \text{ kg}.$$

in case of addition we consider least decimal places.

$$\Rightarrow \quad m_T = 2.3 \text{ kg}. \quad \text{Ans}$$

(b) $\Delta m = 20.\underline{17} - 20.\underline{15} = 0.\underline{02}\ g$ Ans.

- A physical quantity *P* is related to four observables *a*, *b*, *c* and *d* as follows :

  $P = a^3b^2/(\sqrt{c}d)$

  The percentage errors of measurement in *a*, *b*, *c* and d are 1%, 3%, 4% and 2%, respectively. What is the percentage error in the quantity *P* ? If the value of *P* calculated using the above relation turns out to be 3.763, to what value should you round off the result ?

Sol^n: for the relation $P = \frac{a^3b^2}{\sqrt{c}d}$

Maximum fractional error in physical qty P is given as-

$$\frac{\Delta P}{P} = \pm\left[\frac{3\Delta a}{a} + \frac{2\Delta b}{b} + \frac{1}{2}\frac{\Delta c}{c} + \frac{\Delta d}{d}\right]$$

Max % error in P is $\frac{\Delta P}{P}\times 100 = \pm\left[3\times 1 + 2\times 3 + \frac{1}{2}\times 4 + 2\right] = \pm 13\%$ Ans

$$\Rightarrow \Delta P = \frac{13}{100}\times P = 0.13\times P.$$

P should be rounded off upto two SD $\Rightarrow P = [3.763]_R = 3.8$ Ans.

Video Solution

- A book with many printing errors contains four different formulas for the displacement y of a particle undergoing a certain periodic motion :

(a) $y = a \sin 2\pi\, t/T$ ✓

(b) $y = a \sin vt$ ✗

(c) $y = (a/T) \sin t/a$ ✗

(d) $y = (a\sqrt{2})\,(\sin 2\pi t/T + \cos 2\pi t/T)$ ✓

(a = maximum displacement of the particle, v = speed of the particle. T = time-period of motion). Rule out the wrong formulas on dimensional grounds.

Solⁿ: ✓(a) $y = a \sin\left(\frac{2\pi t}{T}\right)$

Dimensions of LHS & RHS. → Dimensionless.

$[L] = [L] \sin[D_0]$

✗(b) $y = a \sin vt$

Dimensions of LHS & RHS

$[L] = [L] \cdot \sin[LT^{-1} \times T]$ → Dimension of [L]

Wrong formula.

✗(c) $y = \frac{a}{T} \sin(t/a)$

D[LHS] & D[RHS] → not dimensionless

$[L] = [LT^{-1}] \sin[TL^{-1}]$

✓(d) $y = a\sqrt{2}\left[\sin\left(\frac{2\pi t}{T}\right) + \cos\left(\frac{2\pi t}{T}\right)\right]$

D[LHS] & D[RHS]

$[L] = [L]\left(\sin[D_0] + \cos[D_0]\right)$

- A famous relation in physics relates 'moving mass' m to the 'rest mass' m_0 of a particle in terms of its speed v and the speed of light, c. (This relation first arose as a consequence of special relativity due to Albert Einstein). A boy recalls the relation almost correctly but forgets where to put the constant c. He writes :

$$m = \frac{m_0}{(1-v^2)^{1/2}}$$

Guess where to put the missing c.

Solⁿ: Every expression must be dimensionally homogeneous.

$$\Rightarrow \quad m = \frac{m_0}{\sqrt{1-v^2}}$$

$$[M] = \frac{[M]}{\sqrt{1 - D[\text{speed}]^2}}$$

for this relation to be correct, denominator on RHS must be a dimensionless qty

$$\Rightarrow \text{Correct relation will be} \quad m = \frac{m_0}{\sqrt{1 - v^2/c^2}}$$

Video Solution

- The unit of length convenient on the atomic scale is known as an angstrom and is denoted by Å: 1 Å = 10^{-10} m. The size of a hydrogen atom is about 0.5 Å. What is the total atomic volume in m^3 of a mole of hydrogen atoms ?

Solⁿ: radius of H-atom $r = 0.5 \times 10^{-10}$ m

Volume of one H-atom $V = \frac{4}{3}\pi r^3 = \frac{4}{3} \times 3.14 \times (5 \times 10^{-11})^3$

$= 5.234 \times 10^{-31}\ m^3$

Volume of 1-mole of H-atoms $= V \times N_{AV}$

$= 5.234 \times 10^{-31} \times 6.023 \times 10^{23}\ m^3$

$= 3.15 \times 10^{-7}\ m^3$

upto 1SD after rounding off we get

$V_T = 3 \times 10^{-7}\ m^3$ Ans.

- One mole of an ideal gas at standard temperature and pressure occupies 22.4 L (molar volume). What is the ratio of molar volume to the atomic volume of a mole of hydrogen ? (Take the size of hydrogen molecule to be about 1Å). Why is this ratio so large ?

Solⁿ: Molar Volume of H-gas is $V_1 = 22.4\,L = 22.4 \times 10^{-3}\,m^3$

atomic volume of 1 mole of H-atoms $V_2 = 3.15 \times 10^{-7}\,m^3$

(Size/radius of H-atom as $r_H = 0.5\,Å$)

Ratio $r = \frac{V_1}{V_2} = \frac{22.4 \times 10^{-3}}{3.15 \times 10^{-7}} = 7.1 \times 10^4$

after rounding off $r = 7 \times 10^4$

r is v. large as in gaseous state atomic separation is v. large that's why molar volume is large. Ans

Video Solution

- **Explain this common observation clearly : If you look out of the window of a fast moving train, the nearby trees, houses etc. seem to move rapidly in a direction opposite to the train's motion, but the distant objects (hill tops, the Moon, the stars etc.) seem to be stationary. (In fact, since you are aware that you are moving, these distant objects seem to move with you).**

Solⁿ:

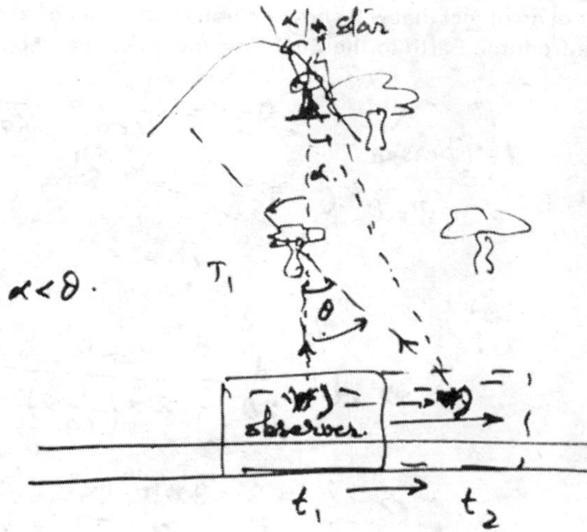

For near by objects the angular position w.r.t. observer is changing more compared to far away objects thats why nearby objects appear to move fast compared to far away object.

- The principle of 'parallax' in section 2.3.1 is used in the determination of distances of very distant stars. The baseline *AB* is the line joining the Earth's two locations six months apart in its orbit around the Sun. That is, the baseline is about the diameter of the Earth's orbit $\approx 3 \times 10^{11}$ m. However, even the nearest stars are so distant that with such a long baseline, they show parallax only of the order of 1" (second) of arc or so. A parsec is a convenient unit of length on the astronomical scale. It is the distance of an object that will show a parallax of 1" (second) of arc from opposite ends of a baseline equal to the distance from the Earth to the Sun. How much is a parsec in terms of metres ?

$$\theta = 1'' = \frac{1^\circ}{3600} = \frac{1}{3600} \times \frac{\pi}{180} \text{ rad}$$

Sol^n

$d = 3 \times 10^{11}$ m.

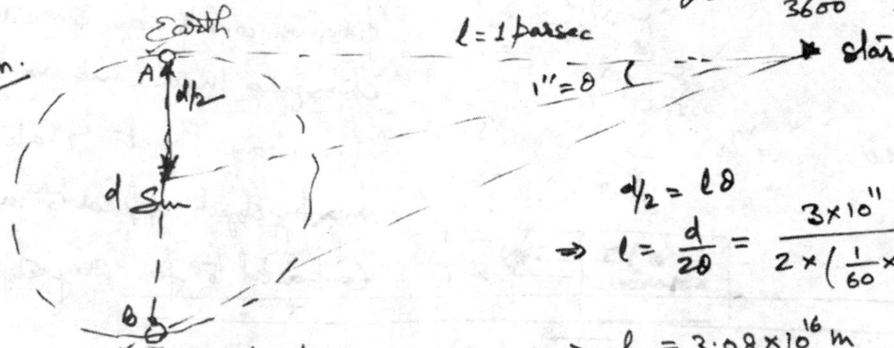

A & B are 6 months apart.

$$d/2 = l\theta$$

$$\Rightarrow l = \frac{d}{2\theta} = \frac{3 \times 10^{11}}{2 \times \left(\frac{1}{60} \times \frac{1}{60} \times \frac{3.14}{180}\right)}$$

$$\Rightarrow l = 3.08 \times 10^{16} \text{ m}$$

after rounding off $l = 3 \times 10^{16}$ m Ans.

Video Solution

- The nearest star to our solar system is 4.29 light years away. How much is this distance in terms of parsecs? How much parallax would this star (named Alpha Centauri) show when viewed from two locations of the Earth six months apart in its orbit around the Sun ?

Sol^n

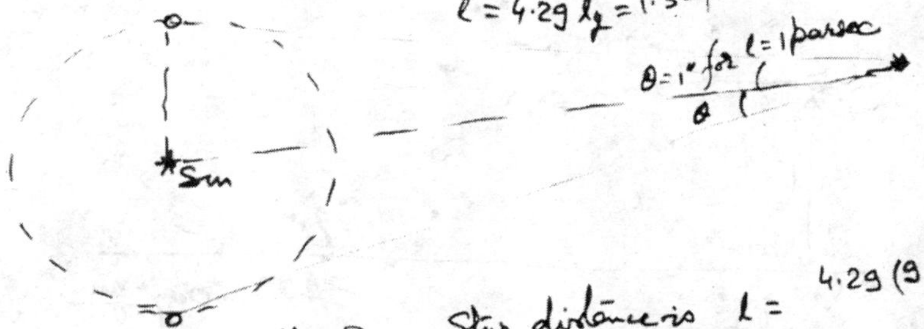

$l = 4.29\ ly = 1.32$ parsec

$\theta = 1''$ for $l = 1$ parsec

As 1 parsec $= 3.08 \times 10^{16}$ m.

1 ly $= 9.46 \times 10^{15}$ m

1 m $= \frac{1}{3.08 \times 10^{16}}$ parsec

$\Rightarrow$ Star distance is $l = 4.29\,(9.46 \times 10^{15}\text{ m})$

$= \frac{4.29 \times 9.46 \times 10^{15}}{3.08 \times 10^{16}}$ parsec

$= 1.318$ parsec $= 1.32$ parsec Ans

here we have parallax $2\theta = 2(1.32) = 2.64''$ Ans

- Precise measurements of physical quantities are a need of science. For example, to ascertain the speed of an aircraft, one must have an accurate method to find its positions at closely separated instants of time. This was the actual motivation behind the discovery of radar in World War II. Think of different examples in modern science where precise measurements of length, time, mass etc. are needed. Also, wherever you can, give a quantitative idea of the precision needed.

Sol: During WW II

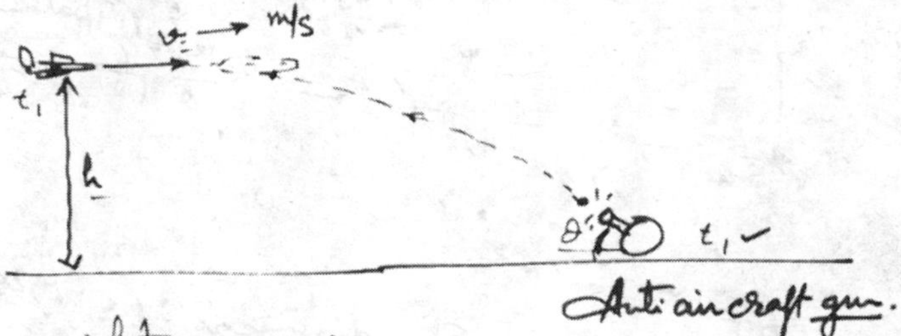

Example: If we wish to measure near point of a defective human eye

↓

precision & accuracy are imp in this measurement as based on these values only next line of action/action plan is decided.

Video Solution

- Just as precise measurements are necessary in science, it is equally important to be able to make rough estimates of quantities using rudimentary ideas and common observations. Think of ways by which you can estimate the following (where an estimate is difficult to obtain, try to get an upper bound on the quantity) :

(a) the total mass of rain-bearing clouds over India during the Monsoon

(b) the mass of an elephant

(c) the wind speed during a storm

(d) the number of strands of hair on your head

(e) the number of air molecules in your classroom.

Sol: (a) Total rains over India = 10 cm (say)

area of India = 3 million sq km = 3×10^6 km^2 (approx)

volume of rain water V = Area × height

$= 3\times10^6\times10^6\times0.1 = 3\times10^{11}$ m^3

approx mass of rainfall $m = V\times d$

$= 3\times10^{11}\times1000$

$= 3\times10^{14}$ kg Ans.

Sol^n (b)

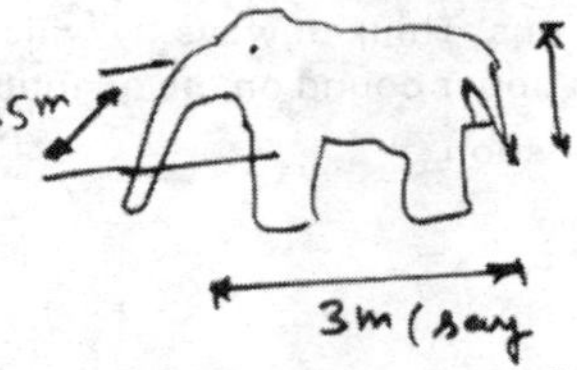

roughly the volume of elephant is

$$V = 3 \times 2 \times 1.5 = 9\,m^3 \text{ (say)}$$

As we know elephant can float in water its avg density is slightly less then water say $d_{elephant} \simeq 800\,kg/m^3$

$\Rightarrow$ approx mass of elephant $m = V \times d = 9 \times 800 = 7200\,kg$ Ans

(2) As a general forecast if storm takes about 1.5 hr in reaching city B

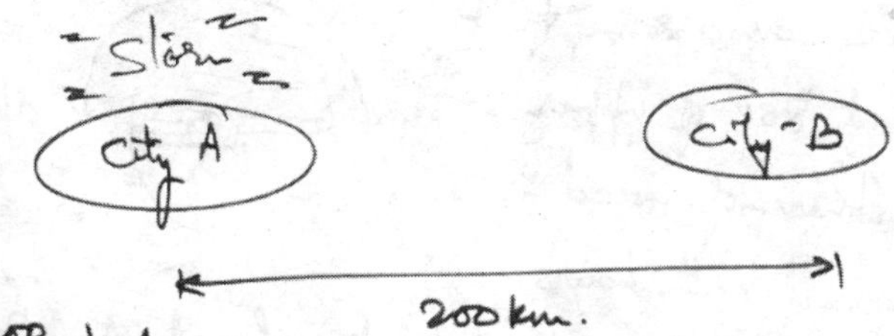

$\Rightarrow$ avg speed of storm

$$v = \frac{\text{distance}}{\text{Time}} = \frac{200}{1.5} \text{ km/hr}$$

$$= \frac{400}{3} \text{ km/hr} \simeq \text{ of the order of } 100 - 150 \text{ km/hr}$$

Ans

(d) We can assume that about 80% of upper hemisphere of head is covered with hairs

approx rad of human head as $r = 10$ cm.

$\Rightarrow$ area of covered part on head $A = \frac{80}{100} \times 2\pi r^2 = 0.8 \times 2 \times 3.14 \times (0.1)^2\ m^2 \times 10^6\ mm^2$

$= 5 \times 10^4\ mm^2$

on an avg of $1\ mm^2$ ($1\ mm \times 1\ mm$) on head we can assume there are 7-8 strands of hair are there $\Rightarrow$

approximate total hair strands on hair are

$5 \times 10^4 \times 8 = 2 \times 10^5$ strands

in general 10^5 to 10^6 strands can be considered.

Video Solution

(c) volume of room

$V = 4 \times 3 \times 3$

$= 36 m^3$

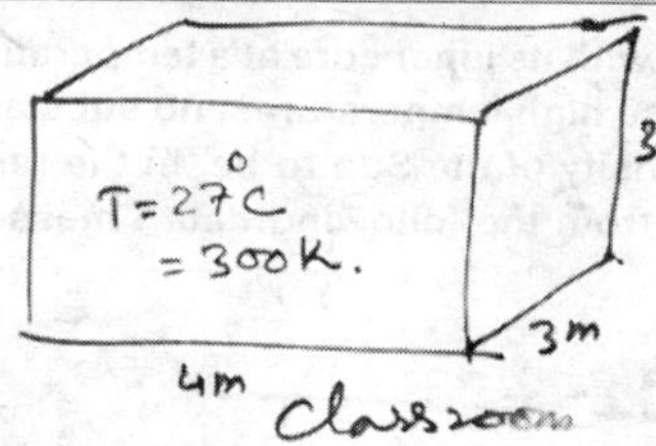

atm pressure

$P = 10^5 N/m^2$

no of air molecules can be directly given by Gas law

$PV = NkT$

$$\Rightarrow N = \frac{PV}{kT} = \frac{10^5 \times 36}{1.38 \times 10^{-23} \times 300} \simeq 8 \times 10^{28} \sim 10^{29} \text{ to } 10^{30} \text{ molecules in room}$$

Ans.

Alternatively you can use the fact that at NTP 6.023×10^{23} molecules (1 mole) occupy 22.4 litre volume.

$\Rightarrow$ using the volume of room we can calculate no of molecules.

- The Sun is a hot plasma (ionized matter) with its inner core at a temperature exceeding 10^7 K, and its outer surface at a temperature of about 6000 K. At these high temperatures, no substance remains in a solid or liquid phase. In what range do you expect the mass density of the Sun to be, in the range of densities of solids and liquids or gases? Check if your guess is correct from the following data : mass of the Sun = 2.0×10^{30} kg, radius of the Sun = 7.0×10^8 m.

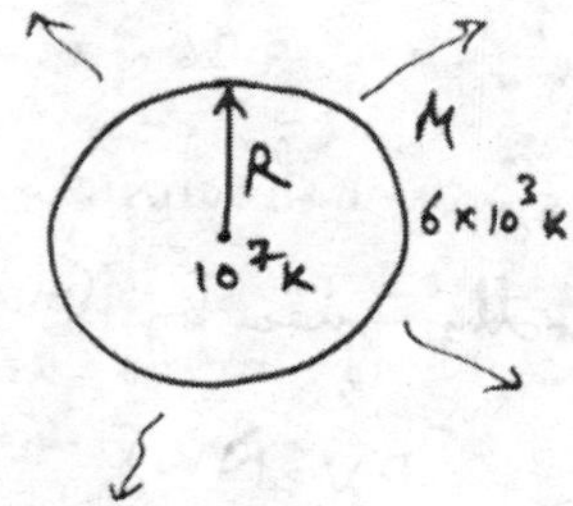

Sol^n: Density of Sun $= \dfrac{\text{mass}}{\text{volume}} = \dfrac{M}{\left(\frac{4}{3}\pi R^3\right)}$

$$= \frac{3 \times 2.0 \times 10^{30}}{4 \times 3.14 \times (7.0 \times 10^8)^3}$$

$$= 1.392 \times 10^3 \text{ kg/m}^3$$

$$= 1.4 \times 10^3 \text{ kg/m}^3 \text{ Ans}$$

This is of the order of solids & liquids not of gases plasma.

- **When the planet Jupiter is at a distance of 824.7 million kilometers from the Earth, its angular diameter is measured to be 35.72" of arc. Calculate the diameter of Jupiter.**

Sol.

In the figure shown we can use

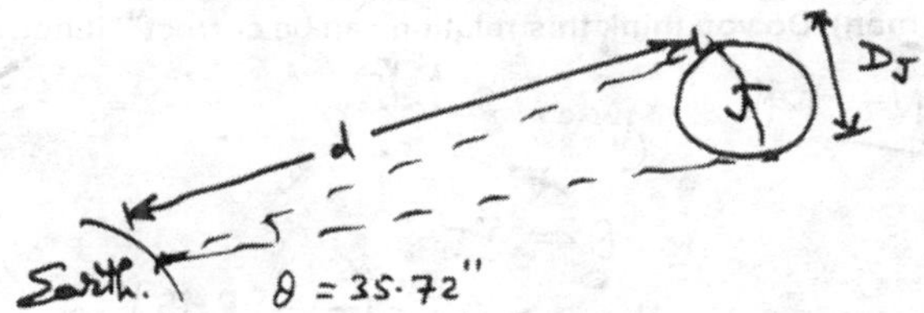

$\theta = 35.72''$

$= 35.72 \times \frac{1}{3600} \times \frac{\pi}{180}$ rad

$D_J = d\theta$

$= 824.7 \times 10^6 \times \frac{35.72 \times 3.14}{3600 \times 180}$ km

$= 1.429 \times 10^5$ km. Ans

- **A man walking briskly in rain with speed *v* must slant his umbrella forward making an angle θ with the vertical. A student derives the following relation between θ and *v* : tan θ = *v* and checks that the relation has a correct limit: as $v \to 0, \theta \to 0$, as expected. (We are assuming there is no strong wind and that the rain falls vertically for a stationary man). Do you think this relation can be correct ? If not, guess the correct relation.**

Solⁿ The given relation

$$\tan\theta = v$$

Dimensionally $D[LHS] = D[RHS]$

dimensionless $\neq [LT^{-1}]$

⇒ relation is not correct.

Correct relation must account for the speed of rain drops also

$$\tan\theta = \frac{v}{v_R}$$

here RHS is also dimensionless

⇒ this formula appear to be Dim correct.

Video Solution

- It is claimed that two cesium clocks, if allowed to run for 100 years, free from any disturbance, may differ by only about 0.02 s. What does this imply for the accuracy of the standard cesium clock in measuring a time-interval of 1 s ?

Sol. $100\text{ yrs} = 100 \times 365 \times 24 \times 3600\text{ s}$

error in 100 yrs is $\Delta t = 0.02\text{ s}$

$\Rightarrow$ error in 1 s duration $= \dfrac{\Delta t}{t} = \dfrac{0.02}{100 \times 365 \times 24 \times 3600} \simeq 6 \times 10^{-12}\text{ s}$

of the order of 10^{-11} to 10^{-12} s. Ans

- Estimate the average mass density of a sodium atom assuming its size to be about 2.5 Å. (Use the known values of Avogadro's number and the atomic mass of sodium). Compare it with the density of sodium in its crystalline phase: 970 kg m^{-3}. Are the two densities of the same order of magnitude ? If so, why ?

Sol^n: volume of one Na atom $V_1 = \frac{4}{3}\pi r^3 = \frac{4}{3} \times 3.14 \times (2.5 \times 10^{-10})^3 = 65.42 \times 10^{-30}\ m^3$

volume of one mole of Na atom $V_{1\,mole} = N_A \times V_1 = 6.023 \times 10^{23} \times 65.42 \times 10^{-30}\ m^3$

$= 3.95 \times 10^{-5}\ m^3$

mass of one mole of Na atoms = 23 gm.

density of Na atoms $= \dfrac{23 \times 10^{-3}}{3.95 \times 10^{-5}} = 584\ kgm/m^3$

here 584 & 970 are of same order.

- The unit of length convenient on the nuclear scale is a fermi : 1 $f = 10^{-15}$ m. Nuclear sizes obey roughly the following empirical relation :

  $r = r_0 A^{1/3}$

  where r is the radius of the nucleus, *A* its mass number, and r_0 is a constant equal to about, 1.2 *f*. Show that the rule implies that nuclear mass density is nearly constant for different nuclei. Estimate the mass density of sodium nucleus. Compare it with the average mass density of a sodium atom obtained in Exercise. 2.27.

Sol^n Volume of a nucleus of mass number A is

$$V = \frac{4}{3}\pi r^3 = \frac{4}{3}\pi (r_0 A^{1/3})^3 = \frac{4}{3}\pi r_0^3 A$$

mass of a Nucleus of mass number A m = avg mass of a nucleon × A (no of nucleons)

$= m_0 A$ $[m_0 = 1.66 \times 10^{-27}$ kg$]$

Average density of nucleus $d = \frac{m}{V} = \frac{m_0 A}{\frac{4}{3}\pi r_0^3 A} = \frac{3m_0}{4\pi r_0^3}$ independent of A ⇒ Constant for all nuclei

for Na or any Nucleus $d = \frac{3 \times 1.66 \times 10^{-27}}{4 \times 3.14 \times (1.2 \times 10^{-15})^3}$

$\simeq 0.3 \times 10^{18}$ kg/m^3 Ans.

Comparing with d_{atom} ⇒ $\frac{d_{Nu}}{d_{atom}} = \frac{0.3 \times 10^{18}}{584} \simeq 10^{15}$ times Ans

- A LASER is a source of very intense, monochromatic, and unidirectional beam of light. These properties of a laser light can be exploited to measure long distances. The distance of the Moon from the Earth has been already determined very precisely using a laser as a source of light. A laser light beamed at the Moon takes 2.56 s to return after reflection at the Moon's surface. How much is the radius of the lunar orbit around the Earth ?

Solⁿ: Laser → EM wave travels at speed of light

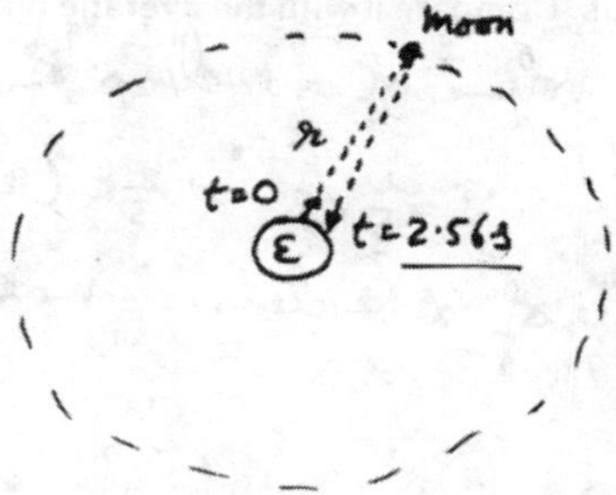

$$\text{Speed} = \frac{\text{distance}}{\text{Time}}$$

$$3\times10^{8} = \frac{2r}{2.56\ s}$$

$$r = \frac{1}{2}\times 2.56\times 3\times10^{8}\ m$$

$$= 3.84\times10^{8}\ m = \underline{3.84\times10^{5}\ km}.\ \text{Ans.}$$

- A SONAR (sound navigation and ranging) uses ultrasonic waves to detect and locate objects under water. In a submarine equipped with a SONAR the time delay between generation of a probe wave and the reception of its echo after reflection from an enemy submarine is found to be 77.0 s. What is the distance of the enemy submarine? (Speed of sound in water = 1450 m s^{-1}).

Sol^n:

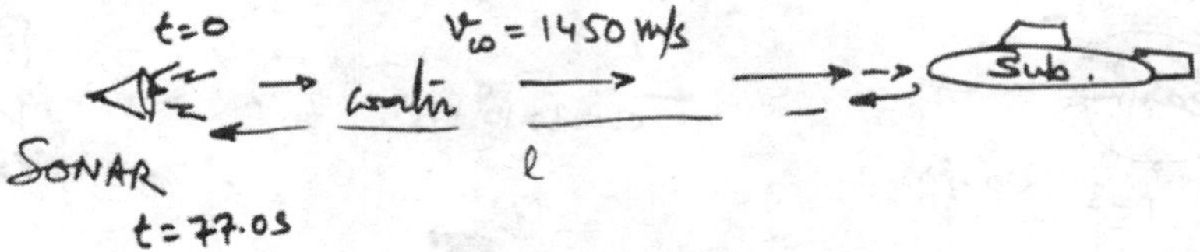

If distance between SONAR & Submarine is l we use -

$$v_w = \frac{2l}{t}$$

$$\Rightarrow l = \frac{1}{2} \times v_w \times t = \frac{1}{2} \times 1450 \times 77.0 = 55825 \text{ m.}$$

$$= 55.825 \text{ km.}$$

$$= 55.8 \text{ km Ans.}$$

Web Reference at www.physicsgalaxy.com

Video Sol. : Class 11th NCERT Solutions | **Sec. -** Mechanics **| Topic -** Units and Measurements

Theory Reference : Grade - 11 & 12 | **Sec. -** Basic Tools **| Topic -** Errors & Measurements

Video Solution

Exercise - 2.31

- The farthest objects in our Universe discovered by modern astronomers are so distant that light emitted by them takes billions of years to reach the Earth. These objects (known as quasars) have many puzzling features, which have not yet been satisfactorily explained. What is the distance in km of a quasar from which light takes 3.0 billion years to reach us?

Sol:

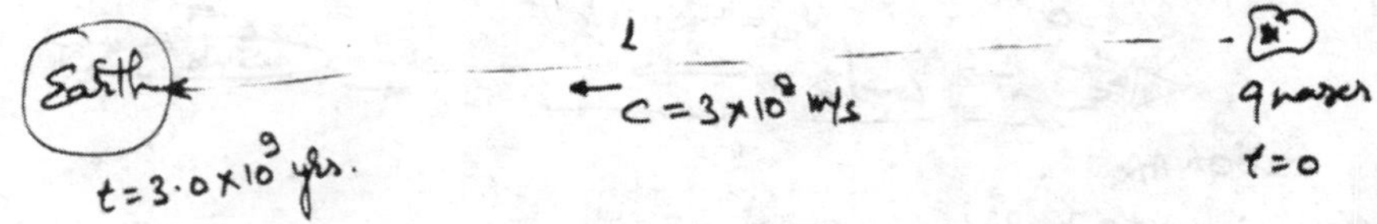

Distance from quasar to Earth. $l = ct$

$= 3\times10^8 \times 3.0 \times 10^9 \times 365 \times 24 \times 3600$ m

$= 2.84 \times 10^{25}$ m

$= 2.8 \times 10^{22}$ km Ans.

- It is a well known fact that during a total solar eclipse the disk of the moon almost completely covers the disk of the Sun. From this fact and from the information you can gather from examples 2.3 and 2.4, determine the approximate diameter of the moon.

Solⁿ: info from Ex 2.3 & 2.4

$r_{moon-Earth\,(ME)} = 3.84 \times 10^{8}$ m

$r_{Sun-Earth\,(SE)} = 1.496 \times 10^{11}$ m.

$d_{Sun} = 1.39 \times 10^{9}$ m.

Solar eclipse

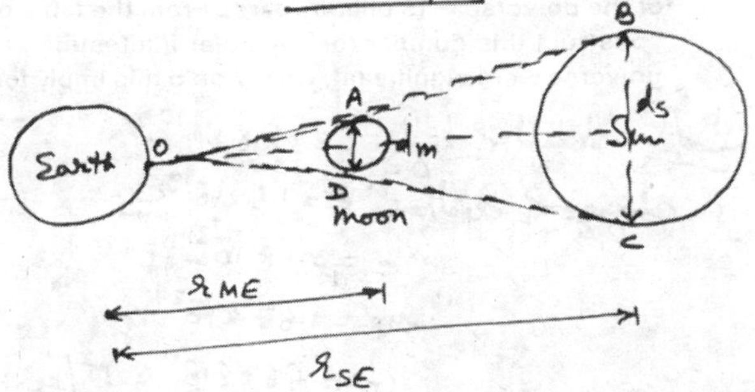

In triangles ΔOAD & ΔOBC

by similarity, we can use

$$\frac{d_m}{d_s} = \frac{r_{ME}}{r_{SE}}$$

diameter of moon ⇒

$$d_m = \frac{r_{ME}}{r_{SE}} \times d_s = \frac{3.84 \times 10^{8}}{1.496 \times 10^{11}} \times 1.39 \times 10^{9} = 3.568 \times 10^{6}\ \text{m}$$

$= 3.568 \times 10^{3}$ km

$= 3.57 \times 10^{3}$ km Ans

- A great physicist of this century (P.A.M. Dirac) loved playing with numerical values of Fundamental constants of nature. This led him to an interesting observation. Dirac found that from the basic constants of atomic physics (*c*, *e*, mass of electron, mass of proton) and the gravitational constant *G*, he could arrive at a number with the dimension of time. Further, it was a very large number, its magnitude being close to the present estimate on the age of the universe (~15 billion years). From the table of fundamental constants in this book, try to see if you too can construct this number (or any other interesting number you can think of). If its coincidence with the age of the universe were significant, what would this imply for the constancy of fundamental constants ?

Sol: Speed of light $c = 3\times10^{8}$ m/s

Charge of electron $e = 1.6\times10^{-19}$ C

$m_e = 9.1\times10^{-31}$ kg

$m_p = 1.67\times10^{-27}$ kg

$G = 6.67\times10^{-11}$ N-m²/kg² (kg m/s²)

Electrostatic Constant $k = \left(\frac{1}{4\pi\epsilon_0}\right) = 9\times10^{9}\ \frac{C^2}{N\text{-}m^2}$

& $\epsilon_0 = 8.85\times10^{-12}$ N-m²/C²

→ after manipulations adjusting constants so that the unit left after using all units of constants is 's' (second) then we get the relation

$$T = \frac{e^4}{16\pi^2\epsilon_0^2\, m_p m_e^2\, c^3 G}$$

($m_p m_e^2$ → m_p^3 or m_e^3 or $m_p^2 m_e$)

$$T = \frac{(1.6\times10^{-19})^4}{16\times(3.14)^2\times(8.85\times10^{-12})^2\times(1.67\times10^{-27})\times(9.1\times10^{-31})^2\times 3\times10^8\times6.67\times10^{-11}}$$

$\simeq 10^{9}$ yr ~ 1 Byr. ✓

Chapter 3

Motion in a Straight Line

QR Code of Link to the Video Lectures of Theory of this chapter Motion in a Straight Line at 'Physics Galaxy' web portal

QR Code of Link to the NCERT textbook Video Solutions of unsolved exercises at the end of each chapter in sequence of this chapter at 'Physics Galaxy' web portal

- In which of the following examples of motion, can the body be considered approximately a point object:

✓(a) a railway carriage moving without jerks between two stations

✓(b) a monkey sitting on top of a man cycling smoothly on a circular track

×(c) a spinning cricket ball that turns sharply on hitting the ground

×(d) a tumbling beaker that has slipped off the edge of a table

Sol^n: (a) If stations are far apart (large distance) compared to size of carriage
⇒ we consider it as a pt mass.

(b) As distance is v large (given that motion is smooth) ⇒ we can consider monkey as a pt mass.

(c)

f is considered only when size of ball is considered
⇒ it cannot be taken as a pt mass.

(d)

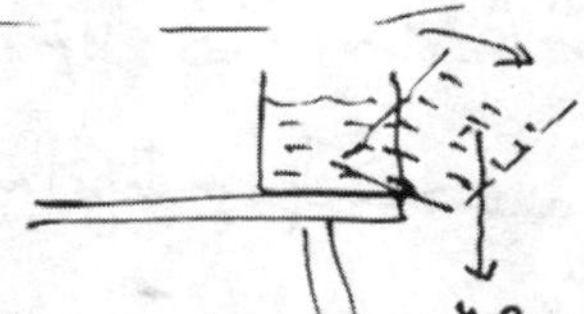

due to size only beaker will topple ⇒ Cannot be taken as a point mass

- The position-time (x-t) graphs for two children A and B returning from their school O to their homes P and Q respectively are shown in figure. Choose the correct entries in the brackets below ;

(a) (A/B) lives closer to the school than (B/A)

(b) (A/B) starts from the school earlier than (B/A)

(c) (A/B) walks faster than (B/A)

(d) A and B reach home at the (same/different) time

(e) (A/B) overtakes (B/A) on the road (once/twice)

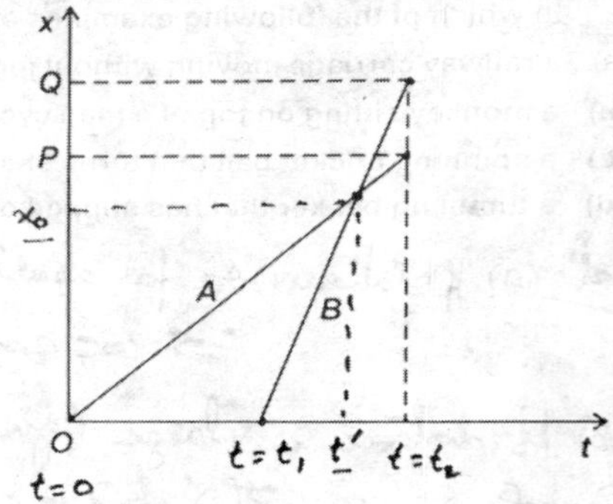

Sol^n: (a) As OQ > OP ⇒ A lives closer to school than B

(b) A starts from school earlier than B.
($t=0$) ($t=t_1$)

(c) As $(\text{slope})_A < (\text{slope})_B \Rightarrow v_A < v_B \Rightarrow$ B walks faster than A

(d) Both A & B are reaching together

(e) B overtakes A on road once.

- A woman starts from her home at 9.00 am, walks with a speed of 5 km h^{-1} on a straight road up to her office 2.5 km away, stays at the office up to 5.00 pm, and returns home by an auto with a speed of 25 km h^{-1}. Choose suitable scales and plot the *x-t* graph of her motion.

Sol: starts at t = 9 am.

reaches office at $t = 9\text{am} + \frac{2.5\text{km}}{5\text{kph}} = 9{:}30\text{am}$

she returns from office at t = 5 pm

time of arrival at home $t = 5\text{pm} + \frac{2.5\text{ km}}{25\text{ km/hr}}$ ($\frac{1}{10}$ hr = 6 min)

= 5:06 pm.

Ans. →

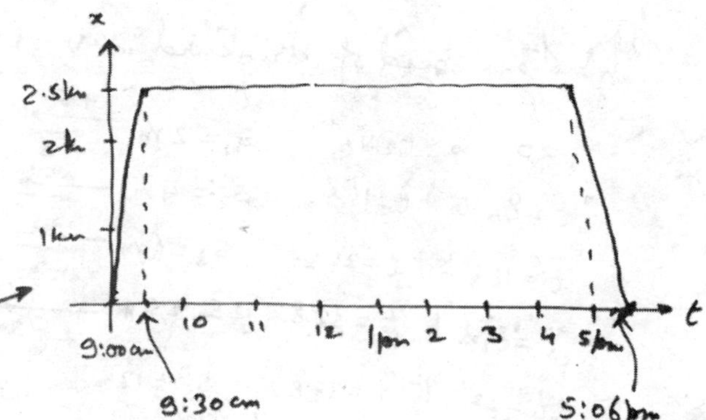

- A drunkard walking in a narrow lane takes 5 steps forward and 3 steps backward, followed again by 5 steps forward and 3 steps backward, and so on. Each step is 1 m long and requires 1 s. Plot the *x-t* graph of his motion. Determine graphically and otherwise how long the drunkard takes to fall in a pit 13 m away from the start.

Sol^n:

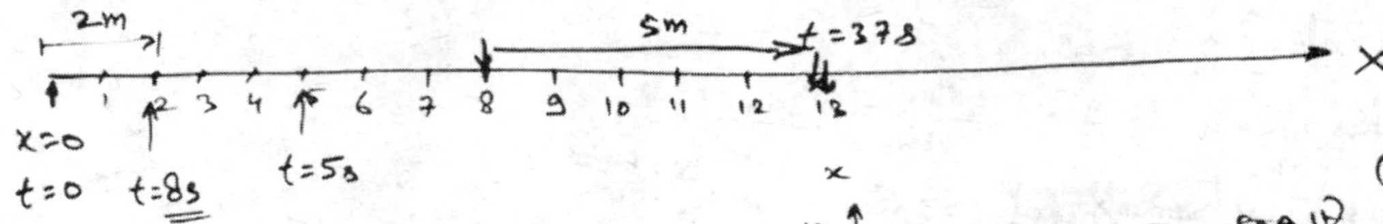

In motion speed of drunkard is $v = 1\ m/s$.

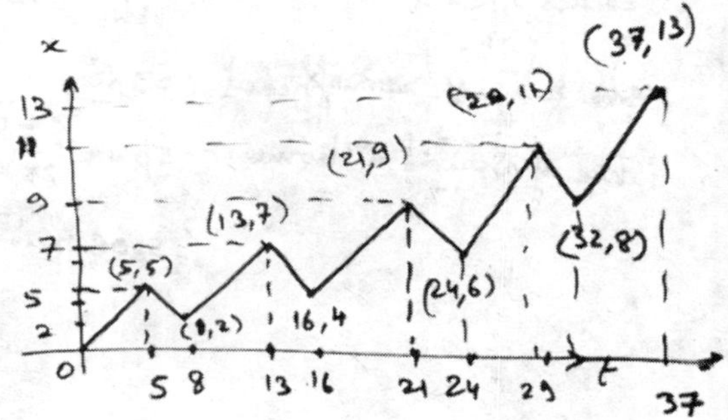

$t = 0$ to $t = 8\ s$ $S_1 = 2\ m$ (+5, −3)

$t = 8\ s$ to $t = 16\ s$ $S_2 = 4\ m$ (+5, −3)

$t = 16\ s$ to $t = 24\ s$ $S_3 = 6\ m$ (+5, −3)

$t = 24\ s$ to $t = 32\ s$ $S_4 = 8\ m$ (+5, $S_5 = 13\ m$, −3 ×)

$t = 32\ s$ to $t = 37\ s$ $S_5 = 13\ m$

falls in pit

Video Solution

- **A jet airplane travelling at the speed of 500 km h^{-1} ejects its products of combustion at the speed of 1500 km h^{-1} relative to the jet plane. What is the speed of the latter with respect to an observer on the ground ?**

Sol^n:

$v_p = 500$ km/hr

$v_{cJ} = 1500$ km/hr w.r.to jet plane.

$\vec{v}_p = 500$ kph

$-$ve ← → +ve

$\vec{v}_{cJ} = -1500$ kph.

If $\vec{v}_c$ is the velocity of combustion products w.r.to ground

$$\Rightarrow \quad \vec{v}_{cJ} = \vec{v}_c - \vec{v}_J$$

$$\vec{v}_c = \vec{v}_{cJ} + \vec{v}_J = -1500 \text{ kph} + 500 \text{ kph} = \underline{\underline{-1000 \text{ kph.}}}$$

Ans.

- A car moving along a straight highway with speed of 126 km h^{-1} is brought to a stop within a distance of 200 m. What is the retardation of the car (assumed uniform), and how long does it take for the car to stop ?

Sol^n:

$u = 126\ km/hr \times \frac{5}{18} = 35\ m/s$

$s = 200\,m$

using speed eq^n $v^2 = u^2 + 2as$

$$a = \frac{v^2 - u^2}{2s} = \frac{0 - (35)^2}{2 \times 200} = -\frac{49}{16}\ m/s^2 = -3.06\ m/s^2 \text{ Ans}$$

using speed eq^n $v = u + at$

$$\Rightarrow t = \frac{v - u}{a} = \frac{0 - (35)}{-49/16} = \frac{80}{7}\ s = 11.4\ s \text{ Ans}$$

Video Solution

- Two trains *A* and *B* of length 400 m each are moving on two parallel tracks with a uniform speed of 72 km h^{-1} in the same direction, with *A* ahead of *B*. The driver of *B* decides to overtake *A* and accelerates by 1 m s^{-2}. If after 50 s, the guard of *B* just brushes past the driver of *A*. what was the original distance between them ?

Sol^n:

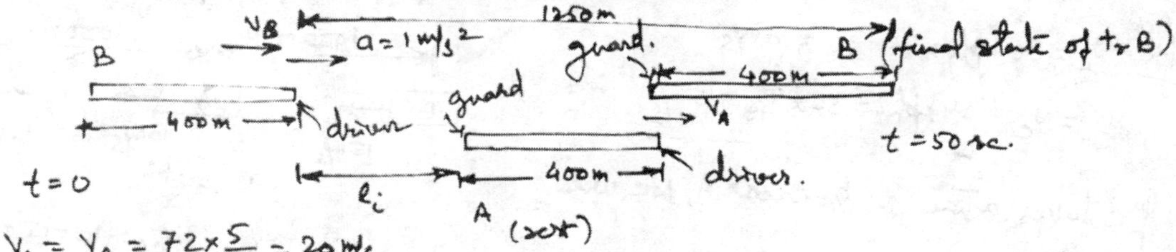

$V_A = V_B = 72 \times \frac{5}{18} = 20$ m/s

If we solve the problem in reference frame of A (relative to A)

w.r.to A vel of B is $v_{BA} = v_B - v_A = 0$

acc^n of B is $a_{BA} = a_B - a_A = 1$ m/s^2

distance travelled by B relative to A in 50 s is

$$d_{BA} = ut + \tfrac{1}{2}at^2 = 0 + \tfrac{1}{2} \times 1 \times (50)^2 = 1250 \text{ m.}$$

initial distance between driver of B & guard of A is $= 1250 - 800 = 450$ m Ans

- On a two-lane road, car *A* is travelling with a speed of 36 km h^{-1}. Two cars *B* and *C* approach car *A* in opposite directions with a speed of 54 km h^{-1} each. At a certain instant, when the distance *AB* is equal to *AC*, both being 1 km, *B* decides to overtake *A* before *C* does. What minimum acceleration of car *B* is required to avoid an accident ?

Solⁿ: $v_A = 36\ kph = 36 \times 5/18 = 10\ m/s$

$v_B = v_C = 54\ kph = 54 \times 5/18 = 15\ m/s$

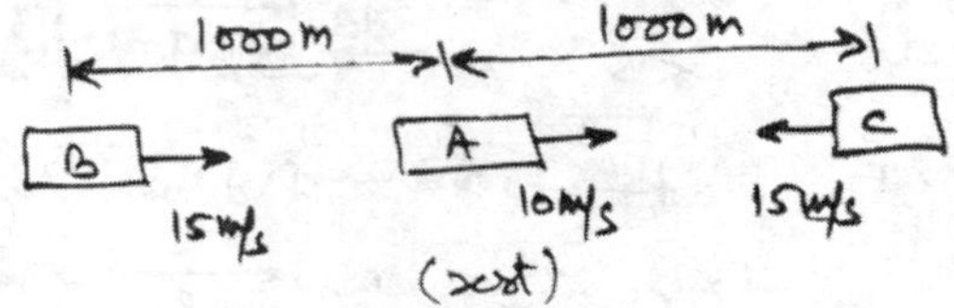

$v_{CA} = 10 + 15 = 25\ m/s$

$v_{BA} = 15 - 10 = 5\ m/s$

If C takes a time t to cross A, we use

$$t = \frac{1000}{25} = 40\ s.$$

To avoid an accident & to overtake car A before car C crosses it, B has to travel 1000 m w.r.to A (wrt) in 40 s.

$\Rightarrow$ using speed eqⁿ $\quad s = ut + \frac{1}{2}at^2$

$$1000 = 5 \times 40 + \frac{1}{2} a \times (40)^2$$

$$800 = 800\, a \quad \Rightarrow \quad a = 1\ m/s^2 \quad \text{Ans.}$$

Video Solution

- Two towns *A* and *B* are connected by a regular bus service with a bus leaving in either direction every *T* minutes. A man cycling with a speed of 20 km h^{-1} in the direction *A* to *B* notices that a bus goes past him every 18 min in the direction of his motion, and every 6 min in the opposite direction. What is the period *T* of the bus service and with what speed (assumed constant) do the buses ply on the road?

Sol^n:

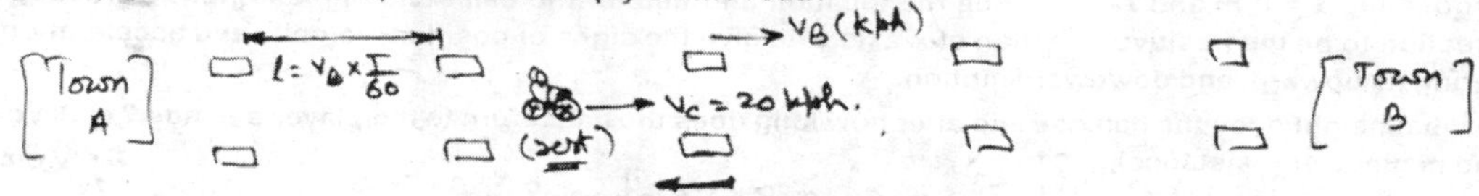

for buses in direction of cyclist are meeting with him at every 18 min.
w.r.to cyclist we use
$$l = (v_B - v_c) \times \frac{18}{60} = v_B \times \frac{T}{60} \quad \text{--- (1)}$$
rel speed of bus w.r.to cyclist.

for buses in opposite dir are meeting every 6 min to cyclist
$\Rightarrow$ w.r.to cyclist we use
$$l = (v_B + v_c) \times \frac{6}{60} = v_B \times \frac{T}{60} \quad \text{--- (2)}$$

from (1) & (2) $(v_B - 20) \times \frac{18}{60} = (v_B + 20) \times \frac{6}{60} \Rightarrow 3v_B - 60 = v_B + 20$

$\Rightarrow v_B = 40$ km/hr Ans.

from eq^n (1) $20 \times \frac{18}{60} = 40 \times \frac{T}{60}$

$\Rightarrow T = 9$ min Ans.

- A player throws a ball upwards with an initial speed of 29.4 m s^{-1}.

(a) What is the direction of acceleration during the upward motion of the ball ?

(b) What are the velocity and acceleration of the ball at the highest point of its motion ?

(c) Choose the $x = 0$ *m* and $t = 0$ *s* to be the location and time of the ball at its highest point, vertically downward direction to be the positive direction of *x*-axis, and give the signs of position, velocity and acceleration of the ball during its upward, and downward motion.

(d) To what height does the ball rise and after how long does the ball return to the player's hands ? (Take $g = 9.8$ m s^{-2} and neglect air resistance).

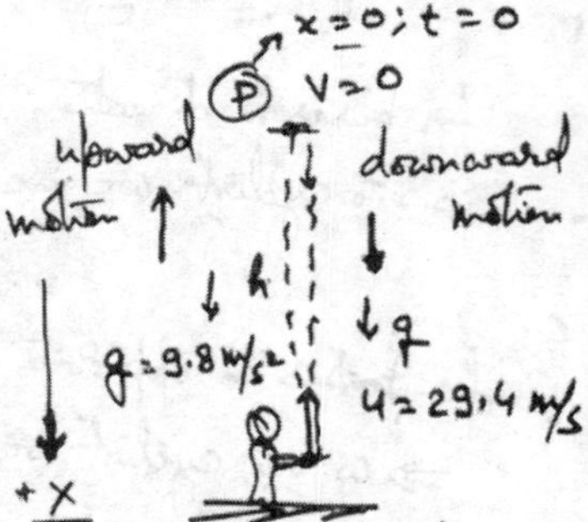

Sol^n: (a) acc^n due to gravity $\rightarrow g = 9.8$ m/s^2 always in downward direction Ans

(b) At highest point P
$v = 0$ (rest)
$a = g = 9.8$ m/s^2 ↓ } Ans

(c) During upward motion $x \rightarrow +ve$; $v^{\uparrow} \rightarrow -ve$; $a = g \downarrow$ +ve

During downward motion $x \rightarrow +ve$; $v_{\downarrow} \rightarrow +ve$; $a = g \downarrow$ +ve.

(d) max height attained by ball $h = \frac{u^2}{2g} = \frac{(29.4)^2}{2 \times 9.8} = 44.1$ m Ans

and time of upward & downward motion $\rightarrow t_{up} = t_{down} = \frac{u}{g} = \frac{29.4}{9.8} = 3$ s

$T = 2t_{up} = 6$ s Ans

Video Solution

- Read each statement below carefully and state with reasons and examples, if it is true or false;
  A particle in one-dimensional motion

(a) with zero speed at an instant may have non-zero acceleration at that instant

(b) with zero speed may have non-zero velocity,

(c) with constant speed must have zero acceleration,

(d) with positive value of acceleration must be speeding up

Sol: (a) at an instant

$v = 0$ & $a \neq 0$ ✓

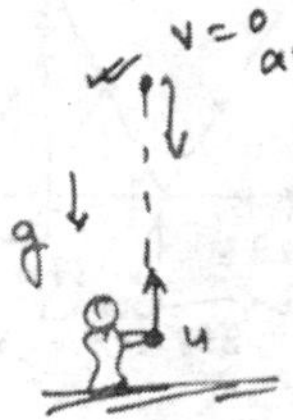

TRUE

(b) at an instant $v = 0$ but $\vec{v} \neq 0$ — not possible

→ v (m/s)

if a particle is in motion $v \neq 0$

$\vec{v} \neq 0$

but at rest $v = 0$

$\Rightarrow \vec{v} = 0$

FALSE.

(c) If v = Const, $a = 0$ ×

If a particle has constant speed but changing its direction

$\Rightarrow \vec{v} \neq$ Constant

$\vec{a} = \frac{d\vec{v}}{dt} \neq 0$

$\vec{v}$ changing but $|\vec{v}|$ = Constant

$\vec{a} \neq 0$.

FALSE.

(d) If a = +ve

$\Rightarrow v$ increases ×

→ +x

v +ve, a +ve

$\Rightarrow$ speeding up

→ +x

v −ve, a +ve

$\Rightarrow v$ decreases

FALSE.

Web Reference at www.physicsgalaxy.com

Video Sol. : Class 11th NCERT Solutions | **Sec. -** Mechanics | **Topic -** Motion in a Straight Line

Theory Reference : Grade - 11 & 12 | **Sec. -** Mechanics | **Topic -** Motion in One Dimensions

Video Solution

- A ball is dropped from a height of 90 m on a floor. At each collision with the floor, the ball loses one tenth of its speed. Plot the speed-time graph of its motion between $t = 0$ to 12 s.

Sol:

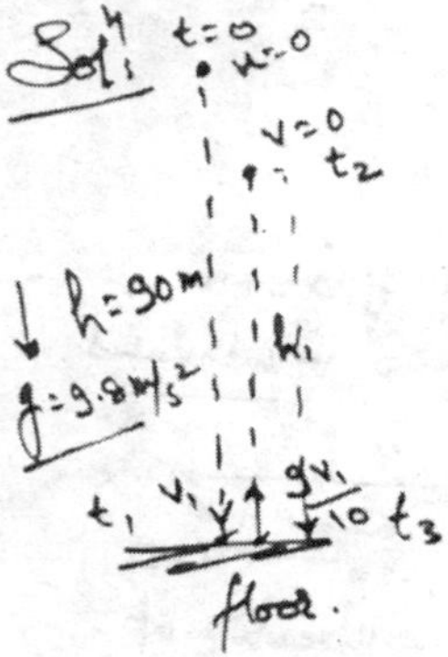

at first collision $t_1 = \sqrt{\frac{2h}{g}} = \sqrt{\frac{2\times 90}{9.8}} = 4.28\,s$

$v_1 = \sqrt{2gh} = \sqrt{2\times 90\times 9.8} = 42\,m/s$

rebound speed $= \frac{9v_1}{10} = \frac{9}{10}\times 42 = 37.8\,m/s$

rebound height $h_1 = \frac{u^2}{2g} = \frac{(37.8)^2}{2\times 9.8} = 72.9\,m.$

rebounce time $t_2 = \sqrt{\frac{2h_1}{g}} = \sqrt{\frac{2\times 72.9}{9.8}} \simeq 3.857\,s$

down time after reaching top ↓ upto second collision $t_3 = t_2 = 3.857\,s.$

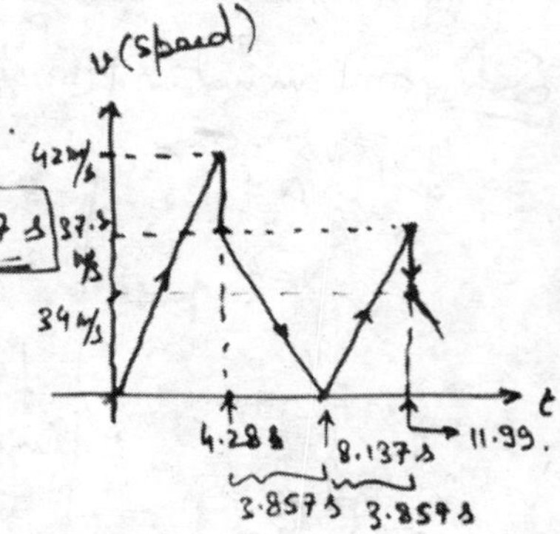

time spent till second collision $= t_1 + t_2 + t_3$

$= 4.28 + 3.857 + 3.857\,s$

$= 11.99 \simeq 12\,s$

speed after second collision $= \frac{9}{10}\times 37.8 \cong 34\,m/s$

- Explain clearly, with examples, the distinction between :

(a) magnitude of displacement (sometimes called distance) over an interval of time, and the total length of path covered by a particle over the same interval;

(b) magnitude of average velocity over an interval of time, and the average speed over the same interval. [Average speed of a particle over an interval of time isdefined as the total path length divided by the time interval]. Show in both (a) and (b) that the second quantity is either greater than or equal to the first. When is the equality sign true ? [For simplicity, consider one-dimensional motion only].

Sol^n(a)

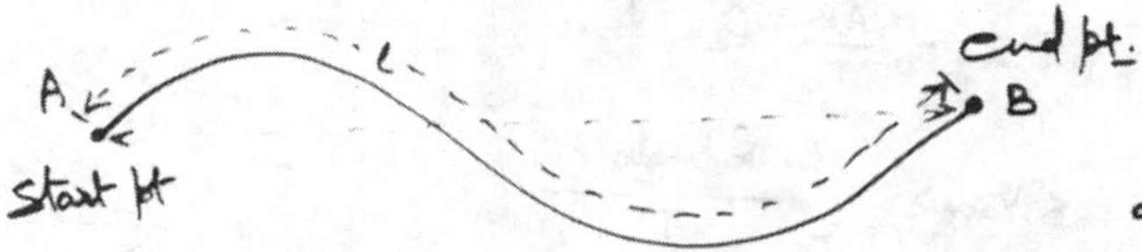

displacement = AB

distance travelled = length of path from A to B.

always path length ≥ displacement

Motion in a st line

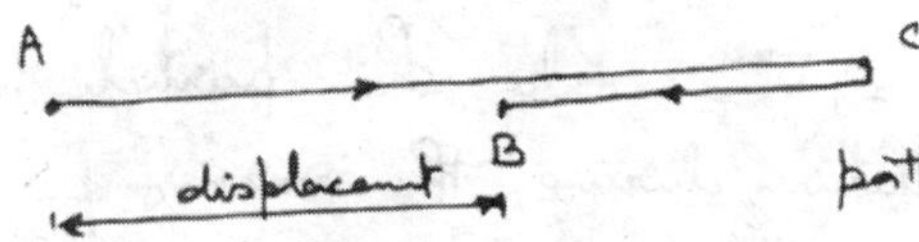

path length = AC + CB

If particle is moving along a st line & does not return ⇒ path length = displacement

(b)

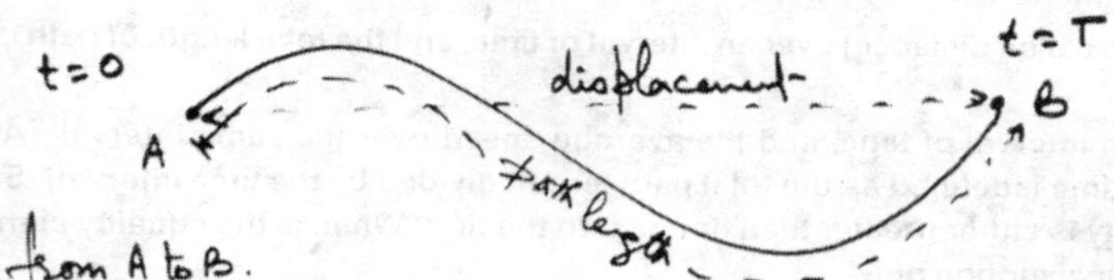

from A to B.

average velocity $\vec{v}_{avg} = \frac{AB}{T}\,\hat{AB}$

average speed $\langle v_{avg} \rangle = \frac{\text{path length } AB}{T}$

As path length AB > AB. $\Rightarrow \quad \langle v_{avg} \rangle \geq |\vec{v}_{avg}|$

here $\langle v_{avg} \rangle = |\vec{v}_{avg}|$ only when particle is moving in a st line & it does not return during the journey.

for 1D motion

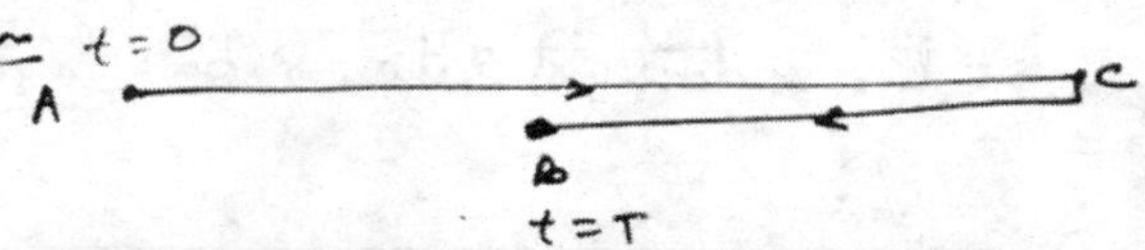

$|\vec{v}_{avg}| = \frac{AB}{T}$

$\langle v_{avg} \rangle = \frac{AC + CB}{T}$

- A man walks on a straight road from his home to a market 2.5 km away with a speed of 5 km h^{-1}. Finding the market closed, he instantly turns and walks back home with a speed of 7.5 km h^{-1}. What is the

(a) magnitude of average velocity, and

(b) average speed of the man over the interval of time (i) 0 to 30 min, (ii) 0 to 50 min, (iii) 0 to 40 min ? [Note: You will appreciate from this exercise why it is better to define average speed as total path length divided by time, and not as magnitude of average velocity. You would not like to tell the tired man on his return home that his average speed was zero !]

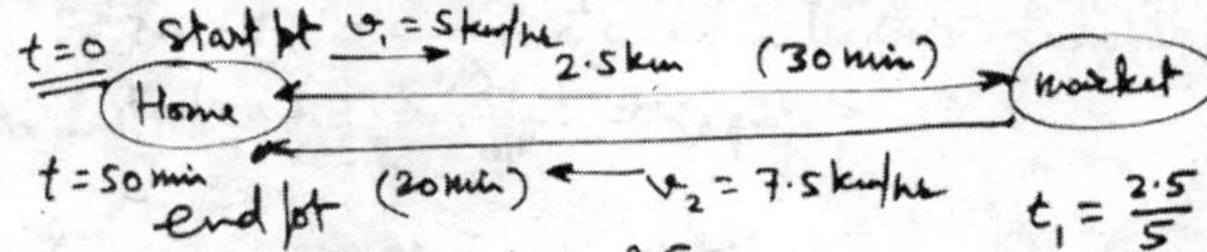

Sol (a) Total displacement of man

$d = 0$

average velocity $\vec{v}_{avg} = \frac{0}{T} = 0$ m/s Ans

$t_1 = \frac{2.5}{5} = \frac{1}{2}$ hr $= 30$ min

$t_2 = 30\text{ min} + \frac{2.5}{7.5}$

$30\text{ min} + \frac{1}{3}\text{ hr} = 30\text{ min} + 20\text{ min} = 50\text{ min}.$

(b)(i) 0 to 30 min

$\langle v_{avg_1} \rangle = |\vec{v}_{avg_1}| = \frac{2.5}{(1/2)} = 5$ km/hr Ans.

(ii) 0 to 50 min

$\langle v_{avg_2} \rangle = \frac{2.5 + 2.5}{(5/6\text{ hr})} = 6$ km/hr Ans

(iii) 0 to 40 min (0 to 30 is onward journey & 30 to 40 min is return journey)
10 min

distance covered by man in 10 min during return journey $= v_2 t = 7.5 \times \frac{10}{60}$
$= 1.25$ km

Total distance covered in the 0 to 40 min $= 2.5 + 1.25 = 3.75$ km.

$$\langle v_{avg3} \rangle = \frac{3.75}{4/6} = 5.625 \text{ km/hr}$$ Ans.

- **In Exercises 3.13 and 3.14, we have carefully distinguished between average speed and magnitude of average velocity. No such distinction is necessary when we consider instantaneous speed and magnitude of velocity. The instantaneous speed is always equal to the magnitude of instantaneous velocity. Why ?**

Sol^n:

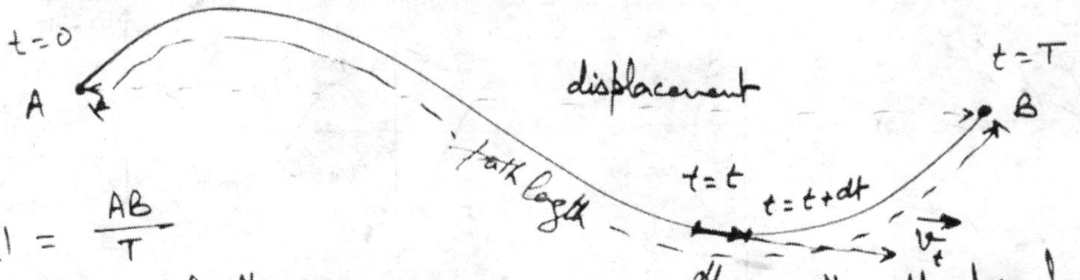

(being small, it is always taken a st line)

$$|\vec{v}_{avg}| = \frac{AB}{T}$$

$$\langle v_{avg} \rangle = \frac{\text{path length } AB}{T}$$

In an elemental duration t to t + dt, if particle travels a distance dl

⇒ at instant t its instantaneous speed is $v = \frac{dl}{dt}$ ← velocity of particle at that t

as in duration 'dt' particle does not return & considered to be moving in a st line ⇒ (instantaneous speed) = (inst velocity magnitude)

- Look at the graphs (a) to (d) (figure) carefully and state, with reasons, which of these cannot possibly represent one-dimensional motion of a particle.

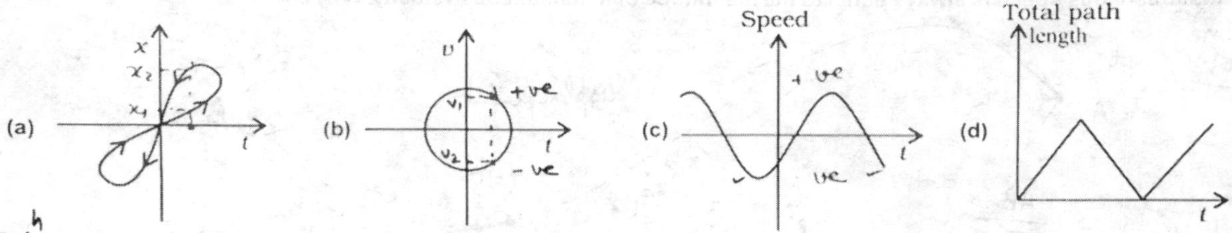

Sol^n

(a) Not possible as At one instant two positions of a particle cannot be there.

(b) Not possible as at one instant a particle cannot have two velocities in opposite direction.

(c) Not possible as Speed of a particle is always +ve, it cannot be –ve as in Speed we do not associate direction

(d) Not possible as path length in any motion always increases with time.

- Figure shows the *x* - *t* plot of one-dimensional motion of a particle. Is it correct to say from the graph that the particle moves in a straight line for $t < 0$ and on a parabolic path for $t > 0$? If not, suggest a suitable physical context for this graph.

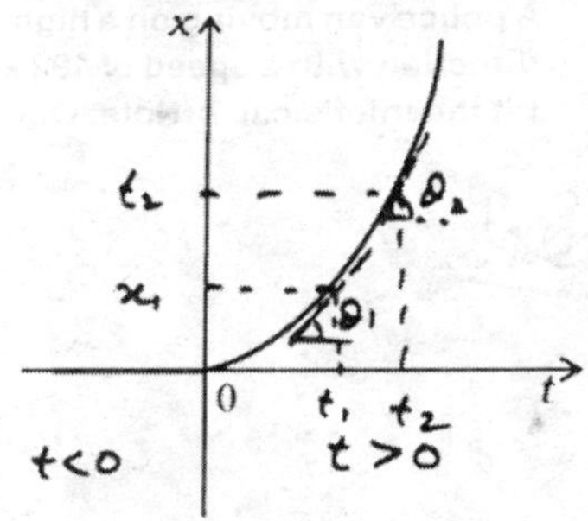

Sol^n: No.

here as $t_2 > t_1$

& we can see $\theta_2 > \theta_1$

⇒ As slope of graph is increasing with time

↓ "velocity of particle"

⇒ this curve represent accelerated motion

$v_1 = \tan\theta_1$

$v_2 = \tan\theta_2$

$v_2 > v_1$

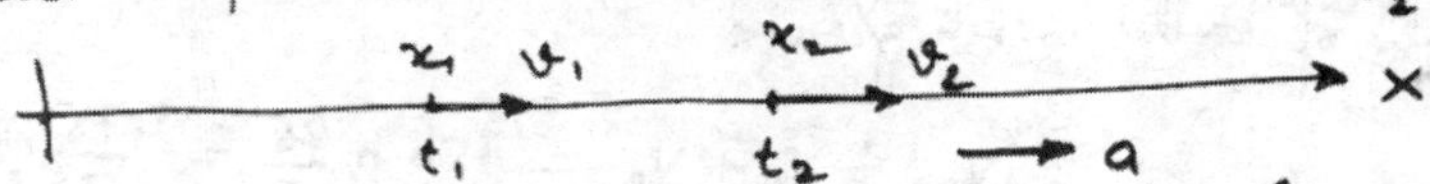

the graph can be of a one dimentional accelerated motion (like a freefall)

Web Reference at www.physicsgalaxy.com

Video Sol. : Class 11th NCERT Solutions | **Sec. -** Mechanics | **Topic -** Motion in a Straight Line

Theory Reference : Grade - 11 & 12 | **Sec. -** Mechanics | **Topic -** Motion in One Dimensions

Video Solution

- A police van moving on a highway with a speed of 30 km h^{-1} fires a bullet at a thief's car speeding away in the same direction with a speed of 192 km h^{-1}. If the muzzle speed of the bullet is 150 m s^{-1}, with what speed does the bullet hit the thief's car ? (Note: Obtain that speed which is relevant for damaging the thief's car).

Sol^n

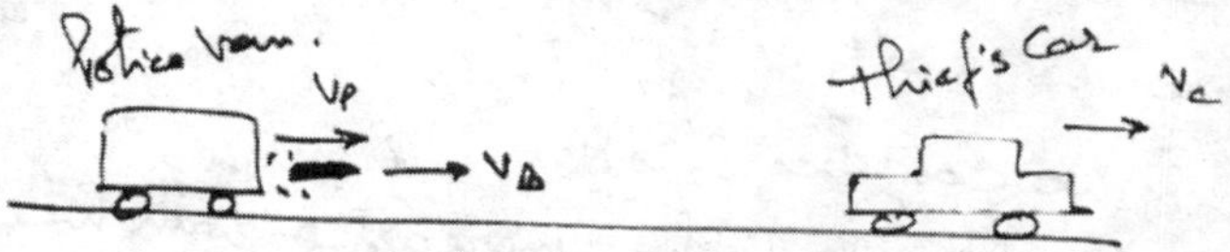

$$v_p = 30 \times \frac{5}{18} = \frac{25}{3} \text{ m/s}$$

$$v_c = 192 \text{ km/hr} = 192 \times \frac{5}{18} = \frac{160}{3} \text{ m/s}$$

$v_B = 150$ m/s relative to van.

velocity of bullet w.r.t ground

$$v_{BG} = v_B + v_p = 150 + \frac{25}{3} = \frac{475}{3} \text{ m/s}$$

velocity of bullet w.r.t. thief's car is $v_{BC} = v_{BG} - v_c = \frac{475}{3} - \frac{160}{3} = 105 \text{ m/s}$ Ans

Video Solution

- **Suggest a suitable physical situation for each of the following graphs (figure):**

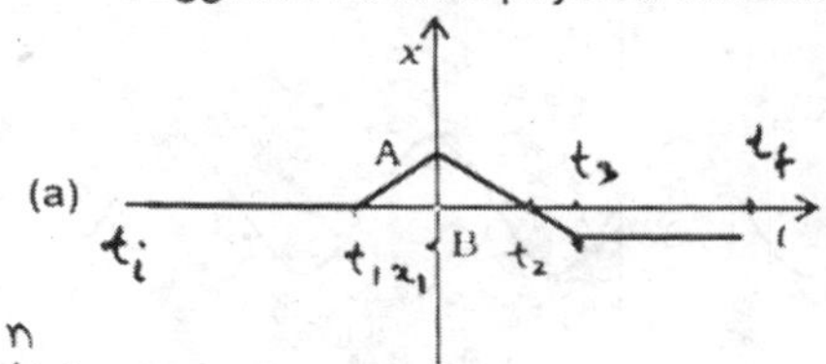

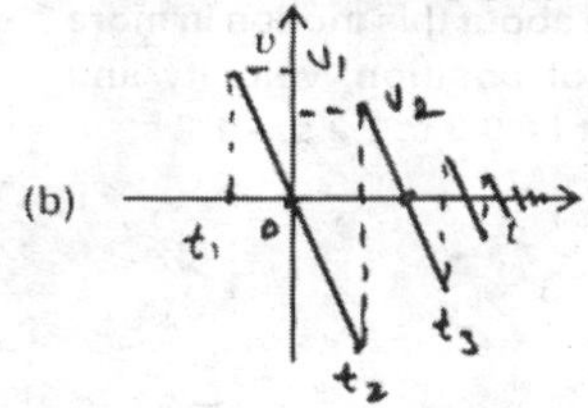

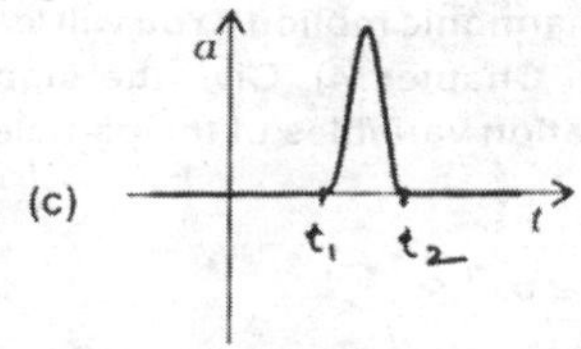

Sol^n(a)

from $t = t_i$ to t_1 → particle is at rest

$t = t_1$ to 0 → particle moves at uniform velocity

$t = 0$ to t_3 → particle moves at uniform velocity in opposite dir

$t = t_3$ to $\infty (t_f)$ → rest

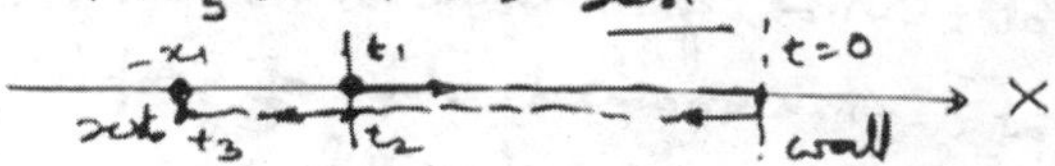

(b)

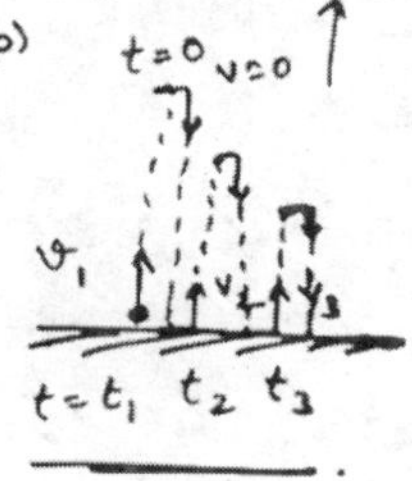

(c) upto time t_1 $a = 0$

$\Rightarrow v = \text{Constant}$

Case-I

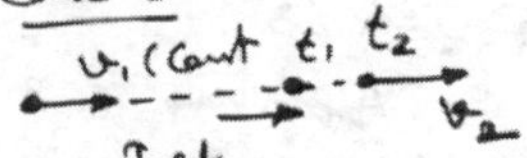

$\Delta v = v_2 - v_1 = \text{area of } a\text{-}t \text{ graph}$

Case-II

$\Delta v = v_2 + v_1 = \text{area of } a\text{-}t \text{ graph}$

- Figure gives the *x- t* plot of a particle executing one-dimensional simple harmonic motion. (You will learn about this motion in more detail in Chapter14). Give the signs of position, velocity and acceleration variables of the particle at $t = 0.3$ s, 1.2 s, – 1.2 s.

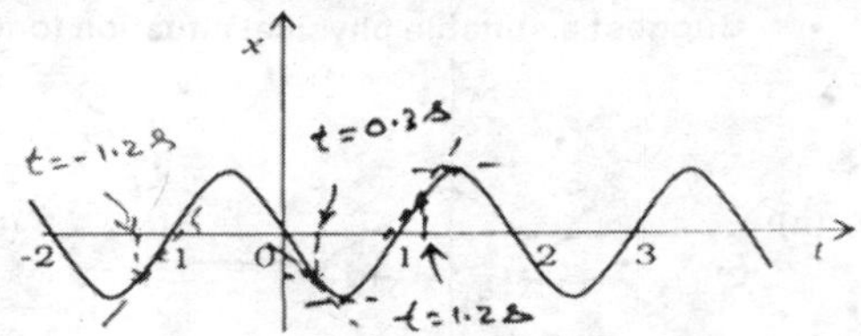

Sol^n:

At $t = 0.3$s
position $x = -ve$
velocity $v = -ve$
acc^n $a = +ve$

At $t = 1.2$s
position $x = +ve$.
vel. $v = +ve$
acc^n. $a = -ve$

At $t = -1.2$s
position $x = -ve$
velocity $v = +ve$
acc^n $a = +ve$.

at $t = 0.3$s, graph slope is -ve.
at $t = 0.3$s onward slope of graph is decreasing ⇒ particle is retarding

at $t = 1.2$s, slope of graph is +ve
at $t = 1.2$s onward slope of graph is decreasing ⇒ particle is retarding
at $t = -1.2$s, graph slope is +ve
at $t = -1.2$s onward slope of graph is increasing ⇒ particle is accelerating

- **Figure gives the *x*- *t* plot of a particle in one-dimensional motion. Three different equal intervals of time are shown. In which interval is the average speed greatest, and in which is it the least ? Give the sign of average velocity for each interval.**

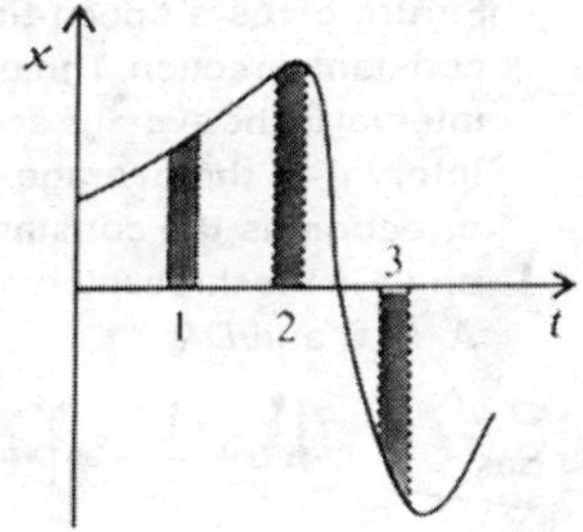

Sol^n: Average velocity → average value of slope of x-t curve in the given interval.

from graph it is clear that

$$(\text{slope})_3 > (\text{slope})_1 > (\text{slope})_2$$

$$(\text{avg speed})_3 > (\text{avg speed})_1 > (\text{avg speed})_2$$

$$\left(\begin{array}{l}\bar{v}_1 \text{ \& } \bar{v}_2 \rightarrow +ve \\ \bar{v}_3 \rightarrow -ve\end{array}\right) \text{ Ans.}$$

- Figure gives a speed-time graph of a particle in motion along a constant direction. Three equal intervals of time are shown. In which interval is the average acceleration greatest in magnitude ? In which interval is the average speed greatest ? Choosing the positive direction as the constant direction of motion, give the signs of *v* and *a* in the three intervals. What are the accelerations at the points *A*, *B*, *C* and *D* ?

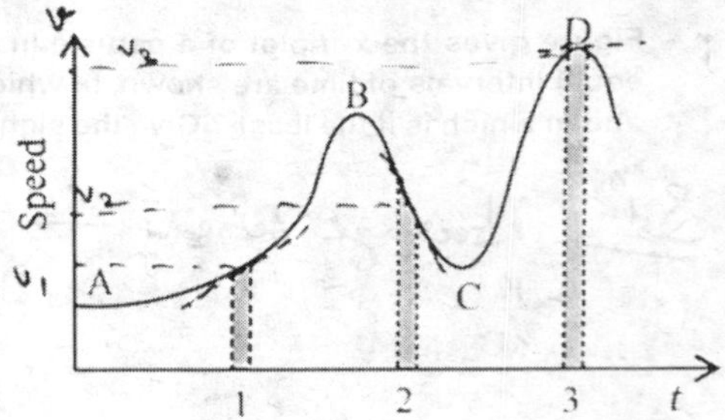

Sol^n: About speed for all regions

1, 2 and 3 $v = +ve$

Slope of graph
1 → slope +ve ⇒ $a = +ve$
2 → slope -ve ⇒ $a = -ve$
3 → slope zero ⇒ $a = 0$

at pts A, B, C & D as slope is zero ⇒ $a = 0$ at all these pts.

in the 3 regions avg speed is greatest in Region (3)

in the 3 regions avg acceleration is greatest in region (2) (tangent-2 is steepest)

- A three-wheeler starts from rest, accelerates uniformly with 1 m s^{-2} on a straight road for 10 s, and then moves with uniform velocity. Plot the distance covered by the vehicle during the nth second (n = 1,2,3...) versus n. What do you expect this plot to be during accelerated motion : a straight line or a parabola ?

Sol^n: Distance covered by particle in n^{th} second of motion (a = Constant) is given as

$$S_n = u + \frac{a}{2}(2n-1)$$

given here that $u = 0$ $\Rightarrow$ $S_n = \frac{a}{2}(2n-1) = 0.5(2n-1)$ m.

for $n=1 \rightarrow S_1 = 0.5$ m

$n=2 \rightarrow S_2 = 1.5$ m

$n=3 \rightarrow S_3 = 2.5$ m

$n=4 \rightarrow S_4 = 3.5$ m

⋮

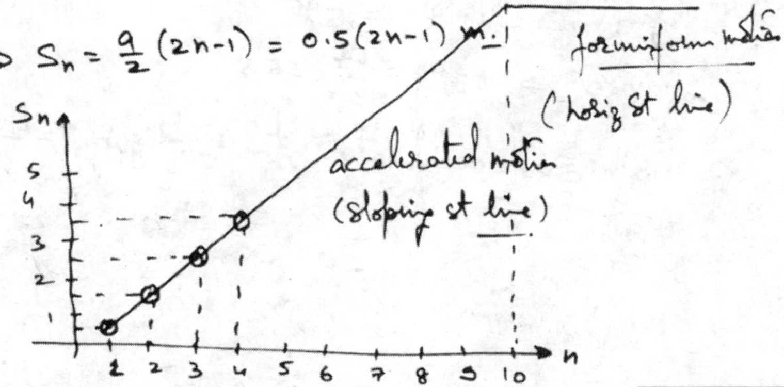

- A boy standing on a stationary lift (open from above) throws a ball upwards with the maximum initial speed he can, equal to 49 m s^{-1}. How much time does the ball take to return to his hands? If the lift starts moving up with a uniform speed of 5 m s^{-1} and the boy again throws the ball up with the maximum speed he can, how long does the ball take to return to his hands ?

Sol^n: Case I: for stationary lift.

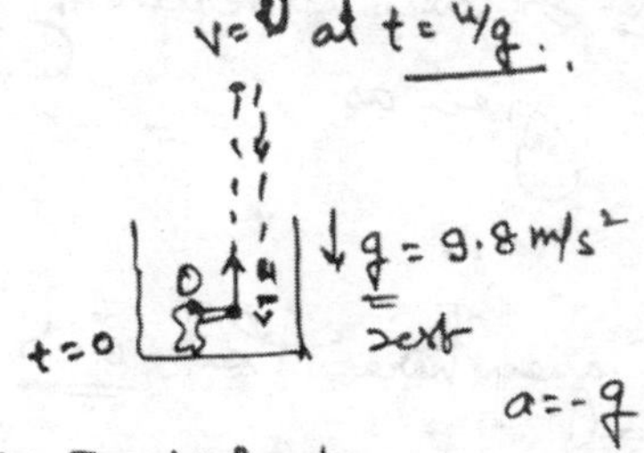

$u = 49\, m/s$

using $v = u + at = u - gt$

at $v = 0 \Rightarrow t = u/g = \frac{49}{9.8} = 5\, s$

with same acceleration time of flight $T = \frac{2u}{g} = 2 \times 5 = 10\, s$. Ans

Case-II: lift is going up at 5 m/s

⇒ Due to motion of lift ball will also be moving initially at 5 m/s.

→ at the time of throw, vel of ball w.r.to lift $v_{BL} = 49\text{ m/s}$ (53 m/s − 5 m/s)

$u = 49 + 5 = 53\text{ m/s}$

acc^n of ball w.r.to lift $a_{BL} = a_B - a_L = 9.8 - 0 = 9.8\text{ m/s}^2$

w.r.to lift, the time of flight of ball

$$T_{ball} = \frac{2u_{BL}}{a_{BL}} = \frac{2\times 49}{9.8} = 10\text{ s Ans.}$$

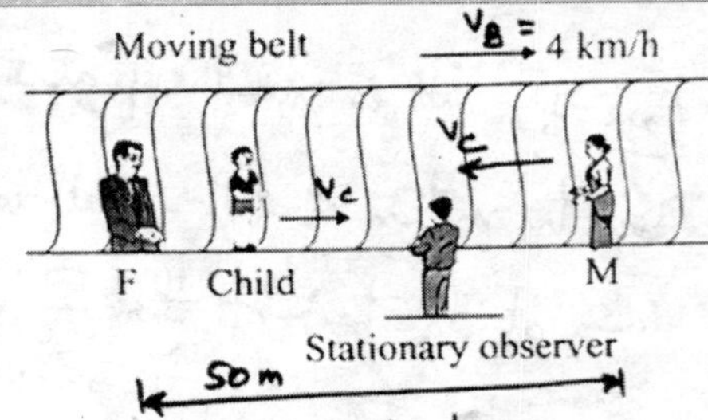

- On a long horizontally moving belt (figure), a child runs to and fro with a speed 9 km h^{-1} (with respect to the belt) between his father and mother located 50 m apart on the moving belt. The belt moves with a speed of 4 km h^{-1}. For an observer on a stationary platform outside, what is the

(a) speed of the child running in the direction of motion of the belt ?

(b) speed of the child running opposite to the direction of motion of the belt ?

(c) time taken by the child in (a) and (b) ?

Which of the answers alter if motion is viewed by one of the parents ?

$V_c = 9$ km/hr

Sol^n: (a) vel of child as seen from ground frame

$$V_{CG} = V_c + V_B = 9 + 4 = 13 \text{ km/hr Ans} \text{ (toward right)}$$

(b) if child moves/runs in opp dir

$$V_{CG} = V_c - V_B = 9 - 4 = 5 \text{ km/hr Ans. (toward left)}$$

(c) $$t_A = \frac{\text{distance}}{\text{speed}} = \frac{50}{9 \times 5/18} = 20 \text{ s. Ans}$$

t_B " (same) — w.r.to belt or w.r.to ground frame

w.r.to parents (in frame of belt) answer to part (a) & (b) will be same at 9 km/hr.

Video Solution

- Two stones are thrown up simultaneously from the edge of a cliff 200 m high with initial speeds of 15 m s^{-1} and 30 m s^{-1}. Verify that the graph shown in figure correctly represents the time variation of the relative position of the second stone with respect to the first. Neglect air resistance and assume that the stones do not rebound after hitting the ground. Take $g = 10$ m s^{-2}. Give the equations for the linear and curved parts of the plot.

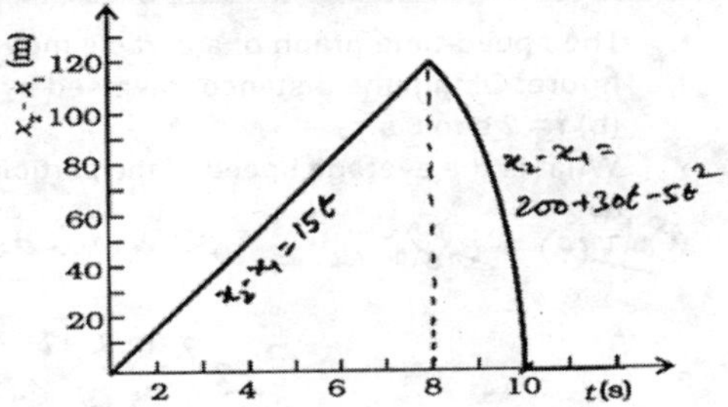

Sol^n: For first stone $\quad y_1 = 200 + (u_1 t - \frac{1}{2} g t^2)$

$= 200 + 15t - 5t^2$

if at $t = t_1$, $y_1 = 0 \Rightarrow \quad 200 + 15t_1 - 5t_1^2 = 0$

$t_1^2 - 3t_1 - 40 = 0$

$(t-8)(t+5) = 0 \Rightarrow t_1 = -5$ or $8s$

For second stone $\quad y_2 = 200 + (u_2 t - \frac{1}{2} g t^2)$

$= 200 + 30t - 5t^2 = 0$

at $t = t_2$, $y_2 = 0 \Rightarrow \quad t^2 - 6t - 40 = 0$

$(t-10)(t+4) = 0 \Rightarrow t = -4$ or $10s$

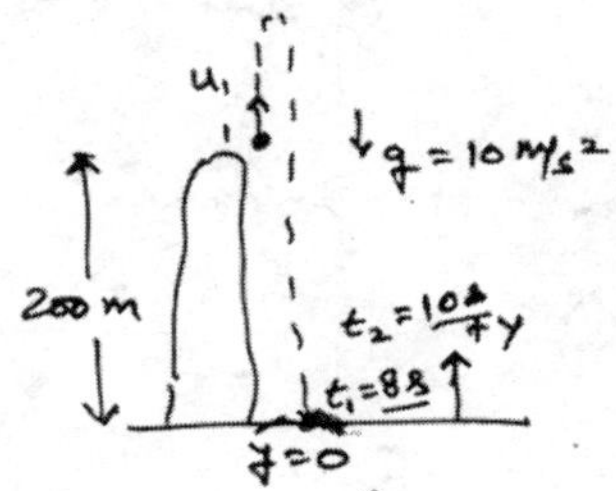

For relative motion of the two stones

$y_2 - y_1 = (200 + 30t - 5t^2) - (200 + 15t - 5t^2)$

$\boxed{y_2 - y_1 = 15t}$ Ans. valid upto $t = 8$ sec only

after 8s as $y_1 = 0 \Rightarrow \boxed{y_2 - y_1 = 200 + 30t - 5t^2}$ Ans. valid for $8s < t < 10s$

- The speed-time graph of a particle moving along a fixed direction is shown in figure. Obtain the distance traversed by the particle between (a) $t = 0$ s to 10 s, (b) $t = 2$ s to 6 s.
  What is the average speed of the particle over the intervals in (a) and (b) ?

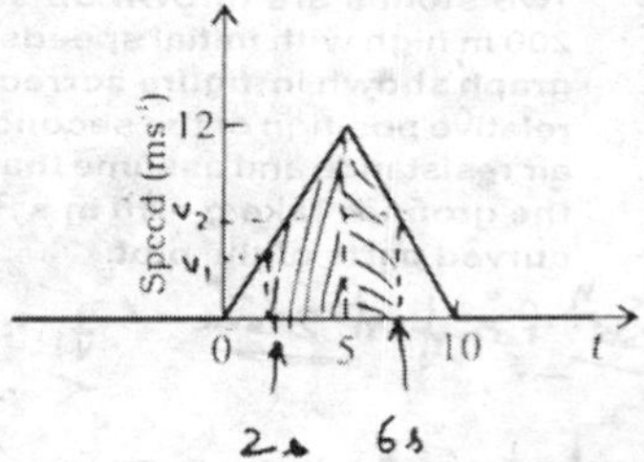

Solⁿ: (a) Distance = area under v-t curve

$$= \frac{1}{2} \times 10 \times 12 = 60\text{ m} \quad \text{Ans.}$$

$$\text{avg speed} = \frac{\text{distance}}{\text{Time}} = \frac{60}{10} = 6\text{ m/s} \quad \text{Ans}$$

(b) Distance = area from $t = 2$ to 5 s + area from $t = 5$ to 6 s.

$$= \frac{1}{2} \times 3 \times \left(12 + \frac{24}{5}\right) + \frac{1}{2} \times 1 \left(12 + \frac{48}{5}\right)$$

$$= \frac{3 \times 84}{2 \times 5} + \frac{108}{2 \times 5} = 25.2 + 10.8 = 36\text{ m} \quad \text{Ans}$$

$$\text{avg speed} = \frac{\text{distance}}{\text{time}} = \frac{36}{4} = 9\text{ m/s} \quad \text{Ans.}$$

by properties of Similar triangles

① $\frac{v_1}{2} = \frac{12}{5}$

$\Rightarrow v_1 = \frac{24}{5}$ m/s

② $\frac{v_2}{4} = \frac{12}{5}$

$\Rightarrow v_2 = \frac{48}{5}$ m/s

Video Solution

- The velocity-time graph of a particle in one-dimensional motion is shown in figure. Which of the following formulae are correct for describing the motion of the particle over the time-interval t_1 to t_2:

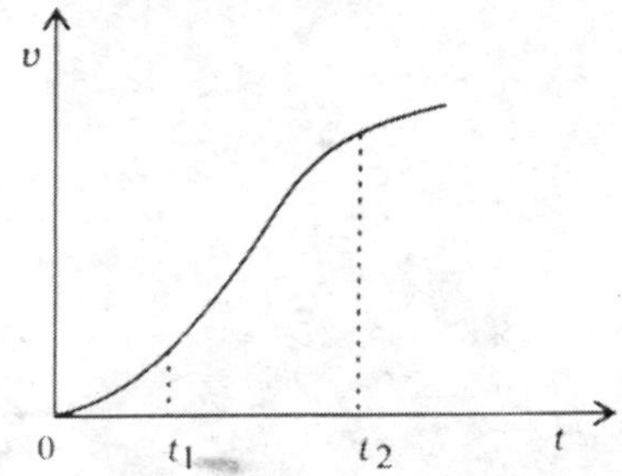

(a) $x(t_2) = x(t_1) + v(t_1)(t_2 - t_1) + (½) a(t_2 - t_1)^2$ ✗

(b) $v(t_2) = v(t_1) + a(t_2 - t_1)$ ✗

(c) $v_{average} = (x(t_2) - x(t_1)) / (t_2 - t_1)$ ✓

(d) $a_{average} = (v(t_2) - v(t_1)) / (t_2 - t_1)$ ✓

(e) $x(t_2) = x(t_1) + v_{average}(t_2 - t_1) + (½) a_{average}(t_2 - t_1)^2$ ✗

(f) $x(t_2) - x(t_1)$ = area under the *v-t* curve bounded by the *t*-axis and the dotted line shown ✓

Sol^n: from t_1 to t_2 → acceleration is non uniform. (varying)
⇓
Speed eq^n for constant acc^n are not applicable.

(a) & (b) are not applicable here

(c) avg velocity = $\frac{\text{displacement}}{\text{time}} = \frac{x_2 - x_1}{t_2 - t_1}$

(d) avg acc^n = $\frac{\Delta v}{\Delta t} = \frac{v_2 - v_1}{t_2 - t_1}$

(e) is wrong. (f) displacement is always area under v-t curve.

Chapter 4

Motion in a Plane

QR Code of Link to the Video Lectures
of Theory of this chapter Motion in Plane
at 'Physics Galaxy' web portal

QR Code of Link to the NCERT textbook Video Solutions
of unsolved exercises at the end of each chapter in sequence
of this chapter at 'Physics Galaxy' web portal

- State, for each of the following physical quantities, if it is a scalar or a vector : volume, mass, speed, acceleration, density, number of moles, velocity, angular frequency, displacement, angular velocity.

Solⁿ:

Scalars: Volume, mass, speed, density, number of moles, ang frequency

Vectors: Acceleration, velocity, displacement, angular velocity.

- Pick out the two scalar quantities in the following list : force, angular momentum, work, current, linear momentum, electric field, average velocity, magnetic moment, relative velocity.

Sol^n:

Vectors → Force, Angular momentum, linear momentum, electric field, angular velocity, magnetic moment, relative velocity

Scalar → Work, current

- Pick out the only vector quantity in the following list : Temperature, pressure, impulse, time, power, total path length, energy, gravitational potential, coefficient of friction, charge.

Vector qty.

Impulse $\vec{J} = \vec{F}\Delta t = \Delta\vec{P}$

change in momentum.

- State with reasons, whether the following algebraic operations with scalar and vector physical quantities are meaningful : (a) adding any two scalars, (b) adding a scalar to a vector of the same dimensions, (c) multiplying any vector by any scalar, (d) multiplying any two scalars, (e) adding any two vectors, (f) adding a component of a vector to the same vector.

Sol^n:

(a) adding any two scalars : unless these two scalars have same dimensions/units then only it is meaning full.

adding energy to time

J + s. → no meaning

(b) adding a scalar to a vector of same dimension : No meaning as both will represent different physical quantities

(c) multiplying a scalar & a vector: Yes it can be done & the product will give another physical qty

$$\underline{F} = m\,a \quad (m: \text{scalar},\ a: \text{vect})$$

m ↓ mass (in kg)

a ↓ acc^n (m/s^2)

(d) multiplying any two scalars: Yes it can be done as the product will be another physical qty

$$\text{mass} = \text{volume} \times \text{density}$$

mass ↓ (kg); volume (m^3); density (kg/m^3)

(e) adding any two vector : can't be done unless both vectors have same (dimensions) (units)

mass + time ⟶ No meaning

(f) Component of a vector is a part of this vector

⇒ Component can't be added to the full vector again.

Adding of a component to same vector → can't be done.

Video Solution

- Read each statement below carefully and state with reasons, if it is true or false :
  (a) The magnitude of a vector is always a scalar, (b) each component of a vector is always a scalar, (c) the total path length is always equal to the magnitude of the displacement vector of a particle. (d) the average speed of a particle (defined as total path length divided by the time taken to cover the path) is either greater or equal to the magnitude of average velocity of the particle over the same interval of time, (e) Three vectors not lying in a plane can never add up to give a null vector.

Sol^n: (a) Magnitude of a vector → numerical value → scalar ⟹ True

(b) Components of a vector → vectors sum of which gives the base vector ⟹ False.

(c)

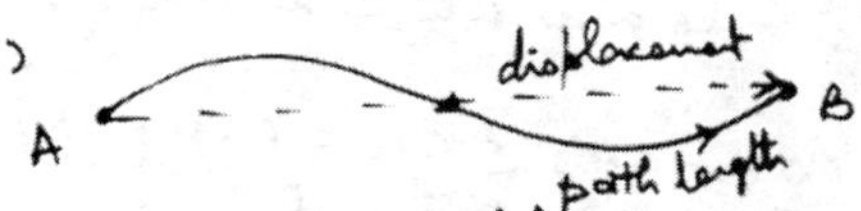

⟹ False

(d) avg speed = $\frac{\text{path length}}{\text{time taken}}$; avg velocity = $\frac{\text{displacement}}{\text{time taken}}$

As path length ≥ displacement

⟹ avg speed ≥ avg velocity ⟹ True.

(e) 3 vectors if add up to a null vector that means these are forming a closed path & in a plane only that's possible.

$\vec{R} = 0$ (only in a plane)

⟹ True.

Web Reference at www.physicsgalaxy.com

Video Sol. : Class 11th NCERT Solutions | **Sec. -** Mechanics | **Topic -** Motion in a Plane

Theory Reference : Grade - 11 & 12 | **Sec. -** Basic Tools | **Topic -** Basics of Vectors

Video Solution

- **Establish the following vector inequalities geometrically or otherwise :**

(a) $|\vec{a}+\vec{b}| \le |\vec{a}|+|\vec{b}|$ (b) $|\vec{a}+\vec{b}| \ge ||\vec{a}|-|\vec{b}||$ (c) $|\vec{a}-\vec{b}| \le |\vec{a}|+|\vec{b}|$ (d) $|\vec{a}-\vec{b}| \ge ||\vec{a}|-|\vec{b}||$

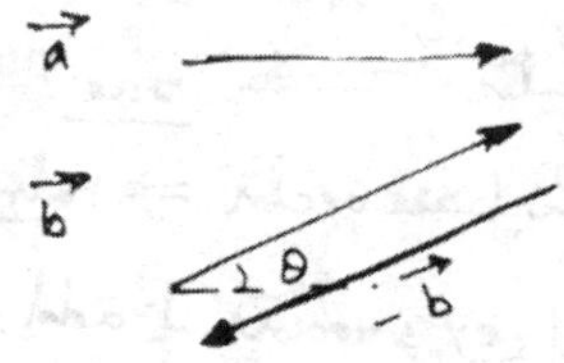

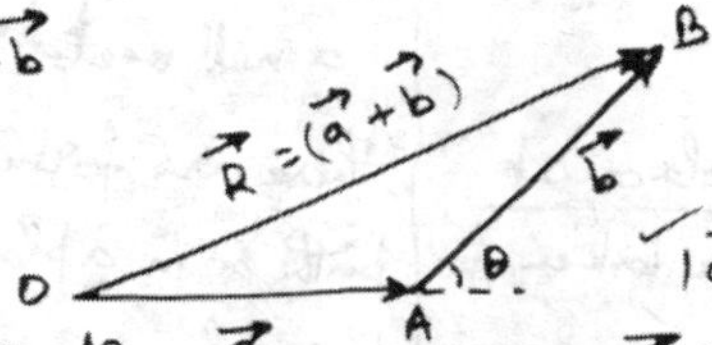

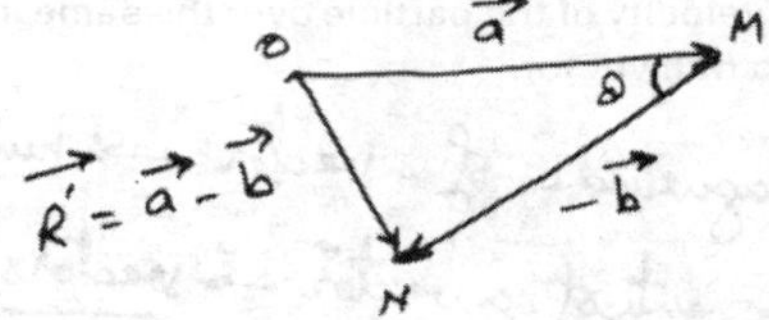

by properties of a triangle we have

$(OA - AB) \le OB \le (OA + AB)$

$|\vec{a}+\vec{b}| \le |\vec{a}|+|\vec{b}|$ ✓

$|\vec{a}+\vec{b}| \ge ||\vec{a}|-|\vec{b}||$ ✓

here also we can use

$(OM - ON) \le ON \le (OM + ON)$

$|\vec{a}-\vec{b}| \ge ||\vec{a}|-|\vec{b}||$ ✓

$|\vec{a}-\vec{b}| \le |\vec{a}|+|\vec{b}|$ ✓

Video Solution

- Given $\vec{a}+\vec{b}+\vec{c}+\vec{d}=0$, which of the following statements are correct :

(a) $\vec{a}, \vec{b}, \vec{c}$ and $\vec{d}$ must each be a null vector,

(b) The magnitude of $(\vec{a}+\vec{c})$ equals the magnitude of $(\vec{b}+\vec{d})$,

(c) The magnitude of $\vec{a}$ can never be greater than the sum of the magnitudes of $\vec{b}$, $\vec{c}$, and $\vec{d}$.

(d) $\vec{b}+\vec{c}$ must lie in the plane of $\vec{a}$ and $\vec{d}$ if $\vec{a}$ and $\vec{d}$ are not collinear, and in the line of $\vec{a}$ and $\vec{d}$, if they are collinear?

Sol^n: (a) Not necessary.

(b) $\vec{a}+\vec{b} = -(\vec{c}+\vec{d}) \Rightarrow |\vec{a}+\vec{b}| = |\vec{c}+\vec{d}|$

(c) $\vec{a} = -(\vec{b}+\vec{c}+\vec{d}) \Rightarrow |\vec{a}| = |\vec{b}+\vec{c}+\vec{d}| \leq |\vec{b}|+|\vec{c}|+|\vec{d}|$

(d) $(\vec{b}+\vec{c}) = -(\vec{a}+\vec{d})$

if $\vec{a}$ & $\vec{d}$ are collinear.

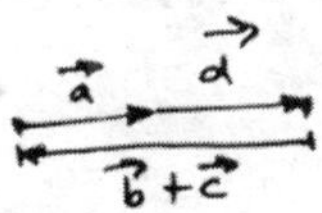

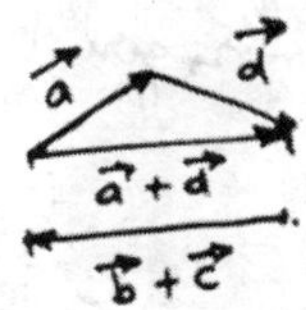

- Three girls skating on a circular ice ground of radius 200 m start from a point *P* on the edge of the ground and reach a point *Q* diametrically opposite to *P* following different paths as shown in figure. What is the magnitude of the displacement vector for each ? For which girl is this equal to the actual length of path skate ?

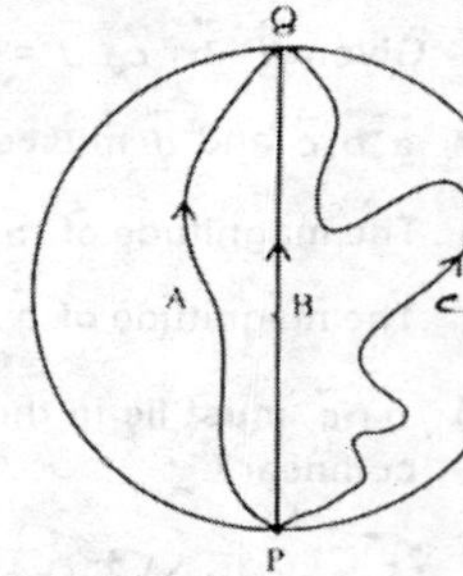

Sol[n] displacement = length of line joining Starting & end pt

= diameter of circular ground

$= 2 \times R = 2 \times 200 = 400\text{m}$ Ans

for girl B, the path length is equal to the displacement PQ.

- A cyclist starts from the centre O of a circular park of radius 1 km, reaches the edge *P* of the park, then cycles along the circumference, and returns to the centre along *QO* as shown in figure. If the round trip takes 10 min, what is the (a) net displacement, (b) average velocity, and (c) average speed of the cyclist ?

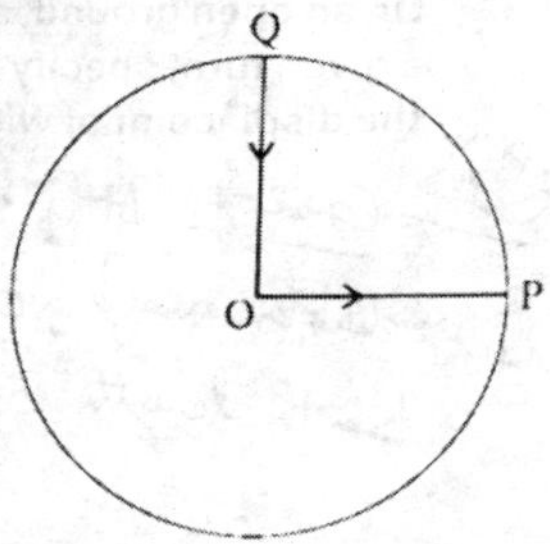

Sol^n: (a) As cyclist return to initial point

Thus displacement = 0 Ans

(b) Average velocity = $\frac{\text{displacement}}{\text{time taken}} = \frac{0}{10} = 0$ Ans

R = 1 km.

(c) Average speed = $\frac{\text{path length}}{\text{time taken}}$

path length = OP + PQ + QO

$= R + \frac{1}{4} \times 2\pi R + R$

$= 1 + \frac{1}{2} \times 3.14 \times 1 + 1$ km

$= 2 + 1.57 = 3.57$ km.

→ Avg speed = $\frac{3.57 \text{ km}}{10 \times \frac{1}{60} \text{ hr}}$

$= 3.57 \times 6$ km/hr

$= 21.42$ kph Ans

- On an open ground, a motorist follows a track that turns to his left by an angle of 60° after every 500 m. Starting from a given turn, specify the displacement of the motorist at the third, sixth and eighth turn. Compare the magnitude of the displacement with the total path length covered by the motorist in each case.

Sol^n: Case-I: At Third turn

displacement OC = 1000 m

path length OABC = 1500 m.

$$\frac{OC}{OABC} = \frac{1000}{1500} = \frac{2}{3}$$

displacement $= \frac{2}{3}$ path length.

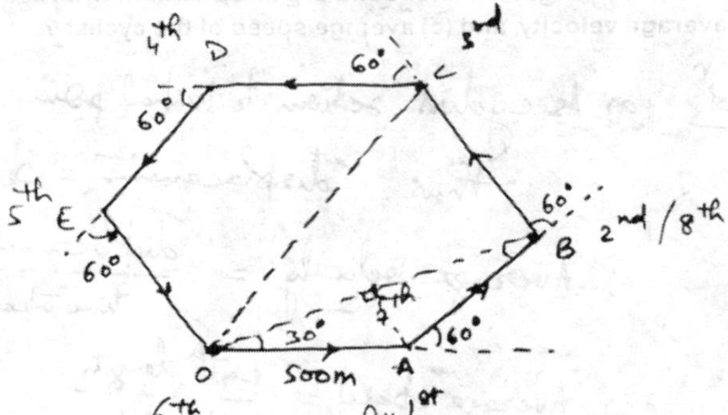

Case-II: At sixth turn

Displacement = 0

path length = 500 × 6 = 3000 m.

$$\frac{\text{Disp}}{\text{path length}} = \frac{0}{3000} = 0$$

Case-III: At Eighth turn

Displacement $OB = 2 \times OA \cos 30^\circ$

$= 2 \times 500 \times \frac{\sqrt{3}}{2} = 500\sqrt{3}$ m at 30° to OA

path length = 4000 m

$$\frac{\text{Disp}}{\text{path length}} = \frac{500\sqrt{3}}{4000} = \frac{\sqrt{3}}{8}$$ Ans

- A passenger arriving in a new town wishes to go from the station to a hotel located 10 km away on a straight road from the station. A dishonest cabman takes him along a circuitous path 23 km long and reaches the hotel in 28 min. What is (a) the average speed of the taxi, (b) the magnitude of average velocity ? Are the two equal ?

Solⁿ:

$t = 0$

$t = 28\text{ min} = \frac{28}{60} = \frac{7}{15}\text{ hr}$

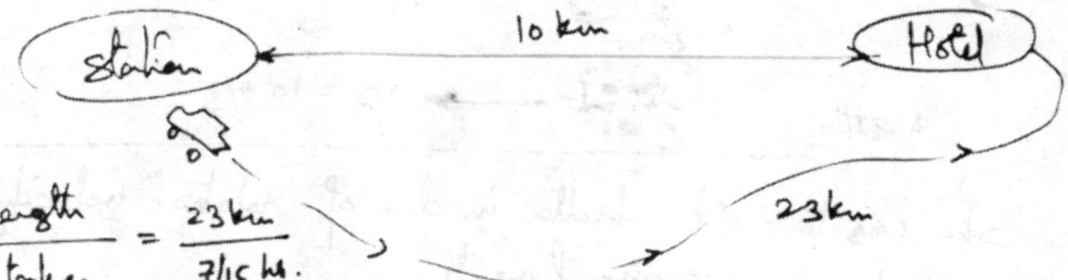

(a) Avg Speed of taxi

$$\langle v \rangle = \frac{\text{path length}}{\text{time taken}} = \frac{23\text{ km}}{7/15\text{ hr}}$$

$$= \frac{23 \times 15}{7} = 49.3\text{ km/hr. Ans}$$

(b) Avg velocity

$$\bar{v}_{avg} = \frac{\text{displacement}}{\text{time taken}} = \frac{10\text{ km}}{7/15\text{ hr}} = \frac{150}{7}\text{ km/hr} = 24.43\text{ km/hr Ans.}$$

- Rain is falling vertically with a speed of 30 m s^{-1}. A woman rides a bicycle with a speed of 10 m s^{-1} in the north to south direction. What is the direction in which she should hold her umbrella ?

Sol^n

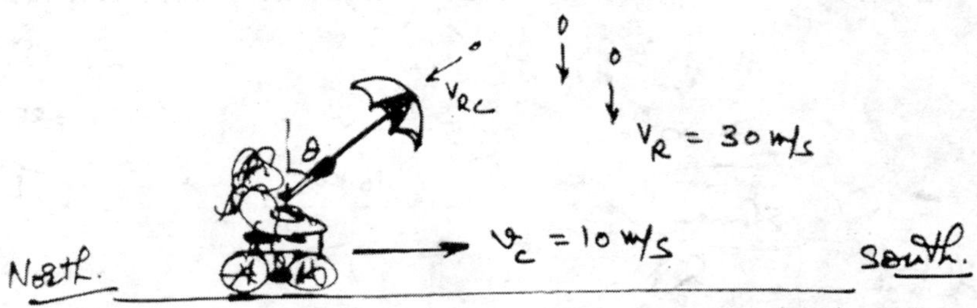

She has to hold umbrella in dir of relative velocity of rain drops w.r.to bicycle to save herself.

rel vel of rain w.r.to bicycle $\vec{v}_{RC} = \vec{v}_R - \vec{v}_c$

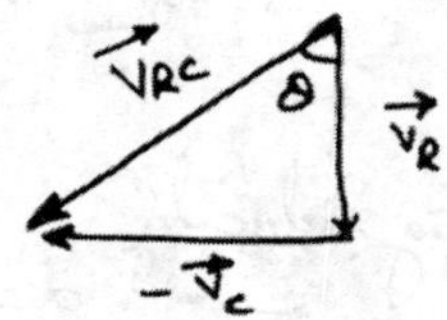

from vector triangle $\theta = \tan^{-1}\left(\left|\frac{v_c}{v_R}\right|\right) = \tan^{-1}\left(\frac{10}{30}\right)$

$= \tan^{-1}(1/3)$ Ans

$\simeq 18^\circ$.

Video Solution

- A man can swim with a speed of 4.0 km/h in still water. How long does he take to cross a river 1.0 km wide if the river flows steadily at 3.0 km/h and he makes his strokes normal to the river current? How far down the river does he go when he reaches the other bank ?

Sol^n

crossing vel of swimmer $= V_S = 4$ km/hr

drift vel of swimmer $= u_R = 3$ km/hr

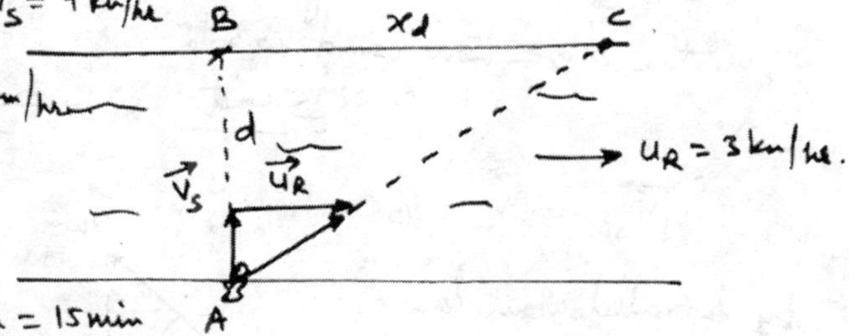

time to cross the river

$$t = \frac{d}{V_S} = \frac{1\text{ km}}{4\text{ km/hr}} = \frac{1}{4}\text{ h} = 15\text{ min}$$ Ans

drift along river current

$$x_d = u_R \times t = 3\text{ km/hr} \times 1/4\text{ hr} = 3/4\text{ km} = 750\text{ m}$$ Ans.

- In a harbour, wind is blowing at the speed of 72 km/h and the flag on the mast of a boat anchored in the harbour flutters along the *N-E* direction. If the boat starts moving at a speed of 51 km/h to the north, what is the direction of the flag on the mast of the boat?

Solⁿ: Flag on a boat always flutters in the direction wind w.r.to Boat.

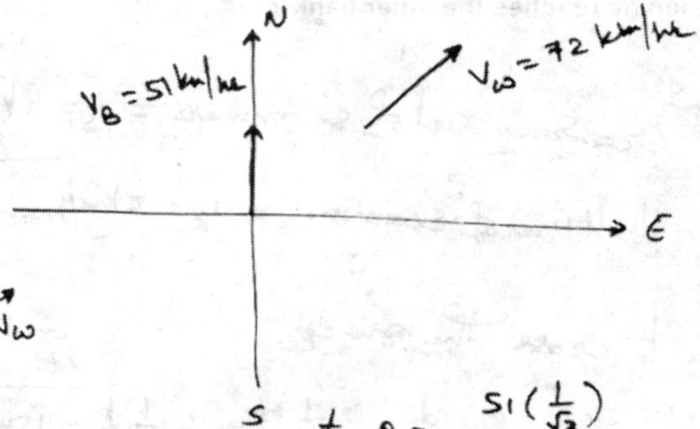

$$\vec{V}_{\omega B} = \vec{V}_\omega - \vec{V}_B$$

by parallelogram law of vector addition, we use

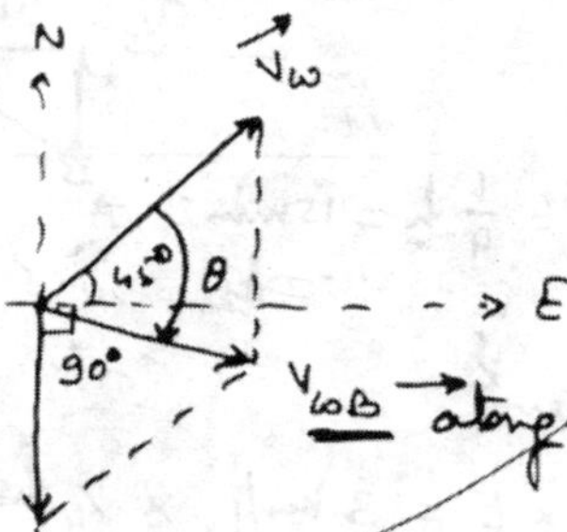

$$\tan\theta = \frac{V_B \sin(135^\circ)}{V_\omega + V_B \cos(135^\circ)}$$

$$\tan\theta = \frac{51\left(\frac{1}{\sqrt{2}}\right)}{72 + 51\left(-\frac{1}{\sqrt{2}}\right)}$$

$$\tan\theta = \frac{51}{72 \times 1.414 - 51} = 1.003$$

$$\theta = \tan^{-1}(1) = \underline{45^\circ}$$

⇒ Flag on boat flutters along east direction Ans.

Video Solution

- The ceiling of a long hall is 25 m high. What is the maximum horizontal distance that a ball thrown with a speed of 40 m s^{-1} can go without hitting the ceiling of the hall ?

Solⁿ: for $H_{max} = 25$, we use

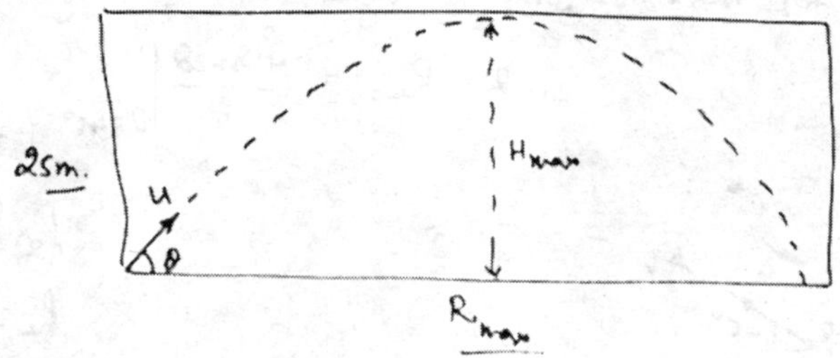

$$H_{max} = \frac{u^2 \sin^2\theta}{2g}$$

$$25 = \frac{(40)^2 \sin^2\theta}{2 \times 9.8}$$

$$\sin^2\theta = \frac{25 \times 2 \times 9.8}{1600} = 0.306$$

$$\sin\theta = 0.5531 \Rightarrow \theta \simeq 34^\circ$$

max Range at $\theta = 34^\circ \longrightarrow R = \frac{u^2 \sin 2\theta}{g} = \frac{(40)^2 \sin 2(34)}{9.8}$

$$= \frac{1600}{9.8} \times \sin 68^\circ = \frac{1600}{9.8} \times 0.922 = 150.5\,m$$

Ans.

- A cricketer can throw a ball to a maximum horizontal distance of 100 m. How much high above the ground can the cricketer throw the same ball ?

Solⁿ for max horizontal Range $\theta = 45^\circ$

$$\& \quad R_{max} = \left.\frac{u^2 \sin 2\theta}{g}\right|_{\theta=45^\circ} = \frac{u^2}{g} = 100\,m$$

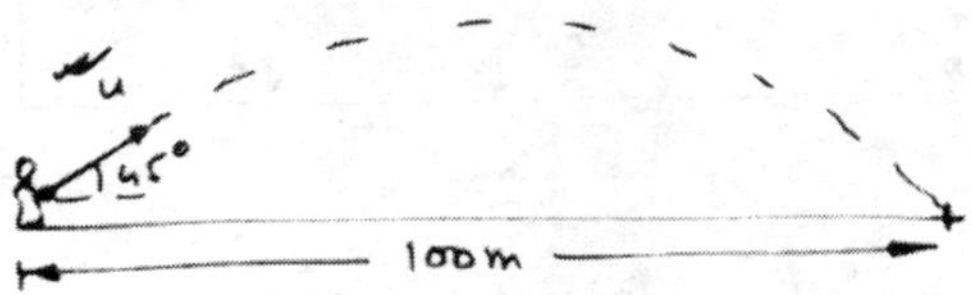

for max height above the ground he has to throw the ball vertically up.

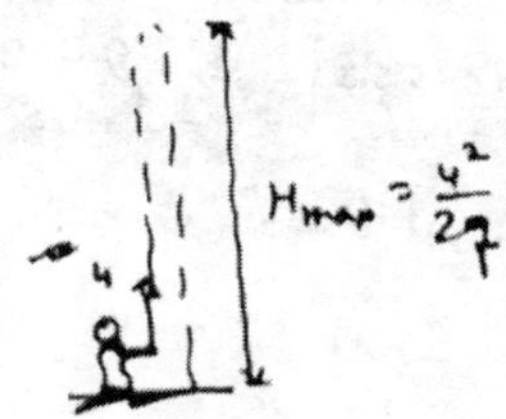

max height in case of vertically upward throw is

$$H_{max} = \frac{u^2}{2g} = \frac{100}{2} = 50\,m$$

Ans.

- A stone tied to the end of a string 80 cm long is whirled in a horizontal circle with a constant speed. If the stone makes 14 revolutions in 25 s, what is the magnitude and direction of acceleration of the stone ?

Solⁿ. for UCM the acceleration is only normal (or centripetal) & will Continuously act toward Centre of Circle & it's magnitude is given as-

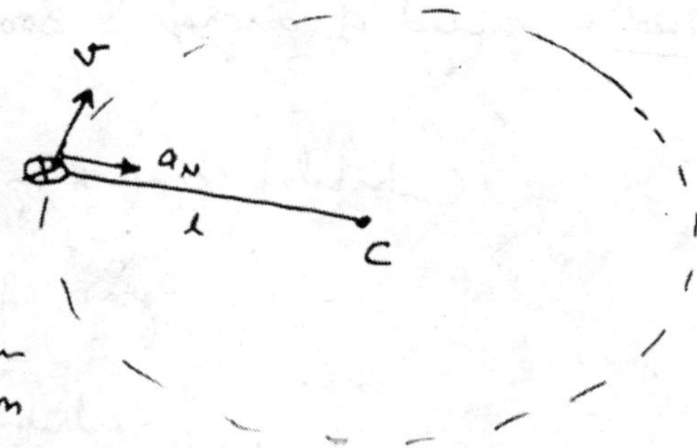

$$a_N = \omega^2 r$$

$r = l = 80\text{cm} = 0.8\text{m}$

angular speed $\omega = 2\pi n = 2\pi\left(\frac{14}{25}\right) = \frac{28\pi}{25}$ rad/s

Centripetal acceleration $a_N = \left(\frac{28 \times 3.14}{25}\right)^2 \times 0.8 = 9.9\ \text{m/s}^2$ Ans

- An aircraft executes a horizontal loop of radius 1.00 km with a steady speed of 900 km/h. Compare its centripetal acceleration with the acceleration due to gravity.

Sol^n speed of aircraft $= 900\ km/hr \times \frac{5}{18} = 250\ m/s$

Centripetal acceleration of aircraft $a_r = \frac{v^2}{R} = \frac{(250)^2}{1000} = 62.5\ m/s^2$

$a_{grav} = g = 9.8\ m/s^2$

$$\frac{\text{Centripetal acc}^n}{\text{acc}^n \text{ due to gravity}} = \frac{62.5}{9.8} = 6.38$$

Centripetal acc^n $= 6.38g$ Ans.

- Read each statement below carefully and state, with reasons, if it is true or false :

(a) The net acceleration of a particle in circular motion is always along the radius of the circle towards the centre

(b) The velocity vector of a particle at a point is always along the tangent to the path of the particle at that point

(c) The acceleration vector of a particle in uniform circular motion averaged over one cycle is a null vector

Sol^n: (a) False.

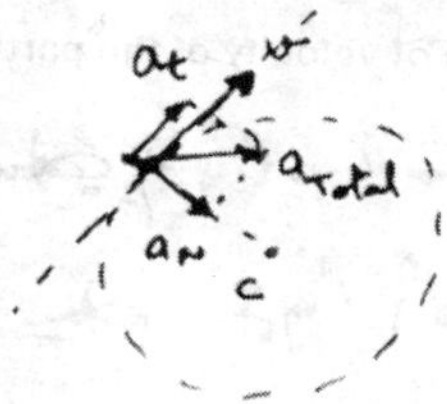

If it is UCM then $a_t = 0$ & total acc^n will be a_N only which acts along radius.

(b) True. as velocity in circular motion is always along the tangent of circle.

(c) True as in UCM $a_t = 0$ & $\vec{v}_i = \vec{v}_f$ at starting pt & after completing the cycle at the same point

$$\vec{a}_{avg} = \frac{\vec{v}_f - \vec{v}_i}{t} = 0$$

- The position of a particle is given by

  $\vec{r} = 3.0t\,\hat{i} - 2.0t^2\,\hat{j} + 4.0\hat{k}m$

  where t is in seconds and the coefficients have the proper units for $\vec{r}$ to be in metres.

(a) Find the $\vec{v}$ and $\vec{a}$ of the particle?

(b) What is the magnitude and direction of velocity of the particle at $t = 2.0$ s ?

Solⁿ: (a) $\vec{v} = \frac{d\vec{r}}{dt} = 3.0\hat{i} - 4.0t\,\hat{j}$ m/s Ans

& $\vec{a} = \frac{d\vec{v}}{dt} = -4.0\hat{j}$ m/s² Ans.

(b) $\vec{v}\Big|_{t=2.0} = 3.0\hat{i} - 8.0\hat{j}$ m/s

$|\vec{v}| = \sqrt{(3.0)^2 + (8.0)^2} = \sqrt{9 + 64} = \sqrt{73} = 8.54$ m/s Ans

Angle of $\vec{v}$ with x axis is $\theta = \tan^{-1}\left(\frac{-8.0}{3.0}\right) = -\tan^{-1}(8/3) = -69.7° \approx -70°$

Ans

- A particle starts from the origin at $t = 0$ s with a velocity of $10.0\hat{j}$ m/s and moves in the x-y plane with a constant acceleration of $(8.0\hat{i} + 2.0\hat{j})$ m s^{-2}.

(a) At what time is the x-coordinate of the particle 16 m? What is the y-coordinate of the particle at that time?

(b) What is the speed of the particle at the time ?

Sol^n: (a) Initial speed along x-dir $u_x = 0$

acc^n along x-dir $a_x = 8.0\ m/s^2$ (Constant)

we use $x = u_x t + \frac{1}{2} a_x t^2$

$16 = \frac{1}{2}(8.0)t^2 \Rightarrow t^2 = 4 \Rightarrow t = 2\ s$ Ans.

in y direction $u_y = 10\ m/s$ & $a_y = 2.0\ m/s^2$ (Constant)

we use $y = u_y t + \frac{1}{2} a_y t^2 = 10(2) + \frac{1}{2}(2.0)(2)^2 = 20 + 4 = 24\ m$ Ans

(b) speed of particle along x & y direction are given as-

$$\left.\begin{aligned} v_x &= u_x + a_x t = 0 + (8.0)(2) = 16 \\ v_y &= u_y + a_y t = 10 + (2.0)(2) = 14 \end{aligned}\right] \Rightarrow v = \sqrt{v_x^2 + v_y^2} = \sqrt{(16)^2 + (14)^2} = 21.26\ m/s^2$$ Ans.

- $\hat{i}$ and $\hat{j}$ are unit vectors along x- and y- axis respectively. What is the magnitude and direction of the vectors $\hat{i} + \hat{j}$, and $\hat{i} - \hat{j}$? What are the components of a vector $\vec{A} = 2\hat{i} + 3\hat{j}$ along the directions of $\hat{i} + \hat{j}$ abd $\hat{i} - \hat{j}$? [You may use graphical method]

Sol.

$\vec{r}_1 = \hat{i} + \hat{j}$

$|\vec{r}_1| = \sqrt{(1)^2 + (1)^2} = \sqrt{2}$ Ans.

$\theta_1 = \tan^{-1}\left(\frac{1}{1}\right) = 45^\circ$ with x axis Ans

$\vec{r}_2 = \hat{i} - \hat{j}$

$|\vec{r}_2| = \sqrt{(1)^2 + (-1)^2} = \sqrt{2}$ Ans.

$\theta_2 = \tan^{-1}\left(\frac{-1}{1}\right) = -45^\circ$ with x axis

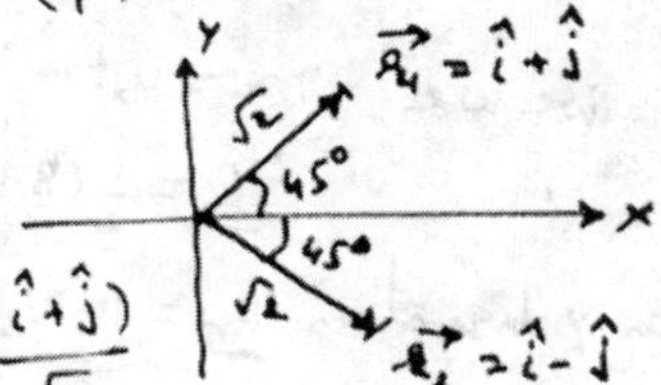

As we know Components of a vector $\vec{A}$ along the direction of $\vec{r}_1$ and $\vec{r}_2$

$$A_{\text{along } r_1} = \vec{A}\cdot\hat{r}_1 = (2\hat{i} + 3\hat{j})\cdot\frac{\vec{r}_1}{r} = (2\hat{i} + 3\hat{j})\cdot\frac{(\hat{i} + \hat{j})}{\sqrt{2}}$$

$$= \frac{2+3}{\sqrt{2}} = \frac{5}{\sqrt{2}} \text{ Ans}$$

$$\vec{A}_{\text{along } \vec{r}_1} = \frac{5}{\sqrt{2}}\cdot\hat{r} = \frac{5}{\sqrt{2}}\left(\frac{\hat{i} + \hat{j}}{\sqrt{2}}\right)$$

$$= \frac{5}{2}(\hat{i} + \hat{j}) \text{ Ans.}$$

Video Solution

here $A_{along\, r_2} = \vec{A}\cdot\hat{r}_2 = (2\hat{i}+3\hat{j})\cdot\frac{\vec{r}_2}{r_2} = (2\hat{i}+3\hat{j})\cdot\frac{(\hat{i}-\hat{j})}{\sqrt{2}} = \frac{2-3}{\sqrt{2}} = -\frac{1}{\sqrt{2}}$ Ans

$$\vec{A}_{along\, \vec{r}_2} = -\frac{1}{\sqrt{2}}\cdot\hat{r}_2 = -\frac{1}{\sqrt{2}}\cdot\left(\frac{\hat{i}-\hat{j}}{\sqrt{2}}\right) = -\frac{1}{2}(\hat{i}-\hat{j})$$ Ans.

- For any arbitrary motion in space, which of the following relations are true :

(a) $\vec{v}_{average} = (1/2)\ (\vec{v}(t_1) + \vec{v}(t_2))$

(b) $\vec{v}_{average} = [\vec{r}(t_2) - \vec{r}(t_1)]/(t_2 - t_1)$

(c) $\vec{v}(t) = \vec{v}(0) + \vec{a}\, t$

(d) $\vec{r}(t) = \vec{r}(0) + \vec{v}(0)\, t + (1/2)\ \vec{a}\, t^2$

(e) $\vec{a}_{average} = [\vec{v}(t_2) - \vec{v}(t_1)]\ /\ (t_2 - t_1)$

(The 'average' stands for average of the quantity over the time interval t_1 to t_2)

Sol^n: (a) False. — it can be true only if acc^n is uniform.

(b) True as $\vec{v}_{avg} = \frac{\vec{\Delta r}}{\Delta t}$ ✓

(c) False — as speed eq^n are only valid for uniform acc^n.

(d) False — as speed eq^n are only valid for uniform acc^n.

(e) True as $\vec{a}_{avg} = \frac{\vec{\Delta v}}{\Delta t}$

Video Solution

- Read each statement below carefully and state, with reasons and examples, if it is true or false :

  A scalar quantity is one that

(a) is conserved in a process

(b) can never take negative values

(c) must be dimensionless

(d) does not vary from one point to another in space

(e) has the same value for observers with different orientations of axes

Sol^n: (a) False — energy is not always conserved in every system.

mass ————.

temperature ————

(b) False — A scalar can take up any +ve & -ve values depending upon type of physical qty.

temperature → +40°c / -70°c - - -

energy → +100 J / -35 J (Pot^n energy)

(c) False — A scalar can have magnitude as well as dimensions.

Energy → in Joule. [D(energy)] → $[MLT^{-2}][L] = [ML^2T^{-2}]$

(d) False — Scalars can have variable values in space

(e) True — as a scalar does not have a direction.

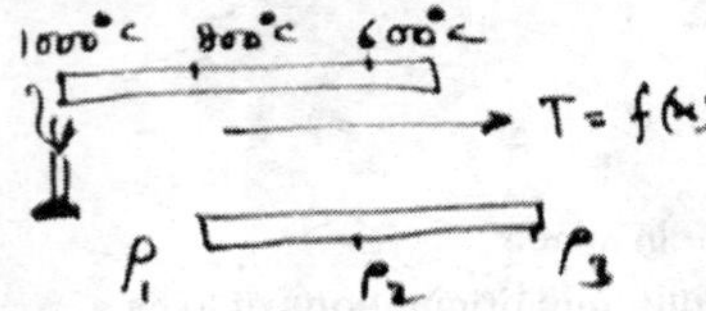

density varying

- An aircraft is flying at a height of 3400 m above the ground. If the angle subtended at a ground observation point by the aircraft positions 10.0 s apart is 30°, what is the speed of the aircraft ?

Sol[n]: Case I: If initially aircraft is overhead above the observer

$\tan 30^\circ = \frac{AB}{OA}$

$AB = OA \tan 30^\circ$

$v_a t = OA \tan 30^\circ$

$v_a = \frac{OA \tan 30^\circ}{t} = \frac{3400(1/\sqrt{3})}{10} = \frac{340}{\sqrt{3}}$ m/s

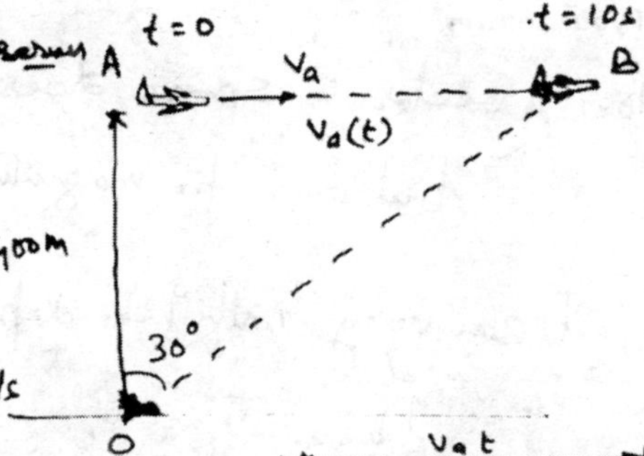

Ans

Case II → if aircraft is flying symmetrically above the observer.

From figure

$\frac{\frac{v_a t}{2}}{3400} = \frac{AC}{OC} = \tan 15^\circ \Rightarrow v_a = \frac{3400 \tan 15^\circ}{10} \times 2 = 680 \tan 15^\circ$ Ans

$= 680 \times 0.2679$

$= 182.20$ m/s Ans

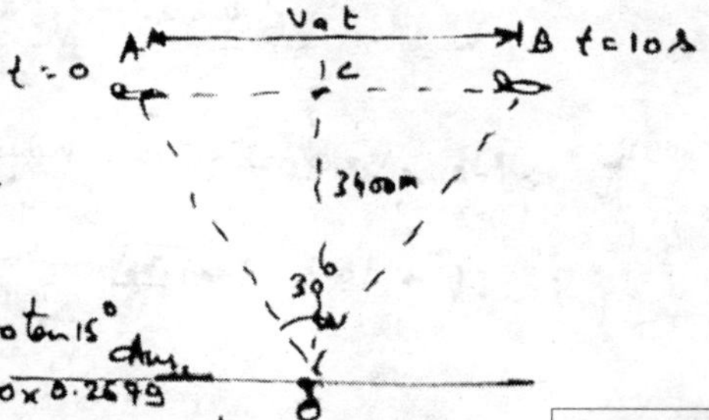

- **A vector has magnitude and direction. Does it have a location in space ? Can it vary with time ? Will two equal vectors $\vec{a}$ and $\vec{b}$ at different locations in space necessarily have identical physical effects? Give examples in support of your answer.**

Sol^n: • No. A vector in space does not have a fixed location but has fix magnitude & direction at an instant.

• Yes. it can vary with time depending upon the physical qty

like $\vec{v}_t = \vec{u}_t + \vec{a}_t \cdot t$

• No. vectors can have different physical effects

$\vec{F}_1 = 10N \longrightarrow \boxed{2kg} \longrightarrow a = \frac{10}{2} = 5 m/s^2$ $\vec{F}_2 = 10N \longrightarrow \boxed{5kg} \longrightarrow a = \frac{10}{5} = 2 m/s^2$

$\vec{F}_1 = \vec{F}_2$

in some specific cases vectors have similar effects

- A vector has both magnitude and direction. Does it mean that anything that has magnitude and direction is necessarily a vector ? The rotation of a body can be specified by the direction of the axis of rotation, and the angle of rotation about the axis. Does that make any rotation a vector ?

Solⁿ No. A vector has both mag and direction & also it follows the laws specified in vector algebra (Subtraction / addition / Multiplication)

Rotation of a body by some angle.

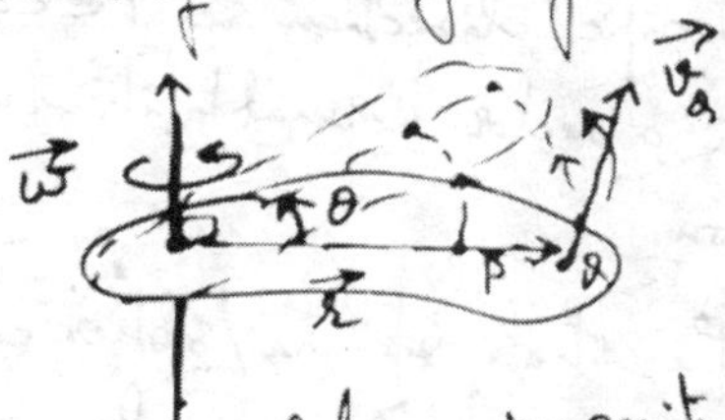

$\vec{v}_Q = \vec{\omega} \times \vec{r}$

inst velocity $\quad v_Q = \frac{d\theta}{dt} \cdot r$

$\vec{\omega} = \frac{d\vec{\theta}}{dt}$

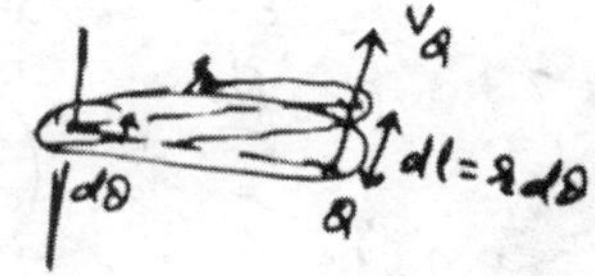

θ has a magnitude and also a direction but it is a Scaler qty

$d\theta$ is a vector qty.

Exercise - 4.28

- Can you associate vectors with (a) the length of a wire bent into a loop, (b) a plane area, (c) a sphere ? Explain.

Sol^n:

(a) No.

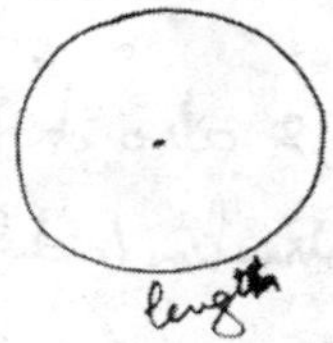

vector cannot be associated with length as it is not oriented in a specific direction

(b) YES

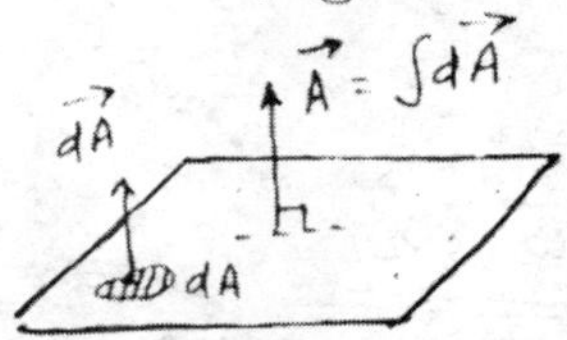

As a plane surface is always oriented in a specific direction so we can associate a vector normal to its surface as shown.

(c) No.

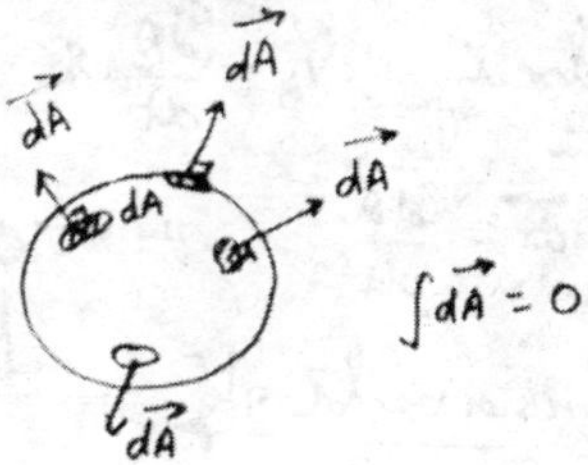

For the whole sphere/spherical surface we cannot associate a single vector however every element on surface will be having the elemental area vectors associated.

- A bullet fired at an angle of 30° with the horizontal hits the ground 3.0 km away. By adjusting its angle of projection, can one hope to hit a target 5.0 km away ? Assume the muzzle speed to be fixed, and neglect air resistance.

Sol.ⁿ Horizontal Range $R = \frac{u^2 \sin 2\theta}{g}$

$$3000 = \frac{u^2}{g}\sin(60^\circ) \Rightarrow \frac{u^2}{g} = \frac{6000}{\sqrt{3}}$$

max horizontal range of bullet ($\theta = 45^\circ$)

$$R_{max} = \frac{u^2}{g} = \frac{6000}{\sqrt{3}} = 2000\sqrt{3} \simeq 3464\text{ m.} \simeq 3.46\text{ km.}$$

As max possible range of bullet is 3.46 km

$\Rightarrow$ it is NOT possible to hit a target at 5 km.

Ans.

- **A fighter plane flying horizontally at an altitude of 1.5 km with speed 720 km/h passes directly overhead an anti-aircraft gun. At what angle from the vertical should the gun be fired for the shell with muzzle speed 600 m s^{-1} to hit the plane ? At what minimum altitude should the pilot fly the plane to avoid being hit ? (Take g = 10 m s^{-2}).**

Sol^n: velocity of fighter plane

$$V_p = 720 \times \frac{5}{18} = 200\ m/s$$

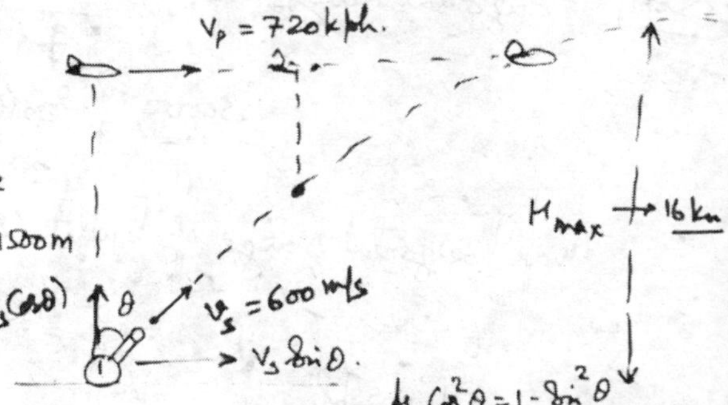

for shell to hit the plane we must have

$$V_p = V_s \sin\theta$$

$$\Rightarrow \sin\theta = \frac{V_p}{V_s} = \frac{200}{600} = \frac{1}{3}$$

$$\Rightarrow \theta = \sin^{-1}(1/3) \simeq 19^\circ \text{ Ans.}$$

As $\cos^2\theta = 1 - \sin^2\theta$
$= 1 - 1/9 = 8/9$

max. height by the shell in its motion $H_{max} = \frac{(V_s \cos\theta)^2}{2g} = \frac{(600)^2 \times \cos^2(19)}{2 \times 10}$

$$= \frac{(600)^2 \times 8/9}{20} = 16000\,m = 16\,km$$

Ans.

Video Solution

- A cyclist is riding with a speed of 27 km/h. As he approaches a circular turn on the road of radius 80 m, he applies brakes and reduces his speed at the constant rate of 0.50 m/s every second. What is the magnitude and direction of the net acceleration of the cyclist on the circular turn ?

Sol^n: Given that tangential acceleration of cyclist is $a_t = 0.5\ m/s^2$

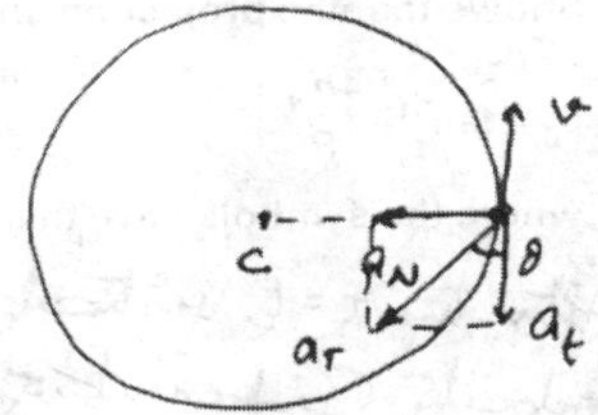

Normal acceleration $a_N = \frac{v^2}{R} = \frac{(15/2)^2}{80}$

$a_N = \frac{225}{320} = 0.7\ m/s^2$

here $v = 27 \times \frac{5}{18} = \frac{15}{2}\ m/s$

Total acceleration of cyclist $a_T = \sqrt{a_t^2 + a_N^2}$

$= \sqrt{(0.5)^2 + (0.7)^2} = 0.86\ m/s^2$ Ans.

angle between total acc^n & tangent is given as $\theta = \tan^{-1}\left(\frac{a_N}{a_t}\right) = \tan^{-1}\left(\frac{7}{5}\right) = 54.5^\circ$ Ans

Web Reference at www.physicsgalaxy.com

Video Sol. : Class 11th NCERT Solutions | **Sec. -** Mechanics | **Topic -** Motion in a Plane

Theory Reference : Grade - 11 & 12 | **Sec. -** Mechanics | **Topic -** Circular Motion

Video Solution

- **(a)** **Show that for a projectile the angle between the velocity and the *x*-axis as a function of time is given by**

  $$\theta(t) = \tan^{-1}\left(\frac{v_{0y} - gt}{v_{0x}}\right)$$

  (b) **Shows that the projection angle θ_0 for a projectile launched from the origin is given by**

  $$\theta_0 = \tan^{-1}\left(\frac{4h_m}{R}\right)$$

  where the symbols have their usual meaning.

Solⁿ (a) After time t = t, vertical velocity Component of projectile is given as

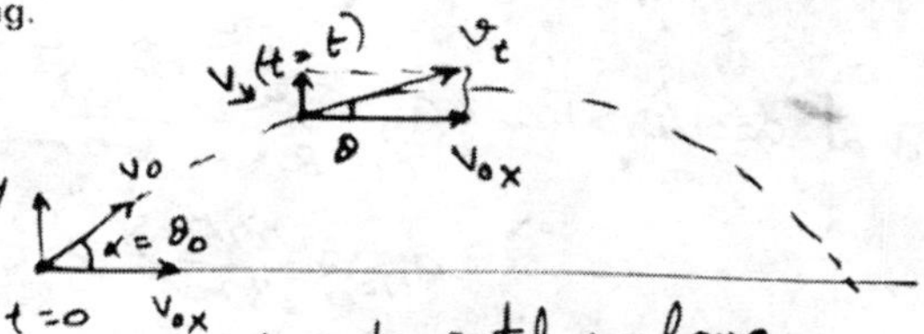

$$v_{y(t)} = v_{0y} - gt \quad (a_y = -g)$$

from figure $\tan\theta = \frac{v_{yt}}{v_{xt}} = \frac{v_{0y} - gt}{v_{0x}}$

$$\Rightarrow \theta = \tan^{-1}\left(\frac{v_{0y} - gt}{v_{0x}}\right)$$

hence proved!

(b) For a projectile we have

$$h_m = \frac{v_0^2 \sin^2\theta_0}{2g} \text{ — (1)} \quad \& \quad R = \frac{v_0^2 \sin 2\theta_0}{g} \text{ — (2)}$$

$$= \frac{v_0^2}{g} \times 2\sin\theta_0 \cos\theta_0$$

$$\frac{h_m}{R} = \frac{1}{4}\tan\theta_0 \Rightarrow \tan\theta_0 = \frac{4h_m}{R}$$

$$\Rightarrow \theta_0 = \tan^{-1}\left(\frac{4h_m}{R}\right)$$

Video Solution

Chapter 5

Laws of Motion

QR Code of Link to the Video Lectures of Theory of this chapter Laws of Motion at 'Physics Galaxy' web portal

QR Code of Link to the NCERT textbook Video Solutions of unsolved exercises at the end of each chapter in sequence of this chapter at 'Physics Galaxy' web portal

- Give the magnitude and direction of the net force acting on

(a) a drop of rain falling down with a constant speed,

(b) a cork of mass 10 g floating on water,

(c) a kite skillfully held stationary in the sky,

(d) a car moving with a constant velocity of 30 km/h on a rough road,

(e) a high-speed electron in space far from all material objects, and free of electric and magnetic fields.

(take $g = 10 \text{ m s}^{-2}$)

Solⁿ: (a) As constant speed $\Rightarrow \vec{a} = 0 \Rightarrow \vec{F} = 0$

(b) floating $\Rightarrow$ cork is at rest $\Rightarrow \vec{a} = 0 \Rightarrow \vec{F} = 0$

(c) kite is stationary $\Rightarrow$ at rest $\Rightarrow \vec{a} = 0 \Rightarrow \vec{F} = 0$

(d) Constant velocity $\Rightarrow \vec{a} = 0 \Rightarrow \vec{F} = 0$

(e) As no gravitational, electric or magnetic force is acting on electron

$\Rightarrow \vec{F}_{net} = 0.$

- A pebble of mass 0.05 kg is thrown vertically upwards. Give the direction and magnitude of the net force on the pebble,

(a) during its upward motion,

(b) during its downward motion,

(c) at the highest point where it is momentarily at rest. Do your answers change if the pebble was thrown at an angle of 45° with the horizontal direction?

Ignore air resistance.

(take $g = 10 \text{ m s}^{-2}$)

Sol^n:

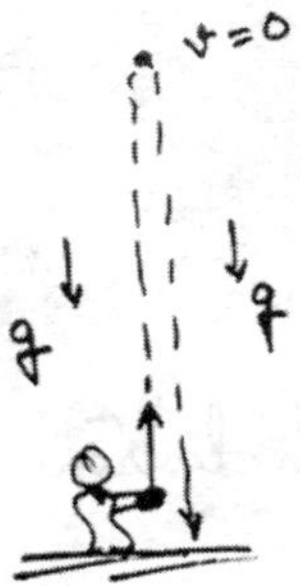

net force on pebble during motion at all instants of (a), (b) & (c) is the force of gravity

$F = mg = 0.05 \times 10 = 0.5 \text{ N}$. Ans.

at all instants of projectile motion the net force is mg only.

Ans.

Video Solution

- Give the magnitude and direction of the net force acting on a stone of mass 0.1 kg,

(a) just after it is dropped from the window of a stationary train,

(b) just after it is dropped from the window of a train running at a constant velocity of 36 km/h,

(c) just after it is dropped from the window of a train accelerating with 1 m s^{-2}

(d) lying on the floor of a train which is accelerating with 1 m s^{-2}, the stone being at rest relative to the train

Neglect air resistance throughout.
(take $g = 10$ m s^{-2})

Sol.ⁿ (a) after dropping stone is in free fall motion

$F = mg = 0.1 \times 10 = 1N$

(b) $v = 36 \times 5/18 = 10$ m/s.

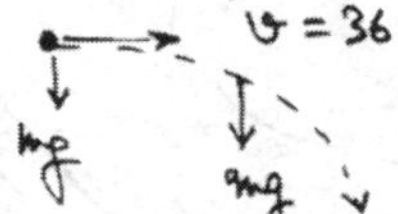

$F = mg = 0.1 \times 10 = 1N.$

(c) from an accelerating frame when a body is detached, only vel of frame is transferred to body

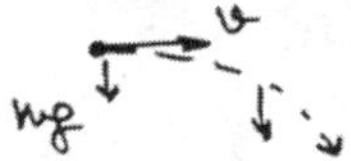

$F = mg = 0.1 \times 10 = 1N$

(d)

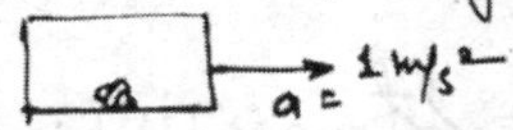

net force on stone $F = ma = 0.1 \times 1 = 0.1$ N

Ans

Web Reference at www.physicsgalaxy.com

Video Sol. : Class 11th NCERT Solutions | Sec. - Mechanics | Topic - Laws of Motion

Theory Reference : Grade - 11 & 12 | Sec. - Mechanics | Topic - Newton's Laws of Motion

Video Solution

- One end of a string of length l is connected to a particle of mass m and the other to a small peg on a smooth horizontal table. If the particle moves in a circle with speed v the net force on the particle (directed towards the centre)

(i) T (ii) $T - \frac{mv^2}{l}$ (iii) $T + \frac{mv^2}{l}$ (iv) 0

T is the tension in the string. [Choose the correct alternative].
(take $g = 10$ m s^{-2})

Sol^n: Here tension T on mass provides the necessary centripetal force for its circular motion

$$T = \frac{mv^2}{l}$$

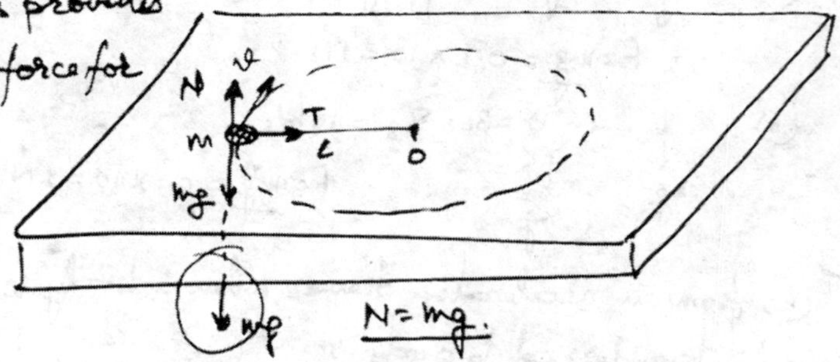

Correct option is (i) T.

- A constant retarding force of 50 N is applied to a body of mass 20 kg moving initially with a speed of 15 m s^{-1}. How long does the body take to stop ?
(take $g = 10$ m s^{-2})

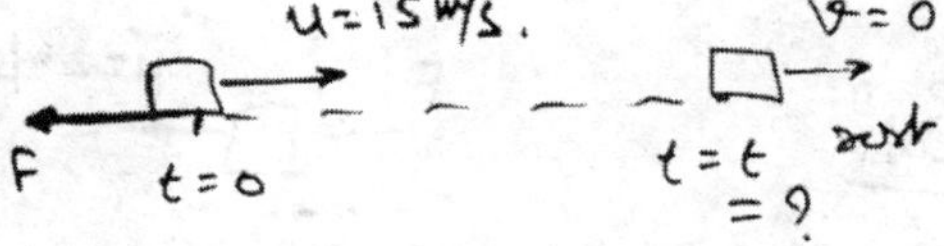

Sol^n: force on body $F = -50N$.

$$\Rightarrow \quad a = \frac{F}{m} = -\frac{50}{20} = -2.5 \, m/s^2$$

using speed eq^n $\quad v = u + at$

$$0 = 15 - 2.5(t)$$

$$\Rightarrow \quad t = \frac{15}{2.5} = 6\,s \quad \text{Ans.}$$

- A constant force acting on a body of mass 3.0 kg changes its speed from 2.0 m s^{-1} to 3.5 m s^{-1} in 25 s. The direction of the motion of the body remains unchanged. What is the magnitude and direction of the force ? (take $g = 10$ m s^{-2})

Sol^n:

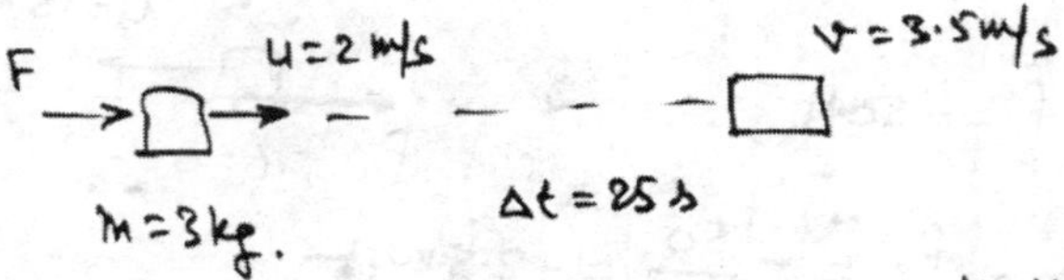

By speed equation $v = u + at \Rightarrow a = \frac{v - u}{t} = \frac{3.5 - 2}{25}$

$= \frac{1.5}{25}$ m/s^2

net force on body is $F = ma = (3.0) \times \frac{1.5}{25} = 0.18$ N Ans.

- **A body of mass 5 kg is acted upon by two perpendicular forces 8 N and 6 N. Give the magnitude and direction of the acceleration of the body.**
  (take $g = 10\ \text{m s}^{-2}$)

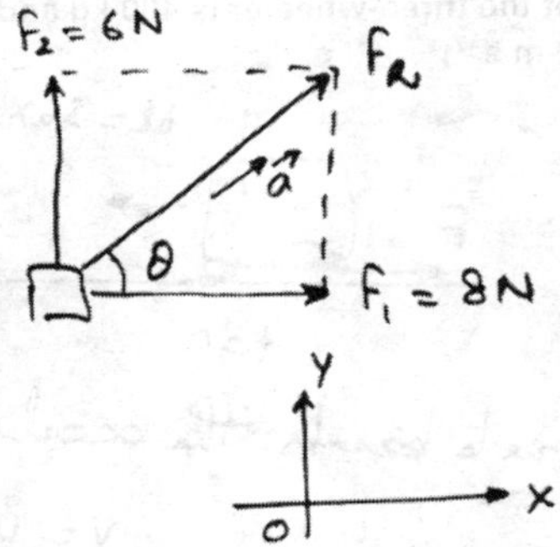

Sol^n: for forces in ⊥ direction resultant is given as

$$\vec{F}_1 = 8\hat{i} \quad ; \quad \vec{F}_2 = 6\hat{j}$$

$$\vec{F}_R = 8\hat{i} + 6\hat{j}$$

magnitude of force (net) on body

$$|\vec{F}_R| = \sqrt{(8)^2 + (6)^2} = \sqrt{64+36} = \sqrt{100} = 10\,N.$$

& here $\tan\theta = \frac{6}{8} = 3/4 \Rightarrow \theta = \tan^{-1}(3/4) = 37^\circ$

→ acc^n of body

$$a = \frac{F_R}{m} = \frac{10}{5} = 2\ m/s^2$$

in dir 37° with the 8 N force line of action

Ans.

- The driver of a three-wheeler moving with a speed of 36 km/h sees a child standing in the middle of the road and brings his vehicle to rest in 4.0 s just in time to save the child. What is the average retarding force on the vehicle ? The mass of the three-wheeler is 400 kg and the mass of the driver is 65 kg. (take $g = 10\ m\ s^{-2}$)

Solⁿ:

$u = 36 \times 5/18 = 10\ m/s$

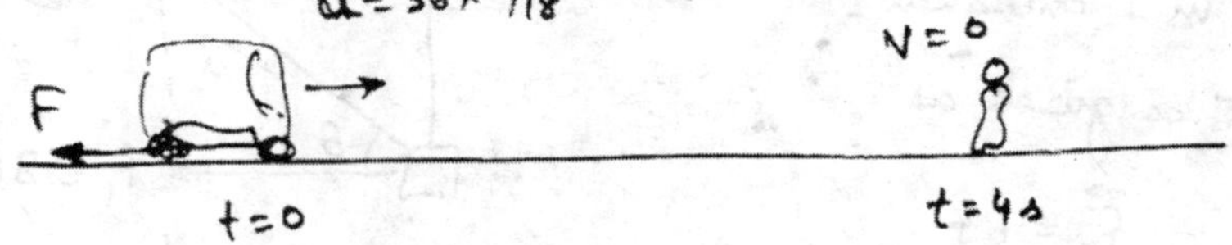

Due to breaks the acceleration of three-wheeler is a, we use

$$v = u + at$$

$$0 = 10 + a(4) \Rightarrow a = -\frac{10}{4} = -2.5\ m/s^2$$

↑ opp dir / retardation

Total mass of three-wheeler $m = 400 + 65 = 465\ kg$.

net retarding force $F = ma = 465 \times 2.5 = 1162.5\ N$

$= 1163\ N$ Ans

$= 1.2 \times 10^3\ N.$

Video Solution

- **A rocket with a lift-off mass 20,000 kg is blasted upwards with an initial acceleration of 5.0 m s^{-2}. Calculate the initial thrust (force) of the blast.**
  (take g = 10 m s^{-2})

Sol^n: Just after lift off, we use equation of motion of rocket as

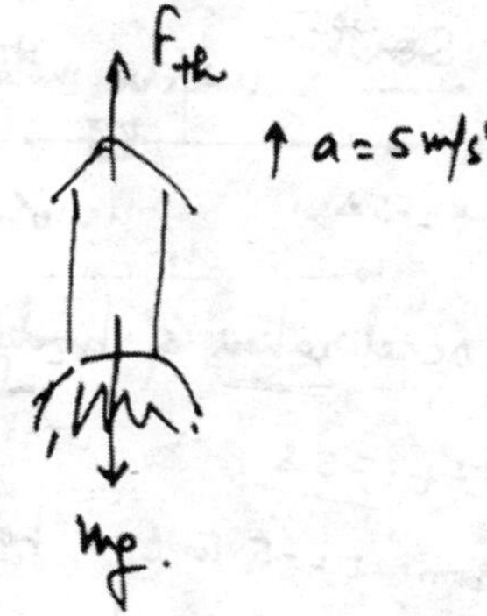

$$F_{th} - mg = ma.$$

$$\Rightarrow F_{th} = mg + ma$$

$$= m(g+a)$$

$$= 20000\,(10+5) = 3\times10^5\ \text{N} \quad \text{Ans.}$$

- A body of mass 0.40 kg moving initially with a constant speed of $10\ m\ s^{-1}$ to the north is subject to a constant force of 8.0 N directed towards the south for 30 s. Take the instant the force is applied to be $t = 0$, the position of the body at that time to be $x = 0$, and predict its position at $t = -5$ s, 25 s, 100 s.

Sol^n:

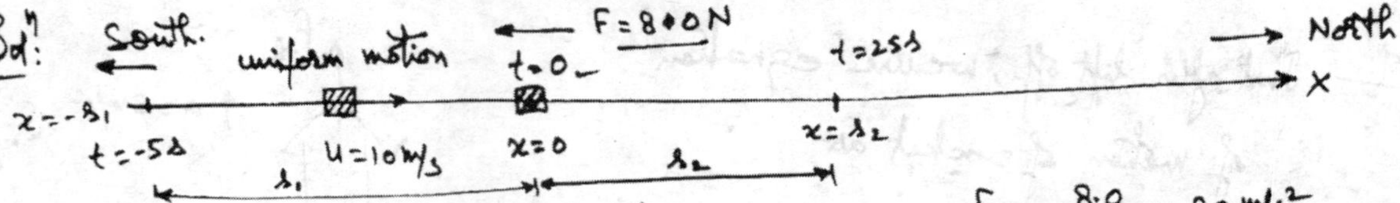

acceleration of body after $t=0$ upto $t = 30s$ is $a = \frac{F}{m} = \frac{8.0}{0.40} = 20\ m/s^2$ (−ve)

(i) At $t = -5s$.

from $t=-5$ to $t=0$ body can be consider in uniform motion

$\Rightarrow$ distance from $x=0$ at $t=-5s$ is $s_1 = ut = 10 \times 5 = 50m$

position of body at $t=-5s$ is $x = -50m$. Ans

(ii) At $t = 25s$ we use $s_2 = ut + \frac{1}{2}at^2 = 10(25) + \frac{1}{2}(-20)(25)^2 = 250 - 6250$

$= -6000\ m = -6\ km$ Ans

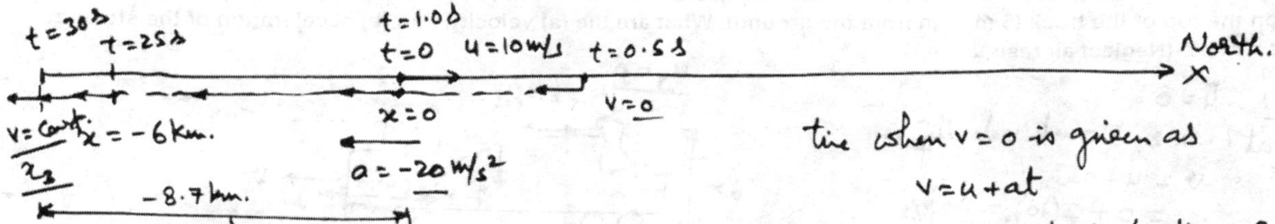

time when $v = 0$ is given as

$$v = u + at$$

$$0 = 10 - 20t \Rightarrow t = 1/2 = 0.5\,s$$

(iii) At $t = 100\,s$

upto 30 sec the position of body is $x_3 = ut + \frac{1}{2}at^2$

$$= 10(30) + \frac{1}{2}(-20)(30)^2 = 300 - 9000 = 8700\,m$$

at 30 sec the velocity of body is $v = u + at = 10 + (-20)(30) = 10 - 600 = -590\,m/s$

distance covered in next 70 s is $s_4 = -590 \times 70 = -41300\,m$ | Total distance $= -8.7 - 41.3 = -50\,km$ Ans

- A truck starts from rest and accelerates uniformly at 2.0 m s^{-2}. At t = 10 s, a stone is dropped by a person standing on the top of the truck (6 m high from the ground). What are the (a) velocity, and (b) acceleration of the stone at t = 11s ? (Neglect air resistance.)

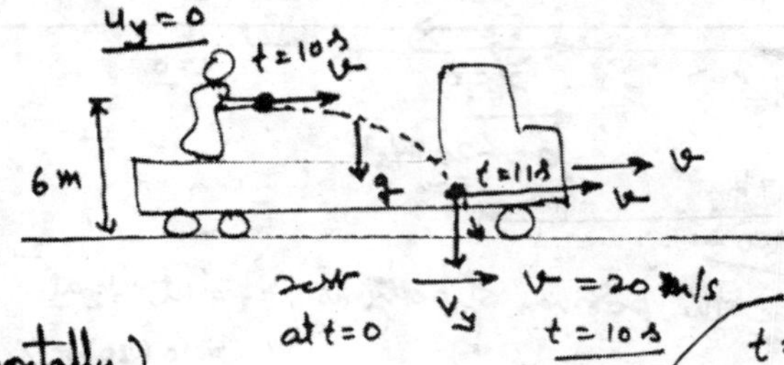

Solⁿ: $u = 0$

at $t = 10$ s, truck velocity is

$v = u + at$

$= 0 + 2(10) = 20$ m/s

At the time of release the stone has velocity of truck (20 m/s horizontally)

then it follows projectile motion as shown & hit the ground.

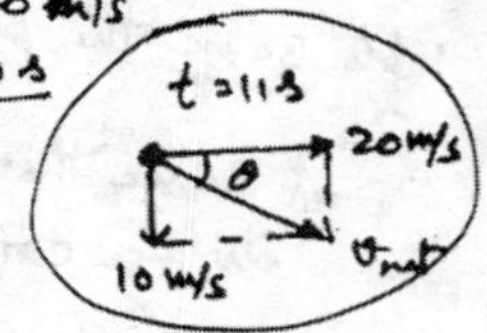

At $t = 11$ s, distance stone will fall in 1 s. $y = \frac{1}{2}gt^2 = \frac{1}{2} \times 10 \times 1 = 5$ m.

At $t = 11$ s, vertical velocity of stone is $v_y = u_y + gt = 0 + 10(1) = 10$ m/s

net velocity of stone at $t = 11$ s is $v_{net} = \sqrt{(20)^2 + (10)^2} = \sqrt{500} = 22.4$ m/s Ans

here $\theta = \tan^{-1}(10/20) = \tan^{-1}(1/2)$ Ans

As stone is in free fall motion its accⁿ $a = 10$ m/s^2 only due to gravity (g) Ans

Video Solution

- A bob of mass 0.1 kg hung from the ceiling of a room by a string 2 m long is set into oscillation. The speed of the bob at its mean position is 1 m s^{-1}. What is the trajectory of the bob if the string is cut when the bob is (a) at one of its extreme positions, (b) at its mean position.

Sol:

(a) At extreme position
$v = 0 \Rightarrow$ rest
here if string is cut,
bob will fall down in
free fall motion

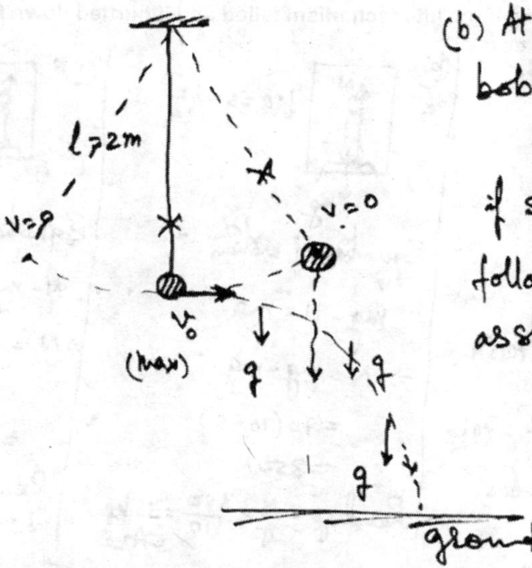

(b) At mean position
bob is moving
horizontally & here
if string is cut, bob
follows a projectile motion
as shown in parabolic
trajectory.

- A man of mass 70 kg stands on a weighing scale in a lift which is moving

(a) upwards with a uniform speed of 10 m s^{-1},

(b) downwards with a uniform acceleration of 5 m s^{-2},

(c) upwards with a uniform acceleration of 5 m s^{-2}. What would be the readings on the scale in each case?

(d) What would be the reading if the lift mechanism failed and it hurtled down freely under gravity ?

Sol^n: (a)

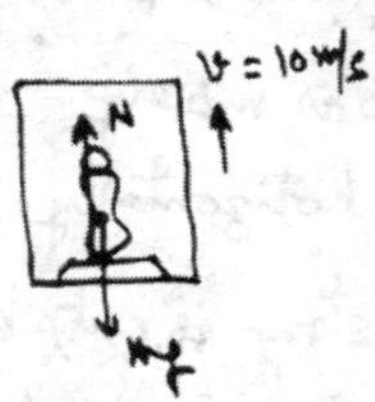

as $a = 0$

we use

$N = mg = 70 \times 10 = 700\,N$

$\text{Reading} = \frac{N}{g} = \frac{700}{10} = 70\,kg$

Ans.

(b)

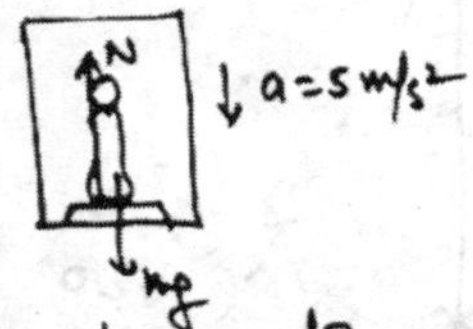

Equation of motion

$mg - N = ma$

$\Rightarrow N = mg - ma$

$= 70(10 - 5)$

$= 350\,N.$

$\text{Reading} = \frac{N}{g} = \frac{350}{10} = 35\,kg$

Ans

(c)

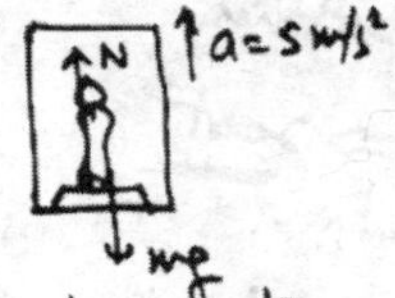

Equation of motion

$N - mg = ma$

$\Rightarrow N = m(g + a)$

$= 70(10 + 5)$

$= 1050\,N$

$\text{Reading} = \frac{N}{g} = \frac{1050}{10} = 105\,kg$

Ans

(d)

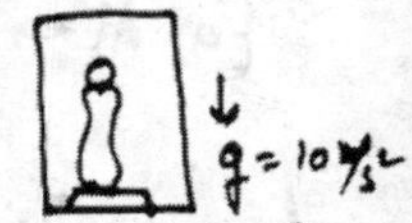

$N = 0$ as both lift & man are in free fall.

$\Rightarrow \text{Reading} = 0\,kg$

Ans.

Video Solution

- Figure shows the position-time graph of a particle of mass 4 kg. What is the

(a) force on the particle for $t < 0$, $t > 4$ s, $0 < t < 4$ s?

(b) impulse at $t = 0$ and $t = 4$ s ? (Consider one-dimensional motion only).

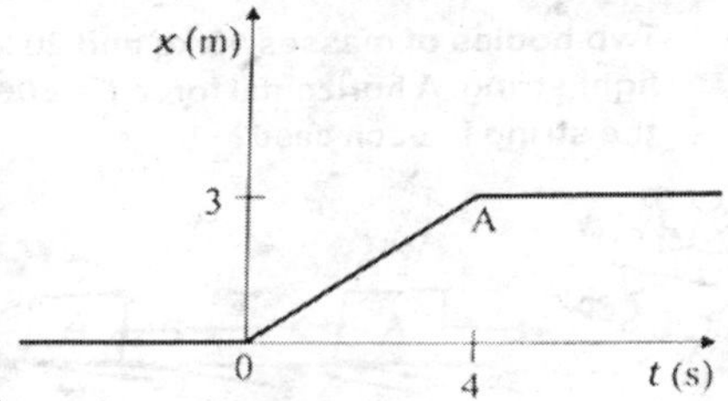

Sol^n: (a) Throughout motion $t<0$, $v=0 \Rightarrow a=0$

$t>4s$, $v=0 \Rightarrow a=0$

$0<t<4s$, v = slope of x-t curve

$= 3/4 = 0.75$ m/s → Constant $\Rightarrow a=0$

$\Rightarrow$ acc^n of particle during all time is $a=0$.

$\Rightarrow$ at all times force on particle $F = ma = 0$ Ans

(b) Impulse = change in momentum

at $t=0$ we use impulse $J_1 = mv_{0+} - mv_{0-} = 4(0.75-0) = 3$ kg m/s Ans → $\vec{J_1} = 3\hat{i}$ kg m/s

at $t=4s$ we use impulse $J_2 = mv_{4+} - mv_{4-} = 4(0-0.75) = -3$ kg m/s Ans → $\vec{J_2} = -3\hat{i}$ kg m/s.

- **Two bodies of masses 10 kg and 20 kg respectively kept on a smooth, horizontal surface are tied to the ends of a light string. A horizontal force F = 600 N is applied to (i) A, (ii) B along the direction of string. What is the tension in the string in each case?**

Sol^n (i)

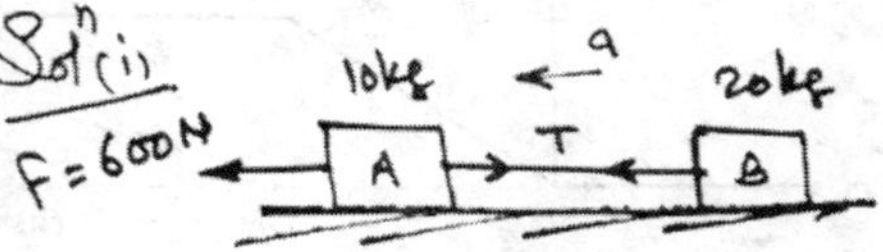

acc^n of system (A+B) is

$$a = \frac{F}{m_A + m_B} = \frac{600}{10+20} = 20\ m/s^2$$

equation of motion of 20kg block

$$T = m_B a = 20 \times 20$$

$$= 400\ N \quad \text{Ans}$$

(ii)

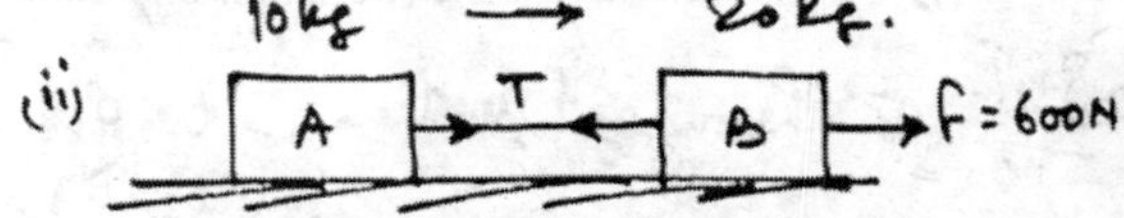

acc^n of system (A+B) is

$$a = \frac{F}{m_A + m_B} = \frac{600}{10+20} = 20\ m/s^2$$

equation of motion of 20kg mass

$$F - T = m_B a$$

$$600 - T = 20 \times 20$$

$$\Rightarrow T = 600 - 400 = 200\ N \quad \text{Ans}$$

Video Solution

- Two masses 8 kg and 12 kg are connected at the two ends of a light inextensible string that goes over a frictionless pulley. Find the acceleration of the masses, and the tension in the string when the masses are released.

Sol^n: Equations of motion for m_1 & m_2

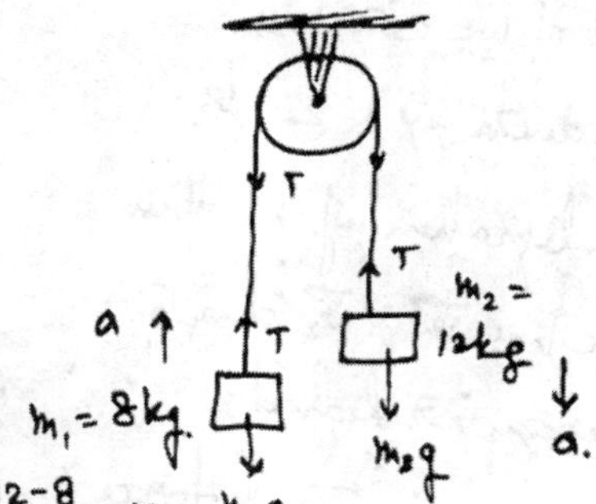

$$T - m_1 g = m_1 a \quad \text{——} (1)$$

$$m_2 g - T = m_2 a \quad \text{——} (2)$$

(1) + (2) $\quad (m_2 - m_1) g = (m_1 + m_2) a.$

$$\Rightarrow a = \frac{m_2 - m_1}{m_1 + m_2} \cdot g. = \frac{12-8}{12+8} \times 10$$

$$= 2 \text{ m/s}^2 \text{ Ans.}$$

from eq^n (1)

$$T = m_1 g + m_1 \left(\frac{m_2 - m_1}{m_1 + m_2} \right) g = \frac{2 m_1 m_2}{m_1 + m_2} \times g.$$

$$= \frac{2 \times 12 \times 8}{8 + 12} \times 10 = 12 \times 8 = 96 \text{ N} \quad \text{Ans.}$$

- **A nucleus is at rest in the laboratory frame of reference. Show that if it disintegrates into two smaller nuclei the products must move in opposite directions.**

Sol^n: If we consider products Y & Z from disintegration of X attain velocities $\vec{v}_1$ & $\vec{v}_2$ due to energy released.

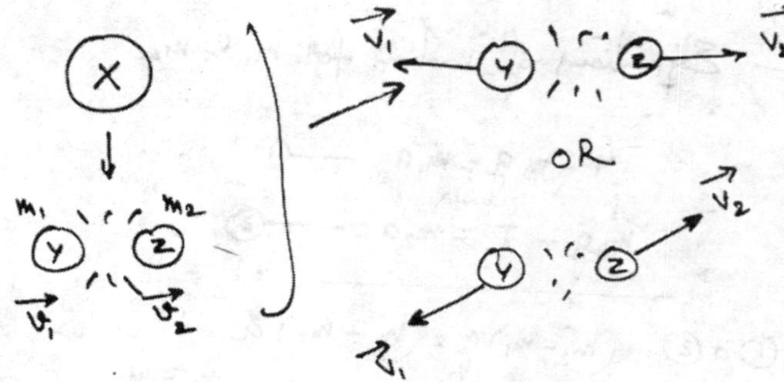

& As no external force is present in this situation, the linear momentum of system will remain conserved

$$\vec{P}_i \qquad \vec{P}_f$$

$$\Rightarrow 0 = m_1\vec{v}_1 + m_2\vec{v}_2 \Rightarrow \vec{v}_2 = -\frac{m_1}{m_2}\vec{v}_1$$

–ve sign indicates that $\vec{v}_2$ is in opposite dir to that of $\vec{v}_1$

hence prooved!

- Two billiard balls each of mass 0.05 kg moving in opposite directions with speed 6 m s^{-1} collide and rebound with the same speed. What is the impulse imparted to each ball due to the other ?

Sol^n:

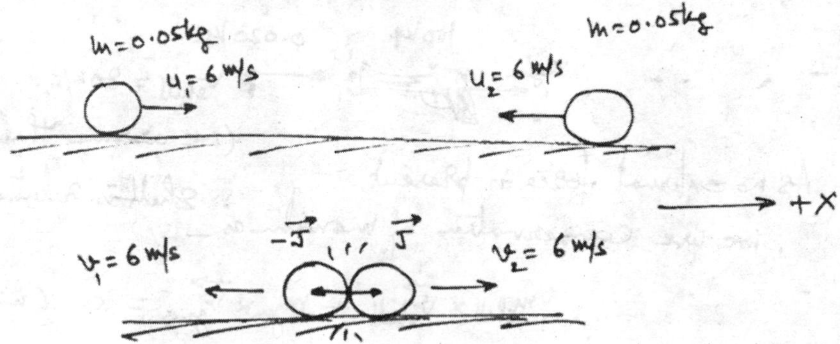

$\vec{u_1} = 6\hat{i}$ m/s

$\vec{u_2} = -6\hat{i}$ m/s

$\vec{v_1} = -6\hat{i}$ m/s

$\vec{v_2} = 6\hat{i}$ m/s

for ball-1: Impulse = change in momentum

$$= m(\vec{v_1} - \vec{u_1}) = 0.05(-6\hat{i} - 6\hat{i}) = -0.6\hat{i} \text{ kg m/s}^2$$

for ball-2:

$$= m(\vec{v_2} - \vec{u_2}) = 0.05(6\hat{i} - (-6\hat{i})) = 0.6\hat{i} \text{ kg m/s}^2$$

Ans.

- **A shell of mass 0.020 kg is fired by a gun of mass 100 kg. If the muzzle speed of the shell is 80 m s^{-1}, what is the recoil speed of the gun ?**

Sol^n:

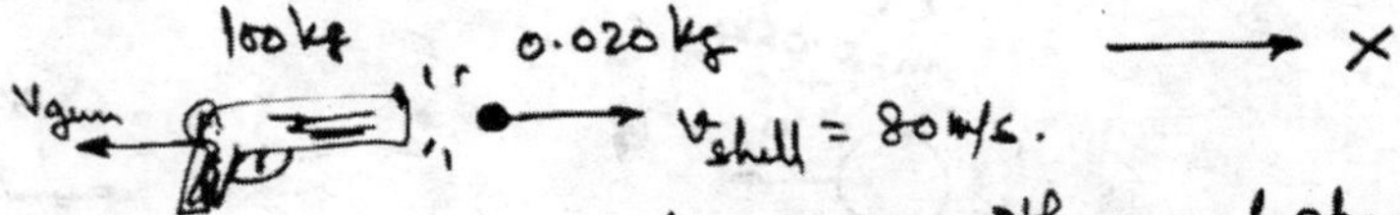

(we assume the muzzle speed of shell is relative to initial state of gun)

As no external force is present, we use conservation of momentum as –

$$m_{shell} \times \vec{v}_{shell} + m_{gun} \times \vec{v}_{gun} = 0 \quad \text{(initial momentum before firing)}$$

$$\vec{v}_{gun} = -\frac{m_{shell}}{m_{gun}} \times \vec{v}_{shell}$$

$$= -\frac{0.020}{100} \times 80\hat{i} = -0.016\hat{i} \text{ m/s}$$

$$|\vec{v}_{gun}| = 1.6 \text{ cm/s} \quad \text{Ans}$$

Video Solution

- A batsman deflects a ball by an angle of 45° without changing its initial speed which is equal to 54 km/h. What is the impulse imparted to the ball ? (Mass of the ball is 0.15 kg.)

Sol^n: speed of ball = 54 kph = $54 \times \frac{5}{18}$

$= 15\ m/s$

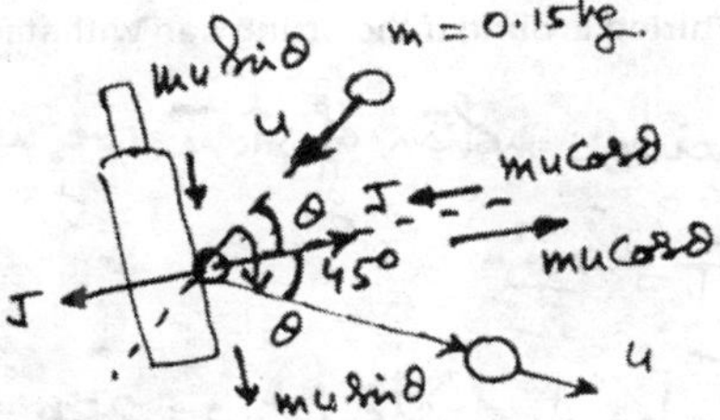

momentum of ball

① → along the bat = $mu\sin\theta$

② → normal to the bat = $mu\cos\theta$

here $2\theta = 45°$

$\theta = 22.5°$

after collision of ball with bat, momentum of ball.

① → along the bat = $mu\sin\theta$ (No change)

② → normal to the bat = $mu\cos\theta$ (reversed.)

Impulse = change in momentum

$J = (mu\cos\theta) - (-mu\cos\theta)$

$= 2mu\cos\theta$

$= 2 \times 0.15 \times 15 \times \cos 22.5°$

$= 4.5 \times 0.9239 = 4.16\ kg\,m/s$

$= 4.2\ kg\,m/s$ Ans

- A stone of mass 0.25 kg tied to the end of a string is whirled round in a circle of radius 1.5 m with a speed of 40 rev./min in a horizontal plane. What is the tension in the string ? What is the maximum speed with which the stone can be whirled around if the string can withstand a maximum tension of 200 N ?

Solⁿ: For circular motion of stone we use

$$T = \frac{mv^2}{r}$$

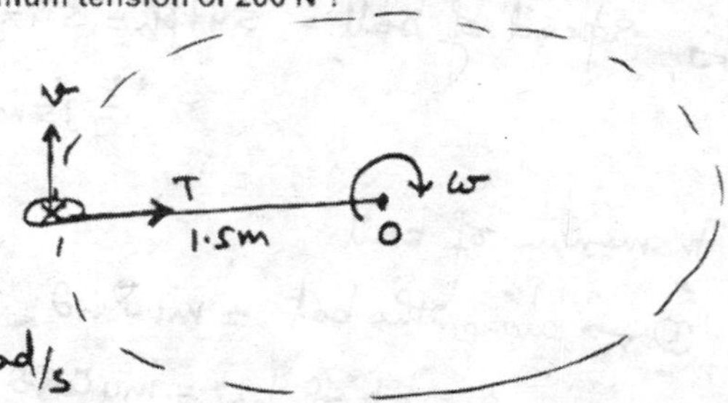

Angular speed of stone $\omega = 2\pi n$

$$= 2\pi\left(\frac{40}{60}\right) \text{ rad/s}$$

$$= \frac{4\pi}{3} \text{ rad/s} \Rightarrow v = r\omega = 1.5 \times \frac{4\pi}{3} = 2\pi \text{ m/s}$$

$$\Rightarrow T = \frac{0.25 \times (2 \times 3.14)^2}{1.5} = 6.6 \text{ N Ans.}$$

for max tension of 200N, we use

$$200 = \frac{mv_{max}^2}{r} \Rightarrow v_{max} = \sqrt{\frac{200 \times 1.5}{0.25}} = \sqrt{1200} = 34.6 \text{ m/s}$$

$$= 35 \text{ m/s Ans}$$

- **If, in Exercise 5.21, the speed of the stone is increased beyond the maximum permissible value, and the string breaks suddenly, which of the following correctly describes the trajectory of the stone after the string breaks :**

(a) the stone moves radially outwards,

(b) the stone flies off tangentially from the instant the string breaks,

(c) the stone flies off at an angle with the tangent whose magnitude depends on the speed of the particle ?

Sol^n:

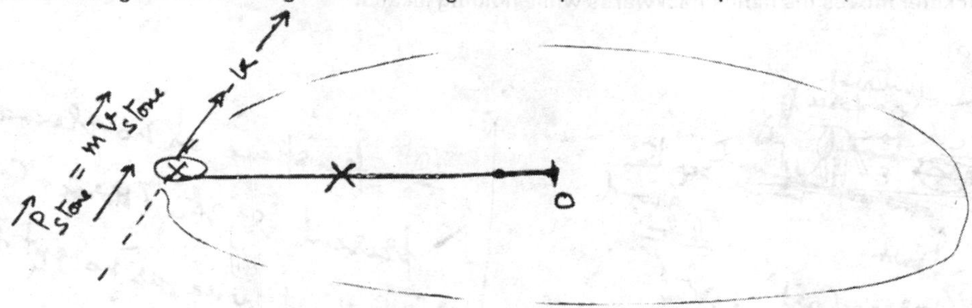

Just after string breaks, as no external force is acting on stone, its momentum will remain Conserved (in magnitude & direction)

$\Rightarrow$ stone will Continue its motion along tangent of circular path

- Explain why

(a) a horse cannot pull a cart and run in empty space,

(b) passengers are thrown forward from their seats when a speeding bus stops suddenly,

(c) it is easier to pull a lawn mower than to push it,

(d) a cricketer moves his hands backwards while holding a catch.

Sol: (a)

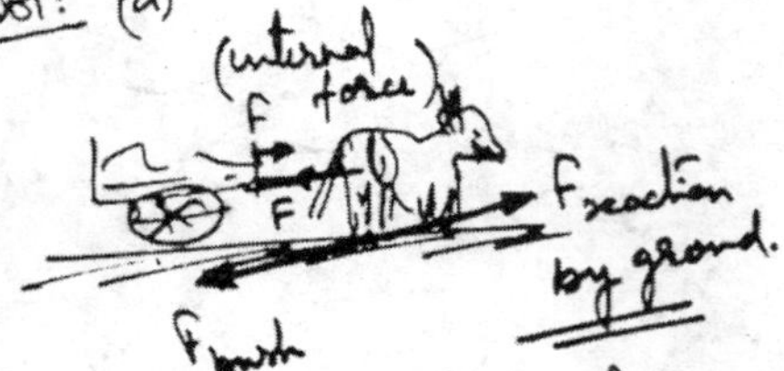

On (Horse + Cart) system the force of reaction by ground is the external force which causes the system to move forward.

In free space as no ground is present system (Horse + Cart) will not move as no ext force will be there.

& by internal forces any system can not gain motion/momentum.

Sol^n (b)

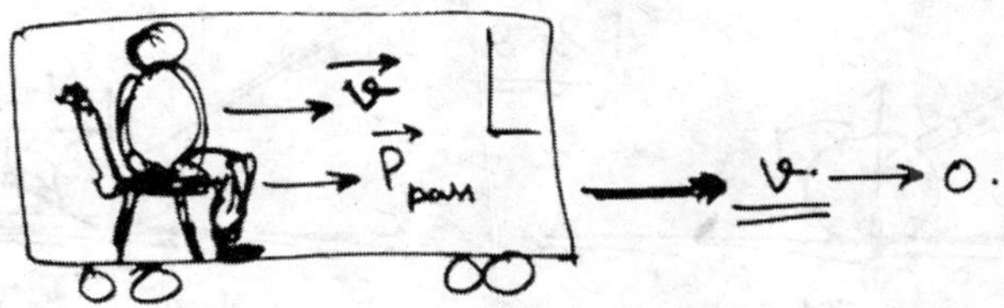

As passengers also have same velocity of bus will have momentum in dir of bus motion.

As bus is suddenly stopped passengers still move at $\vec{v}$ with same momentum & due to inertia in absence of direct external forces passengers are thrown forward due to their initial momentum.

Sol^n (c)

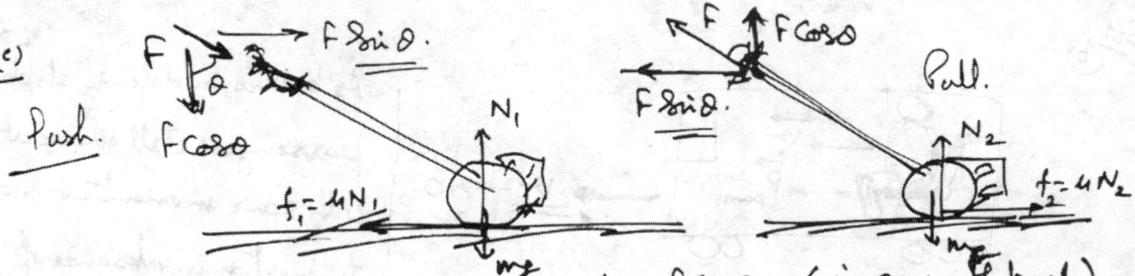

Normal Contact force on mover $N_1 = mg + F\cos\theta$ (in case of push)

$N_2 = mg - F\cos\theta$ (in case of pull)

$\Rightarrow f_2 < f_1 \Rightarrow$ it will be easier to pull

Sol(a)

When a cricketer moves his hands backward, it increases time of catch & impulse required to catch is

J = change in momentum of ball

$= mv - 0 = \underline{mv}$ (0 after catch (rest))

F = force by man on ball during catch.

We also use $J = \underline{F \cdot \Delta t}$

for catch timings $\underline{\Delta t_1}$ & $\underline{\Delta t_2}$ we use

$F_1 \Delta t_1 = F_2 \Delta t_2$ so if $\underline{\Delta t}$ is large less force is required.

- Figure shows the position-time graph of a body of mass 0.04 kg. Suggest a suitable physical context for this motion. What is the time between two consecutive impulses received by the body ? What is the magnitude of each impulse ?

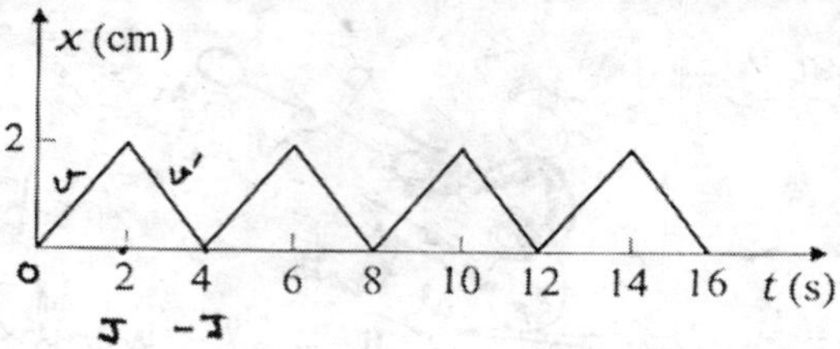

Sol^n: velocity of mass changes due to impulse & the time between two consecutive impulses is

$$\Delta t = 2\,s \quad \text{Ans}$$

velocity from $t = 0$ to $t = 2\,s$

$$v = \text{slope of } x\text{-}t \text{ curve}$$

$$= \frac{2}{2} = 1\,cm/s = 0.01\,m/s$$

velocity from $t = 2\,s$ to $t = 4\,s$

$$v' = -\frac{2}{2} = -1\,cm/s = -0.01\,m/s$$

impulse imparted at $t = 2\,sec$

$$J = \Delta mv = m(v - v')$$

$$= 0.04\,(0.01 - (-0.01))$$

$$= 0.04 \times 0.02\ kg\,m/s$$

$$= 8 \times 10^{-4}\ kg\,m/s \quad \text{Ans}$$

Physical context

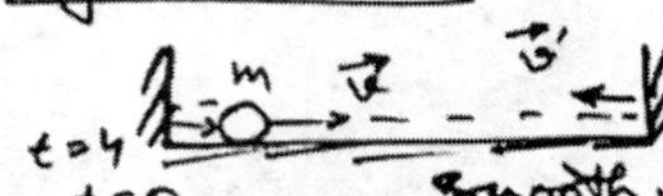

- Figure shows a man standing stationary with respect to a horizontal conveyor belt that is accelerating with 1 m s^{-2}. What is the net force on the man? If the coefficient of static friction between the man's shoes and the belt is 0.2, up to what acceleration of the belt can the man continue to be stationary relative to the belt ? (Mass of the man = 65 kg.)

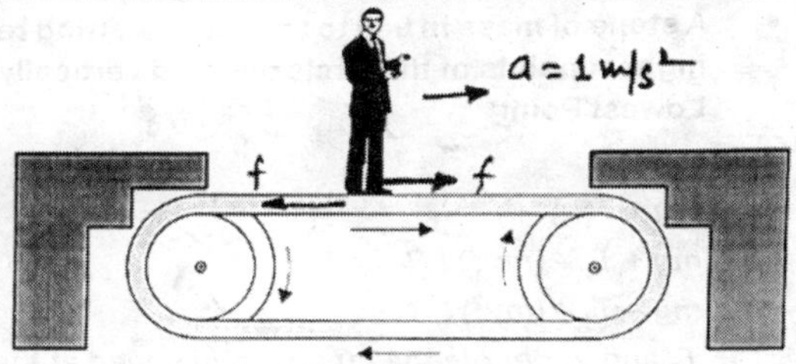

Sol^n: The force on man due to friction is

$$f = ma = 65 \times 1 = 65\ N \quad \text{Ans.}$$

limiting friction on man shoes is $f_L = \mu N = \mu mg = 0.2 \times 65 \times 10$

$$= 130\ N. \ (\text{max})$$

The maximum acc^n upto which man will be stationary on belt (without skidding) can be given as-

$$a_{max} = \frac{f_L}{m} = \frac{\mu mg}{m} = \mu g = 0.2 \times 10 = 2\ m/s^2 \quad \text{Ans.}$$

for $a < 2\ m/s^2$ man will be at rest on belt.

- **A stone of mass m tied to the end of a string revolves in a vertical circle of radius R. The net forces at the lowest and highest points of the circle directed vertically downwards are : [Choose the correct alternative]**

	Lowest Point	Highest Point
✓(a)	$mg - T_1$	$mg + T_2$
(b)	$mg + T_1$	$mg - T_2$
(c)	$mg + T_1 - (mv_1^2)/R$	$mg - T_2 (mv_1^2)/R$
(d)	$mg - T_1 - (mv_1^2)/R$	$mg + T_2 + (mv_1^2)/R$

T_1 and v_1 denote the tension and speed at the lowest point. T_2 and v_2 denote corresponding values at the highest point.

Sol^n.

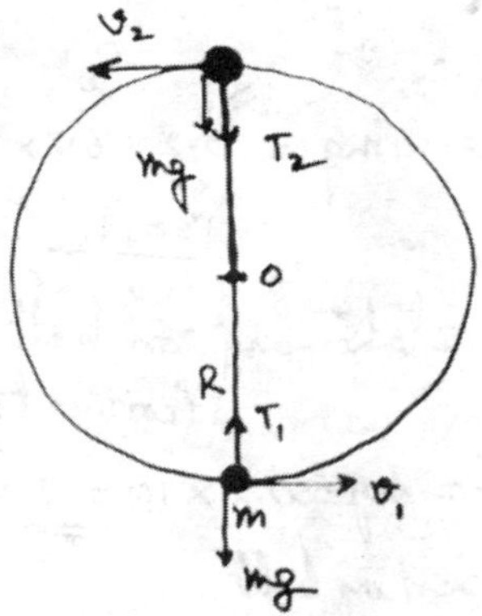

net force at lowest point is

$$F_{net} = T_1 - mg = \frac{mv_1^2}{R}$$

net force at highest point is

$$F_{net} = T_2 + mg = \frac{mv_2^2}{R}$$

$\Rightarrow$ option (a) is Correct.

Video Solution

- A helicopter of mass 1000 kg rises with a vertical acceleration of 15 m s^{-2}. The crew and the passengers weigh 300 kg. Give the magnitude and direction of the

(a) force on the floor by the crew and passengers,

(b) action of the rotor of the helicopter on the surrounding air,

(c) force on the helicopter due to the surrounding air.

Sol^n: $m_1 = 300$ kg

$m_2 = 1000$ kg

(a) FBD of crew & passengers

eq^n of motion

$N_1 - m_1 g = m_1 a$

$\Rightarrow N_1 = m_1(g+a) = 300(10+15) = 7500$ N Ans $\uparrow$

(b) eq^n of motion for helicopter

$F_{lift} - (m_1+m_2)g = (m_1+m_2)a$

$F_{lift} = (m_1+m_2)(g+a) = 1300 \times 25 = 32500$ N $\downarrow$ Ans

(c) According to Newton's III law

F_{lift} will be same by air on helicopter

$F_{lift} = 32500$ N $\uparrow$ Ans

- A stream of water flowing horizontally with a speed of 15 m s^{-1} gushes out of a tube of cross-sectional area 10^{-2} m^2, and hits a vertical wall nearby. What is the force exerted on the wall by the impact of water, assuming it does not rebound ?

Sol^n:

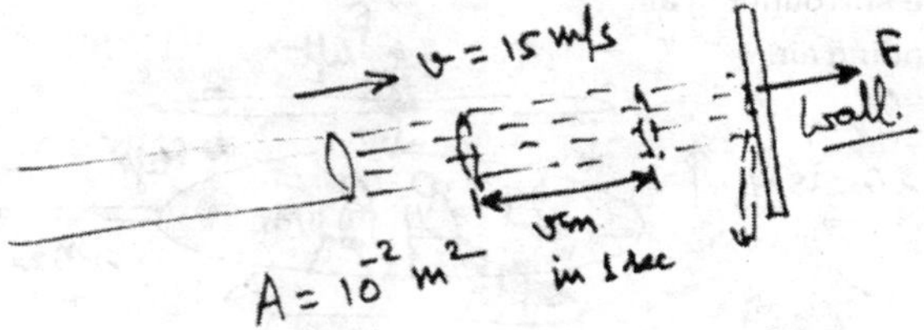

force on wall due to water impact = momentum supplied/sec

$= \underbrace{\rho (vA)}_{\text{mass striking/sec}} \times v = \rho A v^2$

$= 1000 \times 10^{-2} \times (15)^2$

$= 2250$ N Ans.

- Ten one-rupee coins are put on top of each other on a table. Each coin has a mass *m*. Give the magnitude and direction of

(a) the force on the 7th coin (counted from the bottom) due to all the coins on its top,

(b) the force on the 7th coin by the eighth coin,

(c) the reaction of the 6th coin on the 7th coin.

Sol^n: (a) For equilibrium of top 3 coins we use

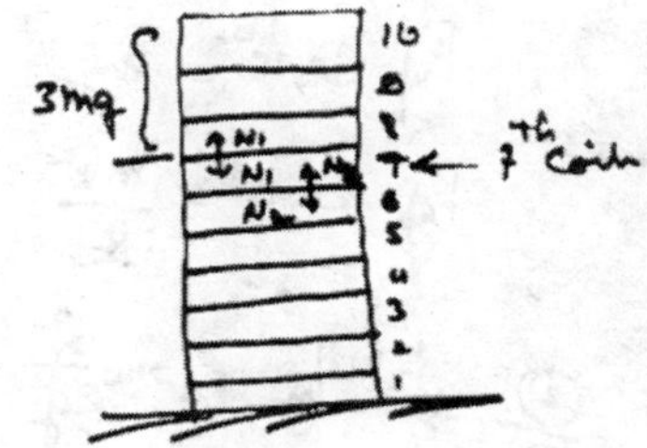

$N_1 = 3mg$ Ans.

(b) It is also N_1 which is applied by 8th coin only

$3mg$ Ans

(c) for equilibrium of 7th coin

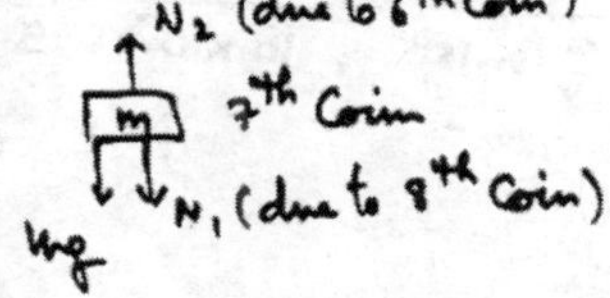

$N_2 = mg + N_1 = 4mg$ Ans.

- **An aircraft executes a horizontal loop at a speed of 720 km/h with its wings banked at 15°. What is the radius of the loop ?**

Sol:
For equilibrium of aircraft, we use

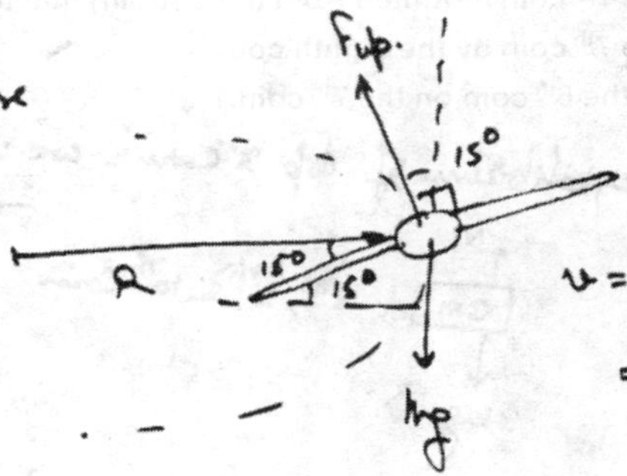

$$F_{up}\cos 15^\circ = mg \quad \text{—} ①$$

$$F_{up}\sin 15^\circ = \frac{mv^2}{R} \quad \text{—} ②$$

$v = 720\text{ km/h} \times \frac{5}{18} = 200\text{ m/s}$

$$\frac{②}{①} \Rightarrow \tan 15^\circ = \frac{v^2}{Rg}$$

$$\Rightarrow R = \frac{v^2}{g\tan 15^\circ} = \frac{(200)^2}{10 \times 0.2679} = 15\text{ km} \quad \text{Ans.}$$

Video Solution

- A train runs along an unbanked circular track of radius 30 m at a speed of 54 km/h. The mass of the train is 10^6 kg. What provides the centripetal force required for this purpose — The engine or the rails ? What is the angle of banking required to prevent wearing out of the rail ?

<u>Sol</u>

Sol^n: The force on outer rail by train due to its motion inertia causes this outer rail to push the flanges of wheels in direction toward the centre of circular track.

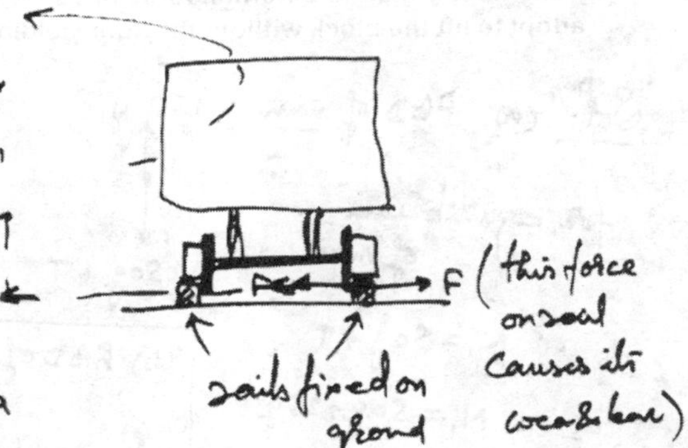

$v = 54 \times \frac{5}{18} = 15 \text{ m/s}$

Banking angle for a given speed v for a circular turn of radius R is given as–

$$\tan\theta = \frac{v^2}{Rg}$$

$$\theta = \tan^{-1}\left(\frac{v^2}{Rg}\right) = \tan^{-1}\left(\frac{(15)^2}{30\times10}\right) = \tan^{-1}\left(\frac{3}{4}\right) = 37^\circ \quad \text{Ans.}$$

- A block of mass 25 kg is raised by a 50 kg man in two different ways as shown in figure. What is the action on the floor by the man in the two cases ? If the floor yields to a normal force of 700 N, which mode should the man adopt to lift the block without the floor yielding ?

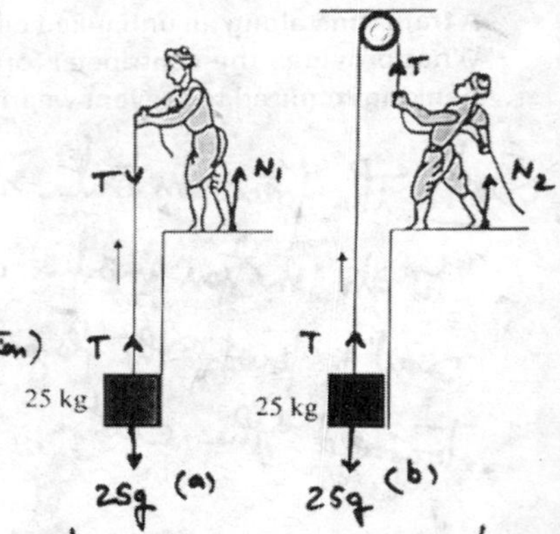

(mass is being raised slowly)

Sol^n: (a) FBD of man.

N_1 (up), $50g + T$ (down)

for equilibrium of man

we have for block at rest (slow motion)

$T = 25g$

$N_1 = 50g + T$

$N_1 = 50g + 25g$

$= 75g = 750\text{N}$. Ans

(b) FBD of man

$T + N_2$ (up), $50g$ (down)

for equilibrium of man.

$T + N_2 = 50g$

$N_2 = 50g - 25g = 25g = 250\text{N}$ Ans.

in Case (b) $N_2 < 700\text{N}$.

$\Rightarrow$ mode (b) should be adopted by man.

- A monkey of mass 40 kg climbs on a rope (figure) which can stand a maximum tension of 600 N. In which of the following cases will the rope break: the monkey

(a) climbs up with an acceleration of 6 m s^{-2}

(b) climbs down with an acceleration of 4 m s^{-2}

(c) climbs up with a uniform speed of 5 m s^{-1}

(d) falls down the rope nearly freely under gravity?

(Ignore the mass of the rope).

Solⁿ: (a) FBD of monkey: T upward, 40g downward, $\uparrow a = 6\ m/s^2$

$\Rightarrow T - 40g = 40a$

$\Rightarrow T = 400 + 240 = 640N\ (>600N)$

$\Rightarrow$ rope will break.

(b) FBD of monkey: T upward, 40g downward, $\downarrow a = 4\ m/s^2$

$\Rightarrow 40g - T = 40a$

$\Rightarrow T = 400 - 160 = 240N\ (<600N)$

$\Rightarrow$ rope will not break.

(c) FBD of monkey: T upward, 40g downward, $a = 0$

$\Rightarrow T = 40g = 400N\ (<600N)$

$\Rightarrow$ rope will not break.

(d) under free fall $T = 0$ $\Rightarrow$ rope will not break

- Two bodies *A* and *B* of masses 5 kg and 10 kg in contact with each other rest on a table against a rigid wall (figure). The coefficient of friction between the bodies and the table is 0.15. A force of 200 N is applied horizontally to *A*. What are (a) the reaction of the partition (b) the actionreaction forces between *A* and *B* ? What happens when the wall is removed? Does the answer to (b) change, when the bodies are in motion? Ignore the difference between μ_s and μ_k.

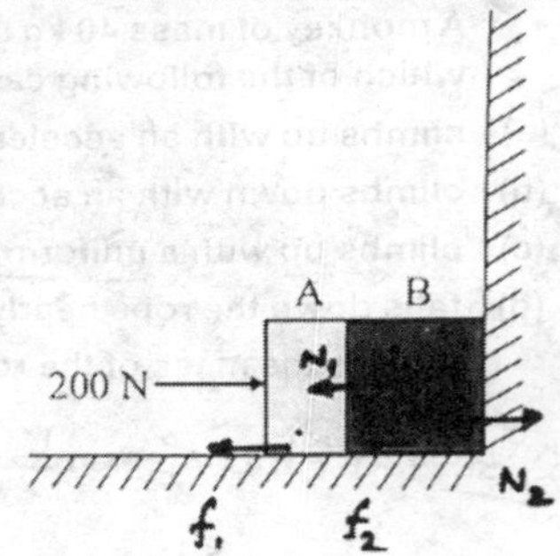

Sol^n (a) Both A & B are at rest

FBD of A

$f_{1L} = 7.5N$

FBD of B.

$f_{2L} = 15N$

$f_{1L} = \mu m_A g = 0.15 \times 5 \times 10 = 7.5N$

$f_{2L} = \mu m_B g = 0.15 \times 10 \times 10 = 15N$

(b) $200 = N_1 + 7.5$

$N_1 = 192.5N$ Ans

(a) $N_2 + 15 = N_1$

$N_2 = 177.5N$ Ans.

If partition is not there, both bodies will set in motion & their equations of motion will be —

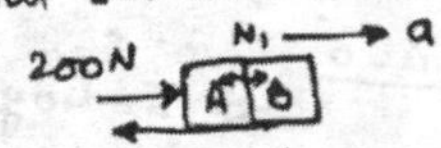

$f_1 + f_2 = 22.5N$

$\Rightarrow 200 - 22.5 = 15a$

$\Rightarrow a = \frac{177.5}{11} \approx 11.8 m/s^2$

for (A) we use $200 - 7.5 - N_1 = 5 \times 11.8 \Rightarrow N_1 = 130N$ Ans.

Video Solution

- A block of mass 15 kg is placed on a long trolley. The coefficient of static friction between the block and the trolley is 0.18. The trolley accelerates from rest with 0.5 m s^{-2} for 20 s and then moves with uniform velocity. Discuss the motion of the block as viewed by (a) a stationary observer on the ground, (b) an observer moving with the trolley.

Sol^n: limiting friction on block $= \mu mg = 0.18 \times 15 \times 10 = 27\,N$

(a) In first 20 s w.r.to stationary observer on ground

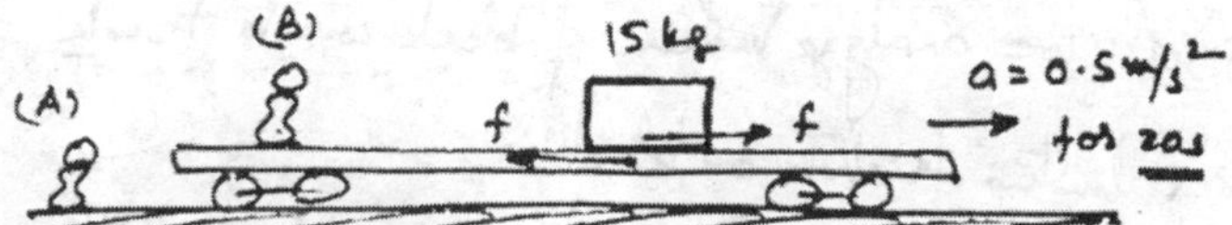

as 15 kg mass is also accelerating at 0.5 m/s^2

its motion eq^n is $f = ma = 15 \times 0.5 = 7.5\,N.$ $(< 27\,N)$ ⇒ it is static friction

⇒ block does not slide w.r.to trolley

after 20 s, block also moves at uniform speed ⇒ $f = 0$ & still block moves with trolley.

(b) w.r.to observer on trolley block will always remain at rest.

- The rear side of a truck is open and a box of 40 kg mass is placed 5 m away from the open end as shown in figure. The coefficient of friction between the box and the surface below it is 0.15. On a straight road, the truck starts from rest and accelerates with 2 m s^{-2}. At what distance from the starting point does the box fall off the truck? (Ignore the size of the box).

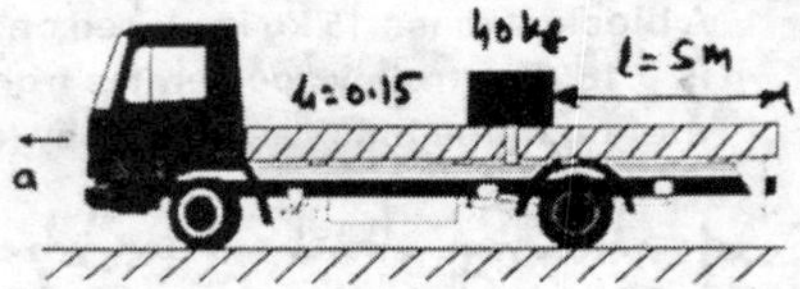

Sol^n: we analyze motion of block w.r.to truck

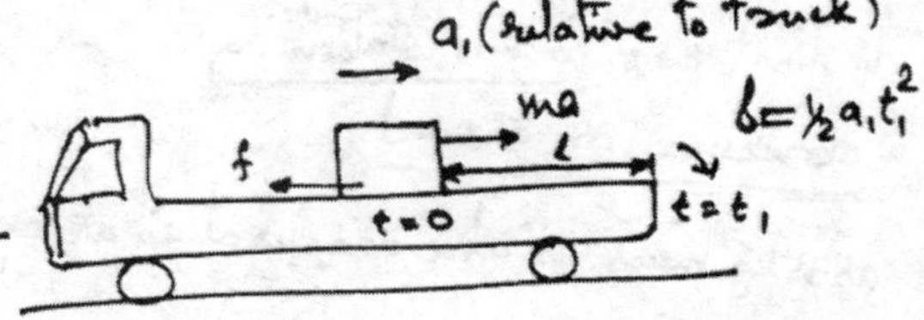

limiting friction on block is

$$f_L = \mu mg = 0.15 \times 40 \times 10 \qquad a = 2\,m/s^2$$
$$= \underline{60\,N}$$

Pseudo force on block w.r.to truck $F_p = ma = 40 \times 2 = \underline{80\,N}$

If block accelerates w.r.to truck at a_1, its motion eq^n we write as

$$ma - f = ma_1$$
$$80 - 60 = 40a_1$$
$$\Rightarrow a_1 = 0.5\,m/s^2$$

Time taken by box to fall off the truck

$$t_1 = \sqrt{\frac{2l}{a_1}} = \sqrt{\frac{2 \times 5}{0.5}} = \underline{\sqrt{20}\,s}$$

Distance travelled by truck $= \frac{1}{2}at_1^2 = \frac{1}{2} \times 2 \times 20$

$= 20\,m$ Ans

- A disc revolves with a speed of $33\frac{1}{3}$ rev/min, and has a radius of 15 cm. Two coins are placed at 4 cm and 14 cm away from the centre of the record. If the co-efficient of friction between the coins and the record is 0.15, which of the coins will revolve with the record ?

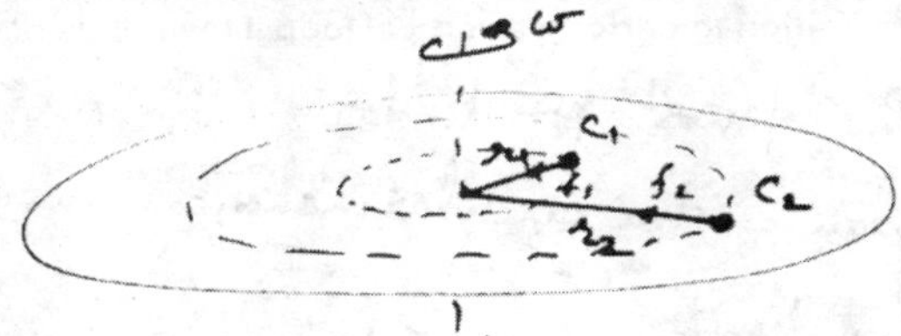

Sol^n: Angular speed $\omega = 2\pi n$

$$= 2\times\frac{22}{7}\left(\frac{100}{3}\times\frac{1}{60}\right)$$

$$= \frac{220}{63} \text{ rad/s}$$

to revolve around the same axis on record the friction on coins must impart necessary centripetal acc^n.

max acc^n friction can impart is $a_{max} = \mu g = 0.15\times 10 = 1.5 \text{ m/s}^2$

for CM, acc^n at angular speed ω are

for C_1 $a_N = \omega^2 r_1 = \left(\frac{220}{63}\right)^2 \times 0.04 = 0.49 \text{ m/s}^2$ $(< 1.5 \text{ m/s}^2)$ ⇒ Coin C_1 can revolve in CM with record.

for C_2 $a_N = \omega^2 r_2 = \left(\frac{220}{63}\right)^2 \times 0.14 = 1.7 \text{ m/s}^2$ $(> 1.5 \text{ m/s}^2)$ ⇒ Coin C_2 will not revolve with record & it will start slipping on it

- You may have seen in a circus a motorcyclist driving in vertical loops inside a 'death-well' (a hollow spherical chamber with holes, so the spectators can watch from outside). Explain clearly why the motorcyclist does not drop down when he is at the uppermost point, with no support from below. What is the minimum speed required at the uppermost position to perform a vertical loop if the radius of the chamber is 25 m ?

Sol: At the topmost point for maintaing the circular motion we must have

$$mg + N = \frac{mv^2}{R}$$

$$\Rightarrow \quad v = \sqrt{\frac{(mg+N)R}{m}}$$

$$v_{min} = \sqrt{gR} \quad \text{(we consider } N = 0\text{)}$$

$$= \sqrt{10 \times 25} = \sqrt{250} = 16 \text{ m/s} \quad \text{Ans.}$$

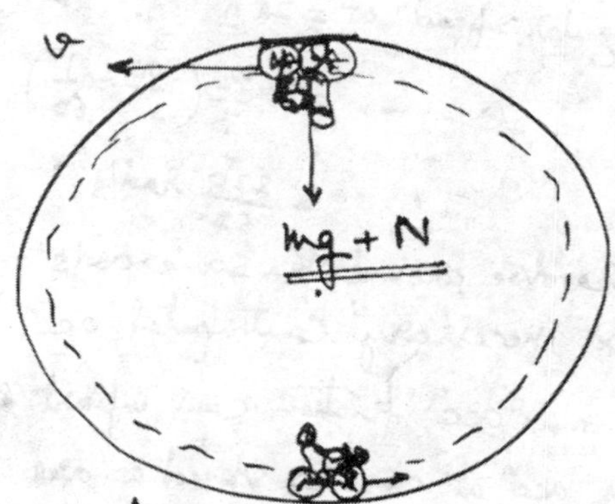

Video Solution

- A 70 kg man stands in contact against the inner wall of a hollow cylindrical drum of radius 3 m rotating about its vertical axis with 200 rev/min. The coefficient of friction between the wall and his clothing is 0.15. What is the minimum rotational speed of the cylinder to enable the man to remain stuck to the wall (without falling) when the floor is suddenly removed ?

Sol^n: In the frame of drum, man experiences a Centrifugal force (Pseudo force) in outward direction, so for equilibrium of man.

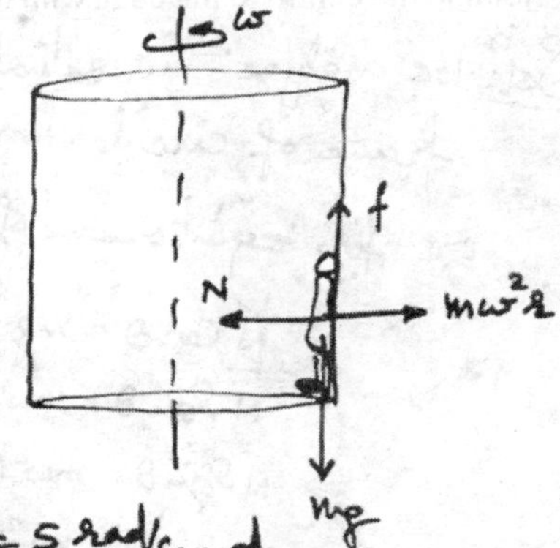

$$mg = f \quad \& \quad N = m\omega^2 r$$

$$mg < f_L = \mu N$$

$$\Rightarrow \quad mg < \mu m\omega^2 r$$

$$\Rightarrow \quad \omega_{min} > \sqrt{\frac{g}{\mu r}} = \sqrt{\frac{10}{0.15\times 3}} = \sqrt{\frac{10}{0.45}} = 5 \text{ rad/sec Ans.}$$

for the given situation $\omega = 2\pi\left(\frac{200}{60}\right) = \frac{20}{3}\times\frac{22}{7} = \frac{440}{21}$ rad/sec $\Rightarrow$ man is Safe.

- A thin circular loop of radius R rotates about its vertical diameter with an angular frequency ω. Show that a small bead on the wire loop remains at its lowermost point for $\omega \le \sqrt{g/R}$. What is the angle made by the radius vector joining the centre to the bead with the vertical downward direction for $\omega = \sqrt{2g/R}$? Neglect friction.

Sol^n: We analyze this situation in frame of circular wire as shown –

for equilibrium of bead, we use

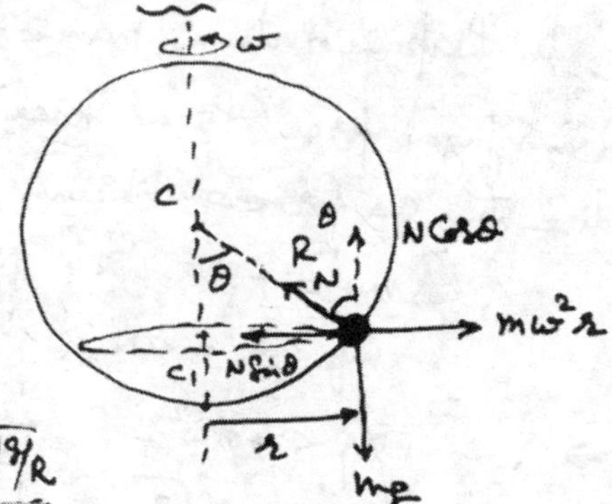

$$N\cos\theta = mg \quad \text{— (1)}$$

$$N\sin\theta = m\omega^2 r \quad \text{— (2)}$$

$$\Rightarrow N\sin\theta = m\omega^2(R\sin\theta)$$

$$N = m\omega^2 R$$

$r = R\sin\theta$

from (1) $\Rightarrow (m\omega^2 R)\cos\theta = mg$

$$\Rightarrow \cos\theta = g/\omega^2 R$$

for $\omega = \sqrt{g/R}$

$\Rightarrow \cos\theta = 1 \Rightarrow \theta = 0°$

for all $\omega \le \sqrt{g/R}$

for $\omega = \sqrt{\frac{2g}{R}} \Rightarrow \cos\theta = 1/2 \Rightarrow \theta = \cos^{-1}(1/2) = 60°$ Ans.

Video Solution

Chapter 6

Work, Energy and Power

QR Code of Link to the Video Lectures
of Theory of this chapter Work, Energy and Power
at 'Physics Galaxy' web portal

QR Code of Link to the NCERT textbook Video Solutions
of unsolved exercises at the end of each chapter in sequence
of this chapter at 'Physics Galaxy' web portal

- The sign of work done by a force on a body is important to understand. State carefully if the following quantities are positive or negative:

(a) work done by a man in lifting a bucket out of a well by means of a rope tied to the bucket

(b) work done by gravitational force in the above case,

(c) work done by friction on a body sliding down an inclined plane,

(d) work done by an applied force on a body moving on a rough horizontal plane with uniform velocity,

(e) work done by the resistive force of air on a vibrating pendulum in bringing it to rest

Sol^n: (a)

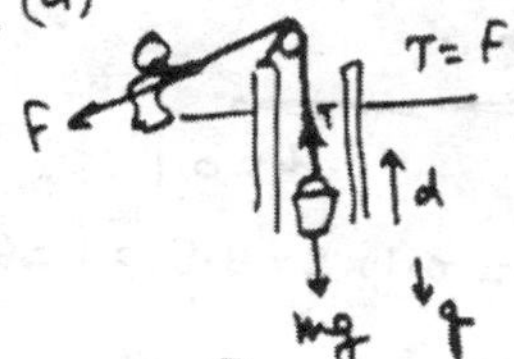

$W = \vec{F}\cdot\vec{d} = +ve$

as F & d are in same dir.

(b) $W_g = m\vec{g}\cdot\vec{d}$
$= -ve$

as $m\vec{g}$ & $\vec{d}$ are opposite

(c)

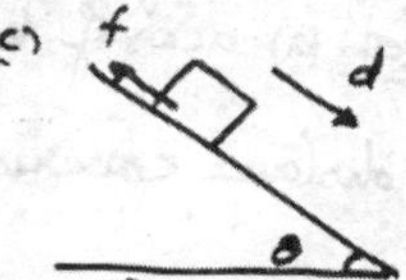

$W = \vec{f}\cdot\vec{d} = -ve$

as $\vec{f}$ & $\vec{d}$ are opposite

(d) $\vec{d}$, v = Constant | a = 0

rough horizontal plane

As a = 0 ⇒ F = f.

$W = \vec{F}_{ext}\cdot\vec{d} = +ve$ as F_{ext} & $\vec{d}$ are in same direction

(e)

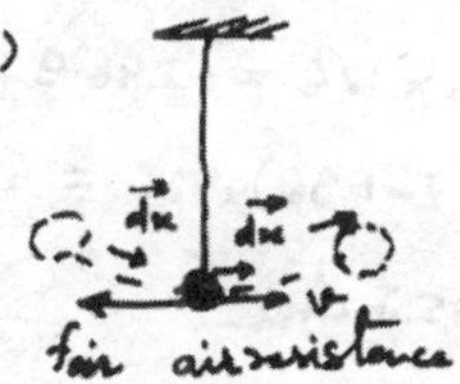

$dW = \vec{f}_{air}\cdot\vec{dx}$

$W = \int dW = -ve$ as always $\vec{f}_{air}$ & $\vec{dx}$ are opposite.

- A body of mass 2 kg initially at rest moves under the action of an applied horizontal force of 7 N on a table with coefficient of kinetic friction = 0.1. Compute the

(a) work done by the applied force in 10 s,

(b) work done by friction in 10 s,

(c) work done by the net force on the body in 10 s,

(d) change in kinetic energy of the body in 10 s,

and interpret your results.

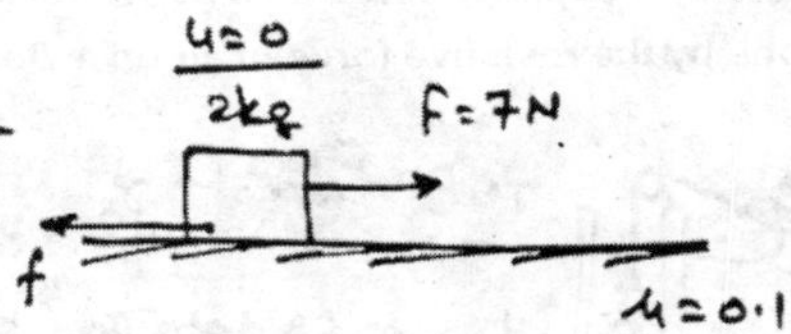

Sol^n: (a) acc^n of body $a = \frac{F-f}{m} = \frac{7-1.96}{2} = 2.52\ m/s^2$

$f = \mu mg = 0.1 \times 2 \times 9.8 = 1.96\ N$

distance covered in 10 s $l_1 = \frac{1}{2}at^2 = \frac{1}{2} \times 2.52 \times (10)^2$

$= 126\ m$

Work done by ext force $W = F.l_1 = 7 \times 126 = 882\ J$ Ans

(b) $W_f = \vec{f}.\vec{l}_1 = -1.96 \times 126 = -246.9\ J \simeq -247\ J$ Ans

(c) $W_{net} = (F-f).l_1 = (7-1.96) \times 126 = 635.04 = 635\ J$ Ans

(d) $\Delta K = W_{net} = 635\ J$ Ans.

Video Solution

- Given in figure are examples of some potential energy functions in one dimension. The total energy of the particle is indicated by a cross on the ordinate axis. In each case, specify the regions, if any, in which the particle cannot be found for the given energy. Also, indicate the minimum total energy the particle must have in each case. Think of simple physical contexts for which these potential energy shapes are relevant.

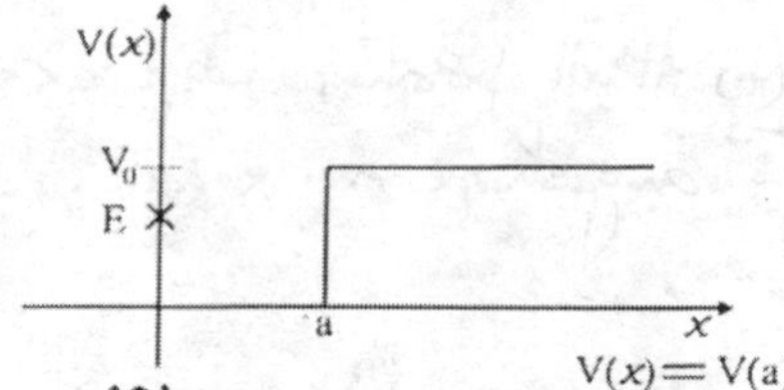

(a)

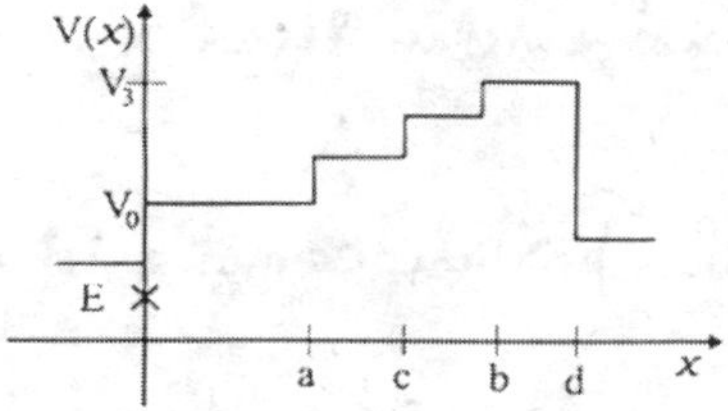

(b)

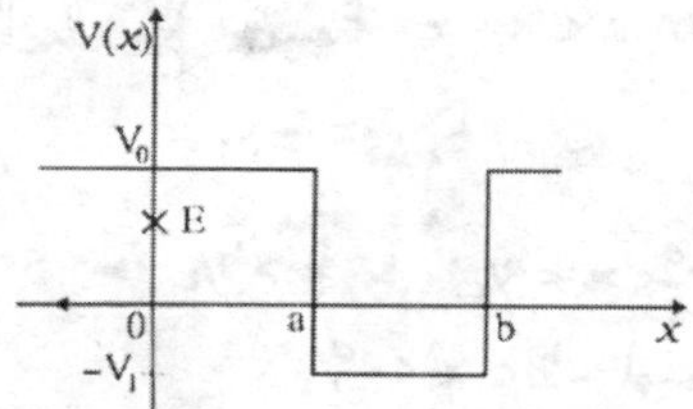

(c)

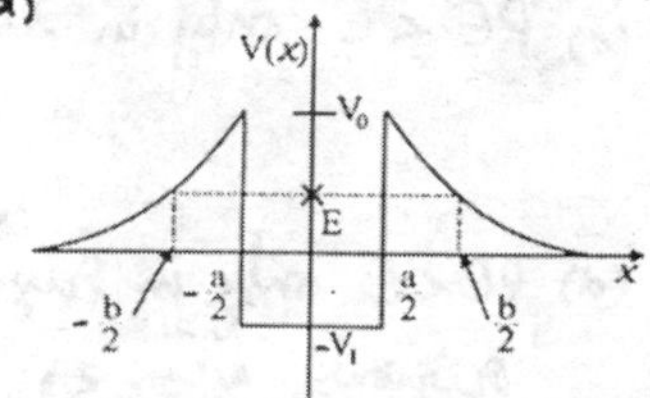

(d)

Soln:

(a) As Total energy = $\underline{KE}$ (+ve) + $\underline{PE}$ ⇒ always PE < E

beyond $x > a$; $V_0 > E \Rightarrow KE$ -ve (not possible) ⇒ in region $x > a$ particle cannot exist

⇒ for $x < a$ the min energy particle can have at rest $E_{min} = 0$ (KE = 0)

(b) At all position $-\infty < x < \infty$, we can see $PE > E \Rightarrow$ particle cannot exist anywhere on x axis.

$$E_{min} = V_1$$

(c) $PE < E$ only in region $a < x < b$ hence particle cannot exist in region $x > a$ & $x < b$

$$E_{min} = -V_1$$

(d) $PE < E$ only in region $-\frac{a}{2} < x < a/2$ & $x > b/2$ & $x < -b/2$ thus particle cannot exist in regions $a/2 < x < b/2$ and $-\frac{b}{2} < x < -a/2$

$$E_{min} = -V_1$$

- The potential energy function for a particle executing linear simple harmonic motion is given by $V(x) = kx^2 / 2$, where k is the force constant of the oscillator. For $k = 0.5\ N\ m^{-1}$, the graph of $V(x)$ versus x is shown in figure. Show that a particle of total energy 1 J moving under this potential must 'turn back' when it reaches $x = \pm 2$ m.

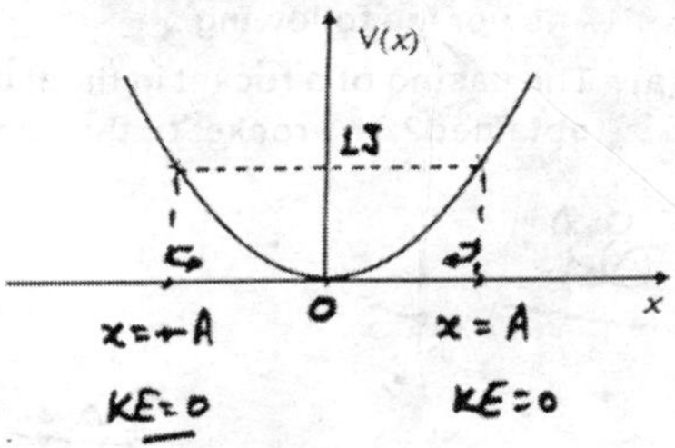

Sol^n: Total energy of particle $E_T = 1J$

$$E_T = KE + PE$$

In oscillation at extreme positions we use $KE = 0$

$$\Rightarrow \quad E_T = 0 + PE$$

$$1 = 0 + \frac{1}{2}kA^2 \quad (\text{at } x = \pm A)$$

$$\Rightarrow \quad A^2 = \frac{2}{k} = \frac{2}{0.5} = 4$$

$$\Rightarrow \quad A = \pm 2\ m. \text{ Ans.}$$

- Answer the following :

(a) The casing of a rocket in flight burns up due to friction. At whose expense is the heat energy required for burning obtained? The rocket or the atmosphere?

Sol^n:

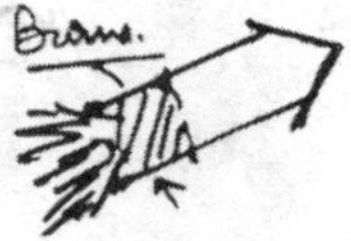

for burning the casing energy is supplied by rocket due to which its mass decreases & it speeds up further.

- Answer the following :

(b) Comets move around the sun in highly elliptical orbits. The gravitational force on the comet due to the sun is not normal to the comet's velocity in general. Yet the work done by the gravitational force over every complete orbit of the comet is zero. Why ?

Solⁿ:

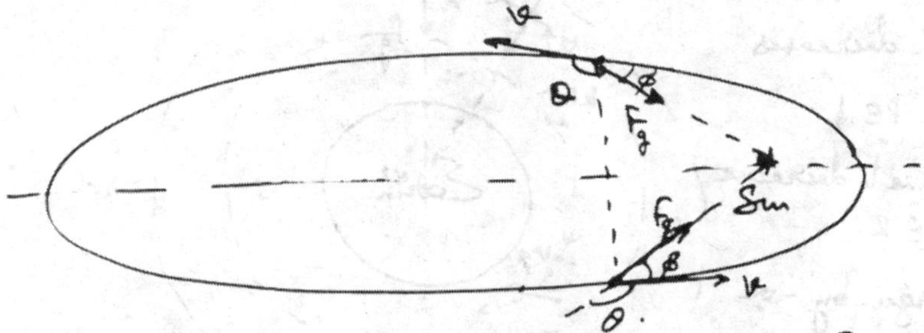

As grav force is conservative so W/D by any Conservative force depends upon initial & final position which are same in a closed path so W/D is always zero.

- Answer the following :

(c) An artificial satellite orbiting the earth in very thin atmosphere loses its energy gradually due to dissipation against atmospheric resistance, however small. Why then does its speed increase progressively as it comes closer and closer to the earth ?

Sol^n: As distance between Satellite & Earth decreases during motion its PE ↓

⇒ KE ↑ due to decrease in PE &

the loss of energy by -ve W/D of resistance is v. small.

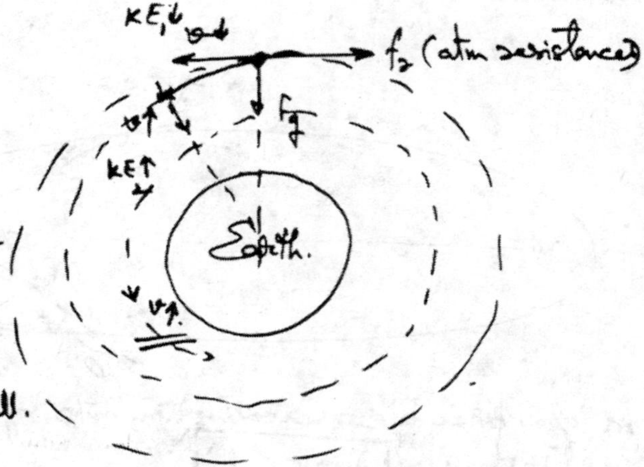

As $KE_2\uparrow > KE_1\downarrow$

⇒ as sat gets close to earth its KE overall increases

- Answer the following :

(d) In figure (i) the man walks 2 m carrying a mass of 15 kg on his hands. In figure (ii), he walks the same distance pulling the rope behind him. The rope goes over a pulley, and a mass of 15 kg hangs at its other end. In which case is the work done greater ?

(i) (ii)

Sol^n: In case (i)

Slow movement

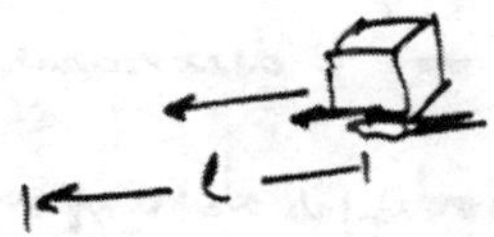

WD_1 = friction by hand (static friction) (v. small) $\times l$.

In Case (ii)

WD_2 = tension in string $\times l$.

↓

force by man $= 15g = 150N$.

As $WD_2 > WD_1$, the man in case ii, has to supply more energy.

- Underline the correct alternative :

(a) When a conservative force does positive work on a body, the potential energy of the body increases / decreases / remains unaltered

(b) Work done by a body against friction always results in a loss of its kinetic / potential energy

(c) The rate of change of total momentum of a many-particle system is proportional to the external force / sum of the internal forces on the system

(d) In an inelastic collision of two bodies, the quantities which do not change after the collision are the total kinetic energy / total linear momentum / total energy of the system of two bodies

Sol. (a) As we know $\vec{F} = -\frac{dU}{dx}\hat{i} \Rightarrow dU = -\vec{F}\cdot\vec{dx} \Rightarrow$ U decreases

(b) 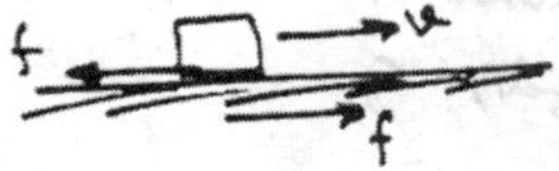

W/D by f on a body is always -ve relative to surface.

$\Rightarrow KE \downarrow$.

(c) $\vec{F}_{ext} = \frac{dP_{total}}{dt} \Rightarrow$ external force causes change in total momentum of system

(d) If $\vec{F}_{ext} = 0$ & bodies are isolated from surrounding then in case $e<1$ (here $e=0$) always total linear momentum & total system energy remain conserved.

Video Solution

- State if each of the following statements is true or false. Give reasons for your answer.

(a) In an elastic collision of two bodies, the momentum and energy of each body is conserved.

(b) Total energy of a system is always conserved, no matter what internal and external forces on the body are present.

(c) Work done in the motion of a body over a closed loop is zero for every force in nature.

(d) In an inelastic collision, the final kinetic energy is always less than the initial kinetic energy of the system.

Sol^n (a)

not necessarily $\begin{bmatrix} u_1 = v_1 \\ u_2 = v_2 \end{bmatrix}$

FALSE. $\Rightarrow$ KE of each body will be changing

(b) FALSE if due to some forces in system energy is dissipated to surrounding system total energy will not be conserved.

(c) FALSE only by conservative forces W/D depends on initial & final states. by non-conservative forces (friction) this work is non-zero.

(d) if $e = 1 \Rightarrow$ elastic
$e = 0 \Rightarrow$ inelastic

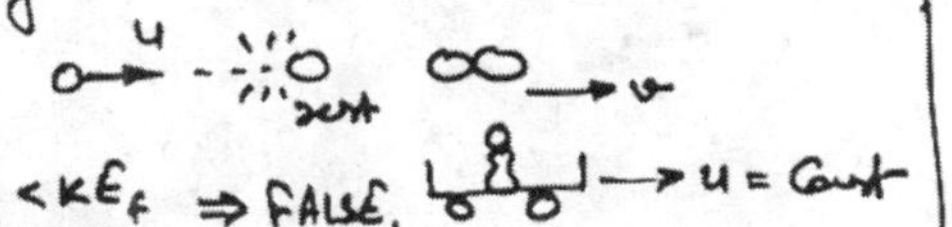

in some ref frame we can have $KE_i < KE_f$ $\Rightarrow$ FALSE.

in frame of trolley
$KE_i = 0 + \frac{1}{2}mu^2$
$KE_f = \frac{1}{2}(2m)(v-u)^2$
here $KE_i < KE_f$.

- **Answer carefully, with reasons :**

(a) **In an elastic collision of two billiard balls, is the total kinetic energy conserved during the short time of collision of the balls (i.e. when they are in contact) ?**

Sol.ⁿ No. during collision time (Contact duration)

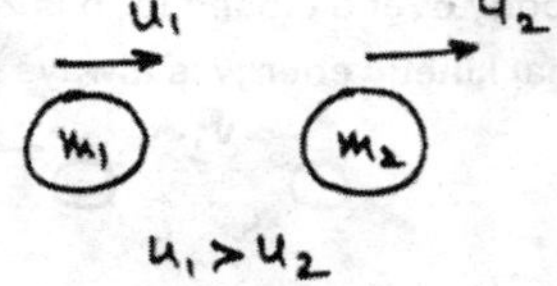

$KE_{system} < KE_i$ as PE↑ then ↓

PE↑ & KE↓

⇒ Total KE is not Conserved in Contact duration

- **Answer carefully, with reasons :**

(b) Is the total linear momentum conserved during the short time of an elastic collision of two balls ?

Sol^n: Yes.

As no external force is acting on system its total linear momentum remain conserved.

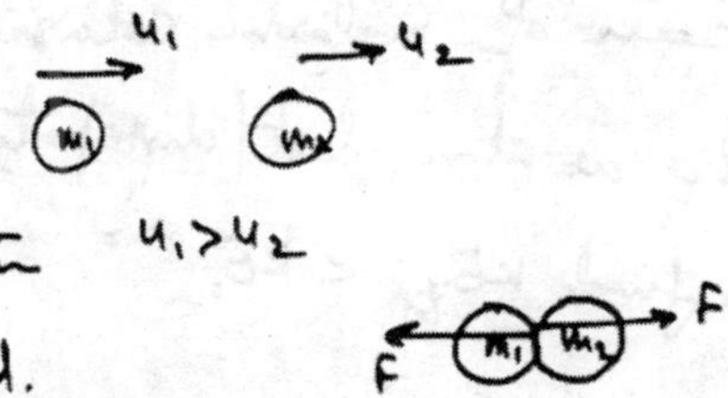

- **Answer carefully, with reasons :**

(c) What are the answers to (a) and (b) for an inelastic collision ?

Sol^n: Incase of inelastic collision no PE is stored in deformation of bodies as it is lost/dissipated.

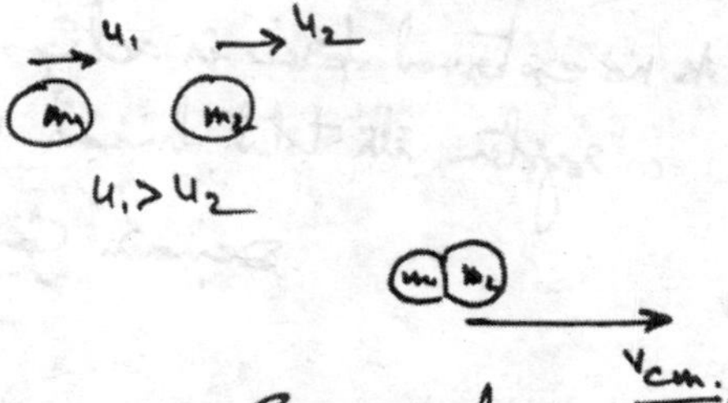

No. & final $KE_{tot} < KE_i$

As no ext force is present

Yes. $\Rightarrow$ linear momentum remain conserved.

Video Solution

- Answer carefully, with reasons :

(d) If the potential energy of two billiard balls depends only on the separation distance between their centres, is the collision elastic or inelastic ? (Note, we are talking here of potential energy corresponding to the force during collision, not gravitational potential energy)

Sol^n:

As $PE = f(r)$ ⇒ the internal force between balls is conservative

⇒ after separation whole PE will be recovered as KE_f (the final KE of balls)

$$\Rightarrow \quad KE_i = KE_f$$

⇒ Collision is elastic.

- **A body is initially at rest. It undergoes one-dimensional motion with constant acceleration. The power delivered to it at time *t* is proportional to**

(i) $t^{1/2}$ ✓(ii) t (iii) $t^{3/2}$ (iv) t^2

Sol^n:

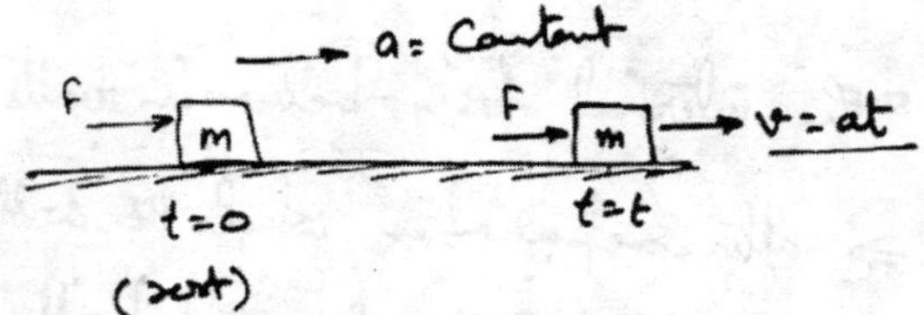

Power supplied at time t is $P = \vec{F}\cdot\vec{v} = Fv$ $(\theta = 0^\circ)$

$F = ma$

$= ma(at)$

$= ma^2 t$

$P \propto t$

Ans

- **A body is moving unidirectionally under the influence of a source of constant power. Its displacement in time *t* is proportional to**

(i) $t^{1/2}$ (ii) t ✓(iii) $t^{3/2}$ (iv) t^2

Sol^n:

$P = \text{Constant}$

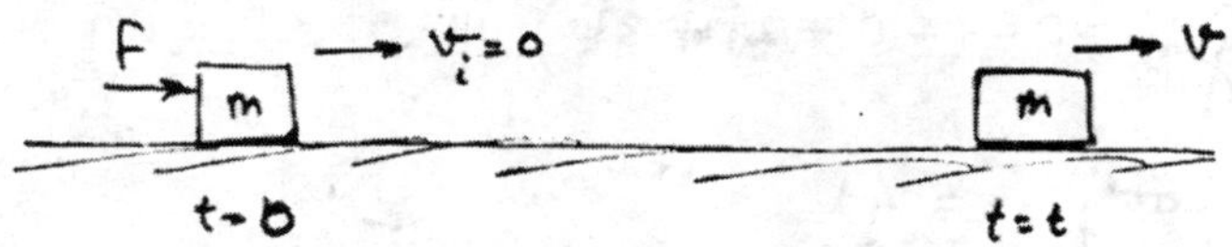

KE gained by body in time $t = 0$ to $t = t$ is equal to total W/D on it

Total W/D on body is $W = Pt = \frac{1}{2}mv^2 \Rightarrow v = \sqrt{\frac{2P}{m}} \cdot \sqrt{t}$

$\Rightarrow \frac{dx}{dt} = \sqrt{\frac{2P}{m}}\sqrt{t}$

or $\int_0^x dx = \sqrt{\frac{2P}{m}}\int_0^t \sqrt{t}\,dt$

$\Rightarrow x = \sqrt{\frac{2P}{m}}\left[\frac{t^{3/2}}{(3/2)}\right]_0^t$

$\Rightarrow x = \frac{2}{3}\sqrt{\frac{2P}{m}} \cdot t^{3/2} \Rightarrow x \propto t^{3/2}$ Ans.

- A body constrained to move along the z-axis of a coordinate system is subject to a constant force $\vec{F}$ given by

$$\vec{F} = -\hat{i} + 2\hat{j} + 3\hat{k} N$$

where $\hat{i}, \hat{j}, \hat{k}$ are unit vectors along the *x*-, *y*- and *z*-axis of the system respectively. What is the work done by this force in moving the body a distance of 4 m along the *z*-axis ?

Sol^n: force on body is $\vec{F} = (-\hat{i} + 2\hat{j} + 3\hat{k})$ N

displacement of body $\vec{s} = 4\hat{k}$

$\Rightarrow$ W/D by the force on body is given as

$$W = \vec{F}\cdot\vec{s} = (-\hat{i} + 2\hat{j} + 3\hat{k})\cdot(4\hat{k})$$

$$= 3\times 4 = 12 \text{ J} \quad \textbf{Ans.}$$

- An electron and a proton are detected in a cosmic ray experiment, the first with kinetic energy 10 keV, and the second with 100 keV. Which is faster, the electron or the proton ? Obtain the ratio of their speeds. (electron mass = 9.11×10^{-31} kg, proton mass = 1.67×10^{-27} kg, 1 eV = 1.60×10^{-19} J).

Solⁿ: For electron, we use $\frac{1}{2}m_e v_e^2 = 10\times10^3\times1.6\times10^{-19}$

$$\Rightarrow v_e = \sqrt{\frac{2\times1.6\times10^{-15}}{9.11\times10^{-31}}}$$

$$v_e = 5.93\times10^7 \text{ m/s} \quad \text{—— (1)}$$

For proton, we use $\frac{1}{2}m_p v_p^2 = 100\times10^3\times1.6\times10^{-19}$

$$\Rightarrow v_p = \sqrt{\frac{2\times1.6\times10^{-14}}{1.67\times10^{-27}}} = 4.38\times10^6 \text{ m/s} \quad \text{—— (2)}$$

from (1) & (2) we see that electron is moving faster.

$$\& \quad \frac{v_e}{v_p} = \frac{5.93\times10^7}{4.38\times10^6} = 13.5 \text{ Ans.}$$

- A rain drop of radius 2 mm falls from a height of 500 m above the ground. It falls with decreasing acceleration (due to viscous resistance of the air) until at half its original height, it attains its maximum (terminal) speed, and moves with uniform speed thereafter. What is the work done by the gravitational force on the drop in the first and second half of its journey ? What is the work done by the resistive force in the entire journey if its speed on reaching the ground is 10 m s^{-1} ?

Soln: mass of rain drop = density × volume $\left(\frac{4}{3}\pi r^3\right)$

$= 1000 \times \frac{4}{3} \times 3.14 \times (2\times10^{-3})^3 = 3.35\times10^{-5}$ kg

grav force on drop is $F = mg = 3.35\times10^{-5}\times 9.8 = 3.28\times10^{-4}$ N

W/D by gravity on drop in 1st half $W = F\times 250$

$= 3.28\times10^{-4}\times250$

$= 0.082$ J Ans

W/D by gravity on 2nd half $W = F\times250 = 0.082$ J Ans

Using W-E theorem we have $K_i + W_g + W_r = K_f$

$0 + mg(500) + W_r = \frac{1}{2}mv_T^2$

$\Rightarrow 0 + 0.164 + W_r = \frac{1}{2}(3.35\times10^{-5})(10)^2 \Rightarrow W_r = -0.162$ J Ans

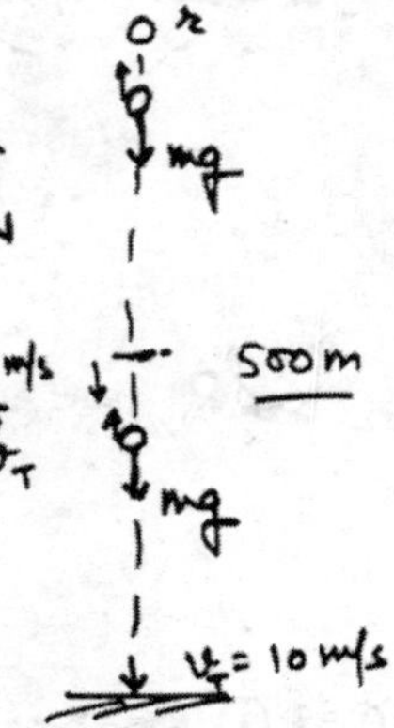

Exercise - 6.14

- A molecule in a gas container hits a horizontal wall with speed 200 m s^{-1} and angle 30° with the normal, and rebounds with the same speed. Is momentum conserved in the collision ? Is the collision elastic or inelastic ?

Sol^n:

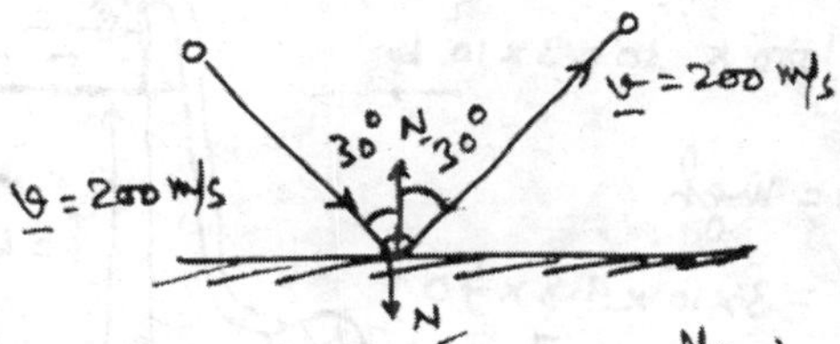

As KE in collision is same ⇒ Collision is elastic.

Yes for ball/Container molecule and container wall, no external force is present so "molecule + wall" as a system their momentum will remain conserved. Here we neglect the momentum attained by wall/Container.

Web Reference at www.physicsgalaxy.com

Video Sol. : Class 11th NCERT Solutions | **Sec. -** Mechanics | **Topic -** Work, Energy and Power

Theory Reference. : Grade - 11 & 12 | **Sec. -** Mechanics | **Topic -** System of Particles - II

Video Solution

- A pump on the ground floor of a building can pump up water to fill a tank of volume 30 m^3 in 15 min. If the tank is 40 m above the ground, and the efficiency of the pump is 30%, how much electric power is consumed by the pump?

Sol^n: mass of water lifted m = density × volume

$= 1000 \times 30 = 3 \times 10^4$ kg.

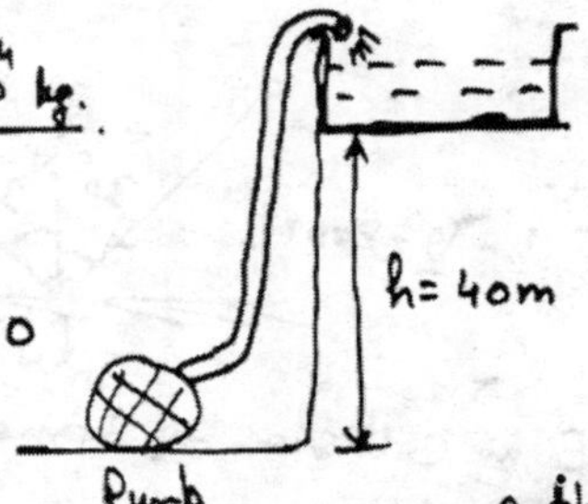

W/D by pump in lifting water $W = mgh$

$= 3\times10^4 \times 9.8 \times 40$

$= 1.176 \times 10^7$ J

Mech. Power of pump $P = \dfrac{\text{work done}}{\text{Time taken}}$ efficiency $\eta = 30\% = \dfrac{\text{Output power}}{\text{input Elect power}} \times 100\%$

$= \dfrac{1.176\times10^7}{15\times60} = 13.07\times10^3$ W $= 13.07$ kW

⇒ Elect Power $= \dfrac{\text{Output power}}{0.3} = \dfrac{13.07}{0.3} = 43.6$ kW Ans.

- Two identical ball bearings in contact with each other and resting on a frictionless table are hit head-on by another ball bearing of the same mass moving initially with a speed *V*. If the collision is elastic, which of the following (figure) is a possible result after collision ?

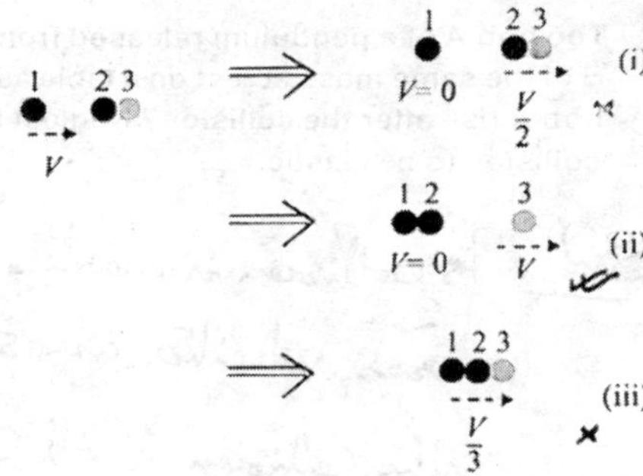

Sol^n: Initial KE of system $K_i = \frac{1}{2} m v^2$

final KE of system

Case (i) $K_{f_1} = \frac{1}{2}(2m)(v/2)^2 = \frac{1}{4} m v^2$ ×

Case (ii) $K_{f_2} = \frac{1}{2} m v^2$

Case (iii) $K_{f_3} = \frac{1}{2}(3m)(v/3)^2 = \frac{1}{6} m v^2$ ×

we can see that $K_{f_2} = K_i \Rightarrow$ in Case (ii) the collision can be taken elastic Ans.

Web Reference at www.physicsgalaxy.com

Video Sol. : Class 11th NCERT Solutions | **Sec.** - Mechanics | **Topic** - Work, Energy and Power

Theory Reference. : **Grade** - 11 & 12 | **Sec.** - Mechanics | **Topic** - System of Particles - II

Video Solution

- The bob *A* of a pendulum released from 30° to the vertical hits another bob *B* of the same mass at rest on a table as shown in figure. How high does the bob *A* rise after the collision? Neglect the size of the bobs and assume the collision to be elastic.

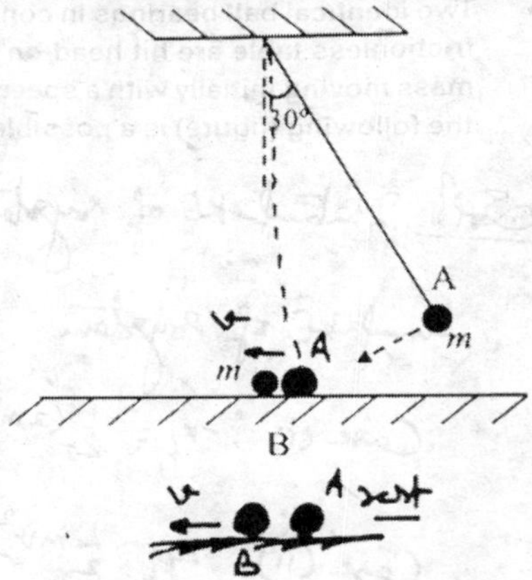

Sol: As collision is elastic for equal masses velocities are swapped so after collision A will come to rest & B moves with velocity of A just before collision.

⇒ After collision A will remain at rest & not rise at all.

Ans

Video Solution

- The bob of a pendulum is released from a horizontal position. If the length of the pendulum is 1.5 m, what is the speed with which the bob arrives at the lowermost point, given that it dissipated 5% of its initial energy against air resistance ?

Solⁿ: By W/E theorem from A to B

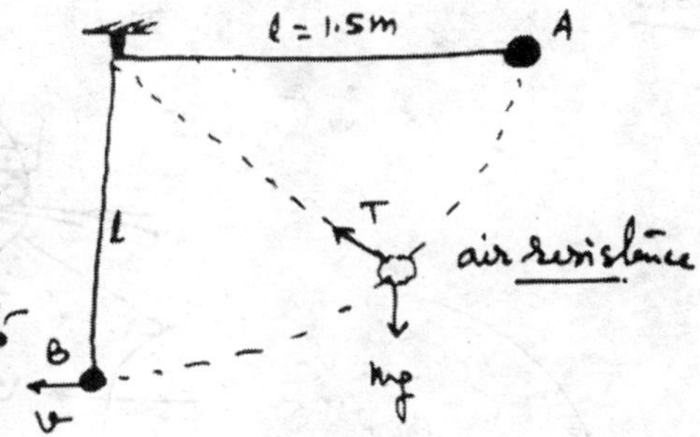

We use

$$\overset{K_i}{0} + mgh = \overset{K_f}{\tfrac{1}{2}mv^2}$$] ideal case without air resistance

$$\downarrow$$

$$\left(mgh - \frac{5}{100}mgh\right)$$ → energy loss due to air resistance

$$\Rightarrow \frac{95}{100}mgh = \frac{1}{2}mv^2$$

$$\Rightarrow v = \sqrt{\frac{95}{50} \times 9.8 \times 1.5} = 5.28\ m/s = 5.3\ m/s \text{ Ans.}$$

- A trolley of mass 300 kg carrying a sandbag of 25 kg is moving uniformly with a speed of 27 km/h on a frictionless track. After a while, sand starts leaking out of a hole on the floor of the trolley at the rate of 0.05 kg s^{-1}. What is the speed of the trolley after the entire sand bag is empty ?

Solⁿ:

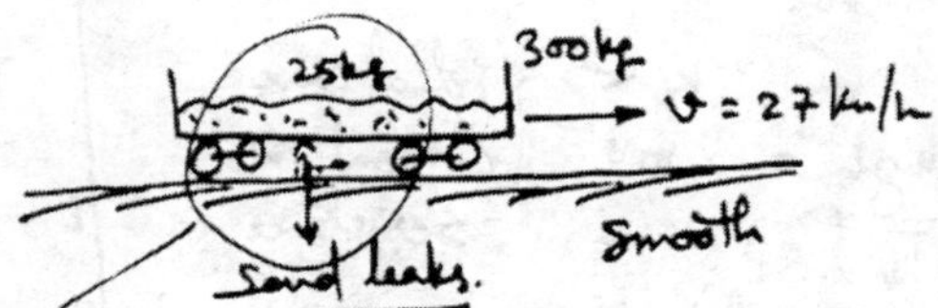

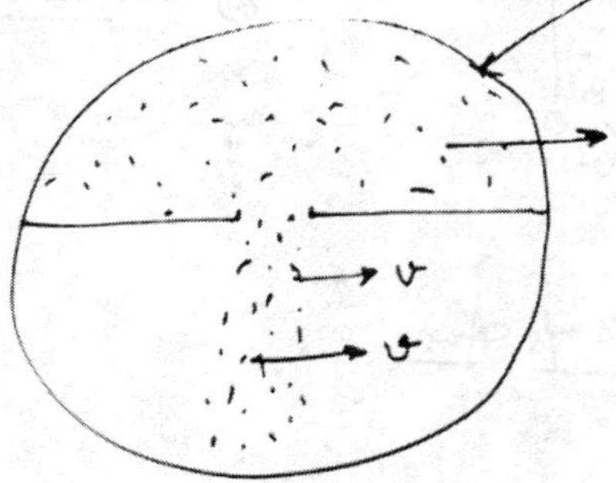

During leakage, no external force is acting on sand (falling) or on trolley so its $acc^n = 0$ & no change in velocity of trolley will be there.

$\Rightarrow v_{trolley} = 27$ km/h **Ans.**

Video Solution

Exercise - 6.20

- A body of mass 0.5 kg travels in a straight line with velocity $v = ax^{3/2}$ where $a = 5\ m^{-1/2}\ s^{-1}$. What is the work done by the net force during its displacement from $x = 0$ to $x = 2$ m ?

Sol^n:

$\rightarrow v = ax^{3/2}$

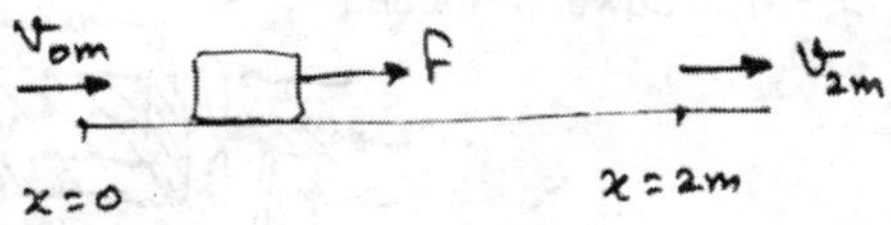

W/D by force = Gain in KE of body

$$= \frac{1}{2} m v_{2m}^2 - \frac{1}{2} m v_{0m}^2$$

$$= \frac{1}{2} m \left[\left\{ a(2)^{3/2} \right\}^2 - \left[a(0)^{3/2} \right]^2 \right]$$

$$= \frac{1}{2} m a^2 (2)^3 = \frac{1}{2} \times 0.5 \times (5)^2 \times (2)^3 = 50\ J \quad \text{Ans.}$$

Web Reference at www.physicsgalaxy.com

Video Sol. : Class 11th NCERT Solutions | **Sec.** - Mechanics | **Topic** - Work, Energy and Power

Theory Reference. : **Grade** - 11 & 12 | **Sec.** - Mechanics | **Topic** - Work, Energy & Power

Video Solution

- The blades of a windmill sweep out a circle of area A.

(a) If the wind flows at a velocity v perpendicular to the circle, what is the mass of the air passing through it in time t?

(b) What is the kinetic energy of the air ?

(c) Assume that the windmill converts 25% of the wind's energy into electrical energy, and that $A = 30\ m^2$, $v = 36$ km/h and the density of air is 1.2 kg m^{-3}. What is the electrical power produced ?

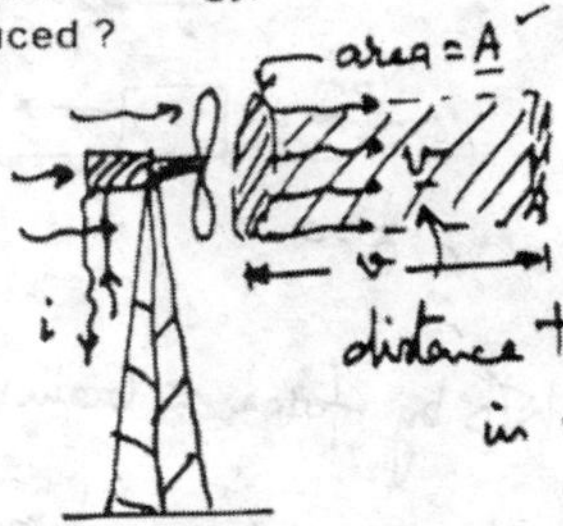

Solⁿ: (a) volume of air passing through the blades circle per second is

$$V_p = Av$$

mass flowing through this cross-section per second is $m_p = Av\rho$ kg/s — density of air.

$v = 36$ km/hr $= 10$ m/s

mass flowing in time t is

$$m = m_p t = Av\rho t \text{ Ans}$$

(b) $K_t = \frac{1}{2}mv^2 = \frac{1}{2}A\rho v^3 t$ Ans

(c) Power produce is (J/s) $\frac{25}{100} \times \frac{1}{2} m_p v^2 = \frac{1}{4} \times \frac{1}{2} \times Av\rho \times v^2 = \frac{1}{8} \times 30 \times (10)^3 \times 1.2 = 4500\ W$
$= 4.5\ kW$ Ans.

Video Solution

- A person trying to lose weight (dieter) lifts a 10 kg mass, one thousand times, to a height of 0.5 m each time. Assume that the potential energy lost each time she lowers the mass is dissipated.

(a) How much work does she do against the gravitational force ?

(b) Fat supplies 3.8×10^7 J of energy per kilogram which is converted to mechanical energy with a 20% efficiency rate. How much fat will the dieter use up?

Sol^n: (a) As she lifts the mass, 1000 times to a height $h = 0.5$ m,

W/D against grav force $W = 1000\,mgh$

$= 1000 \times 10 \times 9.8 \times 0.5$

$= 49000$ J Ans.

(b) 1 kg of mass supplies mechanical energy

$$E_{mech} = \frac{20}{100} \times 3.8 \times 10^7 \text{ J} = 0.76 \times 10^7 \text{ J}$$

Total mass used in this is $m = \frac{W}{E_{mech}} = \frac{49000}{0.76 \times 10^7} = 6.45 \times 10^{-3}$ kg

Ans.

- A family uses 8 kW of power.

(a) Direct solar energy is incident on the horizontal surface at an average rate of 200 W per square meter. If 20% of this energy can be converted to useful electrical energy, how large an area is needed to supply 8 kW?

(b) Compare this area to that of the roof of a typical house

Soln: (a)

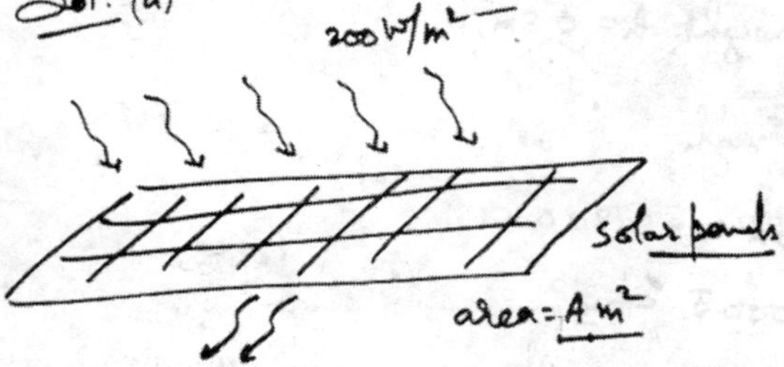

$$\frac{\text{Elect energy}}{\text{sec}} = \frac{20}{100} \times 200\ \text{W/m}^2$$

$$= 40\ \text{W/m}^2$$

Total Elect power produced $= 40 \times A$

Total power req $= 8000\text{W}$

$$40 . A = 8000$$

$$A = 200\ \text{m}^2 . \text{ Ans}$$

(b) In general if we Compare with a decent size large house roof of area 14m × 14m (approx)

$\Rightarrow$ above area is Comparable.

- A bullet of mass 0.012 kg and horizontal speed 70 m s^{-1} strikes a block of wood of mass 0.4 kg and instantly comes to rest with respect to the block. The block is suspended from the ceiling by means of thin wires. Calculate the height to which the block rises. Also, estimate the amount of heat produced in the block.

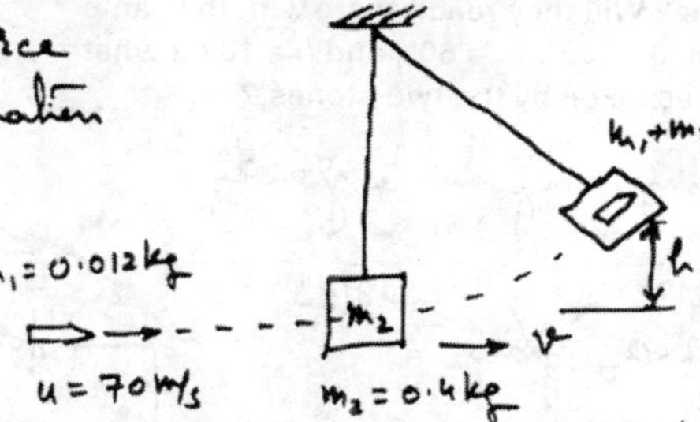

Solⁿ: As no external horizontal force is acting on block, we use Conservation of momentum as-

$$m_1 u + 0 = (m_1+m_2)v$$

$$v = \frac{m_1 u}{m_1+m_2} = \frac{0.012\times 70}{0.4+0.012}$$

$$= 2.04 \text{ m/s}$$

by energy Conservation after collision

$$\frac{1}{2}(m_1+m_2)v^2 - (m_1+m_2)gh = 0$$

$$\Rightarrow \quad h = \frac{v^2}{2g} = \frac{(2.04)^2}{2\times 9.8} = 0.212 \text{ m} = 21.2 \text{ cm}$$

Ans.

→ Heat produced in Collision is -

$$\Delta E_{loss} = \text{Change in KE in Collision}$$

$$= \frac{1}{2}m_1 u^2 - \frac{1}{2}(m_1+m_2)v^2$$

$$= \frac{1}{2}(0.012)(70)^2 - \frac{1}{2}(0.412)(2.04)^2$$

$$= 28.54 \text{ J} = 28.5 \text{ J} \quad \text{Ans.}$$

- Two inclined frictionless tracks, one gradual and the other steep meet at A from where two stones are allowed to slide down from rest, one on each track (figure). Will the stones reach the bottom at the same time? Will they reach there with the same speed ? Explain. Given $\theta_1 = 30°$, $\theta_2 = 60°$, and $h = 10$ m, what are the speeds and times taken by the two stones ?

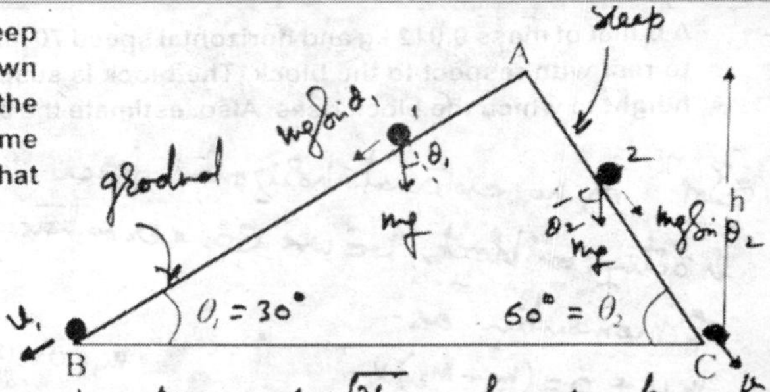

Solⁿ: As stones are falling only due to gravity, their accⁿ are -

$$a_1 = g\sin\theta_1 = g/2 \quad \& \quad a_2 = g\sin\theta_2 = \sqrt{3}g/2$$

As $\theta_1 < \theta_2 \Rightarrow a_1 < a_2$

$\Rightarrow$ Stone 1 will be slow & reach bottom later than stone 2 Ans

$t_2 < t_1$

for stone 1 $t_1 = \sqrt{\frac{2l_1}{a_1}}$ where $l_1 = \frac{h}{\sin 30°} = 20$ m

$$\Rightarrow t_1 = \sqrt{\frac{2\times 20}{9.8/2}} = \sqrt{\frac{80}{9.8}}\ s \simeq 2\sqrt{2}\ s \text{ Ans}$$

for stone 2 $t_2 = \sqrt{\frac{2l_2}{a_2}}$ where $l_2 = \frac{h}{\sin 60°} = \frac{20}{\sqrt{3}}$ m

$$\Rightarrow t_2 = \sqrt{\frac{2\times 20/\sqrt{3}}{\sqrt{3}\,g/2}} = \sqrt{\frac{80}{3\times 9.8}} = 2\sqrt{\frac{2}{3}}\ s \text{ Ans.}$$

by Conservation of energy we use $\frac{1}{2}mv_1^2 = mgh = \frac{1}{2}mv_2^2$

$$\Rightarrow v_1 = v_2 = \sqrt{2gh} = \sqrt{2\times 9.8\times 10} = 14.1\ m/s$$

Video Solution

- A 1 kg block situated on a rough incline is connected to a spring of spring constant 100 N m^{-1} as shown in figure. The block is released from rest with the spring in the unstretched position. The block moves 10 cm down the incline before coming to rest. Find the coefficient of friction between the block and the incline. Assume that the spring has a negligible mass and the pulley is frictionless.

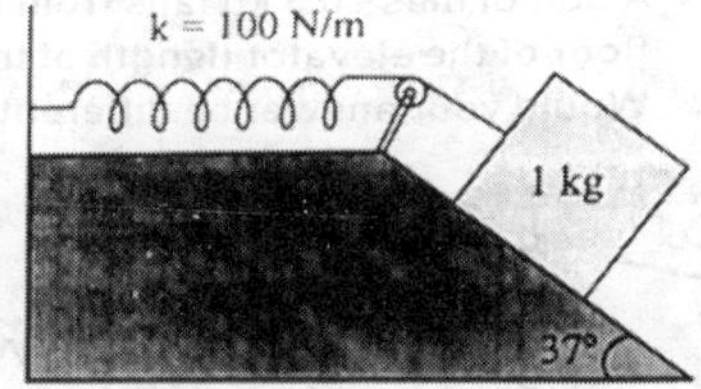

Sol^n: By W/E theorem from pos A to B.

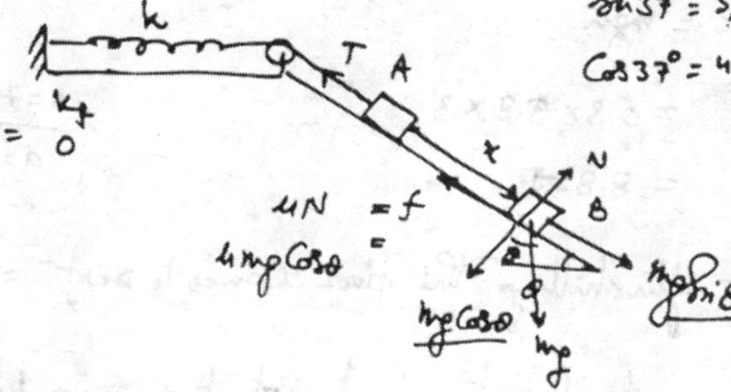

$\sin 37° = 3/5$

$\cos 37° = 4/5$

$$\underset{K_i}{0} + mg\sin\theta . x - \mu mg\cos\theta . x - \frac{1}{2}kx^2 = \underset{K_f}{0}$$

$$\Rightarrow \quad \mu = \frac{2mg\sin\theta - kx}{2mg\cos\theta}$$

$$\mu = \frac{2\times 1\times 10\times 3/5 - 100\times 0.1}{2\times 1\times 10\times 4/5} = 0.125 \text{ Ans.}$$

Web Reference at www.physicsgalaxy.com

Video Sol. : Class 11th NCERT Solutions | **Sec. -** Mechanics **| Topic -** Work, Energy and Power

Theory Reference. : Grade - 11 & 12 | **Sec. -** Mechanics **| Topic -** Work, Energy & Power

Video Solution

Exercise - 6.27

- A bolt of mass 0.3 kg falls from the ceiling of an elevator moving down with an uniform speed of 7 m s^{-1}. It hits the floor of the elevator (length of the elevator = 3 m) and does not rebound. What is the heat produced by the impact? Would your answer be different if the elevator were stationary ?

Sol: In inertial frame of elevator

KE gained by the bolt is-

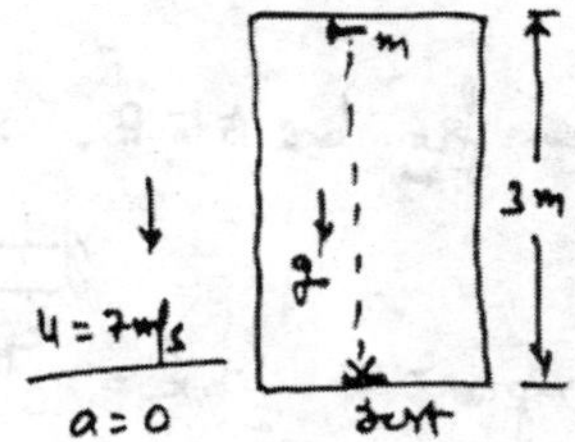

$$\Delta K = mgh$$

$$= 0.3 \times 9.8 \times 3$$

$$= 8.82\text{ J}$$

As bolt after hitting the floor comes to rest $\Rightarrow$ $\Delta K \rightarrow$ lost as heat $= 8.82\text{ J}$ Ans

even if elevator is at rest being an inertial frame g = same

$\Rightarrow \Delta K = \Delta H = 8.82\text{ J}$ Ans

Video Solution

- A trolley of mass 200 kg moves with a uniform speed of 36 km/h on a frictionless track. A child of mass 20 kg runs on the trolley from one end to the other (10 m away) with a speed of 4 m s^{-1} relative to the trolley in a direction opposite to the its motion, and jumps out of the trolley. What is the final speed of the trolley ? How much has the trolley moved from the time the child begins to run ?

Sol^n: As no external force is acting on this system, by conservation of momentum we have

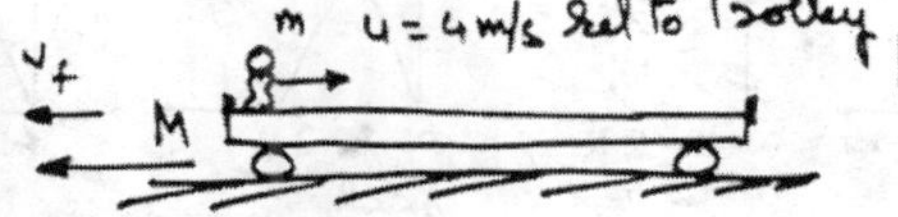

$v_i = 36\ kph \times \frac{5}{18} = 10\ m/s$

$P_i = (M+m)v_i = 220 \times 10 = 2200\ kg\ m/s$

When child starts running if final speed of trolley is v_f then final speed of child w.r.t. ground is $v_f - 4$

$\Rightarrow P_f = Mv_f + m(v_f - 4) = P_i = 2200$

$200v_f + 20v_f - 80 = 2200$

$2200v_f = 2280$

$\rightarrow v_f = \frac{2280}{2200} = 10.36\ m/s$ Ans

time of run $t = l/u = \frac{10}{4} = 2.5\ s$

$\rightarrow$ distance moved by trolley $s = v_f t = 10.36 \times 2.5 = 25.9\ m$ Ans

- **Which of the following potential energy curves in figure cannot possibly describe the elastic collision of two billiard balls ? Here *r* is the distance between centres of the balls.**

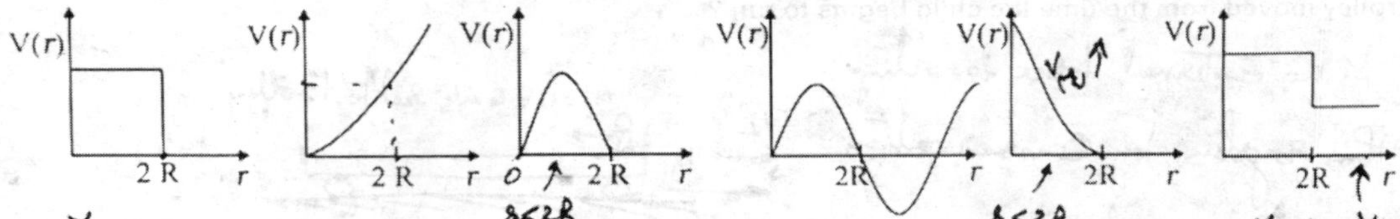

× (a) × (b) × (c) $r<2R$ × (d) (e) $r<2R$ × (f) $V(r)=0$ for $r>2R$.

Sol^n: u_1 → u_2 →

$u_1 > u_2$ ⇒ $r = 2R$ when collision starts; $V(r) = 0$ as no deformation

⇒ when balls are deformed ⇒ $r < 2R$. $V(r)\uparrow$

only possible curve is option (e) Ans.

- Consider the decay of a free neutron at rest : $n \rightarrow p + e^-$.
  Show that the two-body decay of this type must necessarily give an electron of fixed energy and, therefore, cannot account for the observed continuous energy distribution in the β-decay of a neutron or a nucleus (figure).

  [Note: The simple result of this exercise was one among the several arguments advanced by *W.* Pauli to predict the existence of a third particle in the decay products of β-decay. This particle is known as neutrino. We now know that it is a particle of intrinsic spin ½ (like e^-, *p* or *n*), but is neutral, and either massless or having an extremely small mass (compared to the mass of electron) and which interacts very weakly with matter. The correct decay process of neutron is : $n \rightarrow p + e^- + \nu$]

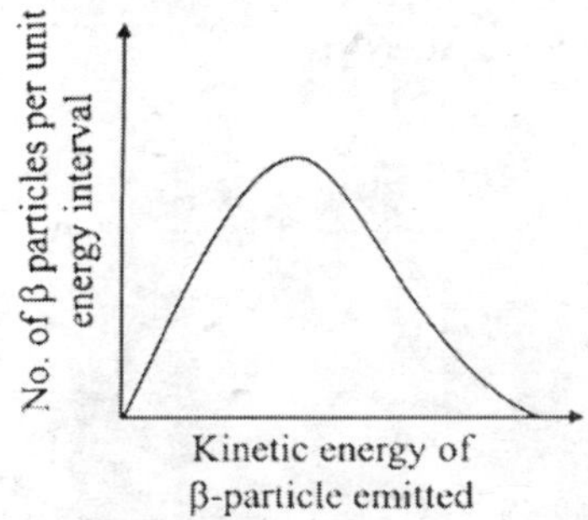

Solⁿ: When a decay occurs in general $X \rightarrow Y + Z + \Delta E_Q$

in nuclear phenomenon we use energy released in above process is

$$\Delta E = \underbrace{[M_X - (M_Y + M_Z)]}_{\text{mass defect}} \times c^2$$

here ΔE_Q is distributed in Y & Z.

$\Rightarrow K_Y + K_Z = \Delta E_Q$ (released energy)

→ in all cases K_Y & K_Z will be constants for all decays of X.

→ In a two body decay always the KE of emitted particles will remain constant.

Chapter 7

System of Particles

QR Code of Link to the Video Lectures of Theory of this chapter System of Particles at 'Physics Galaxy' web portal

QR Code of Link to the NCERT textbook Video Solutions of unsolved exercises at the end of each chapter in sequence of this chapter at 'Physics Galaxy' web portal

- **Give the location of the centre of mass of a (i) sphere, (ii) cylinder, (iii) ring, and (iv) cube, each of uniform mass density. Does the centre of mass of a body necessarily lie inside the body ?**

Solⁿ:
(i) sphere → Centre
(ii) Cylinder → "
(iii) Ring → " → COM lie outside the ring body.
↓
Hollow sphere
Hollow cylinder
(iv) Cube. → "

Geometrically Symmetric
→ COM lie at the geometric Centre of body

- **In the HCl molecule, the separation between the nuclei of the two atoms is about 1.27 Å (1 Å = 10^{-10} m). Find the approximate location of the *CM* of the molecule, given that a chlorine atom is about 35.5 times as massive as a hydrogen atom and nearly all the mass of an atom is concentrated in its nucleus.**

Sol^n:

By COM of two particle system

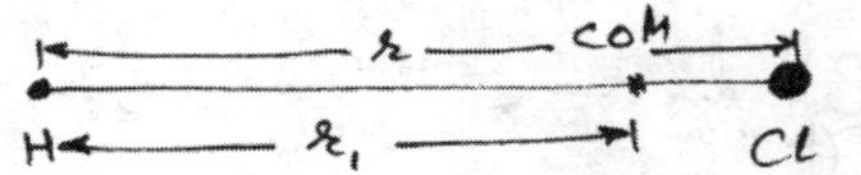

$m_1 = m$ $\quad$ $m_2 = 35.5m$

$$r_1 = \frac{m_2 r}{m_1 + m_2}$$

$$= \frac{35.5m \times 1.27\text{Å}}{36.5m} = \frac{35.5}{36.5} \times 1.27\text{Å} = 1.235 \times 10^{-10}\text{ m}$$

$$\simeq 1.24\text{Å} \quad \text{Ans.}$$

Video Solution

- A child sits stationary at one end of a long trolley moving uniformly with a speed *V* on a smooth horizontal floor. If the child gets up and runs about on the trolley in any manner, what is the speed of the *CM* of the (trolley + child) system ?

Sol.:

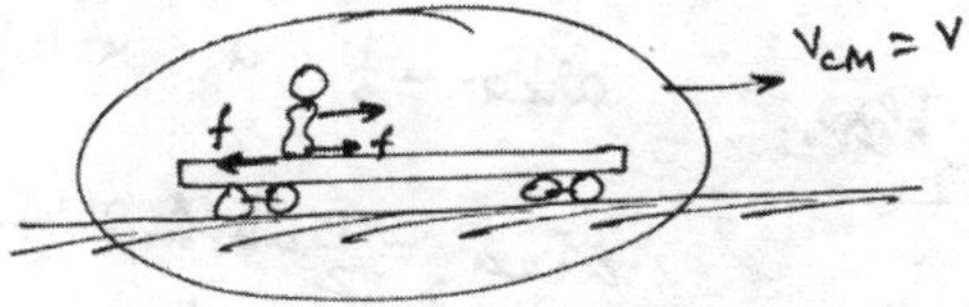

$f \rightarrow$ internal force of (trolly + child) system.

As no ext force is present $\Rightarrow a_{CM} = 0$

$\Rightarrow v_{CM} = V \longrightarrow$ Constant Ans.

- Show that the area of the triangle contained between the vectors $\vec{a}$ and $\vec{b}$ is one half of the magnitude of $\vec{a} \times \vec{b}$.

Sol^n: If altitude of triangle is h.

$\Rightarrow$ area $= \frac{1}{2} \times$ base $\times$ altitude

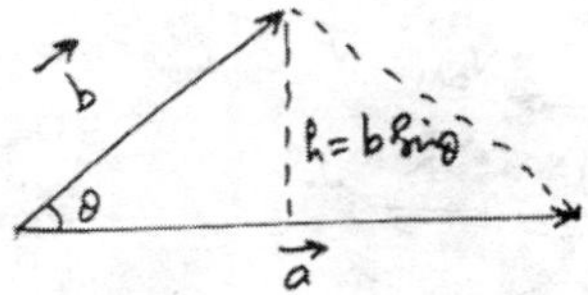

area $= \frac{1}{2} \times a \times b\sin\theta$

area $= \frac{1}{2} ab\sin\theta = \frac{1}{2}|\vec{a} \times \vec{b}|$

by cross product, we have $|\vec{a} \times \vec{b}| = ab\sin\theta$.

- **Show that $\vec{a}\cdot(\vec{b}\times\vec{c})$ is equal in magnitude to the volume of the parallelepiped formed on the three vectors, $\vec{a}$, $\vec{b}$ and $\vec{c}$.**

Sol^n: Volume of parallelepiped is given as

V = area of base (parallelogram) × height

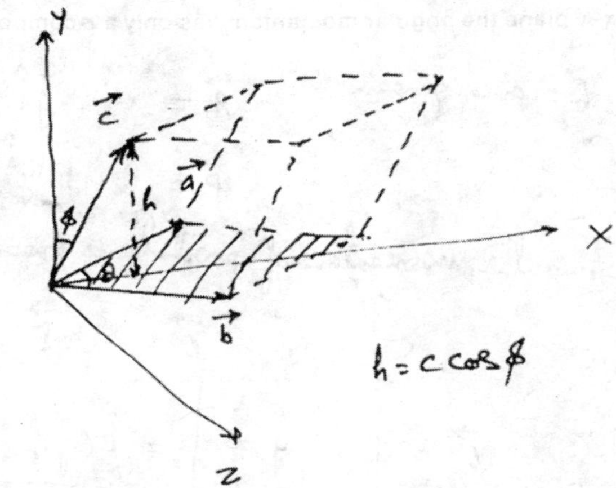

area of base $= |\vec{a}\times\vec{b}|$

$V = |\vec{a}\times\vec{b}|\cdot(c\cos\phi)$

$= (\vec{a}\times\vec{b})\cdot\vec{c} = \vec{a}\cdot(\vec{b}\times\vec{c})$ Hence proved.

- Find the components along the *x*, *y*, *z* axes of the angular momentum $\vec{l}$ of a particle, whose position vector is $\vec{r}$ with components *x*, *y*, *z* and momentum is $\vec{p}$ with components p_x, p_y and p_z. Show that if the particle moves only in the *x*- *y* plane the angular momentum has only a *z*-component.

Sol^n: We are given $\vec{r} = x\hat{i} + y\hat{j} + z\hat{k}$

$$\vec{P} = P_x\hat{i} + P_y\hat{j} + P_z\hat{k}$$

Angular momentum of particle is given as

$$\vec{l} = \vec{r} \times \vec{P} = (x\hat{i} + y\hat{j} + z\hat{k}) \times (P_x\hat{i} + P_y\hat{j} + P_z\hat{k})$$

$$\vec{l} = \begin{vmatrix} \hat{i} & \hat{j} & \hat{k} \\ x & y & z \\ P_x & P_y & P_z \end{vmatrix} = \hat{i}\underbrace{(yP_z - zP_y)}_{l_x} + \hat{j}\underbrace{(zP_x - xP_z)}_{l_y} + \hat{k}\underbrace{(xP_y - yP_x)}_{l_z} \quad \text{Ans}$$

If $z = 0$ (motion is only in x-y plane) & $P_z = 0 \Rightarrow l_x = 0,\ l_y = 0$ & $l_z = xP_y - yP_x$

- Two particles, each of mass *m* and speed *v*, travel in opposite directions along parallel lines separated by a distance *d*. Show that the vector angular momentum of the two particle system is the same whatever be the point about which the angular momentum is taken.

Sol.

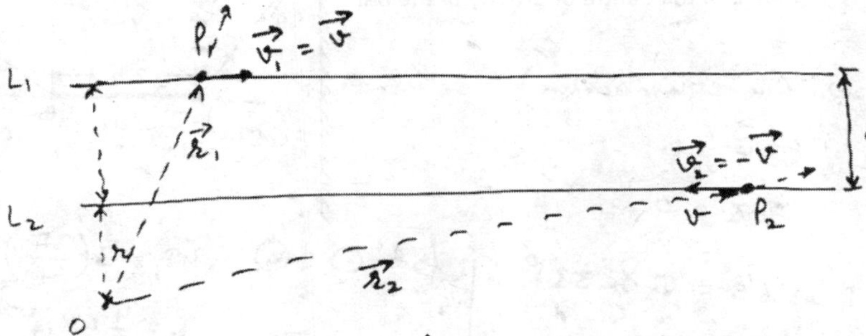

Angular momentum of particles P_1 and P_2 about pt O, it is given as

$$L_0 = \overbrace{mv(r+d)}^{m(\vec{r}_1 \times \vec{v})} - \overbrace{mv(r)}^{[-m(\vec{r}_2 \times \vec{v})]} = \underline{\underline{mvd.}} \quad \text{(Constant)}$$

independent of r

- **A non-uniform bar of weight *W* is suspended at rest by two strings of negligible weight as shown in figure. The angles made by the strings with the vertical are 36.9° and 53.1° respectively. The bar is 2 m long. Calculate the distance *d* of the centre of gravity of the bar from its left end.**

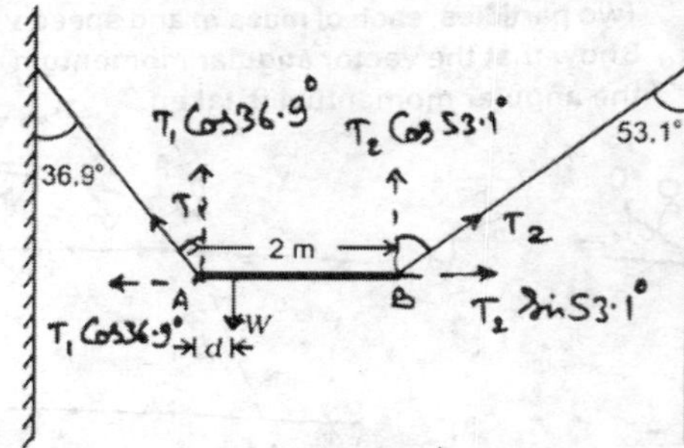

Sol^n: As bar is at rest (in equilibrium)

we consider $\Sigma \vec{F} = 0$

$\Sigma \vec{\tau} = 0$

in horiz dir $T_1 \cos 36.9° = T_2 \sin 53.1°$

$$\frac{3T_1}{5} = \frac{4T_2}{5}$$

$$\Rightarrow 3T_1 = 4T_2 \quad \text{— (1)}$$

in vert dir $\frac{4}{5}T_1 + \frac{3}{5}T_2 = W$

$$\Rightarrow 4T_1 + 3T_2 = 5W \quad \text{— (2)}$$

from (1) & (2) $4T_1 + 3\left(\frac{3T_1}{4}\right) = 5W$

$$\Rightarrow T_1 = \frac{4}{5}W \; \& \; T_2 = \frac{3}{5}W$$

we consider $\Sigma \vec{\tau}_A = 0$

$$\tau_A = Wd - \frac{3}{5}T_2(2) = 0$$

$$\Rightarrow Wd = \frac{3}{5}\left(\frac{3}{5}W\right)(2)$$

$$\Rightarrow d = \frac{18}{25} m = 0.72 m \text{ Ans.}$$

Video Solution

- A car weighs 1800 kg. The distance between its front and back axles is 1.8 m. Its centre of gravity is 1.05 m behind the front axle. Determine the force exerted by the level ground on each front wheel and each back wheel.

Sol^n: As car is at rest

$\Rightarrow$ for static equilibrium, we can use

$$\Sigma \vec{F} = 0$$
$$\Sigma \vec{\tau} = 0$$

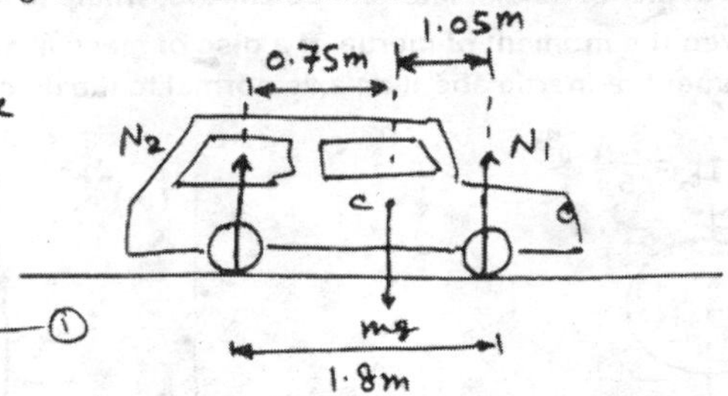

in vertical direction $N_1 + N_2 = 1800g$ — (1)

Considering torque about com, we have

$$\tau_c = N_1 \times 1.05 - N_2 \times 0.75 = 0$$

$$\Rightarrow N_1 = \frac{0.75}{1.05} N_2$$

$$\Rightarrow N_1 = \frac{5}{7} N_2$$

from eq^n (1), we have

$$\left(\frac{5}{7}+1\right) N_2 = 1800 \times 9.8 = 17640$$

$$N_2 = \frac{7}{12} \times 17640 = 10290\,N$$

$$\Rightarrow N_1 = \frac{5}{7} \times 10290 = 7350\,N$$

Force on front wheels $= \frac{N_1}{2} = \frac{7350}{2} = 3675\,N$

Force on Rear wheels $= \frac{N_2}{2} = \frac{10290}{2} = 5145\,N$ Ans

- (a) Find the moment of inertia of a sphere about a tangent to the sphere, given the moment of inertia of the sphere about any of its diameters to be $2MR^2/5$, where M is the mass of the sphere and R is the radius of the sphere.

  (b) Given the moment of inertia of a disc of mass M and radius R about any of its diameters to be $MR^2/4$, find its moment of inertia about an axis normal to the disc and passing through a point on its edge.

Sol (a) $I_c = \frac{2}{5}MR^2$

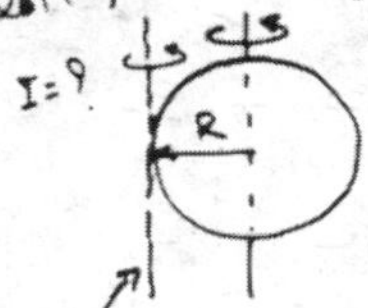

tangential AOR

Using parallel axes theorem we have

$$I = I_c + MR^2$$

$$I = \frac{2}{5}MR^2 + MR^2 = \frac{7}{5}MR^2$$

Ans

(b)

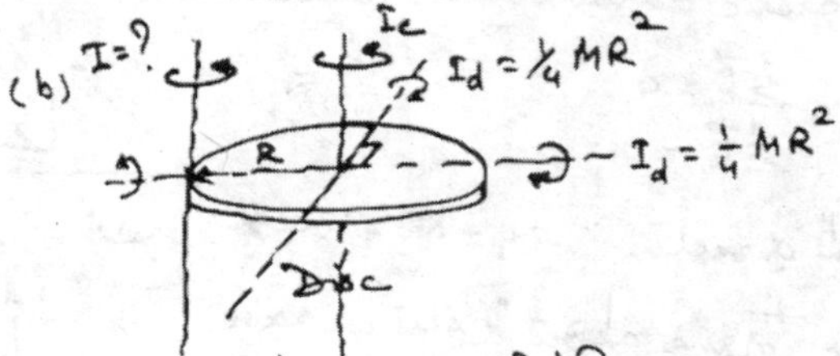

By perpendicular axes theorem, we use

$$I_c = I_d + I_d = 2 \times \frac{1}{4}MR^2 = \frac{1}{2}MR^2$$

By parallel axes theorem, we have

$$I = I_c + MR^2 = \frac{3}{2}MR^2 \quad \text{Ans}$$

- Torques of equal magnitude are applied to a hollow cylinder and a solid sphere, both having the same mass and radius. The cylinder is free to rotate about its standard axis of symmetry, and the sphere is free to rotate about an axis passing through its centre. Which of the two will acquire a greater angular speed after a given time.

Solⁿ: As we know angular speed is given as

$$\omega = \alpha t$$

(α → angular acceleration)

By Newton's laws in rotational motion we use

$$\tau = I\alpha \Rightarrow \alpha = \frac{\tau}{I}$$

(τ → equal for both.)

for a hollow cylinder $I_1 = MR^2$

for a sphere $I_2 = \frac{2}{5}MR^2$

$\Rightarrow I_2 < I_1$

$\Rightarrow \alpha_2 > \alpha_1$

$\Rightarrow \omega_2 > \omega_1$

⇒ sphere will attain greater angular speed. Ans.

- A solid cylinder of mass 20 kg rotates about its axis with angular speed 100 rad s^{-1}. The radius of the cylinder is 0.25 m. What is the kinetic energy associated with the rotation of the cylinder? What is the magnitude of angular momentum of the cylinder about its axis?

Sol: Moment of Inertia of cylinder $I = \frac{1}{2}MR^2 = \frac{1}{2} \times 20 \times (0.25)^2 = 0.625 \text{ kg-m}^2$

Kinetic Energy of Cylinder $K = \frac{1}{2}I\omega^2$

$= \frac{1}{2} \times 0.625 \times (100)^2 = 3125 \text{ J}$ Ans.

Angular momentum magnitude $L = I\omega$

$= 0.625 \times 100 = 62.5 \text{ J-s}$ Ans.

Video Solution

- (a) A child stands at the centre of a turntable with his two arms outstretched. The turntable is set rotating with an angular speed of 40 rev/min. How much is the angular speed of the child if he folds his hands back and thereby reduces his moment of inertia to 2/5 times the initial value ? Assume that the turntable rotates without friction.

  (b) Show that the child's new kinetic energy of rotation is more than the initial kinetic energy of rotation. How do you account for this increase in kinetic energy?

Sol^n (a) As there is no friction ⇒ no external force or torque is acting on turntable
⇓
Angular momentum of turntable remain constant

before folding hands, after folding hands.

$$\Rightarrow I_1\omega_1 = I_2\omega_2$$

ω_1 = 40 rev/min

given that $I_2 = \frac{2}{5} I_1$

$$\Rightarrow \omega_2 = \frac{5}{2}\omega_1 = \frac{5}{2}\times 40 = 100 \text{ rev/min}$$

(b) $KE_{initial} = \frac{1}{2} I_1\omega_1^2 = \frac{1}{2} I_1 (40)^2 = 800 I_1$

$KE_{final} = \frac{1}{2} I_2\omega_2^2 = \frac{1}{2}\left(\frac{2}{5} I_1\right)(100)^2 = 2000 I_1$

$\Rightarrow KE_f > KE_i$

It happens due to the work done by the child in folding his hands. Ans.

- **A rope of negligible mass is wound round a hollow cylinder of mass 3 kg and radius 40 cm. What is the angular acceleration of the cylinder if the rope is pulled with a force of 30 N ? What is the linear acceleration of the rope ? Assume that there is no slipping.**

Sol^n: Moment of inertia of hollow cylinder $I = MR^2$

$= 3 \times (0.4)^2 = 0.48 \text{ kg-m}^2$

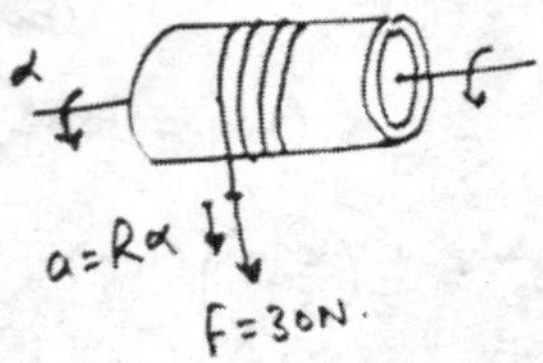

Torque on cylinder due to applied force

$\tau = FR = 30 \times 0.4 = 12 \text{ N-m}$

By Newton's II law in rotation, we use

$\tau = I\alpha$

Angular acc^n $\alpha = \dfrac{\tau}{I} = \dfrac{12}{0.48} = 25 \text{ rad/s}^2$

linear acc^n of rope $a = R\alpha = 0.4 \times 25 = 10 \text{ m/s}^2$ Ans.

- To maintain a rotor at a uniform angular speed of 200 rad s^{-1}, an engine needs to transmit a torque of 180 N m. What is the power required by the engine ?

  (Note: uniform angular velocity in the absence of friction implies zero torque. In practice, applied torque is needed to counter frictional torque). Assume that the engine is 100% efficient.

Sol^n: Power supplied by engine

$$P = \vec{\tau} \cdot \vec{\omega}$$

$$= \tau \omega$$

$$= 180 \times 200 = 36000 \text{ W}$$

$$= 36 \text{ kW} \quad \text{Ans.}$$

- **From a uniform disk of radius *R*, a circular hole of radius *R*/2 is cut out. The centre of the hole is at *R*/2 from the centre of the original disc. Locate the centre of gravity of the resulting flat body.**

Sol: As mass of disc is distributed in its surface area uniformly

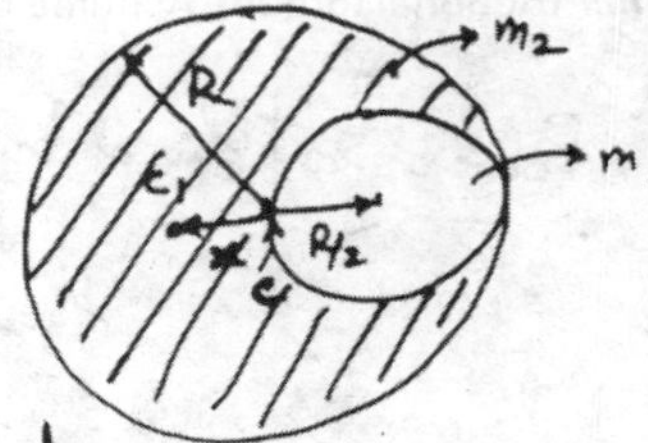

$$\Rightarrow \quad m_1 = \pi (R/2)^2 \times C_0 = \frac{1}{4}\pi R^2 . C_0$$

$$m_2 = \frac{3}{4}\pi R^2 C_0 = 3m_1$$

By the property of mass moments for COM of a body

For the COM of whole disc we use

$$m_1 (R/2) - m_2 x = 0$$

$$\Rightarrow \quad m_1 (R/2) = 3m_1 x \quad \rightarrow \quad x = R/6 \text{ Ans.}$$

Video Solution

- **A metre stick is balanced on a knife edge at its centre. When two coins, each of mass 5 g are put one on top of the other at the 12.0 cm mark, the stick is found to be balanced at 45.0 cm. What is the mass of the metre stick?**

Soln:

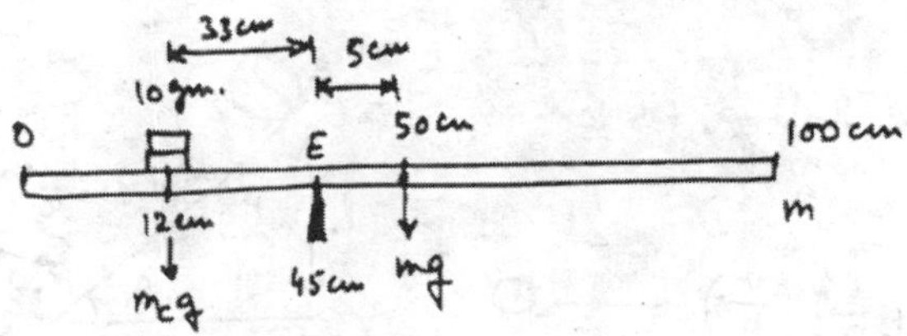

As rod is in static equilibrium we use

$$\sum \vec{F} = 0$$

$$\sum \vec{\tau} = 0$$

We consider torques about knife edge, we have

$$\tau_E = mg \times 5\text{cm} - m_c g \times 33\text{cm} = 0$$

$$\Rightarrow \quad m = \frac{m_c \times 33}{5} = 66\text{ gm Ans.}$$

- **A solid sphere rolls down two different inclined planes of the same heights but different angles of inclination.**

(a) Will it reach the bottom with the same speed in each case?

(b) Will it take longer to roll down one plane than the other?

(c) If so, which one and why?

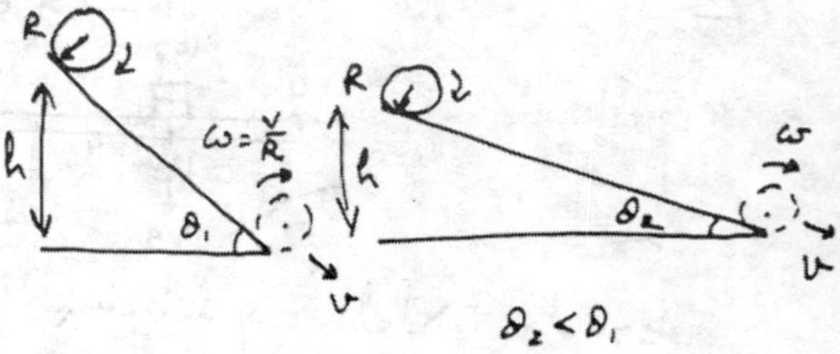

Sol^n(a) Considering pure rolling, we use W/E theoram as

$$Mgh = \frac{1}{2}Mv^2 + \frac{1}{2}I\left(\frac{v}{R}\right)^2 \quad \text{——} (1)$$

Eq^n (1) is independent of $\theta \Rightarrow$

v is same in both case

(b) As accelerations of sphare are different in these two cases, times will be different.

(c) For pure rolling on incline, acceleration of body is grieen as

$$a = \frac{g\sin\theta}{1 + K^2/R^2} \Rightarrow a \propto \sin\theta$$ thus for higher acc^n time will be less

because $\underset{\text{same}}{v} = at \Rightarrow t \propto \frac{1}{a} \Rightarrow$ for $\theta_2\ (<\theta_1)$ the time will be more.

- **A hoop of radius 2 m weighs 100 kg. It rolls along a horizontal floor so that its centre of mass has a speed of 20 cm/s. How much work has to be done to stop it?**

Sol^n:

$\omega = \frac{v}{R}$ (for pure rolling)

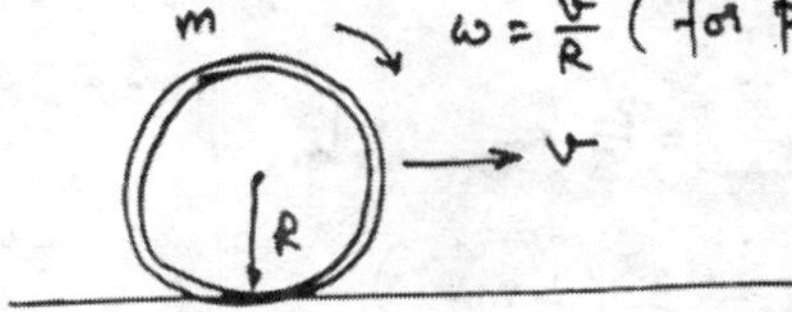

for hoop $I = MR^2$

Kinetic energy of body $= \frac{1}{2}Mv^2 + \frac{1}{2}I\omega^2$

$= \frac{1}{2}(100)(0.2)^2 + \frac{1}{2}(100)(2)^2\left(\frac{0.2}{2}\right)^2$

$= 100 \times 0.04 = \underline{4\ J}$

To stop the hoop W/D on hoop is $W = -\Delta K = -4\ J$ Ans.

W/D by hoop in stopping process $= \underline{4\ J}$.

- **The oxygen molecule has a mass of 5.30×10^{-26} kg and a moment of inertia of 1.94×10^{-46} kg m^2 about an axis through its centre perpendicular to the lines joining the two atoms. Suppose the mean speed of such a molecule in a gas is 500 m/s and that its kinetic energy of rotation is two thirds of its kinetic energy of translation. Find the average angular velocity of the molecule.**

Sol^n: It is given that

$$K_{rotation} = \frac{2}{3} K_{Translation}$$

$$\frac{1}{2} I\omega^2 = \frac{2}{3}\left(\frac{1}{2}mv^2\right)$$

$$\Rightarrow \quad \omega = \sqrt{\frac{2mv^2}{I}}$$

$$= \sqrt{\frac{2 \times 5.30 \times 10^{-26} \times (500)^2}{1.94 \times 10^{-46}}}$$

$$= 6.75 \times 10^{12} \text{ rad/s.} \quad \text{Ans.}$$

Video Solution

- **A solid cylinder rolls up an inclined plane of angle of inclination 30°. At the bottom of the inclined plane the centre of mass of the cylinder has a speed of 5 m/s.**

(a) How far will the cylinder go up the plane?

(b) How long will it take to return to the bottom?

Sol^n (a) For pure rolling acc^n of rolling body on an incline plane is given as

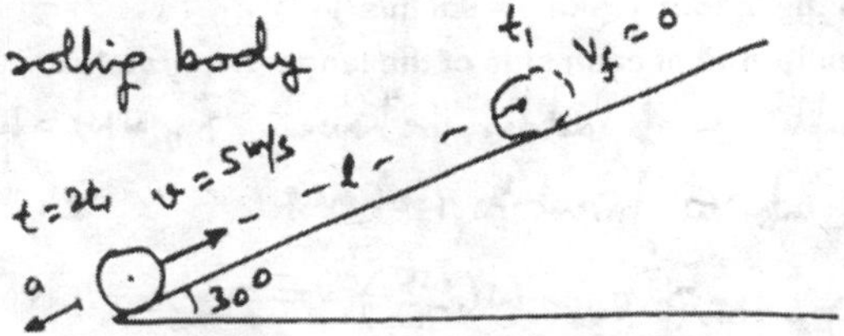

$$a = -\frac{g\sin\theta}{1+\frac{K^2}{R^2}}$$

$K = R/\sqrt{2}$

$$= -\frac{9.8\times 0.5}{1+1/2}$$

$$= -\frac{9.8}{3}\ m/s^2$$

using speed eq^n we have

$$l = \frac{v^2}{2a} = \frac{(5)^2}{2\times 9.8}\times 3$$

$$= 3.83\ m$$

Ans.

(b) Total time of ascending up & then returning journey is given as-

$$T = 2\left(\frac{v}{a}\right) = 2\times\frac{5}{9.8}\times 3$$

$$= \frac{30}{9.8} = 3.06\ s$$

Ans.

Web Reference at www.physicsgalaxy.com

Video Sol. : Class 11th NCERT Solutions | **Sec.** - Mechanics | **Topic** - System of Particles

Theory Reference. : Grade - 11 & 12 | **Sec.** - Mechanics | **Topic** - Rigid Body Dynamics

Video Solution

- **As shown in figure, the two sides of a step ladder *BA* and *CA* are 1.6 m long and hinged at *A*. A rope *DE*, 0.5 m is tied half way up. A weight 40 kg is suspended from a point *F*, 1.2 m from *B* along the ladder *BA*. Assuming the floor to be frictionless and neglecting the weight of the ladder, find the tension in the rope and forces exerted by the floor on the ladder. (Take $g = 9.8\ m/s^2$)**

(Hint: Consider the equilibrium of each side of the ladder separately.)

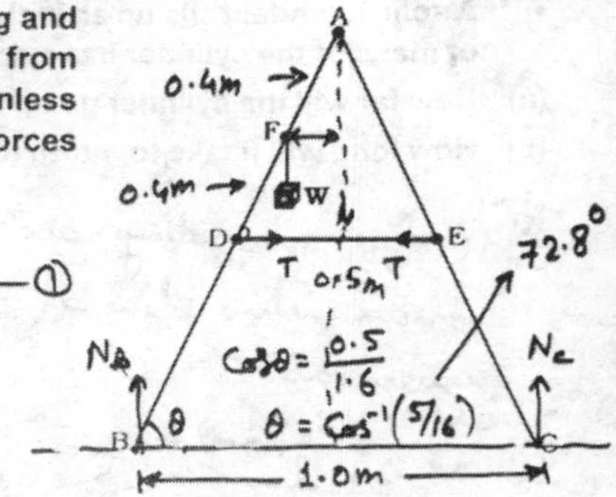

Sol^n: Considering equilibrium of ladder, we have $N_B + N_c = W$ —①

Considering torque about point A, we have

$$\tau_A = N_B(0.5) - N_c(0.5) - W\left(\frac{0.5}{4}\right) = 0$$

$$\Rightarrow N_B - N_c = W/4 \quad —②$$

$$①+② \Rightarrow 2N_B = W/4 + W = \frac{5W}{4}$$

$$\Rightarrow N_B = \frac{5}{4\times 2}\times 40\times 9.8 = 245\text{ N Ans.}$$

from ①

$$N_c = W - N_B = 40\times 9.8 - 245 = 147\text{ N Ans.}$$

for T, we consider torque on ladder AC about point A

$$\tau_A = N_c(0.5) - T(0.8\sin\theta) = 0$$

$$\Rightarrow T = \frac{147\times 0.5}{0.8\times \sin(72.8^\circ)} = \frac{147\times 0.5}{0.8\times 0.9553} = 96.17\text{ N}$$

Ans

Video Solution

- A man stands on a rotating platform, with his arms stretched horizontally holding a 5 kg weight in each hand. The angular speed of the platform is 30 revolutions per minute. The man then brings his arms close to his body with the distance of each weight from the axis changing from 90cm to 20cm. The moment of inertia of the man together with the platform may be taken to be constant and equal to 7.6 kg m^2.

(a) What is his new angular speed? (Neglect friction.)

(b) Is kinetic energy conserved in the process? If not, from where does the change come about?

Sol (a) As no ext torque is present on system ⇒ its Angular momentum remain Conserved

$$\Rightarrow \quad I_1\omega_1 = I_2\omega_2 \quad \text{—— (1)}$$

Here initial MI of system is $I_1 = 7.6 + 2(5)(0.9)^2$

$= 7.6 + 8.1 = 15.7\ kg\text{-}m^2$

$I_m = mr^2$

Final MI of system is $I_2 = 7.6 + 2(5)(0.2)^2$

$= 7.6 + 0.4 = 8.0\ kg\text{-}m^2$

from eq^n (1), we have

$15.7 \times 30 = (8.0).\omega_2 \Rightarrow \omega_2 = \dfrac{15.7 \times 30}{8.0} = 58.9$ rev/m Ans.

(b) KE of system increases due to work done by man in folding his arms.

- **A bullet of mass 10 g and speed 500 m/s is fired into a door and gets embedded exactly at the centre of the door. The door is 1.0 m wide and weighs 12 kg. It is hinged at one end and rotates about a vertical axis practically without friction. Find the angular speed of the door just after the bullet embeds into it.**

  (Hint: The moment of inertia of the door about the vertical axis at one end is $ML^2/3$)

Solⁿ: As no ext force/torque is present on system except at axis of rotation.

So torque about given axis is zero

⇒ system angular momentum remain Conserved.

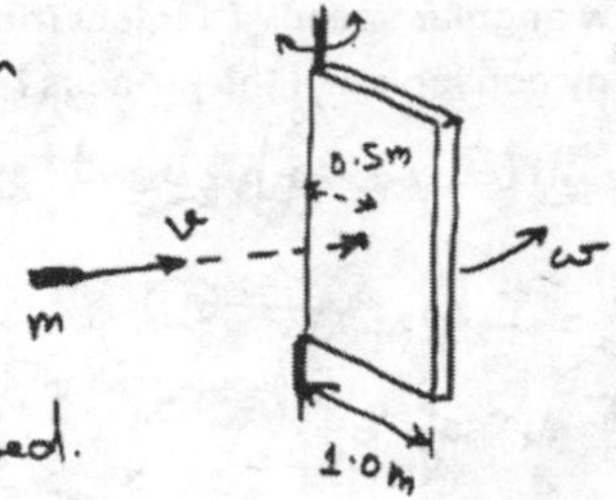

Initial ang momentum = Final angular momentum

$$mvr = I\omega$$

$$\Rightarrow \quad \omega = \frac{mvr}{ML^2/3} = \frac{0.01 \times 500 \times 0.5 \times 3}{12 \times (1)^2} = 0.625 \text{ rad/s}$$

Ans.

Video Solution

- **Two discs of moments of inertia I_1 and I_2 about their respective axes (normal to the disc and passing through the centre), and rotating with angular speeds ω_1 and ω_2 are brought into contact face to face with their axes of rotation coincident.**

(a) What is the angular speed of the two-disc system?

(b) Show that the kinetic energy of the combined system is less than the sum of the initial kinetic energies of the two discs. How do you account for this loss in energy? Take $\omega_1 \neq \omega_2$.

Sol (a) As there is no ext torque acting on this system, here we conserve the angular momentum as

$$I_1\omega_1 + I_2\omega_2 = (I_1 + I_2)\omega_0$$

$$\Rightarrow \omega_0 = \frac{I_1\omega_1 + I_2\omega_2}{I_1 + I_2} \quad \text{Ans}$$

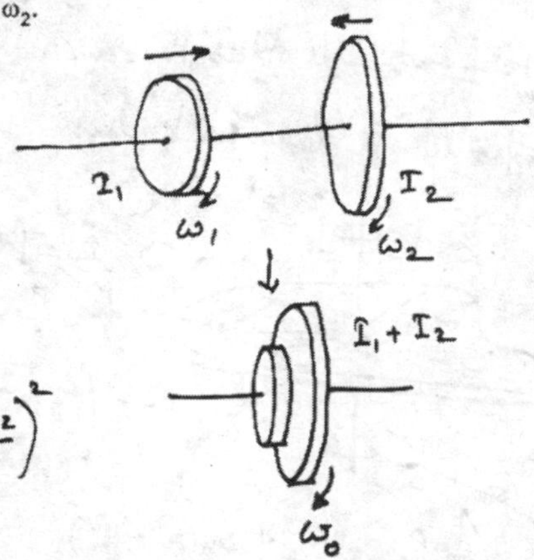

(b) final KE of system $K_f = \frac{1}{2}(I_1 + I_2)\left(\frac{I_1\omega_1 + I_2\omega_2}{I_1 + I_2}\right)^2$

initial KE of system $K_i = \frac{1}{2}I_1\omega_1^2 + \frac{1}{2}I_2\omega_2^2$

change in KE $\Delta K = K_i - K_f = ---- = \frac{1}{2}\left(\frac{I_1 I_2}{I_1 + I_2}\right)(\omega_1 - \omega_2)^2$

+ve

- **(a) Prove the theorem of perpendicular axes.**

  (Hint : Square of the distance of a point (x, y) in the $x - y$ plane from an axis through the origin and perpendicular to the plane is $x^2 + y^2$).

  (b) Prove the theorem of parallel axes.

  (Hint : If the centre of mass is chosen to be the origin $\Sigma m_i \vec{r}_i = 0$)

Sol^n: (a) Perpendicular Axes Theorem.

Valid only for laminar bodies

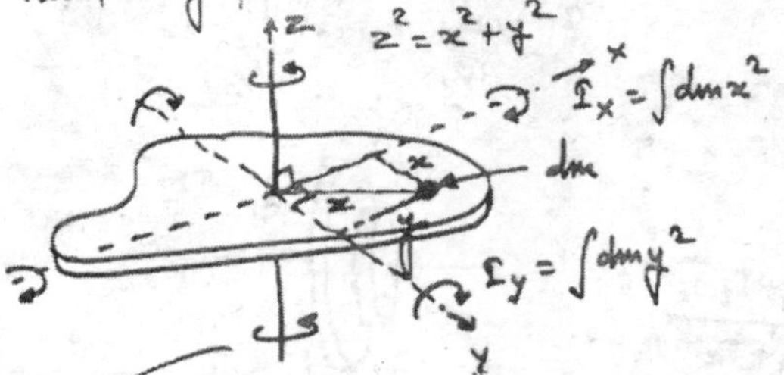

$$I_z = \int dm\, z^2 = \int dm(x^2 + y^2)$$

$$\Rightarrow \boxed{I_z = I_x + I_y}$$

(b) Parallel Axes Theorem.

$I_c = \int dm\, r_1^2$

$I = ?$

$I = \int dm\, r_2^2$

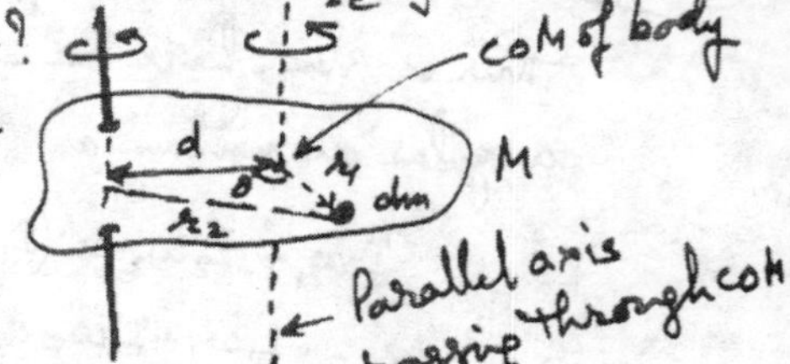

$$I = \int dm(d^2 + r_1^2 - 2dr_1\cos\theta)$$

$$I = I_c + Md^2 - \int dm(2dr_1\cos\theta)$$

$$I = I_c + Md^2 - 2d\int dm\, r_\theta$$

$$\boxed{I = I_c + Md^2}$$

Video Solution

- **Prove the result that the velocity *v* of translation of a rolling body (like a ring, disc, cylinder or sphere) at the bottom of an inclined plane of a height *h* is given by**

$$v^2 = \frac{2gh}{(1+k^2/R^2)}$$

using dynamical consideration (i.e. by consideration of forces and torques). Note *k* is the radius of gyration of the body about its symmetry axis, and *R* is the radius of the body. The body starts from rest at the top of the plane.

Sol^n: Equation of motion of body are

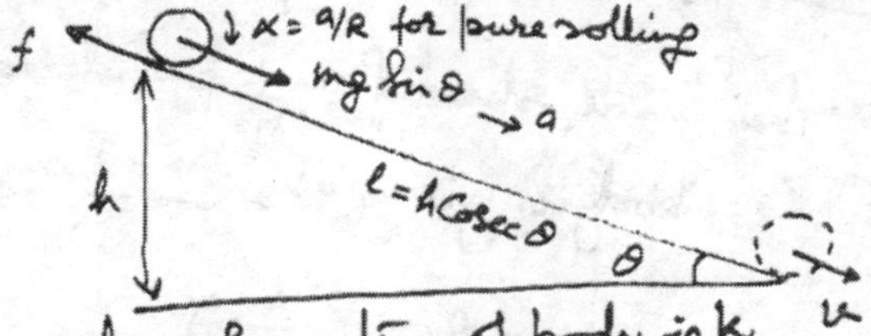

(T) → $mg\sin\theta - f = ma$

(R) → $fR = I\left(a/R^2\right)$

(T) + (R) $mg\sin\theta = a\left(m + \frac{I}{R^2}\right)$

If radius of gyration of body is k

$\Rightarrow I = Mk^2$

$mg\sin\theta = ma\left(1+\frac{k^2}{R^2}\right)$

$\Rightarrow \quad a = \frac{g\sin\theta}{1+k^2/R^2}$

At the bottom of incline, speed of body is given as –

$v^2 = (0)^2 + 2as \Rightarrow v^2 = 2\left(\frac{g\sin\theta}{1+k^2/R^2}\right)h\,\mathrm{cosec}\,\theta$

$\Rightarrow v^2 = 2gh/(1+k^2/R^2)$

- A disc rotating about its axis with angular speed ω_0 is placed lightly (without any translational push) on a perfectly frictionless table. The radius of the disc is R. What are the linear velocities of the points A, B and C on the disc shown in figure ? Will the disc roll in the direction indicated ?

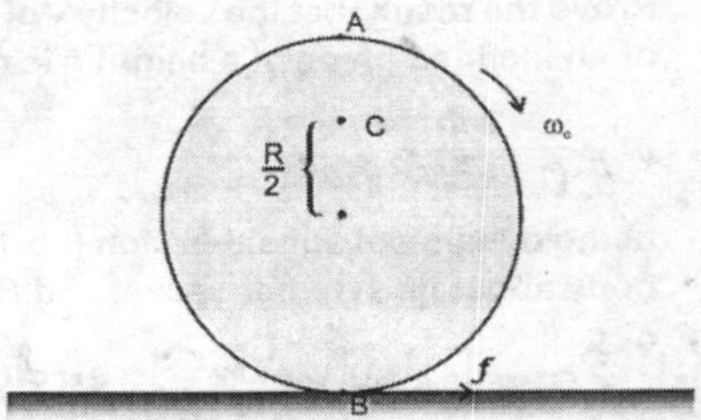

Sol: For any body rotating at angular speed ω, then linear speed of any particle within the body is given as $v = r\omega$. (tangentially)

frictionless $\Rightarrow f = 0$

$$v_A = R\omega_0 \ (\longrightarrow)$$

$$v_B = R\omega_0 \ (\longleftarrow)$$

$$v_C = \frac{R}{2}\omega_0 \ (\longrightarrow)$$

As no friction is there & no other external force is present, COM of disc will remain at rest or disc will not move.

- **Explain why friction is necessary to make the disc in figure roll in the direction indicated.**

(a) **Give the direction of frictional force at *B*, and the sense of frictional torque, before perfect rolling begins**

(b) **What is the force of friction after perfect rolling begins ?**

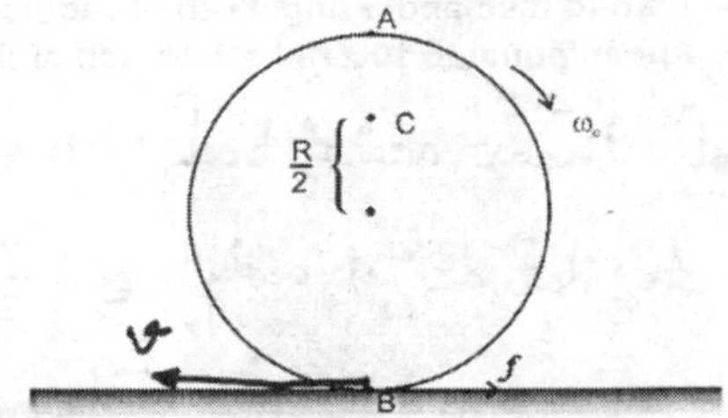

Sol^n: If surface is smooth then body will spin at its initial position only. If surface is rough friction at pt B acts in dir opp to v_B. Due to f body will start moving forward hence its rolling will start.

(a) $f \rightarrow$ rightward direction
Torque due to friction is $\tau = fR$ in ackwise manner & by RHTR $\vec{\tau}$ dir is normal to plane of this figure (outward)

(b) As we know after pure rolling starts friction (static) acts only when some external force is present. Here as $F_{ext} = 0 \Rightarrow f = 0$ after pure rolling begins.

- **A solid disc and a ring, both of radius 10 cm are placed on a horizontal table simultaneously, with initial angular speed equal to 10π rad s^{-1}. Which of the two will start to roll earlier ? The co-efficient of kinetic friction is $\mu_k = 0.2$.**

Solⁿ: linear accⁿ of body $a = \frac{f}{m} = \mu_k g$

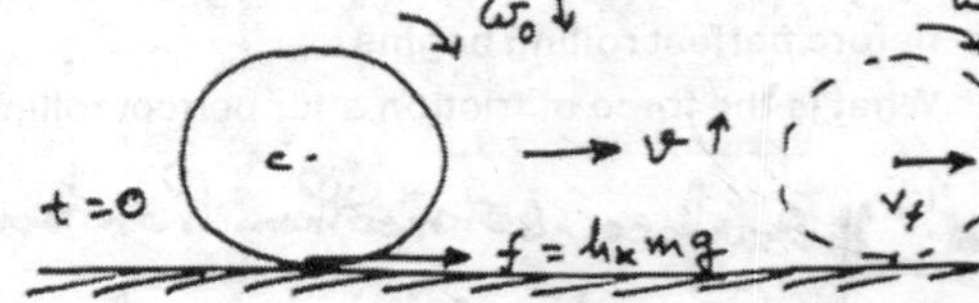

Angular accⁿ of body $\alpha = \frac{\tau}{I} = -\frac{f.R}{I}$

for a Ring $\alpha_1 = -\frac{\mu_k mg.R}{mR^2} = -\frac{\mu_k g}{R}$

for a Disc $\alpha_2 = -\frac{\mu_k mg.R}{\frac{1}{2}mR^2} = -\frac{2\mu_k g}{R}$

$\omega_f = \omega_0 + \alpha t$

pure rolling will start when $v_f = R\omega_f$

using speed eqⁿ, we have

$v_f = 0 + (\mu_k g)t$ — ①

using angular speed eqⁿ, we have →

for a Ring

$\left(\frac{v_f}{R}\right) = \omega_0 - \frac{\mu_k g}{R}.t_1$

$\Rightarrow t_1 = \frac{R\omega_0}{2\mu_k g}$

for a disc

$\frac{v_f}{R} = \omega_0 - \frac{2\mu_k g}{R}.t_2$

$t_2 = \frac{R\omega_0}{3\mu_k g}$

$\Rightarrow t_2 < t_1$ so disc will start rolling first.

Video Solution

- **A cylinder of mass 10 kg and radius 15 cm is rolling perfectly on a plane of inclination 30°. The co-efficient of static friction $\mu_s = 0.25$.**

(a) **How much is the force of friction acting on the cylinder ?**

(b) **What is the work done against friction during rolling ?**

(c) **If the inclination θ of the plane is increased, at what value of θ does the cylinder begin to skid and not roll perfectly ?**

Solⁿ (a) As we know for pure rolling of a body on incline plane, accⁿ is given as

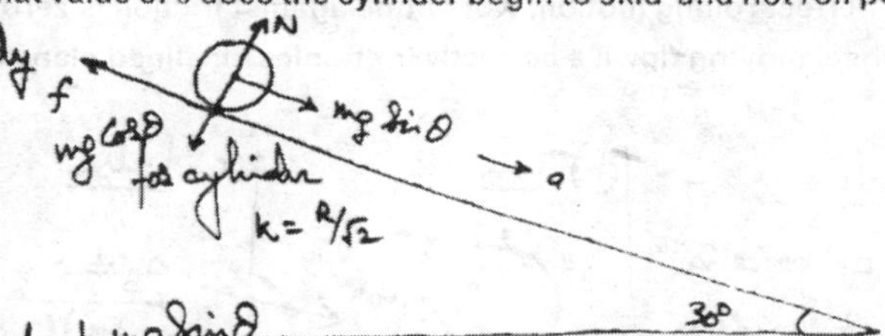

$$a = \frac{g\sin\theta}{1 + k^2/R^2} = \frac{2}{3} g\sin\theta$$

Eqⁿ for cylinder

$$mg\sin\theta - f = ma = \frac{2}{3} mg\sin\theta \Rightarrow f = \frac{1}{3} mg\sin\theta$$

$$= \frac{1}{3} \times (10)(9.8) \times \frac{1}{2} = 16.3\text{ N} \text{ Ans.}$$

(b) For pure rolling always friction is static $\Rightarrow W_{f_s\,\text{rolling}} = 0$ Ans → As bottom contact of cylinder is always at rest.

(c) Cylinder will start slipping when $f \to f_s$

$$\Rightarrow \frac{1}{3} mg\sin\theta = \mu_s N = \mu_s mg\cos\theta$$

$$\Rightarrow \tan\theta = 3\mu_s = 3 \times 0.25 = 0.75$$

$$\Rightarrow \theta = \tan^{-1}(3/4) = 37^\circ \text{ Ans}$$

- Read each statement below carefully, and state, with reasons, if it is true or false;

(a) During rolling, the force of friction acts in the same direction as the direction of motion of the *CM* of the body

(b) The instantaneous speed of the point of contact during rolling is zero

(c) The instantaneous acceleration of the point of contact during rolling is zero

(d) For perfect rolling motion, work done against friction is zero

(e) A wheel moving down a perfectly frictionless inclined plane will undergo slipping (not rolling) motion.

Sol^n:

(a) False

If no ext force is present in rolling ⇓ $f = 0$

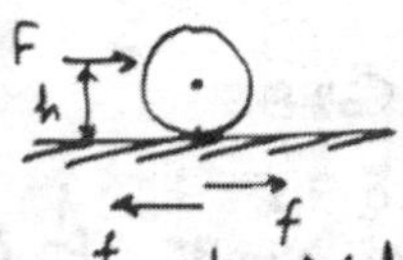

dir of f depends on h.

(b) True

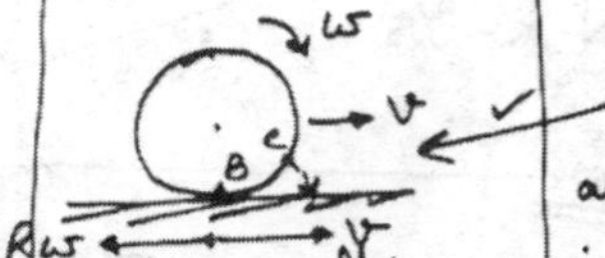

for pure rolling

$v = R\omega$

$v_B = v - R\omega = 0$

(c) False

$a_B \neq 0$

as just after this instant point B will break off from ground & a new contact pt. C will be there

(d) True

As in rolling bottom pt of contact is at rest & friction is static

$\Rightarrow W_f = 0$

$f \times$ displacement (displacement = 0)

(e) True — no rotation

On incline, torque of friction causes rolling which is absent so no rotational motion will be there, it will only slip

- **Separation of Motion of a system of particles into motion of the centre of mass and motion about the centre of mass:**

(a) **Show $\vec{P} = \vec{P_i'} + m_i\vec{V}$ where $\vec{p_i}$ is the momentum of the ith particle (of mass m_i) and $\vec{p_i'} = m_i\vec{v_i'}$. Note $\vec{v_i'}$ is the velocity of the ith particle relative to the centre of mass. Also, prove using the definition of the centre of mass $\sum \vec{P_i'} = 0$**

(Hint : Use the definition of centre of mass and Newton's Third Law. Assume the internal forces between any two particles act along the line joining the particles.)

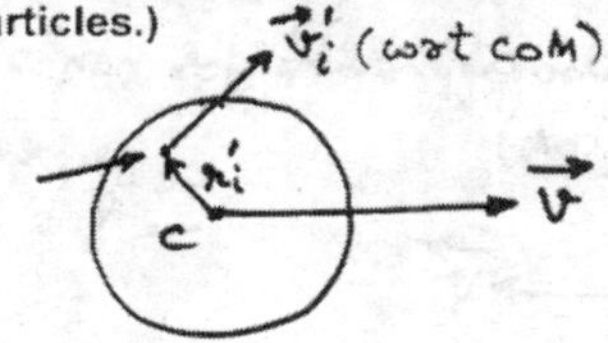

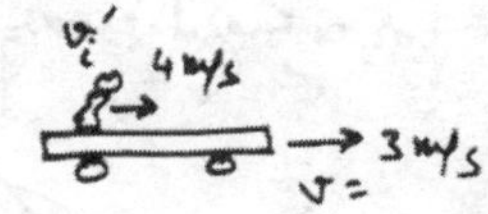

Sol^n: Net velocity of m_i w.r.to ground is given as

$v_{BG} = 4 + 3$

$$\vec{v_i} = \vec{v_i'} + \vec{V}$$

momentum of ith particle in ground frame $\vec{P_i} = m_i\vec{v_i} = m_i(\vec{v_i'} + \vec{V}) = \vec{P_i'} + m_i\vec{V}$

Total momentum of body $\vec{P} = \Sigma\vec{P_i} = \Sigma m_i\vec{v_i'} + \Sigma m_i\vec{V} = \Sigma P_i' + M\vec{V}$

As in frame of COM we know $\Sigma m_i r_i' = 0 \Rightarrow \Sigma m_i v_i' = 0 \Rightarrow \Sigma P_i' = 0$

- **Separation of Motion of a system of particles into motion of the centre of mass and motion about the centre of mass:**

(b) **Show $K = K' + \frac{1}{2}MV^2$ where K is the total kinetic energy of the system of particles, K' is the total kinetic energy of the system when the particle velocities are taken with respect to the centre of mass and $MV^2/2$ is the kinetic energy of the translation of the system as a whole (i.e. of the centre of mass motion of the system). The result has been used in Sec. 7.14.**

(Hint : Use the definition of centre of mass and Newton's Third Law. Assume the internal forces between any two particles act along the line joining the particles.)

Sol.ⁿ For a Rigid Body we use (also applicable for non-rigid bodies or loose particle systems)

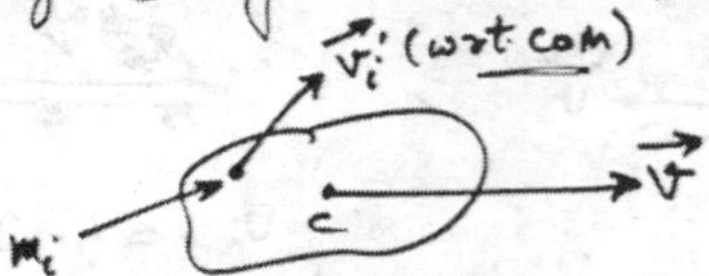

KE of ith particle is $k_i = \frac{1}{2}m_i(\vec{v}_i' + \vec{v})^2$ — ①

if θ is angle between $\vec{v}_i'$ & $\vec{v}$ $\Rightarrow |\vec{v}_i' + \vec{v}| = v_i'^2 + v^2 + 2v_i'v\cos\theta$

from ① we have $k_i = \frac{1}{2}m_i v_i'^2 + \frac{1}{2}m_i v^2 + m v v_i' \cos\theta$

Total energy of body (sop) $K = \sum k_i = \sum \frac{1}{2}m_i v_i'^2 + \sum \frac{1}{2}m_i v^2 + \sum m v_i' v\cos\theta$ (where $\sum m v_i' \to 0$)

$K = K' + \frac{1}{2}Mv^2$

Video Solution

- **Separation of Motion of a system of particles into motion of the centre of mass and motion about the centre of mass:**

(c) **Show where $\vec{L}' = \vec{r}_i' \times \vec{p}_i'$ is the angular momentum of the system about the centre of mass with velocities taken relative to the centre of mass. Remember $\vec{r}_i' = \vec{r}_i - \vec{R}$; rest of the notation is the standard notation used in the chapter. Note $\vec{L}'$ and $M\vec{R} \times \vec{V}$ can be said to be angular momenta, respectively, about and of the centre of mass of the system of particles.**

(Hint : Use the definition of centre of mass and Newton's Third Law. Assume the internal forces between any two particles act along the line joining the particles.)

Sol^n: Angular momentum of body w.r.to O

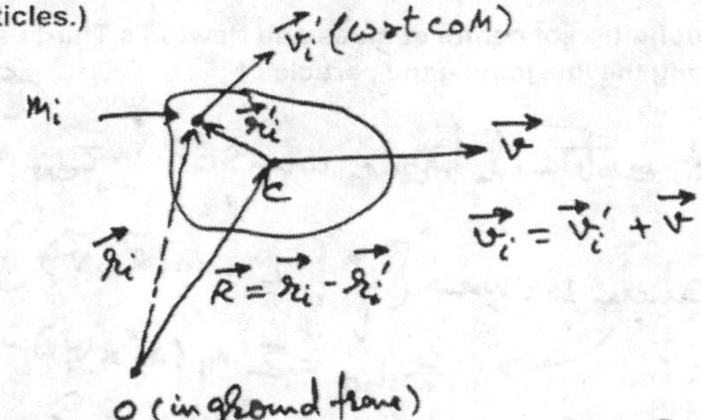

$$\vec{L}_{io} = m_i(\vec{r}_i \times \vec{v}_i)$$

$$\vec{L}_{io} = m_i\left[(\vec{R} + \vec{r}_i') \times (\vec{v}_i' + \vec{V})\right]$$

$$\vec{L}_{io} = m_i(\vec{R} \times \vec{v}_i') + m_i(\vec{r}_i' \times \vec{v}_i') + m_i(\vec{R} \times \vec{V}) + m_i(\vec{r}_i' \times \vec{V})$$

$$\Rightarrow \vec{L} = \Sigma \vec{L}_{io} = 0 + \vec{L}' + M(\vec{R} \times \vec{V}) + 0$$

$$\vec{L} = \vec{L}' + M(\vec{R} \times \vec{V})$$

- **Separation of Motion of a system of particles into motion of the centre of mass and motion about the centre of mass:**

(d) **Show** $\frac{d\vec{L}'}{dt} = \sum \vec{r}_i' \times \frac{d\vec{p}'}{dt}$

Further, show that $\frac{d\vec{L}'}{dt} = \vec{\tau}_{ext}$

where $\vec{\tau}_{ext}$ **is the sum of all external torques acting on the system about the centre of mass.**

(Hint : Use the definition of centre of mass and Newton's Third Law. Assume the internal forces between any two particles act along the line joining the particles.)

Solⁿ: Net external torque on a SOP $\vec{\tau}_{ext} = \vec{r} \times \left(\frac{d\vec{P}_{net}}{dt}\right)$

for i^{th} particle we use $\left[L^{\circ} = L' + M(\vec{R} \times \vec{V})\right] \rightarrow$ for whole body

$\sum L_{io} = \sum m_i (r_i' \times v_i') + \sum m_i (\vec{R} \times \vec{V})$

net torque on body $\tau_0 = \frac{dL}{dt} = \sum r_i' \times \frac{d}{dt} p' \rightarrow p_i' + m_i \vec{V}$

Video Solution

Chapter 8

Gravitation

QR Code of Link to the Video Lectures of Theory of this chapter Gravitation at 'Physics Galaxy' web portal

QR Code of Link to the NCERT textbook Video Solutions of unsolved exercises at the end of each chapter in sequence of this chapter at 'Physics Galaxy' web portal

- Answer the following :

(a) You can shield a charge from electrical forces by putting it inside a hollow conductor. Can you shield a body from the gravitational influence of nearby matter by putting it inside a hollow sphere or by some other means ?

(b) An astronaut inside a small space ship orbiting around the earth cannot detect gravity. If the space station orbiting around the earth has a large size, can he hope to detect gravity ?

(c) If you compare the gravitational force on the earth due to the sun to that due to the moon, you would find that the Sun's pull is greater than the moon's pull. (you can check this yourself using the data available in the succeeding exercises). However, the tidal effect of the moon's pull is greater than the tidal effect of sun. Why ?

Sol^n (a) No. Because grav forces does not depend upon the medium in which bodies are placed, so shielding from grav forces is not possible.

(b) Yes. Because due to large size of spaceship g varies inside the spaceship. & this variation can be detected.

(c) Grav forces $\propto \frac{1}{R^2}$ (inverse square law)

whereas tidal effect on water in oceans $\propto \frac{1}{R^3}$

as Sun-Earth distance >> Moon-Earth distance

- Choose the correct alternative :

(a) Acceleration due to gravity increases/decreases with increasing altitude.

(b) Acceleration due to gravity increases/decreases with increasing depth (assume the earth to be a sphere of uniform density).

(c) Acceleration due to gravity is independent of mass of the earth/mass of the body.

(d) The formula $-G\,Mm(1/r_2 - 1/r_1)$ is more/less accurate than the formula $mg(r_2 - r_1)$ for the difference of potential energy between two points r_2 and r_1 distance away from the centre of the earth.

Sol^n (a) value of g with height above the earth surface is given as-

$$g_h = \frac{g_s}{(1 + h/R_e)^2} \Rightarrow \text{As } h\uparrow \Rightarrow g_h\downarrow$$

(b) value of g at a depth h below earth surface is given as-

$$g_h = g_s\left(1 - \frac{h}{R_e}\right) \Rightarrow \text{As } h\uparrow \Rightarrow g_h\downarrow$$

(c) value of g is given as $g_s = \left(\frac{GM_e}{R_e^2}\right)$

(d) Potential Energy of a body from Earth's centre is given as $U = -\frac{GM_em}{r}$

- **Suppose there existed a planet that went around the sun twice as fast as the earth. What would be its orbital size as compared to that of the earth ?**

Sol^n: If a planet revolves around Sun in an orbit of radius r, then its orbital speed is given as-

$$v = \sqrt{\frac{GM_s}{r}}$$

angular speed of planet $\omega = \frac{v}{r} = \frac{\sqrt{GM_s}}{r^{3/2}}$

for all planets, we have $\omega . r^{3/2} = \text{Constant}$

for Earth & other planet, we use $\underbrace{\omega_1 r_1^{3/2}}_{\text{Earth}} = \underbrace{\omega_2 r_2^{3/2}}_{\text{Planet}}$

We are given that $\omega_2 = 2\omega_1$ $\Rightarrow$ $\omega_1 r_1^{3/2} = 2\omega_1 r_2^{3/2}$

$$\Rightarrow r_2 = \frac{r_1}{(2)^{2/3}} = 0.63 r_1$$

63% of Earth's orbit

- *Io*, one of the satellites of Jupiter, has an orbital period of 1.769 days and the radius of the orbit is 4.22×10^8 m. Show that the mass of Jupiter is about one-thousandth that of the sun.

Sol^n: By Kepler's III law, we have

$$T^2 = \frac{4\pi^2}{GM_J} \cdot r^3$$

We use $T_{JS} = 1.769$ days

$r_{JS} = 4.22 \times 10^8$ m

$$\Rightarrow M_J = \frac{4\pi^2 r^3}{G\,T^2} = \frac{4 \times (3.14)^2 \times (4.22 \times 10^8)^3}{6.67 \times 10^{-11} \times (1.769 \times 86400)^2}$$

$$\simeq 2 \times 10^{27} \text{ kg.}$$

As we know that mass of Sun is $M_s \simeq 2 \times 10^{30}$ kg.

$$\Rightarrow M_J \sim \frac{1}{1000} M_s$$

- Let us assume that our galaxy consists of 2.5×10^{11} stars each of one solar mass. How long will a star at a distance of 50,000 *ly* from the galactic centre take to complete one revolution? Take the diameter of the Milky Way to be 10^5 *ly*.

Sol^n: Total mass in Galaxy $M = 2.5 \times 10^{11} \times \dfrac{2 \times 10^{30}\,\text{kg}}{\text{solar mass}} = 5.0 \times 10^{41}\,\text{kg}$.

Total distance of star from galactic centre is $r = 50000 \times \dfrac{9.46 \times 10^{15}\,\text{m}}{1\,\text{Ly}}$

$= 5 \times 9.46 \times 10^{19}\,\text{m}$

By Kepler's III law, revolution period of star is given as

$$T^2 = \frac{4\pi^2}{GM} \cdot r^3$$

$$T = \sqrt{\frac{4 \times (3.14)^2 \times (5 \times 9.46 \times 10^{19})^3}{6.67 \times 10^{-11} \times 5 \times 10^{41}}} = \frac{(111.96 \times 10^{14}\,\text{s})}{365 \times 86400} \cdot \frac{\text{years}}{\text{days}} = 3.55 \times 10^8\,\text{yr.}$$

Ans.

- **Choose the correct alternative:**

(a) If the zero of potential energy is at infinity, the total energy of an orbiting satellite is negative of its kinetic/potential energy.

(b) The energy required to launch an orbiting satellite out of earth's gravitational influence is more/less than the energy required to project a stationary object at the same height (as the satellite) out of earth's influence.

Sol^n (a) The KE of an orbiting satellite is given as $K = \frac{1}{2}mv^2$

As orbital speed $v = \sqrt{\frac{GM}{x}}$ (x → orbit radius) $= \frac{GMm}{2x}$

PE of an orbiting satellite is given as $P = -\frac{GMm}{x}$ (with zero ref at ∞)

$$\text{Total Energy} = K + P = \frac{GMm}{2x} - \frac{GMm}{x} = -\frac{GMm}{2x}$$

$$TE = -KE.$$

(b) At a distance x from Earth's centre ($x > R_e$)

orbital speed to launch a sat $v = \sqrt{GM/x}$

escape velocity at same pt $v_e = \sqrt{2GM/x}$

As $v_e > v$

⇒ less energy is reqd in launching a Sat.

Video Solution

- **Does the escape speed of a body from the earth depend on (a) the mass of the body, (b) the location from where it is projected, (c) the direction of projection, (d) the height of the location from where the body is launched?**

<u>Sol^n</u>: At escape velocity at a distance R_e (on surface of Earth) from Earth centre the Total energy of body is given as

$$TE = \overset{K}{\frac{1}{2}mv_e^2} + \overset{P}{\left(-\frac{GM_e m}{R_e}\right)} \geq 0 \text{ for body to escape Earth's grav}$$

$$\Rightarrow \quad v_e = \sqrt{\frac{2GM_e}{R_e}}$$

independent of m

independent of longitude or latitude assuming spherical Earth.

R_e ↙ × (if projected from some height)

(a) No

(b) No

(c) No — in any dir as we are not accoing orbital motion of Earth w.r.t. to Sun & rot^n motion

(d) Yes → it depends upon R_e.

- **A comet orbits the sun in a highly elliptical orbit. Does the comet have a constant (a) linear speed, (b) angular speed, (c) angular momentum, (d) kinetic energy, (e) potential energy, (f) total energy throughout its orbit? Neglect any mass loss of the comet when it comes very close to the Sun.**

Sol^n:

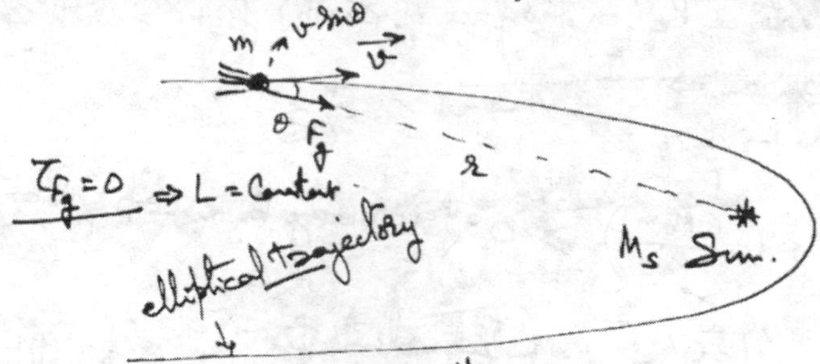

By Conservation of Energy we have

$$\frac{1}{2}mv^2 - \frac{GM_s m}{r} = \text{Constant}$$

($\frac{1}{2}mv^2$ → KE, $\frac{GM_s m}{r}$ → PE)

(a) No as v is changing with r

(b) No as angular speed $\omega = \frac{v\sin\theta}{r}$ as r is changing & θ is also changing

(c) Yes → Angular momentum remain Conserved as No external torque is present.

(d) No → as v is changing

(e) PE → No → as r is changing ; (f) Yes as TE is Conserved.

- **Which of the following symptoms is likely to afflict an astronaut in space (a) swollen feet, (b) swollen face, (c) headache, (d) orientational problem.**

Solⁿ: As in space there is no gravity option (a) is ruled out.

In space pressure << blood pressure of human body

high blood pressure causes swollen face & headache problems.

due to no gravity orientation prob is also there

hence (b), (c) and (d) are likely to affict the astronaut.

- **In the following two exercises, choose the correct answer from among the given ones: The gravitational intensity at the centre of a hemispherical shell of uniform mass density has the direction indicated by the arrow (see figure) (i) a, (ii) b, (iii) c, (iv) 0.**

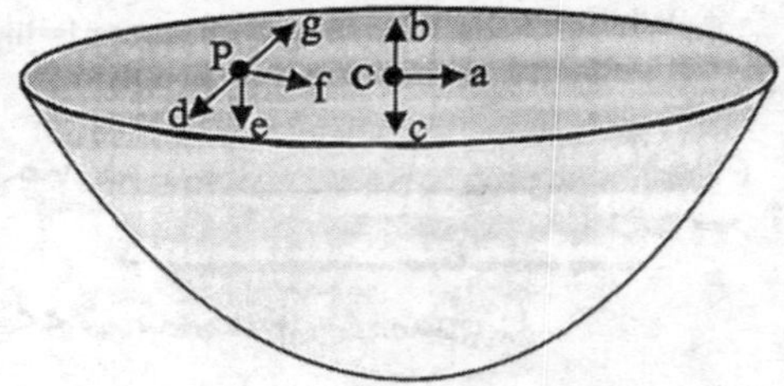

Sol^n: As we know inside a spherical shell grav field intensity is zero.

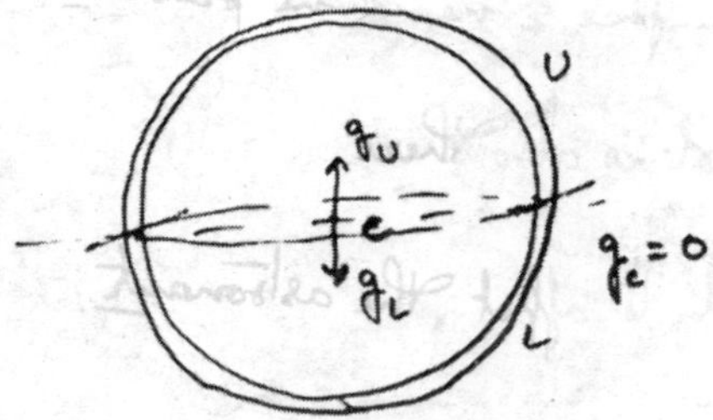

in figure at point c, direction of grav field intensity is along 'c' ↓.

$g_U = g_L$

- **For the above problem, the direction of the gravitational intensity at an arbitrary point *P* is indicated by the arrow (i) d, (ii) e, (iii) f, (iv) g.**

Sol^n: As g_{in} a spherical shell is zero as shown in figure.

g_{in} ↓ at every interior point

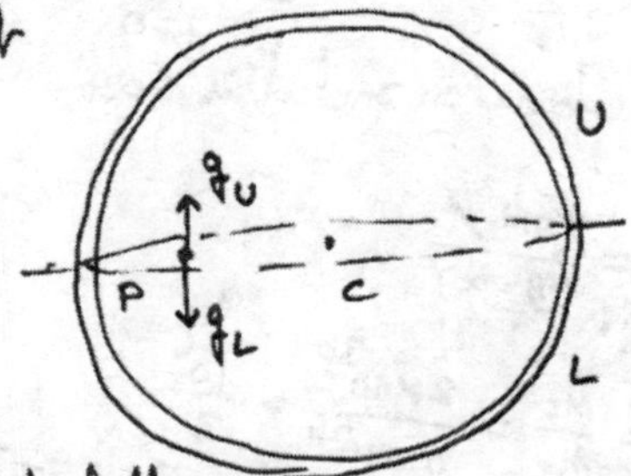

$g_P = 0$

As at P net grav field = 0

due to lower hemispherical shell $g_U = g_L$

⇒ field intensity must be in direction of 'e' ↓.

- **A rocket is fired from the earth towards the sun. At what distance from the earth's centre is the gravitational force on the rocket zero ? Mass of the sun = 2×10^{30} kg, mass of the earth = 6×10^{24} kg. Neglect the effect of other planets etc. (orbital radius = 1.5×10^{11} m).**

Solⁿ:

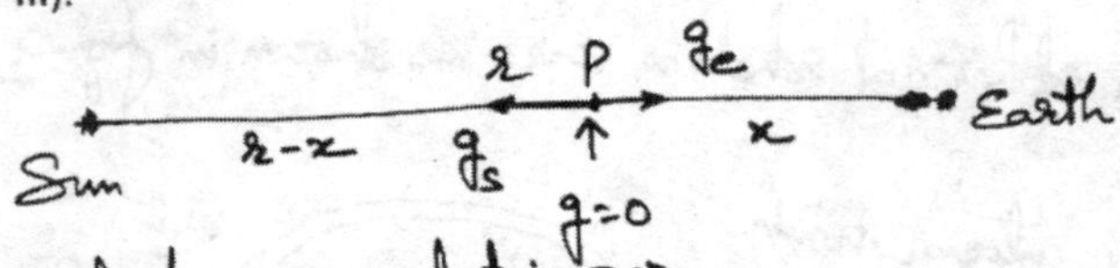

If at pt P the gravitational force on rocket is zero

$\Rightarrow$ we use $\dfrac{GM_e m}{x^2} = \dfrac{GM_s m}{(r-x)^2}$

$$\Rightarrow \left(\frac{r-x}{x}\right)^2 = \frac{M_s}{M_e} = \frac{2\times 10^{30}}{6\times 10^{24}} = \frac{10^6}{3}$$

$$\Rightarrow \frac{r}{x} - 1 = \frac{10^3}{\sqrt{3}} \times \frac{\sqrt{3}}{\sqrt{3}}$$

$$\Rightarrow \frac{r}{x} = \frac{1732}{3} + 1 \Rightarrow$$

$$\Rightarrow x = \frac{3}{1735} \times 1.5 \times 10^{11}\text{ m}$$

$$= 2.59 \times 10^{8}\text{ m} \simeq 2.6 \times 10^{8}\text{ m}$$

Ans.

- How will you 'weigh the sun', that is estimate its mass? The mean orbital radius of the earth around the sun is 1.5×10^8 km.

Sol^n: Using Kepler's III law for orbital motion of earth around Sun, we use

$$T^2 = \frac{4\pi^2}{GM_S} \cdot r^3$$

$$\Rightarrow \quad M_S = \frac{4\pi^2}{GT^2} \cdot r^3$$

$$= \frac{4 \times (3.14)^2 \times (1.5 \times 10^{11})^3}{6.67 \times 10^{-11} \times (365 \times 86400)^2}$$

$$\simeq 2 \times 10^{30} \text{ kg} \quad \underline{\text{Ans.}}$$

- A saturn year is 29.5 times the earth year. How far is the saturn from the sun if the earth is 1.50×10^8 km away from the sun ?

Sol. Using Kepler's III law for planetary motion, we have-

$$T^2 = \left(\frac{4\pi^2}{GM_s}\right) r^3$$

for Earth & Saturn, we use

$$\frac{T_e^2}{T_s^2} = \frac{r_e^3}{r_s^3}$$

$$\Rightarrow r_s^3 = r_e^3 \times \frac{T_s^2}{T_e^2} = (1.5 \times 10^8)^3 \times \left(\frac{29.5}{1}\right)^2$$

$$\Rightarrow r_s^3 = 2.937 \times 10^{27} \text{ Km.}$$

$$\Rightarrow r_s = 1.43 \times 10^9 \text{ km} = 1.43 \times 10^{12} \text{ m} \quad \text{Ans.}$$

Video Solution

- A body weighs 63 N on the surface of the earth. What is the gravitational force on it due to the earth at a height equal to half the radius of the earth ?

Solⁿ: On Earth surface $mg_s = 63N.$

At a height h above the Earth surce, value of g is given as-

$$g_h = \frac{g_s R_e^2}{(h+R_e)^2}$$

at $h = \frac{R_e}{2} \Rightarrow g_h = \frac{g_s R_e^2}{(3/2 R_e)^2} = \frac{4}{9} g_s$

grav force on the body at the given height is

$$mg_h = m\left(\frac{4}{9} g_s\right) = \frac{4}{9} mg_s = \frac{4}{9} \times 63 = 28N \text{ Ans.}$$

- **Assuming the earth to be a sphere of uniform mass density, how much would a body weigh half way down to the centre of the earth if it weighed 250 N on the surface ?**

Sol^n: On Surface of Earth $mg_s = 250\,N$

value of g at a depth h below the Earth Surface

$$g_h = g_s\left(1 - \frac{h}{R_e}\right)$$

at $h = \frac{R_e}{2}$ $\Rightarrow$ $g_h = g_s\left(1 - \frac{1}{2}\right) = g_s/2$

at half way down, weight of body is given as

$$W_{R_e/2} = mg_{R_e/2} = mg_s/2 = \frac{250}{2} = 125\,N \text{ Ans.}$$

Video Solution

- **A rocket is fired vertically with a speed of 5 km s^{-1} from the earth's surface. How far from the earth does the rocket go before returning to the earth ? Mass of the earth = 6.0 × 10^{24} kg; mean radius of the earth = 6.4 × 10^{6} m; G = 6.67 × 10^{-11} N m^{2} kg^{-2}.**

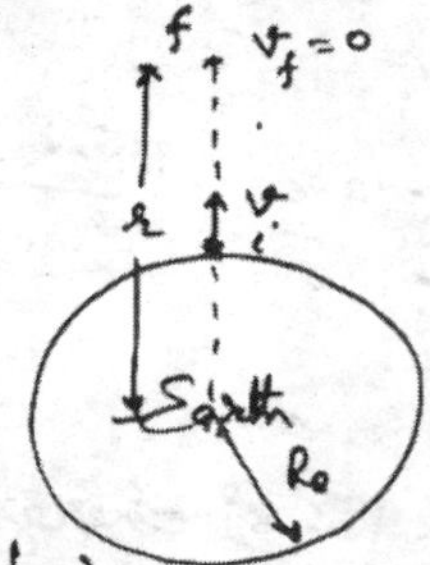

Sol^n: By Energy Conservation —

Initially on Surface of Earth

$$E_i = \frac{1}{2}mv^2 - \frac{GM_e m}{R_e}$$

Finally at a height (distant r from Earth's centre)

$$E_f = -\frac{GM_e m}{r}$$

we use $E_i = E_f$

$$\frac{1}{2}mv^2 - \frac{GM_e m}{R_e} = -\frac{GM_e m}{r}$$

$$\Rightarrow r = \frac{2GM_eR_e}{2GM_e - v^2R_e}$$

$$= \frac{2 \times 6.67 \times 10^{-11} \times 6.0 \times 10^{24} \times 6.4 \times 10^{6}}{(2 \times 6.67 \times 10^{-11} \times 6.0 \times 10^{24}) - (5 \times 10^{3})^2 . 6.4 \times 10^{6}}$$

$$= 7.99 \times 10^{6}\,m \sim 8 \times 10^{6}\,m \text{ Ans.}$$

- The escape speed of a projectile on the earth's surface is 11.2 km s^{-1}. A body is projected out with thrice this speed. What is the speed of the body far away from the earth? Ignore the presence of the sun and other planets.

Sol^n:

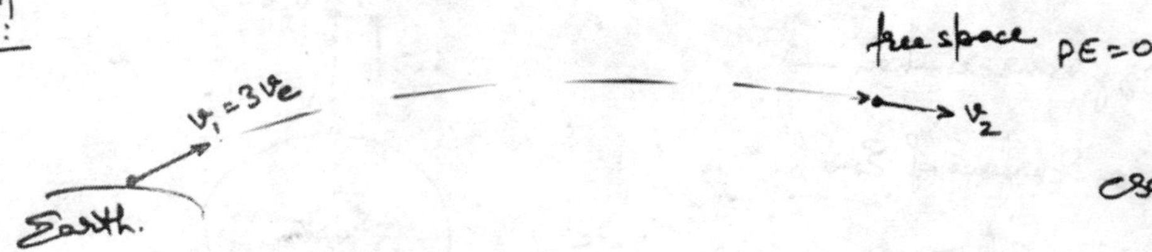

escape velocity is given as

$$\frac{1}{2}mv_e^2 = \frac{GM_em}{R_e}$$

By Conservation of energy

on Earth. far away from Earth.

$$\frac{1}{2}mv_1^2 - \frac{GM_em}{R_e} = \frac{1}{2}mv_2^2$$

$$v_1^2 - v_e^2 = v_2^2$$

$$(3v_e)^2 - v_e^2 = v_2^2$$

$$\rightarrow v_2 = \sqrt{8}\,v_e = 2\sqrt{2} \times 11.2 \text{ km/s}$$

$$= 31.68 \text{ km/s}$$

$$\simeq 31.7 \text{ km/s} \quad \text{Ans.}$$

Video Solution

- A satellite orbits the earth at a height of 400 km above the surface. How much energy must be expended to rocket the satellite out of the earth's gravitational influence? Mass of the satellite = 200 kg; mass of the earth = 6.0×10^{24} kg; radius of the earth = 6.4×10^{6} m; $G = 6.67 \times 10^{-11}$ N m^2 kg^{-2}.

Sol^n: When a satellite is orbiting earth in a radius r, its total energy is given as

$$E = -\frac{GM_e m}{2r}$$

$$r = R_e + h = 6.4\times10^6 + 0.4\times10^6 = 6.8\times10^6 \text{ m}$$

To escape the satellite from earth's grav. pull, its total energy must be increased to zero.

Energy to be supplied is $E_{ext} = \frac{GM_e m}{2r}$

$$= \frac{6.67\times10^{-11}\times6.0\times10^{24}\times200}{2\times6.8\times10^6}$$

$$= 5.9\times10^9 \text{ J} \quad \text{Ans.}$$

- **Two stars each of one solar mass (= 2×10^{30} kg) are approaching each other for a head on collision. When they are a distance 10^9 km, their speeds are negligible. What is the speed with which they collide ? The radius of each star is 10^4 km. Assume the stars to remain undistorted until they collide. (Use the known value of *G*).**

Sol^n:

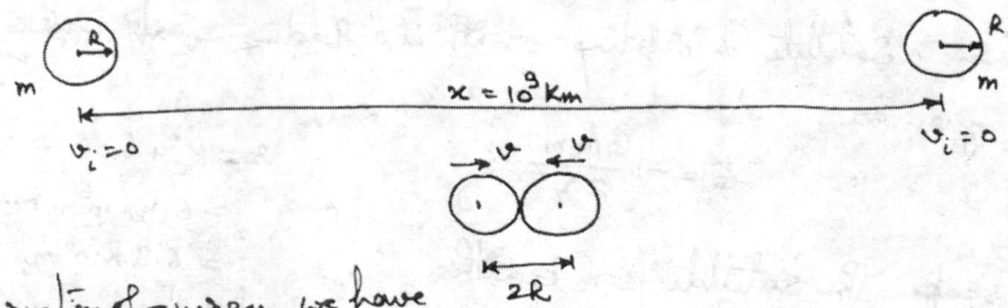

By Conservation of energy, we have

$$\underset{E_i}{-\frac{Gm^2}{r}} = \underset{E_f}{-\frac{Gm^2}{2R} + 2 \times \frac{1}{2} m v^2}$$

$$\Rightarrow \quad v^2 = Gm\left(\frac{1}{2R} - \frac{1}{r}\right) = 6.67 \times 10^{-11} \times 2 \times 10^{30}\left(\frac{1}{2 \times 10^7} - \frac{1}{10^{12}}\right)$$

$$v^2 = 6.67 \times 10^{12}$$

$$v = \sqrt{6.67 \times 10^{12}}$$

$$v = 2.6 \times 10^6 \text{ m/s}$$

Ans.

Video Solution

- Two heavy spheres each of mass 100 kg and radius 0.10 m are placed 1.0 m apart on a horizontal table. What is the gravitational force and potential at the mid point of the line joining the centres of the spheres ? Is an object placed at that point in equilibrium? If so, is the equilibrium stable or unstable ?

Sol^n:

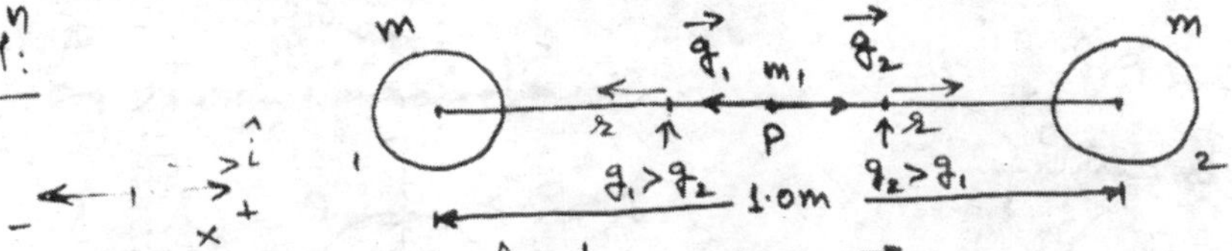

$m = 100\,kg$

$r = \frac{1}{2} = 0.5\,m$

At point P, grav field intensity $g_P = \vec{g}_1 + \vec{g}_2$

$$= \left(-\frac{Gm}{r^2}\right)\hat{i} + \left(\frac{Gm}{r^2}\right)\hat{i} = 0 \text{ Ans}$$

force at mid-point P is $m_1 g_P = 0$

Potential at point P due to spheres $V_P = V_1 + V_2 = \left(-\frac{Gm}{r}\right) + \left(-\frac{Gm}{r}\right) = -\frac{2Gm}{r}$

$$= -\frac{2 \times 6.67 \times 10^{-11} \times 100}{0.5} = -2.7 \times 10^{-8}\ J/kg$$

As $g_P = 0$, m_1 is in equilibrium → Here equilibrium is unstable as in either dir grav potential is [illegible]. Ans.

Web Reference at www.physicsgalaxy.com

Video Sol. : Class 11th NCERT Solutions | **Sec.** - Gravitation | **Topic** - Gravitation

Theory Reference : Grade - 11 & 12 | **Sec.** - Gravitation | **Topic** - Gravitation Theory

Video Solution

- As you have learnt in the text, a geostationary satellite orbits the earth at a height of nearly 36,000 km from the surface of the earth. What is the potential due to earth's gravity at the site of this satellite ? (Take the potential energy at infinity to be zero). Mass of the earth = 6.0×10^{24} kg, radius = 6400 km.

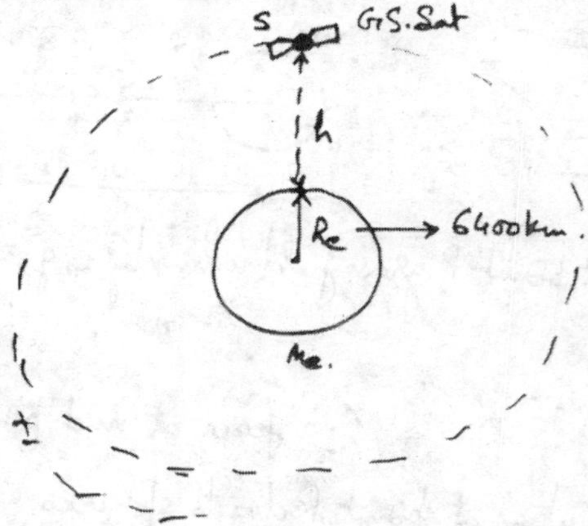

Solⁿ: Grav potential at the location S due to earth is

$$V = -\frac{GM_e}{(R_e+h)}$$

$$= -\frac{6.67\times10^{-11}\times6.0\times10^{24}}{(6400+36000)\times10^{3}}$$

$$= -9.43\times10^{6}\ J/kg \quad \text{Ans.}$$

- **A star 2.5 times the mass of the sun and collapsed to a size of 12 km rotates with a speed of 1.2 rev. per second. (Extremely compact stars of this kind are known as neutron stars. Certain stellar objects called pulsars belong to this category). Will an object placed on its equator remain stuck to its surface due to gravity ? (mass of the sun = 2×10^{30} kg).**

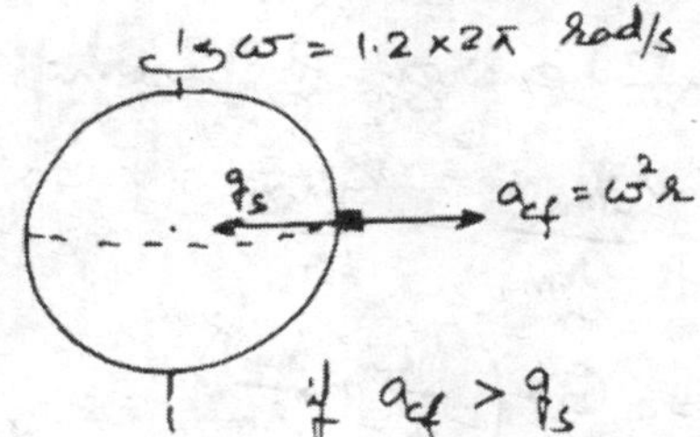

Solⁿ: gravity on surface at equator is

$$g_s = \frac{GM}{R^2} = \frac{6.67 \times 10^{-11} \times 2.5 \times 2 \times 10^{30}}{(12 \times 10^3)^2}$$

$$= 2.3 \times 10^{12} \text{ m/s}^2$$

if $a_{cf} > g_s$ the object will fly off.

Centrifugal accⁿ on equator at surface

$$a_{cf} = \omega^2 r = (1.2 \times 2 \times 3.14)^2 \times (12 \times 10^3)$$

$$\cong 1.1 \times 10^6 \text{ m/s}$$

$\Rightarrow a_{cf} < g_s$ so the object will remain stuck to the star.

- **A spaceship is stationed on Mars. How much energy must be expended on the spaceship to launch it out of the solar system ? Mass of the space ship = 1000 kg; mass of the sun = 2×10^{30} kg; mass of mars = 6.4×10^{23} kg; radius of mars = 3395 km; radius of the orbit of mars = 2.28×10^8 km; $G = 6.67 \times 10^{-11}$ N m^2 kg^{-2}.**

Solⁿ: Potential energy of spaceship in heliocentric refrence frame is given as –

$$PE = -\frac{GM_m m}{r_m} - \frac{GM_s m}{r}$$

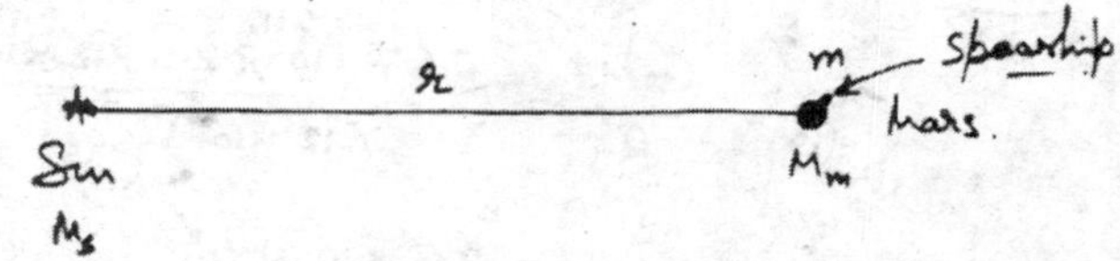

$$= -Gm\left(\frac{M_s}{r} + \frac{M_m}{r_m}\right)$$

Energy to be supplied to spaceship so that it will escape from solar system is given as

$$E_{ext} = |PE| = Gm\left(\frac{M_s}{r} + \frac{M_m}{r_m}\right) = 6.67 \times 10^{-11} \times 1000\left(\frac{2 \times 10^{30}}{2.28 \times 10^{11}} + \frac{6.4 \times 10^{23}}{3.395 \times 10^{6}}\right)$$

$$\simeq 3.1 \times 10^{11} \text{ J} \quad \text{Ans}$$

$\Rightarrow$ TE = 0

- A rocket is fired 'vertically' from the surface of mars with a speed of 2 km s^{-1}. If 20% of its initial energy is lost due to martian atmospheric resistance, how far will the rocket go from the surface of mars before returning to it ? Mass of mars = 6.4×10^{23} kg; radius of mars = 3395 km; G = 6.67×10^{-11} N m^2 kg^{-2}.

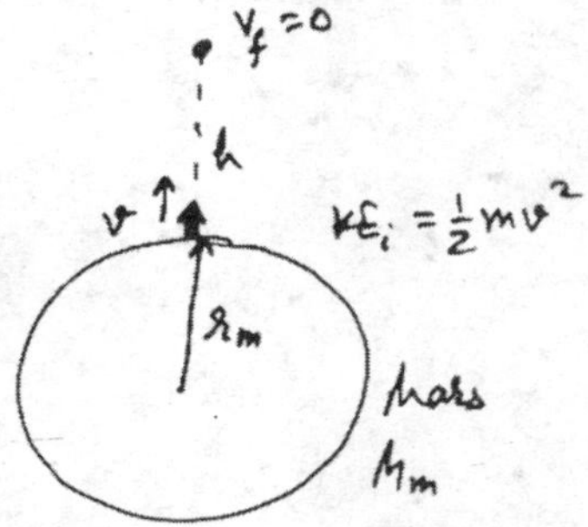

Sol^n: In the given situation using Conservation of energy, we have

E_i (on surface) E_f (at max height)

$$\frac{1}{2}mv^2 \times 0.8 - \frac{GM_m m}{r_m} = -\frac{GM_m m}{r_m + h}$$

$$\Rightarrow \quad r_m + h = \frac{5GM_m r_m}{5GM_m - 2v^2 r_m}$$

$$= \frac{5 \times 6.67 \times 10^{-11} \times 6.4 \times 10^{23} \times 3.395 \times 10^6}{5 \times 6.67 \times 10^{-11} \times 6.4 \times 10^{23} - 2(2 \times 10^3)^2 \times 3.395 \times 10^6} = 3.890 \times 10^6 \text{ m}$$

$$\Rightarrow \quad h = 3890 \text{ km} - 3395 \text{ km} = 495 \text{ km Ans.}$$

Chapter 9

Mechanical Properties of Solids

QR Code of Link to the Video Lectures
of Theory of this chapter Mechanical Properties of Solids
at 'Physics Galaxy' web portal

QR Code of Link to the NCERT textbook Video Solutions
of unsolved exercises at the end of each chapter in sequence
of this chapter at 'Physics Galaxy' web portal

- **A steel wire of length 4.7 m and cross-sectional area 3.0×10^{-5} m^2 stretches by the same amount as a copper wire of length 3.5 m and cross-sectional area of 4.0×10^{-5} m^2 under a given load. What is the ratio of the Young's modulus of steel to that of copper?**

Sol^n: Young's modulus of a wire is given as–

$$Y = \frac{\text{stress}}{\text{strain}} = \frac{F/A}{\Delta l/l} = \frac{Fl}{A\Delta l}$$

here for steel & Copper F & Δl are same

$$\Rightarrow \frac{Y_s}{Y_{cu}} = \frac{l_s \cdot A_{cu}}{l_{cu} \cdot A_s} = \frac{4.7 \times 4.0 \times 10^{-5}}{3.5 \times 3.0 \times 10^{-5}} = 1.8 \text{ Ans.}$$

- **Figure shows the strain-stress curve for a given material. What are (a) Young's modulus and (b) approximate yield strength for this material?**

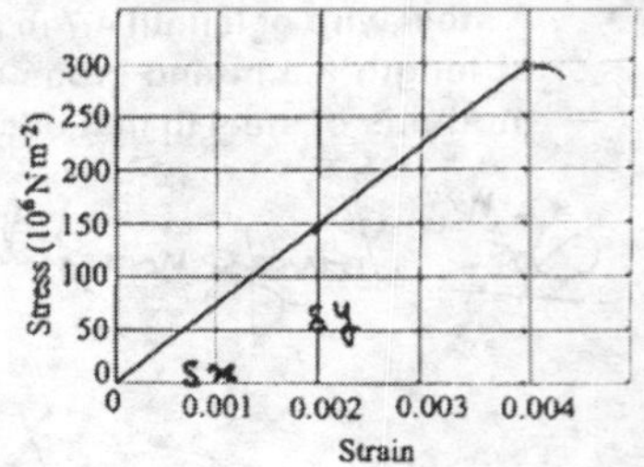

Sol. As we know

(a) Young's modulus $= \frac{\text{stress}}{\text{strain}} \rightarrow$ slope of strain-stress curve

$$= \frac{\delta y}{\delta x} = \frac{150 \times 10^6}{0.002} = 7.5 \times 10^{10}\ N/m^2 \text{ Ans.}$$

(b) Yield strength of material = Max stress which the material can sustain

$$\cong 300 \times 10^6\ N/m^2$$

$$= 3 \times 10^8\ N/m^2 \text{ Ans.}$$

- **The stress-strain graphs for materials *A* and *B* are shown in figure. The graphs are drawn to the same scale.**

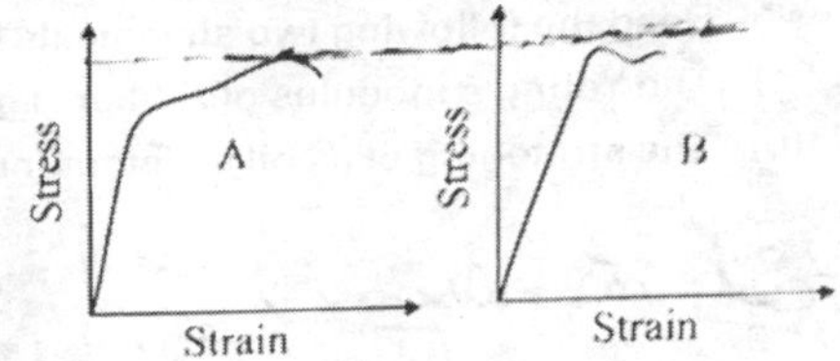

(a) **Which of the materials has the greater Young's modulus?**

(b) **Which of the two is the stronger material?**

Sol^n (a) In a strain-stress curve, Young's modulus is given as

$$Y = \text{slope of strain-stress curve}$$

from the above two graphs $\longrightarrow$ $(\text{slope of curve})_A > (\text{slope of curve})_B$

$$\Rightarrow Y_A > Y_B \quad \text{Ans}$$

(b) The material which can withstand to higher load will be stronger

strength of mat A > strength of mat. B Ans

- **Read the following two statements below carefully and state, with reasons, if it is true or false.**

(a) The Young's modulus of rubber is greater than that of steel;

(b) The stretching of a coil is determined by its shear modulus.

Sol^n: (a) False.

because for a given load (ext force) steel will get less deformed (low strain) compared to rubber

As $Y = \frac{\text{stress}}{\text{strain}}$ ⇒ for same stress if strain is low ⇒ Y is high.

$Y_{steel} > Y_{rubber}$

(b) True

because by applying an ext load (force) it changes the shape of coil not its length or volume ⇒ shape deformation is accounted by shear modulus.

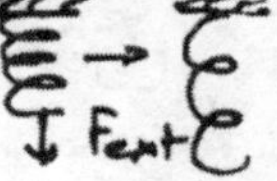

- **Two wires of diameter 0.25 cm, one made of steel and the other made of brass are loaded as shown in figure. The unloaded length of steel wire is 1.5 m and that of brass wire is 1.0 m. Compute the elongations of the steel and the brass wires.**

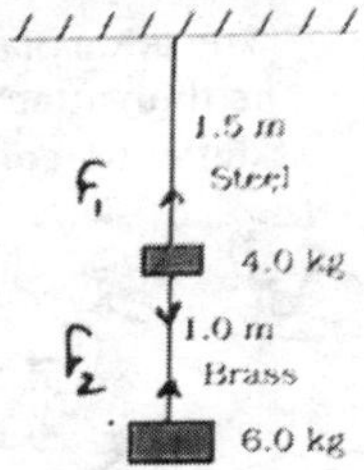

Solⁿ: tension in Steel wire $F_1 = (m_1 + m_2)g = 10 \times 9.8 = 98 N$

Tension in Brass wire $F_2 = m_2 g = 6.0 \times 9.8 = 58.8 N$

By the concept of Young's modulus we have $Y = \frac{Stress}{Strain} = \frac{F/A}{\Delta l / l}$

Elongation in steel wire $(A_s = \pi r^2)$ $\Delta l_s = \frac{F_1 l_1}{Y_s A_s} = \frac{98 \times 1.5}{2.0 \times 10^{11} \times 3.14 (1.25 \times 10^{-3})^2}$

$= 1.5 \times 10^{-4} m$ Ans

Elongation in brass wire $\Delta l_b = \frac{F_2 l_2}{Y_b A_b} = \frac{58.8 \times 1.0}{0.91 \times 10^{11} \times 3.14 (1.25 \times 10^{-3})^2}$

$= 1.3 \times 10^{-4} m$ Ans.

- The edge of an aluminium cube is 10 cm long. One face of the cube is firmly fixed to a vertical wall. A mass of 100 kg is then attached to the opposite face of the cube. The shear modulus of aluminium is 25 GPa. What is the vertical deflection of this face?

Sol^n: By definition of Shear modulus we have –

$$\eta = \frac{\text{Shear stress}}{\text{Shear strain}} = \frac{F/A}{\theta} = \frac{F/A}{x/l}$$

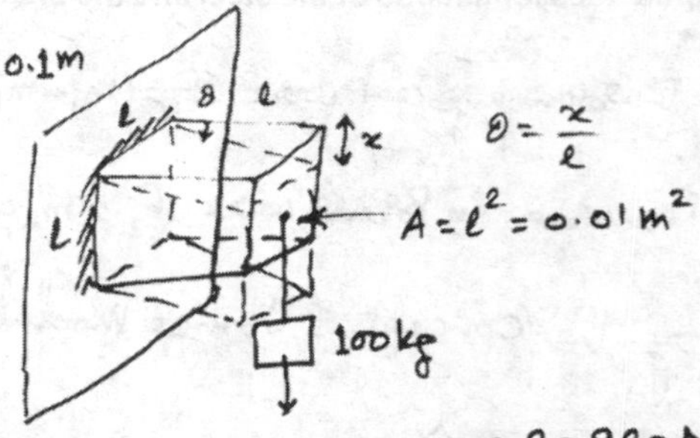

$W = mg = 100 \times 9.8 = 980\ N$

vertical displacement of face

$$x = \frac{Fl}{\eta A} = \frac{980 \times 0.1}{25 \times 10^9 \times 0.01}$$

$$= 3.92 \times 10^{-7}\ m \quad \underline{\text{Ans.}}$$

- **Four identical hollow cylindrical columns of mild steel support a big structure of mass 50,000 kg. The inner and outer radii of each column are 30 and 60 cm respectively. Assuming the load distribution to be uniform, calculate the compressional strain of each column.**

Solⁿ: Total weight supported by 4 Columns is $= mg = 50000 \times 9.8 = 4,90,000\,N.$

weight supported by each Column $= \dfrac{490000}{4} = 122500\,N$

Cross-sectional area of each column. $A = \pi(r_2^2 - r_1^2) = 3.14\left((0.6)^2 - (0.3)^2\right)$

$= 3.14(0.36 - 0.09)$

$= 3.14 \times 0.27\ m^2$

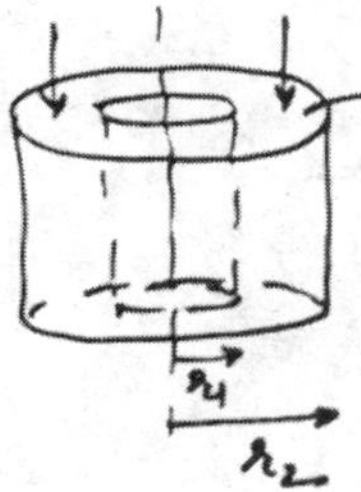

→ area $A = \pi r_2^2 - \pi r_1^2$

By Concept of Young's modulus, we use

$Y = \dfrac{Stress}{Strain} \Rightarrow Strain = \dfrac{Stress}{Y_{steel}} = \dfrac{F/A}{Y_s} = \dfrac{122500}{3.14 \times 0.27 \times 2 \times 10^{11}}$

$= 7.2 \times 10^{-7}$. Ans

- A piece of copper having a rectangular cross-section of 15.2 mm × 19.1 mm is pulled in tension with 44,500 N force, producing only elastic deformation. Calculate the resulting strain?

Solⁿ: The Young's modulus of Copper is given as-

$$Y_c = \frac{\text{Stress}}{\text{Strain}}$$

$$\Rightarrow \quad \text{Strain} = \frac{\text{Stress}}{Y_{cu}} = \frac{F/A}{Y_{cu}} = \frac{44500}{15.2 \times 19.1 \times 10^{-6} \times 1.2 \times 10^{11}}$$

$$= 127.7 \times 10^{-5} \text{ Ans.}$$

- A steel cable with a radius of 1.5 cm supports a chairlift at a ski area. If the maximum stress is not to exceed 10^8 N m^{-2}, what is the maximum load the cable can support ?

Sol^n:

$$\text{maximum stress} = \frac{\text{maximum force (tension)}}{\text{cross sectional area}}$$

$A = \pi r^2$

$$\Rightarrow \text{maximum force} = \text{Max Stress} \times \text{cross sectional area}$$

$$= 10^8 \times 3.14 \times (1.5 \times 10^{-2})^2$$

$$= 7.065 \times 10^4 \text{ N} \quad \text{Ans.}$$

- A rigid bar of mass 15 kg is supported symmetrically by three wires each 2.0 m long. Those at each end are of copper and the middle one is of iron. Determine the ratios of their diameters if each is to have the same tension.

Sol^n: tension in each wire is

$$F = \frac{15g}{3} = 5g$$

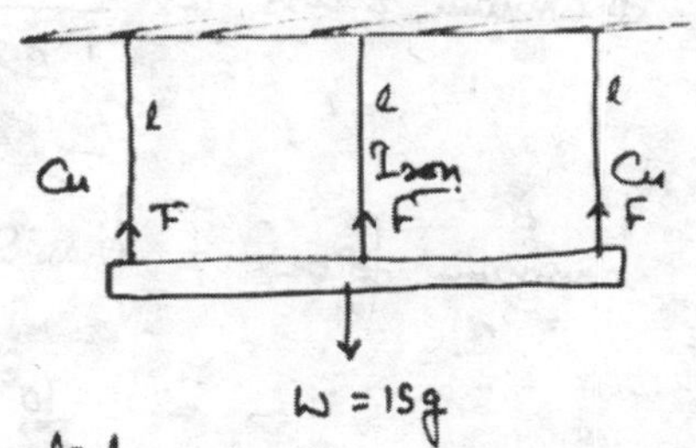

If we consider rod to be horizontal, strain in each wire must be same.

we use

$$Y = \frac{\text{Stress}}{\text{Strain}} = \frac{F/A}{\Delta l/l} \quad \left(A = \pi d^2/4\right) \Rightarrow Y\left(\frac{\pi d^2}{4}\right) = \text{Constant}$$

for Copper & iron wires, we have $Y_{Cu} \cdot d_{Cu}^2 = Y_{iron} \cdot d_{iron}^2$

$$\frac{d_{Cu}}{d_{iron}} = \sqrt{\frac{Y_{iron}}{Y_{Cu}}} = \sqrt{\frac{1.9 \times 10^{11}}{1.2 \times 10^{11}}} = 1.25 \text{ Ans.}$$

Video Solution

- A 14.5 kg mass, fastened to the end of a steel wire of unstretched length 1.0 m, is whirled in a vertical circle with an angular velocity of 2 rev/s at the bottom of the circle. The cross-sectional area of the wire is 0.065 cm^2. Calculate the elongation of the wire when the mass is at the lowest point of its path.

Solⁿ: Tension at lowest point

$$F = mg + m\omega^2 l$$

$$= 14.5 \times 9.8 + 14.5\,(4\pi)^2 \times 1.0$$

$$\simeq 2444.2\ N$$

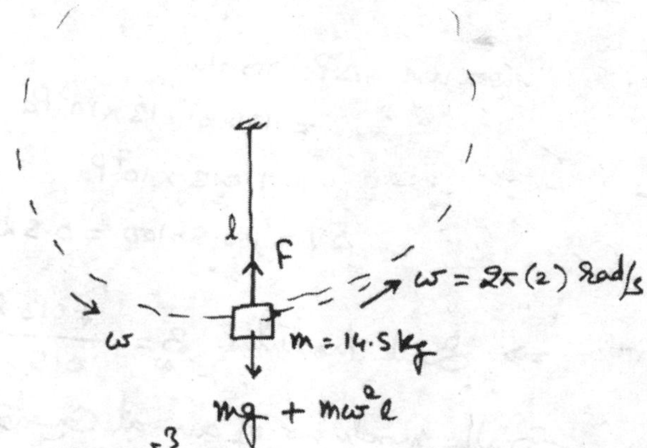

We use by Young's modulus

$$Y = \frac{\text{Stress}}{\text{Strain}} = \frac{F/A}{\Delta l/l}$$

$$\Rightarrow \quad \Delta l = \frac{Fl}{YA} = \frac{2444.2 \times 1.0}{2 \times 10^{11} \times 0.065 \times 10^{-4}} = 1.88 \times 10^{-3}\ m$$

$$= 1.88\ mm \text{ Ans.}$$

- Compute the bulk modulus of water from the following data: Initial volume = 100.0 litre, Pressure increase = 100.0 atm ($1\ atm = 1.013 \times 10^5$ Pa), Final volume = 100.5 litre. Compare the bulk modulus of water with that of air (at constant temperature). Explain in simple terms why the ratio is so large.

Solⁿ: Bulk modulus is given as $B = \left|\frac{\Delta P}{\Delta V/V}\right|$

we use $\Delta P = 100\ atm$

$= 100 \times 1.013 \times 10^5\ Pa$

$= 1.013 \times 10^7\ Pa$

$\Delta V = 100.5 - 100 = 0.5\ litre = 0.5 \times 10^{-3}\ m^3$

$\Rightarrow$ Bulk modulus $B_w = \frac{1.013 \times 10^7 \times 100 \times 10^{-3}}{0.5 \times 10^{-3}} = 2.026 \times 10^9\ Pa$ Ans.

Bulk modulus of air at constant temp is $B_{air} = 10^5\ Pa$.

$\Rightarrow \frac{B_w}{B_{air}} = 2.026 \times 10^4$ (v. high)

because gases/air is highly compressible than liq.

Web Reference at www.physicsgalaxy.com

Video Solution

Video Sol. : Class 11th NCERT Solutions | **Sec. -** Properties of Matter | **Topic -** Mechanical Properties of Solids

Theory Reference. : Grade - 11 & 12 | **Sec. -** Properties of matter | **Topic -** Elasticity

- What is the density of water at a depth where pressure is 80.0 atm, given that its density at the surface is 1.03×10^3 kg m^{-3}?

Sol^n: We consider a mass m of water of which if density at surface is ρ_0 and that at the given depth is ρ_d then we use

volume on surface $V_0 = \frac{m}{\rho_0}$

volume at the depth $V_d = \frac{m}{\rho_d}$

change in volume $\Delta V = V_0 - V_d = m\left(\frac{1}{\rho_0} - \frac{1}{\rho_d}\right)$

$\Rightarrow \Delta V = \frac{m}{\rho_0}\left(1 - \frac{\rho_0}{\rho_d}\right) = V_0\left(1 - \frac{\rho_0}{\rho_d}\right)$

fractional change in volume $\frac{\Delta V}{V_0} = 1 - \frac{\rho_0}{\rho_d}$

→ Bulk modulus of water –

$K = \left|\frac{\Delta P}{\Delta V / V}\right|$

$\Rightarrow K = 2.2 \times 10^9 = \frac{79 \times 1.013 \times 10^5}{1 - \rho_0/\rho_d}$

$\Rightarrow \rho_d = \frac{\rho_0}{1 - \frac{\Delta P}{K}}$

$= \frac{1.03 \times 10^3}{1 - \frac{79 \times 1.013 \times 10^5}{2.2 \times 10^9}} = 1.034 \times 10^3$ kg/m^3 Ans

- **Compute the fractional change in volume of a glass slab, when subjected to a hydraulic pressure of 10 atm.**

Solⁿ: By concept of Bulk modulus, we use

$$K = \left| \frac{\Delta P}{\Delta V/V} \right|$$

⇒ fractional change in volume $\frac{\Delta V}{V} = \left| \frac{\Delta P}{K} \right|$

Bulk modulus of glass $K = 37 \times 10^9$ Pa.

$$\Rightarrow \quad \frac{\Delta V}{V} = \frac{10 \times 1.013 \times 10^5}{37 \times 10^9} = 0.0000274 \text{ Ans.}$$

- **Determine the volume contraction of a solid copper cube, 10 cm on an edge, when subjected to a hydraulic pressure of 7.0×10^6 Pa.**

Sol^n: Bulk modulus is given as $K = \left|\frac{\Delta P}{\Delta V/V}\right|$

→ volume Contraction $\Delta V = \left|\frac{\Delta P V}{K}\right|$

$$= \frac{7 \times 10^6 \times (10 \times 10^{-2})^3}{140 \times 10^9}$$

$$= 5 \times 10^{-8}\ m^3 \text{ Ans}$$

- **How much should the pressure on a litre of water be changed to compress it by 0.10%?**

Sol^n: change in volume is $\Delta V = \frac{0.1}{100} V$

$\Rightarrow$ fractional volume change $\frac{\Delta V}{V} = 10^{-3}$

Bulk modulus of water $K = \left| \frac{\Delta P}{\Delta V/V} \right|$

$$\Rightarrow \quad \Delta P = K \left| \frac{\Delta V}{V} \right|$$

$$= 2.2 \times 10^{9} \times 10^{-3} = 2.2 \times 10^{6}\ N/m^2 \text{ Ans.}$$

- **Anvils made of single crystals of diamond, with the shape as shown in figure, are used to investigate behaviour of materials under very high pressures. Flat faces at the narrow end of the anvil have a diameter of 0.50 mm, and the wide ends are subjected to a compressional force of 50,000 N. What is the pressure at the tip of the anvil?**

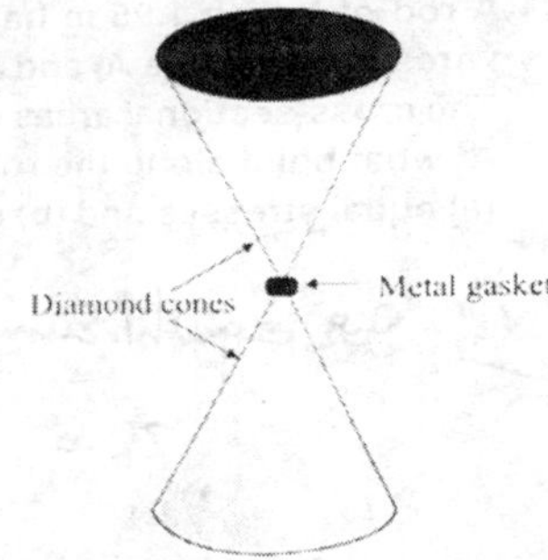

Sol^n: Compressional force $F = 50000\,N$

Area of flat face at narrow end $A = \frac{\pi d^2}{4}$

where diameter $d = 0.5 \times 10^{-3}\,m$

pressure at the tip is $p = \frac{F}{A} = \frac{50000 \times 4}{3.14 \times (0.5 \times 10^{-3})^2}$

$= 2.5 \times 10^{11}\,Pa$ Ans.

- A rod of length 1.05 m having negligible mass is supported at its ends by two wires of steel (wire A) and aluminium (wire B) of equal lengths as shown in figure. The cross-sectional areas of wires A and B are 1.0 mm^2 and 2.0 mm^2, respectively. At what point along the rod should a mass m be suspended in order to produce (a) equal stresses and (b) equal strains in both steel and aluminium wires.

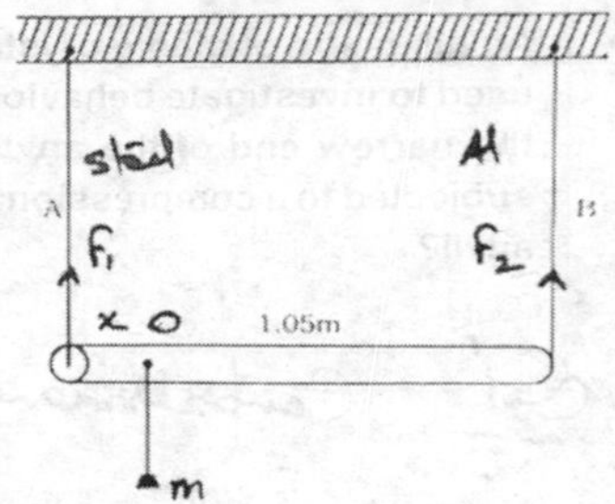

Solⁿ: For equilibrium of rod we use -

$$\tau_0 = F_1 x - F_2(1.05 - x) = 0 \Rightarrow \frac{F_1}{F_2} = \frac{1.05 - x}{x}$$

(a) To produce equal stress in the two wires

we use $\frac{F_1}{A_1} = \frac{F_2}{A_2}$

$$\frac{1.05 - x}{x} = \frac{1}{2}$$

$$\Rightarrow 2.1 - 2x = x \Rightarrow x = \frac{2.1}{3} = 0.7\text{ m Ans.}$$

(b) To produce equal strains in wires

$$\text{strain} = \text{stress}/Y = \frac{F}{AY}$$

$$\Rightarrow \frac{F_1}{A_1 Y_1} = \frac{F_2}{A_2 Y_2} \quad \text{for equal strains}$$

$$\Rightarrow \frac{1.05 - x}{x} = \frac{A_1 Y_1}{A_2 Y_2} = \frac{1}{2} \times \frac{2 \times 10^{11}}{7 \times 10^{10}}$$

on solving, we get $x = 0.43$ m Ans.

- A mild steel wire of length 1.0 m and cross-sectional area 0.50×10^{-2} cm^2 is stretched, well within its elastic limit, horizontally between two pillars. A mass of 100 g is suspended from the mid-point of the wire. Calculate the depression at the midpoint.

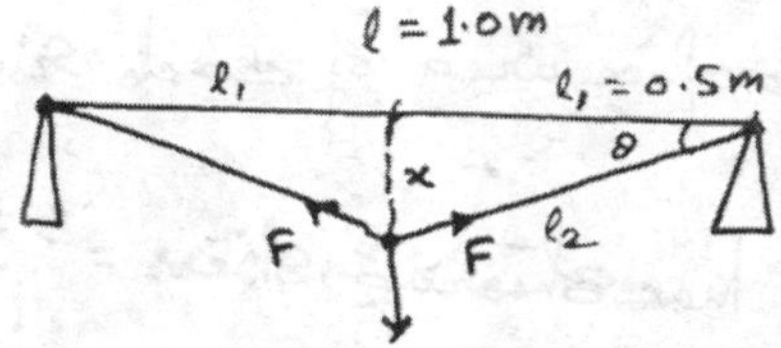

Sol^n: from figure we have

$$\theta = \frac{x}{l_1}$$

elongation in wire $\Delta l = l_2 - l_1$

$$\Delta l = \sqrt{x^2 + l_1^2} - l_1$$

$$\Delta l = l_1\left(1 + \frac{x^2}{l_1^2}\right)^{1/2} - l_1 = \frac{x_1^2}{2l_1}$$

$w = mg = 0.1 \times 9.8 = 0.98$ N

for equilibrium of wt, we use

$$w = 2F\sin\theta \simeq 2F\theta$$

$$\Rightarrow F = \frac{w}{2\theta} = \frac{wl_1}{2x}$$

By using Young's modulus, we have

$$Y = \frac{\text{Stress}}{\text{Strain}} = \frac{F/A}{\Delta l/l_1} = \frac{wl_1^2}{2xA\left(\frac{x_1^2}{2l_1}\right)}$$

$$\Rightarrow x = \sqrt[3]{\frac{wl_1^3}{YA}} = \left[\frac{0.98 \times (0.5)^3}{2\times10^{11} \times 0.5\times10^{-6}}\right]^{1/3} = 0.0107 \text{ m} \quad \text{Ans.}$$

- Two strips of metal are riveted together at their ends by four rivets, each of diameter 6.0 mm. What is the maximum tension that can be exerted by the riveted strip if the shearing stress on the rivet is not to exceed 6.9×10^7 Pa? Assume that each rivet is to carry one quarter of the load.

Sol^n: Surface area of each rivet $A = \frac{\pi d^2}{4}$

$$\text{Max shearing stress} = \frac{\text{Max shearing force}}{\text{area}}$$

If T is the total tension (max) exerted by strip, we use

$$6.9 \times 10^7 = \frac{T/4}{\pi d^2/4}$$

$$\Rightarrow \quad T_{max} = 6.9 \times 10^7 \times 3.14 \times (6 \times 10^{-3})^2$$

$$= 7.79 \times 10^3 \text{ N} \quad \text{Ans.}$$

Video Solution

- The Marina trench is located in the Pacific Ocean, and at one place it is nearly eleven km beneath the surface of water. The water pressure at the bottom of the trench is about 1.1×10^8 Pa. A steel ball of initial volume 0.32 m^3 is dropped into the ocean and falls to the bottom of the trench. What is the change in the volume of the ball when it reaches to the bottom?

Sol^n: we use Bulk modulus of steel -

$$K = \left| \frac{\Delta P}{\Delta V/V} \right|$$

$$\Rightarrow \quad \Delta V = \left| \frac{\Delta P V}{K} \right| = \frac{1.1 \times 10^8 \times 0.32}{1.6 \times 10^{11}}$$

$$= 2.2 \times 10^{-4} \ m^3 \ \text{Ans.}$$

Chapter 10

Mechanical Properties of Fluids

QR Code of Link to the Video Lectures of Theory of this chapter Mechanical Properties of Fluids at 'Physics Galaxy' web portal

QR Code of Link to the NCERT textbook Video Solutions of unsolved exercises at the end of each chapter in sequence of this chapter at 'Physics Galaxy' web portal

- **Explain why**

(a) **The blood pressure in humans is greater at the feet than at the brain**

(b) **Atmospheric pressure at a height of about 6 km decreases to nearly half of its value at the sea level, though the height of the atmosphere is more than 100 km**

(c) **Hydrostatic pressure is a scalar quantity even though pressure is force divided by area**

Soln (a) Pressure due to a liquid column is given as

$P = h\rho g$

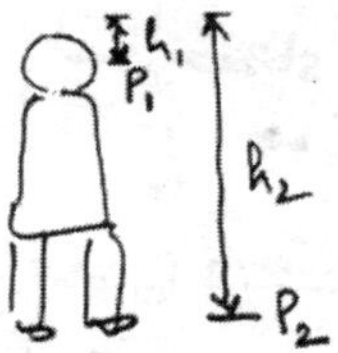

As $h_2 > h_1 \Rightarrow P_2 > P_1$.

(b)

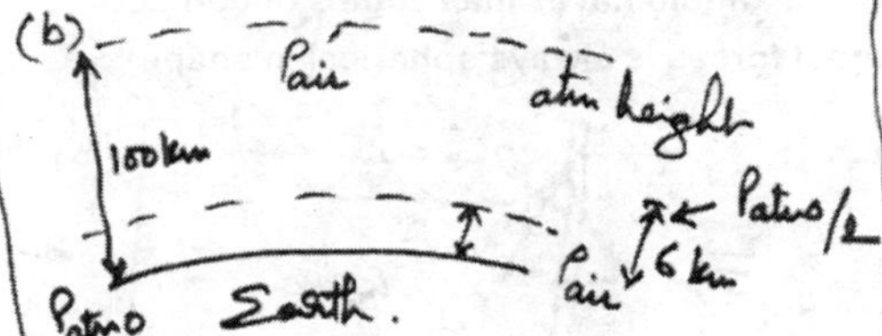

Due to gravity $\rho_{air} >> \rho'_{air}$

So because of high air density in lower altitude atm pressure changes rapidly with height.

(c) Force → vector

Pressure is distributed at a point in directions in a fluid body so there is no specific direction in which pressure acts (all direction) that's why it is a Scalar qty.

- Explain why

(a) The angle of contact of mercury with glass is obtuse, while that of water with glass is acute

(b) Water on a clean glass surface tends to spread out while mercury on the same surface tends to form drops. (Put differently, water wets glass while mercury does not.)

(c) Surface tension of a liquid is independent of the area of the surface

(d) Water with detergent disolved in it should have small angles of contact

(e) A drop of liquid under no external forces is always spherical in shape

Solⁿ (a)

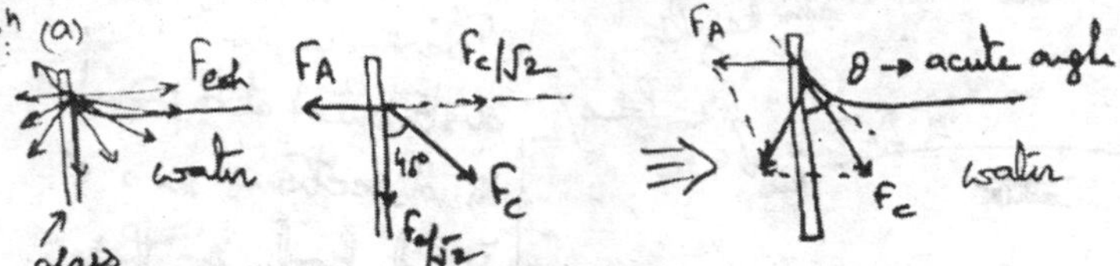

for glass water interface $F_A > F_c/\sqrt{2}$

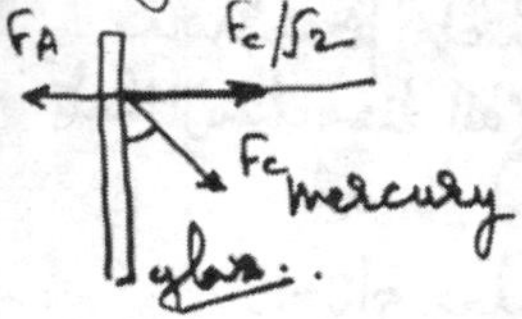

for mercury glass interface $F_c/\sqrt{2} > F_A$

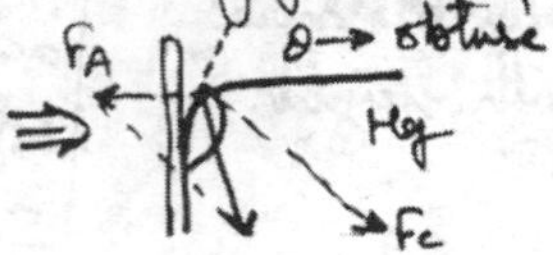

(b)

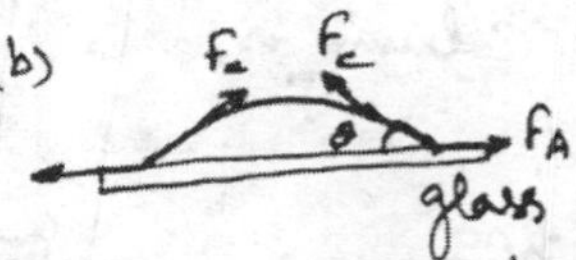

As $F_A > F_c \cos\theta$ in most cases water tends to spread out

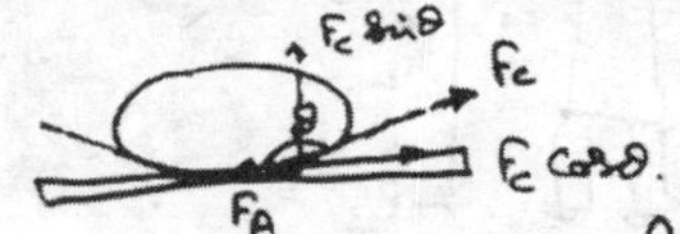

As F_c is more than F_A angle of contact is obtuse Hg will tend to confine in form of a drop.

Video Solution

(c) Surface tension is the force per unit length of any line considered on a liquid surface, normal to it.
$\Rightarrow$ it is independent of surface area.

(d) Capillary height is given as

$$h = \frac{2\sigma \cos\theta}{r\rho g}$$

If θ is small, h is large.
for the penetration of detergent in air capillaries in cloths/fabric will be more if θ is small.

(e) If no ext force is present, shape is only due to surface tension due to which a surface has a tendency to acquire minimum surface area
$\Rightarrow$ spherical drop.

- **Fill in the blanks using the word(s) from the list appended with each statement:**

(a) Surface tension of liquids generally . . . with temperatures (increases / decreases)

(b) Viscosity of gases . . . with temperature, whereas viscosity of liquids . . . with temperature (increases / decreases)

(c) For solids with elastic modulus of rigidity, the shearing force is proportional to . . . , while for fluids it is proportional to . . . (shear strain / rate of shear strain)

(d) For a fluid in a steady flow, the increase in flow speed at a constriction follows (conservation of mass / Bernoulli's principle)

(e) For the model of a plane in a wind tunnel, turbulence occurs at a ... speed for turbulence for an actual plane (greater / smaller)

Solⁿ (a) decreases.

(b) Increases, decreases.

(c) shear strain, rate of shear strain

(d) Conservation of mass.

(e) greater

Video Solution

- Explain why

(a) To keep a piece of paper horizontal, you should blow over, not under, it

(b) When we try to close a water tap with our fingers, fast jets of water gush through the openings between our fingers

(c) The size of the needle of a syringe controls flow rate better than the thumb pressure exerted by a doctor while administering an injection

(d) A fluid flowing out of a small hole in a vessel results in a backward thrust on the vessel

(e) A spinning cricket ball in air does not follow a parabolic trajectory

Sol^n (a)

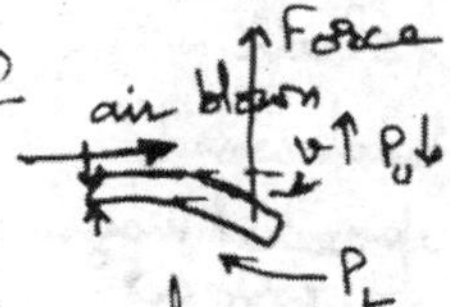

As we have

$$P + \frac{1}{2}\rho v^2 = \text{Constant}$$

due to air blown over the paper $P_U < P_L$

$\Rightarrow$ Force on paper will act upward.

(b)

because of Equation of Continuity, we have

$$A_1 v_1 = A_2 v_2$$

As $A_2 < A_1 \Rightarrow v_2 > v_1$

(c)

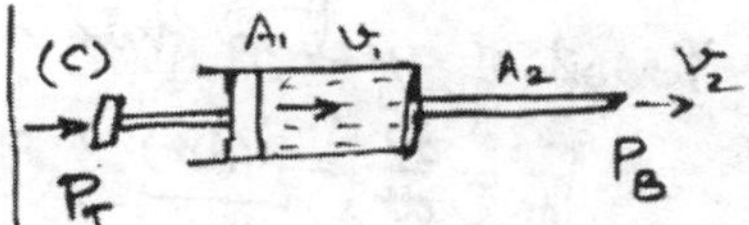

$\rightarrow A_1 v_1 = A_2 v_2$

Equation of Continuity

Bernoulli's Theorem

$\rightarrow P_T + \frac{1}{2} v_1^2 \rho = P_B + \frac{1}{2} v_2^2 \rho$

$A_1 >> A_2 \Rightarrow v_2 >> v_1$

(d)

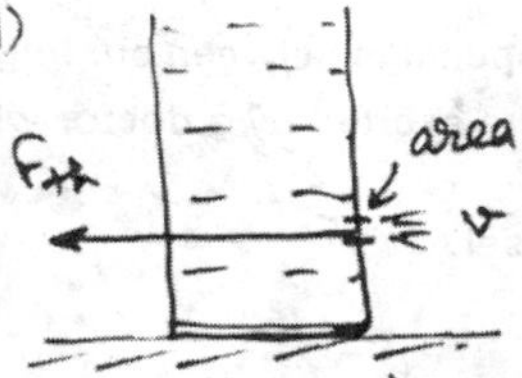

thrust of ejecting fluid is

$$F_{th} = \frac{dP}{dt} = \underbrace{\rho(Av)}_{\text{mass/sec}} \cdot v = \underline{\rho A v^2}.$$

by Conservation of momentum

(e) Thats due to Magnus Effect.

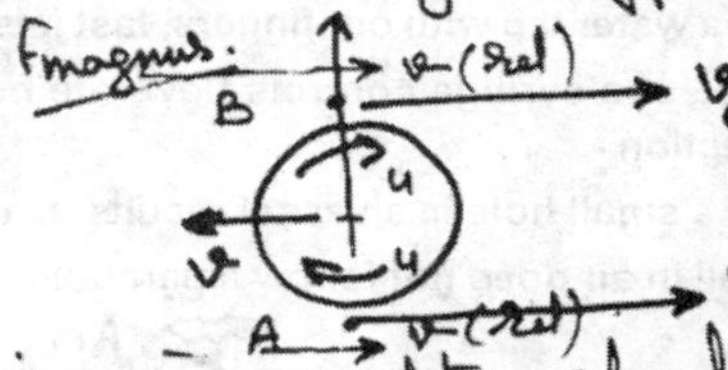

air still

relative speed of air w.r.to ball is backward.

$\underbrace{v_a'}_{\text{at A}} < \underbrace{v_a}_{\text{at B}} \Rightarrow P_A > P_B \Rightarrow$ upward magnus force will act.

Thus ball is not in freefall motion.

- A 50 kg girl wearing high heel shoes balances on a single heel. The heel is circular with a diameter 1.0 cm. What is the pressure exerted by the heel on the horizontal floor ?

Sol^n: Area of heel $A = \pi r^2$

Pressure exerted by heel on floor

$$P = \frac{F}{A} = \frac{mg}{A} = \frac{50 \times 9.8}{3.14 \times (0.5 \times 10^{-2})^2}$$

$$= 6.24 \times 10^6 \text{ Pa}$$ Ans.

- **Toricelli's barometer used mercury. Pascal duplicated it using French wine of density 984 kg m^{-3}. Determine the height of the wine column for normal atmospheric pressure.**

Sol^n: Atm pressure $P_{atm} = 1.013 \times 10^5$ Pa.

A column of height h using french wine creates a pressure

$$P_w = h\rho g = P_{atm}$$

$$h = \frac{P_{atm}}{\rho g} = \frac{1.013 \times 10^5}{984 \times 9.8}$$

$$= 10.5 \text{ m} \quad \text{Ans.}$$

- A vertical off-shore structure is built to withstand a maximum stress of 10^9 Pa. Is the structure suitable for putting up on top of an oil well in the ocean ? Take the depth of the ocean to be roughly 3 km, and ignore ocean currents.

Sol^n: Pressure exerted by water column in ocean is

$$P = h\rho g$$
$$= 3000 \times 1000 \times 9.8$$
$$= 2.94 \times 10^7 \text{ Pa}$$

here $2.94 \times 10^7 < 10^9$ Pa. (max stress) ⇒ This structure is suitable for putting up on top of the oil well in ocean.

- **A hydraulic automobile lift is designed to lift cars with a maximum mass of 3000 kg. The area of cross-section of the piston carrying the load is 425 cm². What maximum pressure would the smaller piston have to bear ?**

Solⁿ: In a hydraulic lift

pressure at smaller piston = pressure at bigger piston

$P_A = P_B$

$$P_A = \frac{mg}{S} = \frac{3000 \times 9.8}{425 \times 10^{-4}}$$

$$= 6.92 \times 10^{5}\ Pa$$

Ans.

- A U-tube contains water and methylated spirit separated by mercury. The mercury columns in the two arms are in level with 10.0 cm of water in one arm and 12.5 cm of spirit in the other. What is the specific gravity of spirit ?

Sol^n: At same level of Hg

$$P_A = P_B$$

$$h_1 \rho_1 g = h_2 \rho_2 g$$

$$\rho_2 = \frac{h_1 \rho_1}{h_2} = \frac{10 \times 1\ gm/cm^3}{12.5}$$

$$= 4/5 = 0.8\ gm/cm^3$$

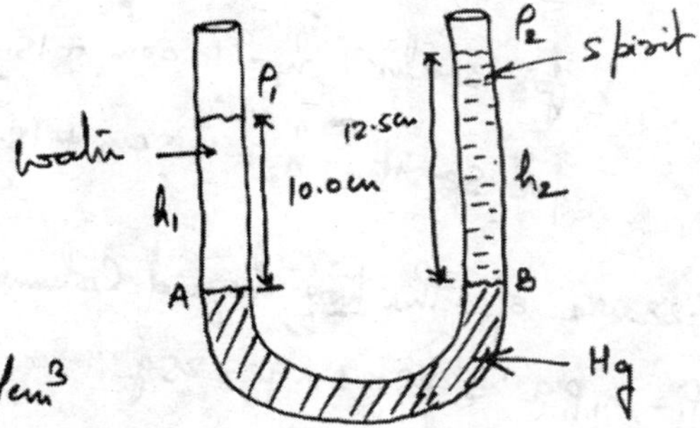

$$\text{sp. gravity of spirit} = \frac{\rho_2}{\rho_1} = 0.8 \text{ Ans.}$$

- In the previous problem, if 15.0 cm of water and spirit each are further poured into the respective arms of the tube, what is the difference in the levels of mercury in the two arms ? (Specific gravity of mercury = 13.6)

Sol^n: After pouring 15.0 cm of water & Spirit, final column heights are

for water $h_1 = 10.0\,cm + 15.0\,cm = 25\,cm.$

for spirit $h_2 = 12.5\,cm + 15.0\,cm = 27.5\,cm.$

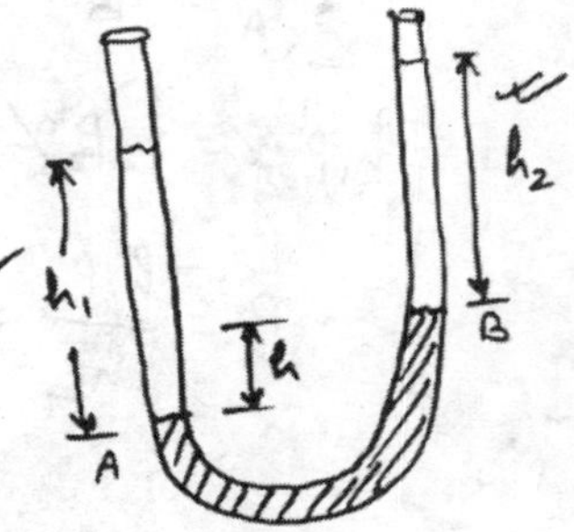

pressure of the two liquid columns are

$A \rightarrow P_1 = h_1 \rho_1 g = 25 \times 1 \times g = 25g$

$B \rightarrow P_2 = h_2 \rho_2 g = 27.5 \times 0.8 \times g = 22g$

for mercury we have $P_A - P_B = h \rho_{Hg} g \Rightarrow (25-22)g = h(13.6)g$

$\Rightarrow h = \frac{3}{13.6} = 0.2206\,cm$ Ans.

- **Can Bernoulli's equation be used to describe the flow of water through a rapid in a river ? Explain.**

Solⁿ:

As Bernoulli's Equation is only applicable for streamline flows of a fluid, in a rapidly flowing river due to turbulence it cannot be applied.

- Does it matter if one uses gauge instead of absolute pressures in applying Bernoulli's equation ? Explain.

Sol^n: If we calculate absolute pressure

$$P_a = P_g + P_{atm}$$

If the two pts where Bernoulli's equation is being used have same atm pressure the no effect if we use P_a or P_g as P_{atm} gets cancelled out in eq^n

If $P_{atm_1} \neq P_{atm_2}$ in case we are using Bernoulli's eq^n at pts 1 & 2 then we must use absolute pressures not gauge pressure.

Video Solution

- Glycerine flows steadily through a horizontal tube of length 1.5 m and radius 1.0 cm. If the amount of glycerine collected per second at one end is 4.0×10^{-3} kg s^{-1}, what is the pressure difference between the two ends of the tube ? (Density of glycerine = 1.3×10^3 kg m^{-3} and viscosity of glycerine = 0.83 Pa s). [You may also like to check if the assumption of laminar flow in the tube is correct].

Solⁿ: For the given tube using Poiseulli's equation we have

volume flow rate $Q = \frac{\pi r^4}{8\eta L} \cdot \Delta P$ here we use $Q = \frac{m}{\rho}$

$$\Rightarrow \Delta P = \frac{8\eta L}{\pi r^4} \cdot \left(\frac{m}{\rho}\right) = \frac{8 \times 0.83 \times 1.5}{3.14 \times (10^{-2})^4} \cdot \frac{4 \times 10^{-3}}{1.3 \times 10^3}$$

$$= 9.8 \times 10^2 \text{ Pa} \quad \text{Ans.}$$

for the flow of Glycerine Reynold's no is given as

$$R_N = \frac{\rho v D}{\eta} = \frac{\rho\left(\frac{Q}{A}\right) \cdot (2r)}{\eta}$$

$$= \frac{1.3 \times 10^3 \times \frac{4 \times 10^{-3}}{1.3 \times 10^3} \times 2}{3.14 \times 10^{-2} \times 0.83} = 0.307$$

As $R_N < 2000$ the flow remain laminar

- **In a test experiment on a model aeroplane in a wind tunnel, the flow speeds on the upper and lower surfaces of the wing are 70 m s^{-1} and 63 m s^{-1} respectively. What is the lift on the wing if its area is 2.5 m^2? Take the density of air to be 1.3 kg m^{-3}.**

Sol^n:

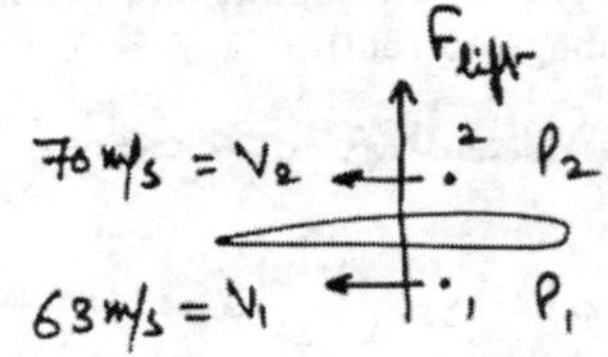

As $v_1 < v_2 \Rightarrow P_1 > P_2$

because wing Bernoulli's eq^n we have

$$P_1 + \frac{1}{2}\rho v_1^2 = P_2 + \frac{1}{2}\rho v_2^2$$

$$\Rightarrow P_1 - P_2 = \frac{1}{2}\rho(v_2^2 - v_1^2)$$

$$F_{lift} = (P_1 - P_2).A$$

$$\Rightarrow F_{lift} = \frac{1}{2}\rho(v_2^2 - v_1^2) \times A$$

$$= \frac{1}{2} \times 1.3 \times ((70)^2 - (63)^2) \times 2.5$$

$$= 1.51 \times 10^3 \text{ N}$$ Ans.

- Figures (a) and (b) refer to the steady flow of a (non-viscous) liquid. Which of the two figures is incorrect ? Why ?

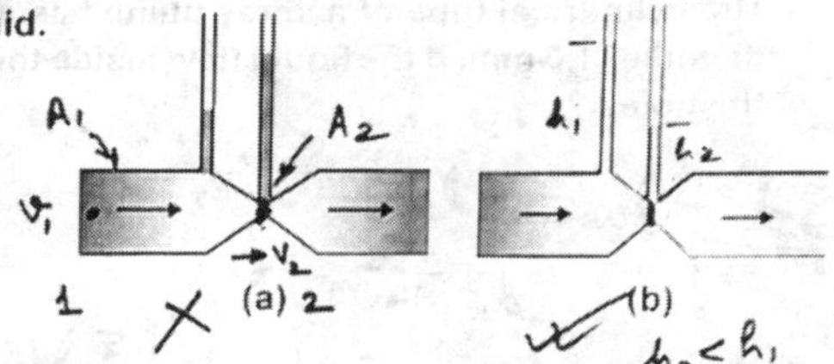

Sol^n: By Bernoulli's eq^n we have

at a given horizontal level. → $P + \frac{1}{2}\rho v^2 = \text{Constant}$

by continuity equation we have $v_1 A_1 = v_2 A_2$

At narrow cross-section we have $v_2 > v_1$ as $A_2 < A_1$

At points 1 & 2 we have $P_1 + \frac{1}{2}\rho v_1^2 = P_2 + \frac{1}{2}\rho v_2^2$

⇒ we use as $v_2 > v_1$ we get $P_2 < P_1$ ⇒ liquid in tube at narrow section (2) will raise to a lower level.

⇒ figure (a) is incorrect.

- The cylindrical tube of a spray pump has a cross-section of 8.0 cm² one end of which has 40 fine holes each of diameter 1.0 mm. If the liquid flow inside the tube is 1.5 m min⁻¹, what is the speed of ejection of the liquid through the holes ?

Solⁿ: Given data

$d = 10^{-3}\ m$

$v_1 = 1.5\ m/min = \frac{1.5}{60}\ m/s = 2.5\times10^{-2}\ m/s$

$A_2 = 40\left(\frac{\pi d^2}{4}\right)$

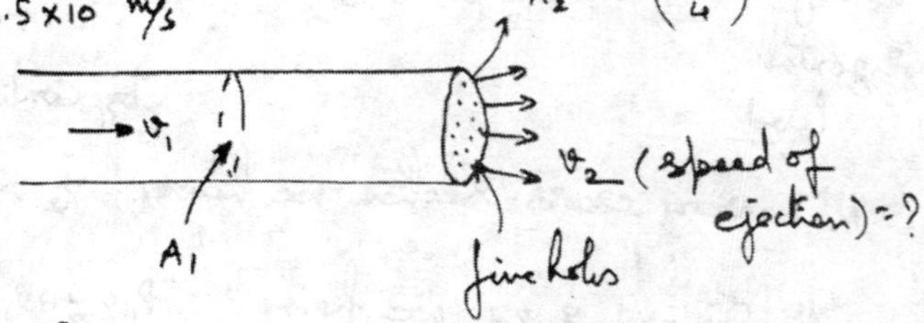

using equation of Continuity, we have

$A_1 v_1 = A_2 v_2$

$\Rightarrow v_2 = \frac{A_1 v_1}{A_2} = \frac{8\times10^{-4}\times2.5\times10^{-2}\times4}{40\times3.14\times(10^{-3})^2} = 0.64\ m/s$ Ans.

- **A U-shaped wire is dipped in a soap solution, and removed. The thin soap film formed between the wire and the light slider supports a weight of 1.5×10^{-2} N (which includes the small weight of the slider). The length of the slider is 30 cm. What is the surface tension of the film ?**

Sol^n: Due to two film surfaces in contact with the slider, the net upward force due to surface tension is given as

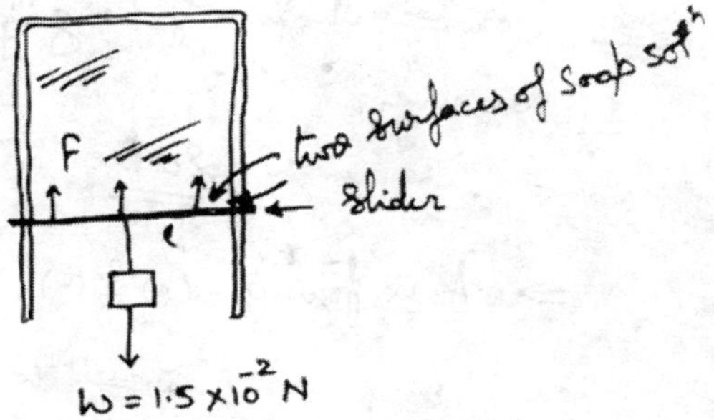

$$F = 2\sigma l$$

for equilibrium of weight, we use

$$2\sigma l = w$$

$$\Rightarrow \quad \sigma = \frac{w}{2l} = \frac{1.5 \times 10^{-2}}{2 \times 0.3} = 2.5 \times 10^{-2}\ \text{N/m} \quad \text{Ans.}$$

- Figure (a) shows a thin liquid film supporting a small weight = 4.5×10^{-2} N. What is the weight supported by a film of the same liquid at the same temperature in figure (b) and (c) ? Explain your answer physically.

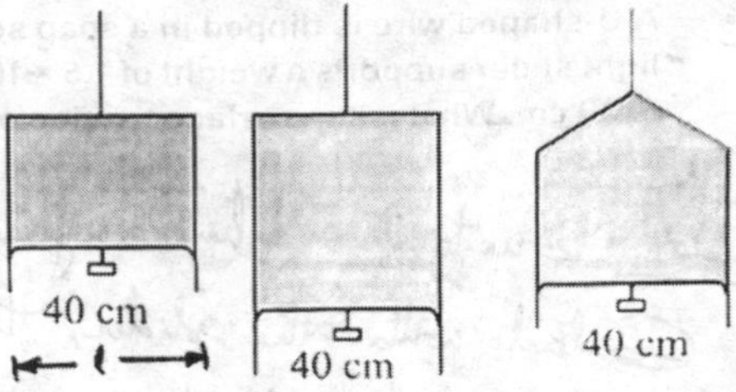

(a) (b) (c)

Sol. For equilibrium of hanging weight we use

$$w = 2\sigma l$$

⇒ As in figures - (b) & (c), l is same

⇒ weight supported in these two cases must remain same 4.5×10^{-2} N.

As σ is Constant (Same liquid at same temp.)

- What is the pressure inside the drop of mercury of radius 3.00 mm at room temperature ? Surface tension of mercury at that temperature (20 °C) is 4.65×10^{-1} N m^{-1}. The atmospheric pressure is 1.01×10^5 Pa. Also give the excess pressure inside the drop.

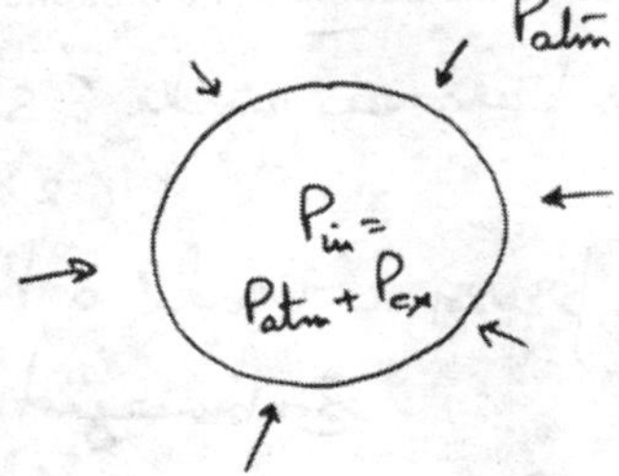

Sol^n: Excess pressure due to surface tension inside a liquid drop is

$$P_{ex} = \frac{2\sigma}{R} = \frac{2 \times 4.65 \times 10^{-1}}{3 \times 10^{-3}}$$

$$= 3.1 \times 10^{2} \text{ Pa} \quad \text{Ans.}$$

inside pressure is $P_{in} = P_{atm} + P_{ex}$

$$= 1.01 \times 10^5 + 3.1 \times 10^2$$

$$= 1.0131 \times 10^5 \text{ Pa} \quad \text{Ans.}$$

- **What is the excess pressure inside a bubble of soap solution of radius 5.00 mm, given that the surface tension of soap solution at the temperature (20 °C) is 2.50 × 10^{-2} N m^{-1} ? If an air bubble of the same dimension were formed at depth of 40.0 cm inside a container containing the soap solution (of relative density 1.20), what would be the pressure inside the bubble ? (1 atmospheric pressure is 1.01 × 10^{5})**

Sol^n: Excess pressure inside a soap bubble (2 surfaces) $P_{ex} = \frac{4\sigma}{R} = \frac{4 \times 2.5 \times 10^{-2}}{5 \times 10^{-3}} = 20\ Pa$ Ans

Excess pressure inside a bubble submerged in a solution (only 1 film surface inside) $P'_{ex} = \frac{2\sigma}{R} = \frac{2 \times 2.5 \times 10^{-2}}{5 \times 10^{-3}} = 10\ Pa.$

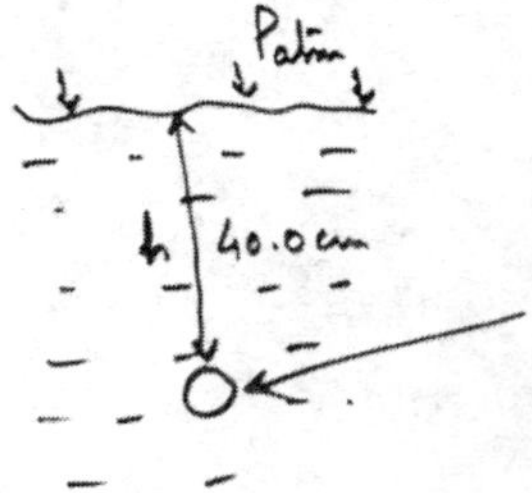

Total inside pressure in bubble is

$$P_{in} = P_{atm} + h\rho g + P'_{ex}$$

$$= 1.01 \times 10^{5} + 0.4 \times 1.2 \times 10^{3} \times 9.8 + 10$$

$$= 1.0571 \times 10^{5}\ Pa \simeq 1.06 \times 10^{5}\ Pa$$ Ans.

Video Solution

- A tank with a square base of area 1.0 m^2 is divided by a vertical partition in the middle. The bottom of the partition has a small-hinged door of area 20 cm^2. The tank is filled with water in one compartment, and an acid (of relative density 1.7) in the other, both to a height of 4.0 m. compute the force necessary to keep the door close.

Sol^n: The pressures on the two sides of hinged door are

$P_1 = h \rho_w g$

$= 4.0 \times 10^3 \times 9.8$

$= 39.2 \times 10^3$ Pa.

$P_2 = h \rho_A g$

$= 4.0 \times 1.7 \times 10^3 \times 9.8$

$= 66.64 \times 10^3$ Pa.

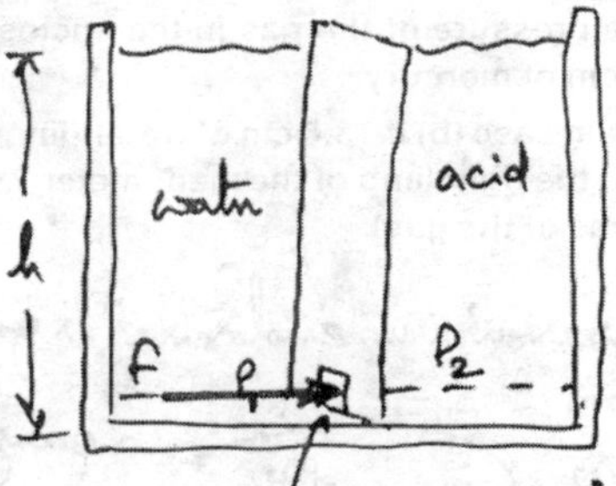

$P_2 > P_1$

To keep the door close, we need an external force from water side to balance the force due to excess pressure, so we have

$F_{ext} = (P_2 - P_1) \cdot A$

$= (66.64 - 39.2) \times 10^3 \times 20 \times 10^{-4}$

$\Rightarrow F_{ext} = 54.88$ N

~ 55 N Ans.

- A manometer reads the pressure of a gas in an enclosure as shown in figure (a) When a pump removes some of the gas, the manometer reads as in figure (b) The liquid used in the manometers is mercury and the atmospheric pressure is 76 cm of mercury.

(a) Give the absolute and gauge pressure of the gas in the enclosure for cases (a) and (b), in units of cm of mercury

(b) How would the levels change in case (b) if 13.6 cm of water (immiscible with mercury) are poured into the right limb of the manometer ? (Ignore the small change in the volume of the gas).

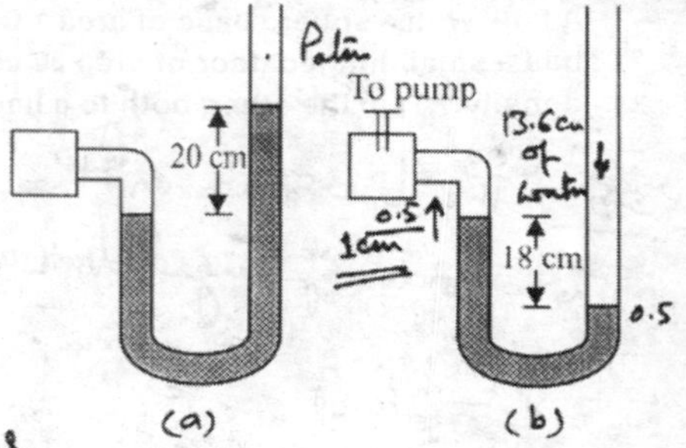

Solⁿ: (a) For case-(a) pressure in enclosure is given as

$$P_{encl} = P_{atm} + 20 \text{ cm of Hg} \rightarrow \text{gauge pressure}$$

$$= 76 + 20 = 96 \text{ cm of Hg Ans}$$

For case-(b) pressure is given as

$$P_{encl} = P_{atm} - 18 \text{ cm of Hg} = 76 - 18 = 58 \text{ cm of Hg Ans}$$

(b) 13.6 cm of water is equivalent to h cm of Hg

$\Rightarrow$ $13.6 \times 1 \times g = h \times 13.6 \times g$

$\Rightarrow$ $h = 1$ cm of Hg.

final level diff will be 19 cm of Hg Ans.

Video Solution

- Two vessels have the same base area but different shapes. The first vessel takes twice the volume of water that the second vessel requires to fill upto a particular common height. Is the force exerted by the water on the base of the vessel the same in the two cases ? If so, why do the vessels filled with water to that same height give different readings on a weighing scale ?

Solⁿ:

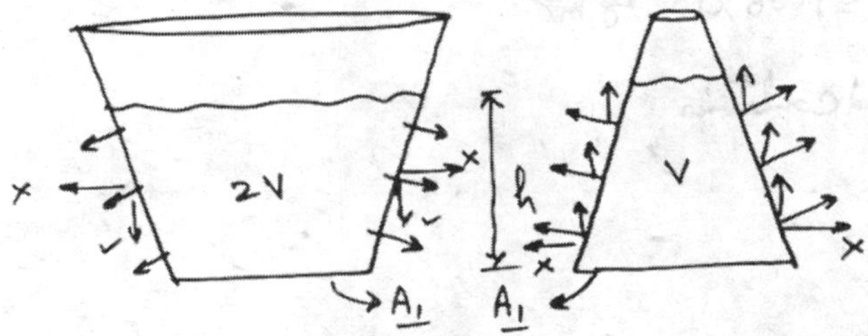

Pressure at bottom of both vessels is $P = P_{atm} + h\rho g$.

As both base have same area, equal pressure exert equal force on the two bases.

Due to vertical components of the force exerted by water on side walls of vessel, the net weight measured by a weighing scale is diff in the two cases.

- During blood transfusion the needle is inserted in a vein where the gauge pressure is 2000 Pa. At what height must the blood container be placed so that blood may just enter the vein ? [Use the density of whole blood from Table 10.1].

Solⁿ: density of blood $\rho_B = 1.06 \times 10^3\ kg/m^3$

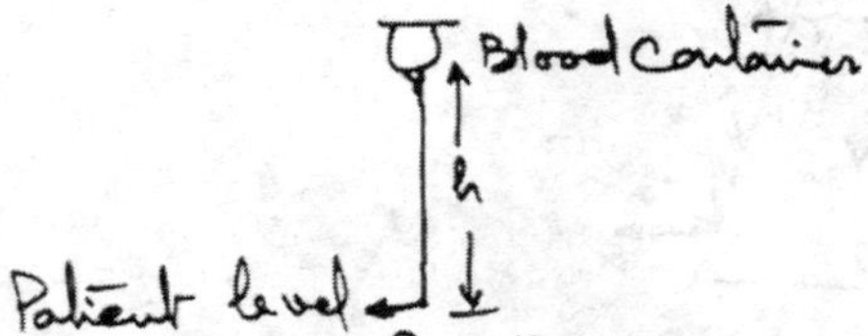

$P_{B\,vein} < P_{B\,needle}$

$\downarrow$

$2000\,Pa < h\rho_B g$

$$\Rightarrow \quad h > \frac{2000}{1.06 \times 10^3 \times 9.8} = 0.2\,m \quad Ans.$$

- In deriving Bernoulli's equation, we equated the work done on the fluid in the tube to its change in the potential and kinetic energy.

(a) How does the pressure change as the fluid moves along the tube, if dissipative forces are present ?

(b) Do the dissipative forces become more important as the fluid velocity increases ? Discuss qualitatively.

Sol^n(a) Due to dissipative forces energy is lost as fluid flows.

if fluid is incompressible its KE depends upon the cross-sectional area of tube as $A\underline{v} = \text{Constant}$ & PE depends upon the height of tube at diff pts.

$\Rightarrow$ the energy loss causes lowering in fluid pressure.

(b) In a viscous fluid the drag force is given as

$F = -\eta A \frac{dv}{dx}$ $\Rightarrow$ for a given level if $v \uparrow$ then $\frac{dv}{dx} \uparrow$ then it causes more viscous force

hence at higher speeds viscous drag becomes more important.

- (a) What is the largest average velocity of blood flow in an artery of radius 2×10^{-3} m if the flow must remain lanimar?

  (b) What is the corresponding flow rate ? (Take viscosity of blood to be 2.084×10^{-3} Pa s).

Sol^n(a) For laminar flow Reynolds no must be kept at or less than 2000.

we have

$$N_R = \frac{\rho v_c D}{\eta}$$

$$\Rightarrow \text{Critical speed } v_c = \frac{N_R \cdot \eta}{\rho D} = \frac{2000 \times 2.084 \times 10^{-3}}{1.06 \times 10^3 \times 4 \times 10^{-3}} = 0.983 \text{ m/s. Ans.}$$

(b) Blood flow rate is given as-

$$Q = A \cdot v = \pi r^2 \cdot v = 3.14 \times (2 \times 10^{-3})^2 \times 0.983$$

$$= 1.24 \times 10^{-5} \text{ m}^3/\text{s Ans.}$$

Video Solution

- A plane is in level flight at constant speed and each of its two wings has an area of 25 m². If the speed of the air is 180 km/h over the lower wing and 234 km/h over the upper wing surface, determine the plane's mass. (Take air density to be 1 kg m⁻³).

Solⁿ:

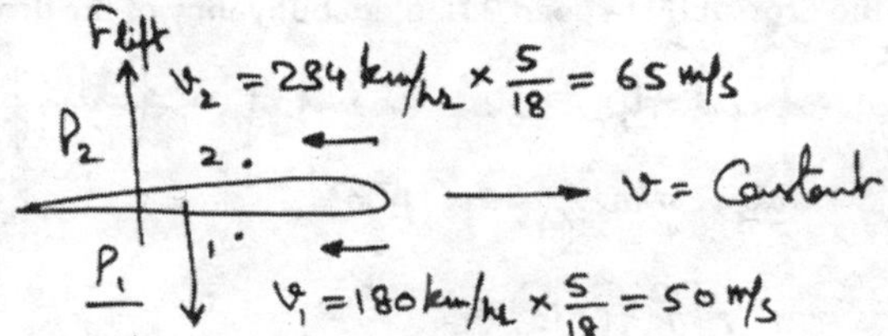

$v_2 = 234\ \text{km/hr} \times \frac{5}{18} = 65\ \text{m/s}$

$v_1 = 180\ \text{km/hr} \times \frac{5}{18} = 50\ \text{m/s}$

$W = (M_{Plane} \cdot g)$

By Bernoulli's eqⁿ we have

$$P_1 + \frac{1}{2}\rho v_1^2 = P_2 + \frac{1}{2}\rho v_2^2$$

$$\Rightarrow P_1 - P_2 = \frac{1}{2}\rho (v_2^2 - v_1^2)$$

$$= \frac{1}{2} \times 1 \times \left((65)^2 - (50)^2\right)$$

$$= 862.5\ \text{Pa.}$$

Net lift force on both wings of plane is

$$F_{lift} = (P_1 - P_2) \times A \times 2$$

$$= 862.5 \times 25 \times 2 = M_{Plane} \times g.$$

$$M_{Plane} = \frac{862.5 \times 25 \times 2}{9.8} = 4400\ \text{kg}$$

Ans.

Web Reference at www.physicsgalaxy.com

Video Sol. : Class 11th NCERT Solutions | **Sec. -** Properties of Matter | **Topic -** Mechanical Properties of Fluids

Theory Reference. : Grade - 11 & 12 | **Sec. -** Properties of matter | **Topic -** Fluid Dynamics

Video Solution

- In Millikan's oil drop experiment, what is the terminal speed of an uncharged drop of radius 2.0×10^{-5} m and density 1.2×10^3 kg m^{-3}. Take the viscosity of air at the temperature of the experiment to be 1.8×10^{-5} Pa s. How much is the viscous force on the drop at that speed ? Neglect buoyancy of the drop due to air.

Sol^n: At terminal speed the final speed of a falling spherical object (drop) in a viscous medium is given as

$$v_T = \frac{2}{9}\left(\frac{r^2(\rho-\rho_0)g}{\eta}\right)$$

$$= \frac{2}{9}\,\frac{(2\times10^{-5})^2(1.2\times10^{3}-0)\times 9.8}{1.8\times10^{-5}} = 5.8\times10^{-2}\ \text{m/s}\ \text{Ans.}$$

At terminal speed, viscous force is given as-

$$F_v = 6\pi\eta r v \quad [\text{Stoke's Rule}]$$

$$= 6\times3.14\times1.8\times10^{-5}\times2\times10^{-5}\times5.8\times10^{-2} = 3.9\times10^{-10}\ \text{N}$$

Ans.

- **Mercury has an angle of contact equal to 140° with soda lime glass. A narrow tube of radius 1.00 *mm* made of this glass is dipped in a trough containing mercury. By what amount does the mercury dip down in the tube relative to the liquid surface outside ? Surface tension of mercury at the temperature of the experiment is 0.465 N m^{-1}. Density of mercury = 13.6×10^3 kg m^{-3}.**

Sol^n: By capillary action the height of liquid fall in capillary tube is given as —

$$h = \frac{2\sigma \cos\theta}{r\rho g}$$

$$= \frac{2 \times 0.465 \times \cos(140^\circ)}{(10^{-3}) \times 13.6 \times 10^3 \times 9.8}$$

[$\cos(140^\circ) = -0.766$]

$$= -5.34 \times 10^{-3} \text{ m}$$

$$= -5.34 \text{ mm. Ans}$$

–ve sign shows the fall of liquid in the tube.

- Two narrow bores of diameters 3.0 mm and 6.0 mm are joined together to form a U-tube open at both ends. If the U-tube contains water, what is the difference in its levels in the two limbs of the tube ? Surface tension of water at the temperature of the experiment is 7.3×10^{-2} N m^{-1}. Take the angle of contact to be zero and density of water to be 1.0×10^{3} kg m^{-3} ($g = 9.8$ m s^{-2}).

Sol^n:

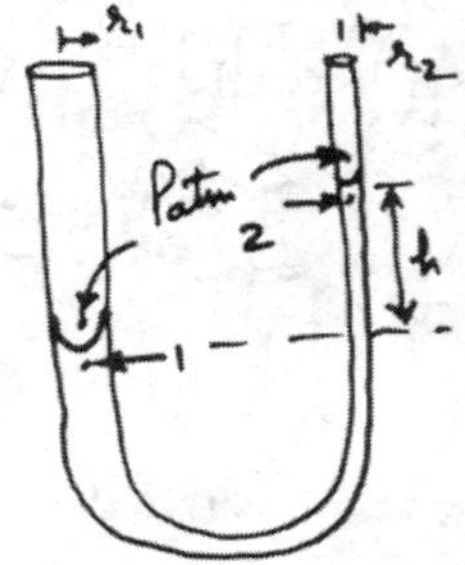

$r_1 = 6.0\,\text{mm}/2 = 3.0\,\text{mm}$

$r_2 = 3.0\,\text{mm}/2 = 1.5\,\text{mm}$

Pressures at pts 1 & 2 are given as-

$$P_1 = P_{atm} - \frac{2\sigma}{r_1}\Big|_{excess}$$

$$P_2 = P_{atm} - \frac{2\sigma}{r_2}\Big|_{excess}$$

for equilibrium of water in the U-tube we have

$$P_1 - P_2 = h\rho g$$

$$\Rightarrow 2\sigma\left(\frac{1}{r_2} - \frac{1}{r_1}\right) = h\rho g$$

$$h = \frac{2\sigma}{\rho g}\left(\frac{1}{r_2} - \frac{1}{r_1}\right)$$

$$= \frac{2 \times 7.3 \times 10^{-2}}{10^{3} \times 9.8}\left(\frac{1}{1.5 \times 10^{-3}} - \frac{1}{3.0 \times 10^{-3}}\right)$$

$$= 4.97 \times 10^{-3}\ \text{m}\ \textbf{Ans.}$$

- (a) It is known that density ρ of air decreases with height y as

  $\rho = \rho_0 e^{-y/y_0}$

  where $\rho_0 = 1.25\ kg\ m^{-3}$ is the density at sea level, and y_0 is a constant. This density variation is called the law of atmospheres. Obtain this law assuming that the temperature of atmosphere remains a constant (isothermal conditions). Also assume that the value of g remains constant.

  (b) A large He balloon of volume $1425\ m^3$ is used to lift a payload of 400 kg. Assume that the balloon maintains constant radius as it rises. How high does it rise ?

  [Take $y_0 = 8000$ m and $\rho_{He} = 0.18\ kg\ m^{-3}$].

Sol^n (a)

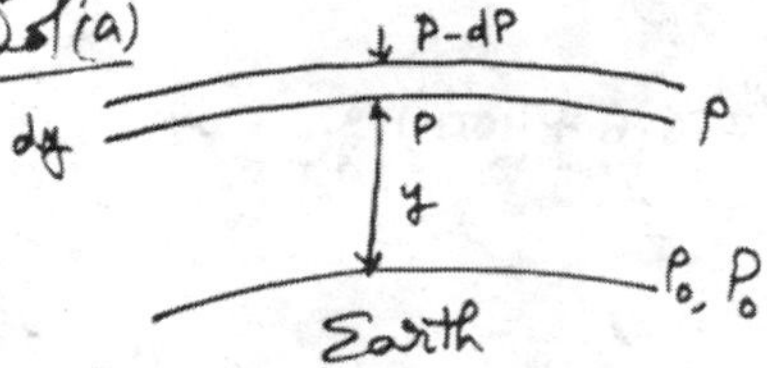

by gas law, we have $\rho = \frac{PM}{RT}$

in the small atm layer of width dy, we use

$$dP = -dy\,\rho g$$

$$\Rightarrow dP = -dy\left(\frac{PM}{RT}\right)\cdot g$$

$$\Rightarrow \int_{P_0}^{P}\frac{dP}{P} = -\frac{Mg}{RT}\int_0^y dy$$

$$\Rightarrow [\ln P]_{P_0}^{P} = -\frac{Mg}{RT}\cdot y$$

$$\ln\left(\frac{P}{P_0}\right) = -\frac{Mgy}{RT}$$

$$P = P_0 e^{-Mgy/RT}$$

$$P = P_0 e^{-y/y_0}$$

$\times\frac{M}{RT}$ $\times\frac{M}{RT}$ where $y_0 = \frac{RT}{Mg}$

$$\boxed{\rho = \rho_0 e^{-y/y_0}}$$

(b) $V = 1425\,m^3$

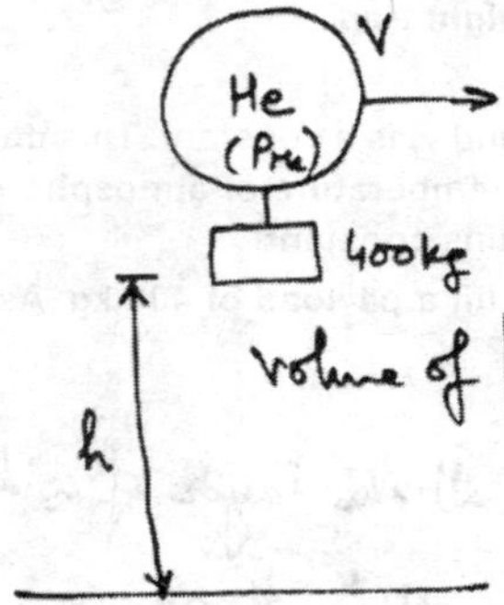

$$m = \rho_{He} \times V = 0.18 \times 1425 \text{ kg}$$
$$= 256.5 \text{ kg}$$

volume of payload is negligible

$$F_{Boyancy} = (256.6 + 400).g$$

At a height h we use

$$V.\rho_{air}\cancel{g} = 656.6\cancel{g}$$

$$1425 \times \rho_0 e^{-y/y_0} = 656.6$$

$$1425 \times 1.25\, e^{-y/8000} = 656.6$$

$$(2.71)^{-y/8000} = (2.71)^{-1} \Rightarrow y = 8000\,m = 8\,km$$

Ans.

Chapter 11

Thermal Properties of Matter

QR Code of Link to the Video Lectures
of Theory of this chapter Thermal Properties of Matter
at 'Physics Galaxy' web portal

QR Code of Link to the NCERT textbook Video Solutions
of unsolved exercises at the end of each chapter in sequence
of this chapter at 'Physics Galaxy' web portal

- The triple points of neon and carbon dioxide are 24.57 K and 216.55 K respectively. Express these temperatures on the Celsius and Fahrenheit scales.

Sol: On Celsius Scale we use $C = K - 273.15$

for neon we have $C_1 = 24.57 - 273.15 = -248.58°C$ Ans

for CO_2 we have $C_2 = 216.55 - 273.15 = -56.60°C$ Ans

On Fahrenheit Scale we use $\frac{F-32}{9} = \frac{K-273.15}{5}$

for neon, we have $F_1 = \frac{9}{5}(24.57 - 273.15) + 32 = -415.44°F$ Ans.

for CO_2, we have $F_2 = \frac{9}{5}(216.55 - 273.15) + 32 = -69.88°F$ Ans

- Two absolute scales *A* and *B* have triple points of water defined to be 200 *A* and 350 *B*. What is the relation between T_A and T_B?

Sol^n: Triple point of water

$$T = 200\,A = 350\,B = 273.15\,K.$$

Size of units for scales A & B are

$$A = \frac{273.15}{200}\,K \quad \& \quad B = \frac{273.15}{350}\,K$$

For a specific temperature if T_A & T_B are readings on scales A & B then in kelvin scale the values are

$$T_{A(K)} = T_A\left(\frac{273.15}{200}\,K\right) \quad \text{and} \quad T_{B(K)} = T_B\left(\frac{273.15}{350}\,K\right)$$

$$\text{As } T_{A(K)} = T_{B(K)} \Rightarrow \frac{T_A}{4} = \frac{T_B}{7} \Rightarrow \frac{T_A}{T_B} = \frac{4}{7} \text{ Ans.}$$

Video Solution

- The electrical resistance in ohms of a certain thermometer varies with temperature according to the approximate law :

$$R = R_0 [1 + \alpha(T - T_0)]$$

The resistance is 101.6 Ω at the triple-point of water 273.16 K, and 165.5 Ω at the normal melting point of lead (600.5 K). What is the temperature when the resistance is 123.4 Ω ?

Sol^n: We use at temperatures 273.16 K and 600.5 K, the resistances are related as –

$$165.5 = 101.6 [1 + \alpha (600.5 - 273.16)]$$

$$\Rightarrow \alpha = \frac{165.5 - 101.6}{101.6 \times 327.34} = \frac{63.9}{101.6 \times 327.34}$$

Again we use resistance 123.4 Ω at temp T′

$$\Rightarrow 123.4 = 101.6 \left[1 + \frac{63.9}{101.6 \times 327.34} (T' - 273.16)\right]$$

$$\Rightarrow T' = 384.83 \text{ K}$$ Ans.

- Answer the following :

(a) The triple-point of water is a standard fixed point in modern thermometry. Why ? What is wrong in taking the melting point of ice and the boiling point of water as standard fixed points (as was originally done in the Celsius scale) ?

(b) There were two fixed points in the original Celsius scale as mentioned above which were assigned the number 0°C and 100°C respectively. On the absolute scale, one of the fixed points is the triple-point of water, which on the Kelvin absolute scale is assigned the number 273.16 K. What is the other fixed point on this (Kelvin) scale ?

(c) The absolute temperature (Kelvin scale) T is related to the temperature t_c on the Celsius scale by

$$t_c = T - 273.15$$

Why do we have 273.15 in this relation, and not 273.16 ?

(d) What is the temperature of the triple-point of water on an absolute scale whose unit interval size is equal to that of the Fahrenheit scale ?

Sol(a) Because ice point & boiling point depend on pressure whereas triple pt of water is fixed

(b) On Kelvin Scale other fix point is absolute zero (0K)

(c) 273.16 is triple pt of water but in °C Scale we use ice pt which 0°C or 273.15K

Triple pt → 0.01°C.

(d) Triple pt of water on Kelvin Scale = 273.16K

no of div on K scale = 100

no of div on F scale = 180

Triple pt of water on an abs scale with 180 div.

$T = 273.16\left(\frac{180}{100}\right) = 491.69$ Ans.

- Two ideal gas thermometers *A* and *B* use oxygen and hydrogen respectively. The following observations are made:

Temperature	Pressure thermometer A	Pressure thermometer B
Triple-point of water	1.250×10^5 Pa	0.200×10^5 Pa
Normal melting point of sulphur	1.797×10^5 Pa	0.287×10^5 Pa

(a) What is the absolute temperature of normal melting point of sulphur as read by thermometers *A* and *B* ?

(b) What do you think is the reason behind the slight difference in answers of thermometers *A* and *B* ? (The thermometers are not faulty). What further procedure is needed in the experiment to reduce the discrepancy between the two readings ?

Sol^n (a) Triple pt of water = 273.16 K

for constant volume gas thermometers, we use

$$\frac{P_1}{T_1} = \frac{P_2}{T_2} \Rightarrow T_2 = \frac{P_2}{P_1} \cdot T_1$$

Reading of 'A':

$$T_2 = \frac{1.797 \times 10^5}{1.250 \times 10^5} \times 273.16$$

$$T_2 = 392.69 \text{ K Ans.}$$

again for thermometer B, we use

$$T_2 = \frac{P_2}{P_1} \cdot T_1 = \frac{0.287 \times 10^5}{0.200 \times 10^5} \times 273.16$$

$$= 391.98 \text{ K Ans.}$$

(b) Readings differ because gases are not ideal at these temp & pressures. To improve accuracy pressure should be lowered.

At v. low pressure gases behave ideally

- A steel tape 1m long is correctly calibrated for a temperature of 27.0 °C. The length of a steel rod measured by this tape is found to be 63.0 cm on a hot day when the temperature is 45.0 °C. What is the actual length of the steel rod on that day ? What is the length of the same steel rod on a day when the temperature is 27.0 °C ? Coefficient of linear expansion of steel = $1.20 \times 10^{-5}\,K^{-1}$.

Sol^n: length of 1 div on steel tape at 45°C is ← $L_f = L_i(1+\alpha\Delta T)$

$$l_{1div} = 1\,cm\,(1 + \alpha(18))$$

$$l_{1div} = 1\,(1 + 1.2\times10^{-5}\times18)$$

$$= 1.000216\,cm.$$

63 cm measured value (no of div) have correct length at 45°C is

$$l_{actual} = l_{meas} \times l_{1div} = 63.0 \times 1.000216\,cm$$

$$= 63.0136\,cm \text{ Ans.}$$

At calibration temp 27°C the actual length of rod will be 63.0 cm Ans.

- A large steel wheel is to be fitted on to a shaft of the same material. At 27 °C, the outer diameter of the shaft is 8.70 cm and the diameter of the central hole in the wheel is 8.69 cm. The shaft is cooled using 'dry ice'. At what temperature of the shaft does the wheel slip on the shaft? Assume coefficient of linear expansion of the steel to be constant over the required temperature range :
$\alpha_{steel} = 1.20 \times 10^{-5}\ K^{-1}$.

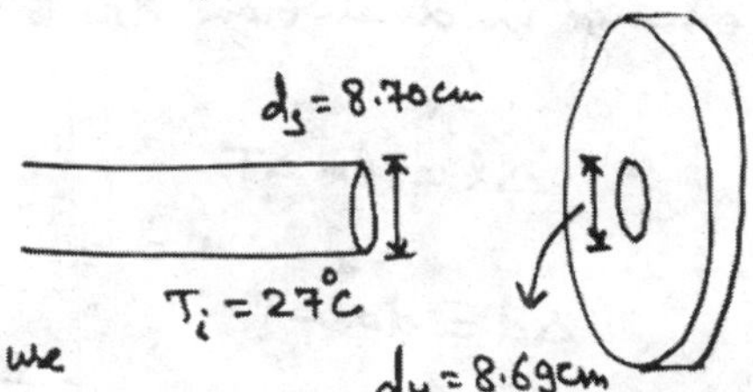

Sol:

By concept of linear expansion, we use

$$d_H = d_s(1 + \alpha \Delta T)$$

$$\Rightarrow 8.69 = 8.70(1 + 1.2 \times 10^{-5} \times \Delta T)$$

$$\Rightarrow \Delta T = -95.78\ K \text{ or } °C$$

→ final temp of the shaft will be

$$T_f = T_i - 95.78$$

$$= 27 - 95.78$$

$$= -68.78°C \approx -69°C$$

Ans.

- A hole is drilled in a copper sheet. The diameter of the hole is 4.24 cm at 27.0 °C. What is the change in the diameter of the hole when the sheet is heated to 227 °C? Coefficient of linear expansion of copper = $1.70 \times 10^{-5} K^{-1}$.

Sol^n: For a given object change in dimension due to heating is given as

$$\Delta l = l\alpha\Delta T$$

here we use $\Delta d = d\alpha\Delta T$

$$= 4.24 \times 1.70 \times 10^{-5} \times 200$$

$$= 1.44 \times 10^{-2}\ cm$$ Ans.

- A brass wire 1.8 m long at 27 °C is held taut with little tension between two rigid supports. If the wire is cooled to a temperature of –39 °C, what is the tension developed in the wire, if its diameter is 2.0 mm ? Co-efficient of linear expansion of brass = $2.0 \times 10^{-5}\,K^{-1}$; Young's modulus of brass = 0.91×10^{11} Pa.

Solⁿ: Young's Modulus is given as

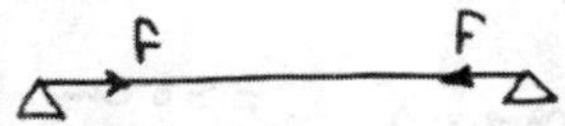

ΔT ↓

$$Y = \frac{\text{Stress}}{\text{Strain}} = \frac{F/A}{\Delta l/l} = \frac{F/A}{\alpha \Delta T}$$

length Contraction $\Delta l = \alpha l \Delta T$

$\Rightarrow$ tension $F = YA\alpha\Delta T$ (with $A = \pi d^2/4$)

$$= 0.91 \times 10^{11} \times \frac{3.14 \times (2 \times 10^{-3})^2}{4} \times 2 \times 10^{-5} \times (39 + 27)$$

$$= 3.77 \times 10^{2}\,N \simeq 3.8 \times 10^{2}\,N \quad \text{Ans.}$$

- A brass rod of length 50 cm and diameter 3.0 mm is joined to a steel rod of the same length and diameter. What is the change in length of the combined rod at 250 °C, if the original lengths are at 40.0 °C? Is there a 'thermal stress' developed at the junction ? The ends of the rod are free to expand (Co-efficient of linear expansion of brass = 2.0×10^{-5} K^{-1}, steel = 1.2×10^{-5} K^{-1}).

Solⁿ: Initial lengths $l_0 = 50$ cm each

final length of brass rod is $l_f = l_0(1+\alpha_b \Delta T)$

$= 50(1 + 2\times10^{-5} \times 210) = 50.21$ cm.

$\Delta l_{brass} = 50.21 - 50 = 0.21$ cm.

final length of steel rod is $l_f = l_0(1+\alpha_s \Delta T)$

$= 50(1 + 1.2\times10^{-5} \times 210) = 50.126$ cm.

$\Delta l_{steel} = 50.126 - 50 = 0.126$ cm.

Total change in length of Combined rod is $\Delta l_T = \Delta l_{brass} + \Delta l_{steel} = 0.21 + 0.126$

$= 0.336$ cm.

As ends are free ⇒ No stress is developed Ans

Video Solution

- The coefficient of volume expansion of glycerin is 49×10^{-5} K^{-1}. What is the fractional change in its density for a 30 °C rise in temperature ?

Sol^n: If initial volume of glycerin is V, final volume after ΔT rise in temp is given as -

$$V_f = V(1 + \gamma \Delta T)$$

fractional change in volume is

$$\frac{\Delta V}{V} = \frac{V_f - V}{V} = \gamma \Delta T = 49 \times 10^{-5} \times 30 = 0.0147$$

for a given mass, we have

$$m = \rho V$$

As m → Const

$$0 = \rho \Delta V + \Delta \rho V$$

fractional change in density ⇒ $$\frac{\Delta \rho}{\rho} = -\frac{\Delta V}{V} = -0.0147 \text{ Ans.}$$

(density is decreasing)

- A 10 kW drilling machine is used to drill a bore in a small aluminium block of mass 8.0 kg. How much is the rise in temperature of the block in 2.5 minutes, assuming 50% of power is used up in heating the machine itself or lost to the surroundings. Specific heat of aluminium = 0.91 J g^{-1} K^{-1}.

Sol: Amount of energy used in rising temperature of Al-block is

$$E_{abs} = 10{,}000\ J/s \times 2.5 \times 60\ \text{seconds} \times \frac{50}{100}$$

$$= 7.5 \times 10^5\ J$$

If temp rise is ΔT, we use

$$E_{abs} = ms\Delta T$$

$$\Rightarrow \Delta T = \frac{E_{abs}}{ms} = \frac{7.5 \times 10^5}{8 \times 0.91 \times 10^3} = 103°C \text{ Ans.}$$

Video Solution

- A copper block of mass 2.5 kg is heated in a furnace to a temperature of 500 °C and then placed on a large ice block. What is the maximum amount of ice that can melt? (Specific heat of copper = $0.39\ J\ g^{-1}\ K^{-1}$; heat of fusion of water = $335\ J\ g^{-1}$).

Sol^n: Maximum amount of heat which can be supplied by Cu-block is

$$\Delta Q = m s \Delta T$$

$$= 2.5 \times 0.39 \times 10^3 \times (500 - 0)$$

if m_i is the amount of ice melted by above heat, we use

$$\Delta Q = m_i . L_f$$

$$\Rightarrow \quad m_i = \frac{\Delta Q}{L_f} = \frac{2.5 \times 390 \times 500}{335 \times 10^3} = 1.455\ kg$$

$$\sim 1.5\ kg \text{ Ans.}$$

- In an experiment on the specific heat of a metal, a 0.20 kg block of the metal at 150 °C is dropped in a copper calorimeter (of water equivalent 0.025 kg) containing 150 cm³ of water at 27 °C. The final temperature is 40 °C. Compute the specific heat of the metal. If heat losses to the surroundings are not negligible, is your answer greater or smaller than the actual value for specific heat of the metal ?

Solⁿ:

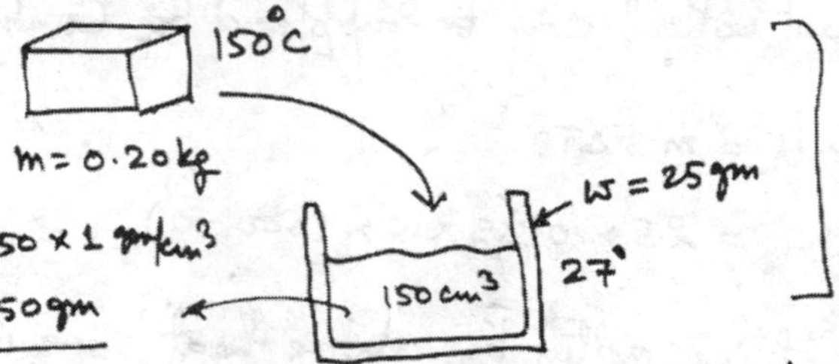

$m_i = 150 \times 1$ gm/cm³

$m_i = 150$ gm

After mixing final temp becomes 40°C.

Total heat loss by block = Heat gain by Calorimeter

$$m_b S_b \Delta T_b = m_w \cdot S_w \Delta T_c$$

$$S_b = \frac{(175 \times 10^{-3}) \times 4.2 \times 10^3 \times (40-27)}{0.20 \times 110} = 0.434 \text{ J/gm-K} \rightarrow 0.434 \times 10^3 \text{ J/kg-K}$$

Ans.

Video Solution

- Given below are observations on molar specific heats at room temperature of some common gases.

Gas	Molar specific heat (C_v) (cal mo1^{-1} K^{-1})
Hydrogen	4.87
Nitrogen	4.97
Oxygen	5.02
Nitric oxide	4.99
Carbon monoxide	5.01
Chlorine	6.17

The measured molar specific heats of these gases are markedly different from those for monatomic gases. Typically, molar specific heat of a monatomic gas is 2.92 cal/mol K. Explain this difference. What can you infer from the somewhat larger (than the rest) value for chlorine ?

Solⁿ: For a general ideal gas C_v is given as $C_v = \frac{fR}{2}$ ($f \rightarrow$ degrees of freedom for gas molecule)

for a monoatomic gas $f = 3$ (Trans.) & for a diatomic gas $f = 5$ (3 Translational DOF + 2 Rotational DOF)

all above gas are diatomic

$$\Rightarrow C_v = \frac{5R}{2} = \frac{5 \times 1.98}{2} \approx 4.95 \text{ Cal/mol-K.}$$

for chlorine the molecules have additional vibrational DOF due to which f is higher by 1. ($f = 6$)

- Answer the following questions based on the *P-T* phase diagram of carbon dioxide:

(a) At what temperature and pressure can the solid, liquid and vapour phases of CO_2 co-exist in equilibrium ?

(b) What is the effect of decrease of pressure on the fusion and boiling point of CO_2?

(c) What are the critical temperature and pressure for CO_2 ? What is their significance ?

(d) Is CO_2 solid, liquid or gas at (a) –70 °C under 1 atm, (b) –60 °C under 10 atm, (c) 15 °C under 56 atm ?

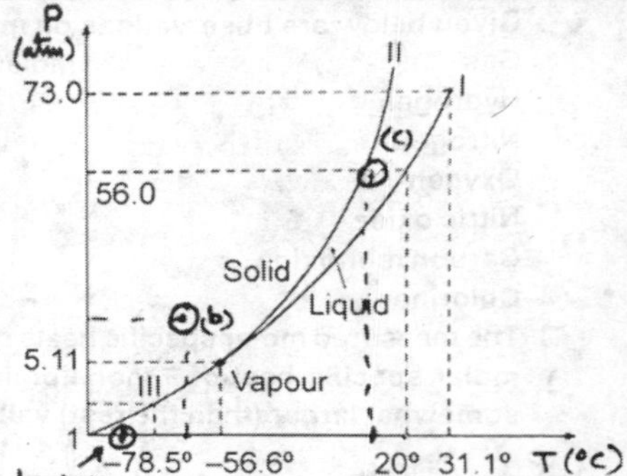

Sol^n (a) It happens at triple point when
$P = 5.11$ atm
$T = -56.6°C$
Ans

(b) from curve, we can see that on decreasing pressure both fusion & boiling point decreases in curve I & II.

(c) From vapourization curve I we can see that critical temp & pressure for CO_2 are
$T_c = 31.1°C$
$P_c = 73.0$ atm
⇒ at $T > T_c$ CO_2 cannot be liquified at any value of pressure.

(d) → (a) $T = -70°C$ at 1atm
⇓
CO_2 is vapour

(b) $-60°C$ at 10 atm
CO_2 is solid

(c) $15°C$ at 56 atm
CO_2 is liquid.

Video Solution

- Answer the following questions based on the $P-T$ phase diagram of CO_2:

(a) CO_2 at 1 atm pressure and temperature – 60 °C is compressed isothermally. Does it go through a liquid phase ?

(b) What happens when CO_2 at 4 atm pressure is cooled from room temperature at constant pressure ?

(c) Describe qualitatively the changes in a given mass of solid CO_2 at 10 atm pressure and temperature –65 °C as it is heated up to room temperature at constant pressure

(d) CO_2 is heated to a temperature 70 °C and compressed isothermally. What changes in its properties do you expect to observe ?

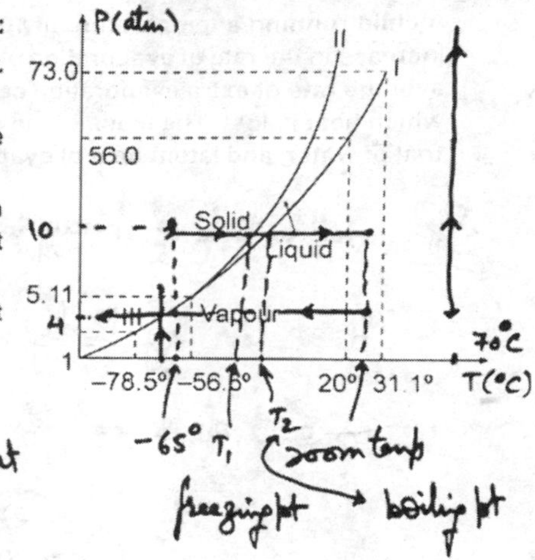

Sol^n (a) No, in this process vapour condenses directly to solid

(b) In this process also vapour condenses directly to solid

(c) it changes first from solid to liquid at T_1 then liquid to vapour at T_2

(d) As $T > 31.1°C\ (T_c)$ here CO_2 will not liquify and remain in vapour phase but as temp is constant, on increasing pressure its behaviour will drift toward more non-ideal nature.

- A child running a temperature of 101°F is given an antipyrin (i.e. a medicine that lowers fever) which causes an increase in the rate of evaporation of sweat from his body. If the fever is brought down to 98 °F in 20 min, what is the average rate of extra evaporation caused, by the drug. Assume the evaporation mechanism to be the only way by which heat is lost. The mass of the child is 30 kg. The specific heat of human body is approximately the same as that of water, and latent heat of evaporation of water at that temperature is about 580 cal g^{-1}.

Sol^n. fall in temp of body in °C is $\Delta T = \frac{5}{9}(101-98) = \frac{5}{3}\,°C$

Heat lost by body is $\Delta Q = ms\Delta T = 30 \times 4.2 \times 10^3 \times 5/3$

amount of sweat evaporated in 20 min is m_s then we use

$$\Delta Q = m_s \cdot L_f = m_s\,(580 \times 4.2 \times 10^3)$$

Rate of extra evaporation of sweat —

$$r = \frac{m_s}{t} = \frac{30 \times 4.2 \times 10^3 \times 5/3}{580 \times 4.2 \times 10^3 \times 20} = 4.3 \times 10^{-3}\ \text{kg/min}$$

$$= 4.3\ \text{gm/min}\ \text{Ans.}$$

- A 'thermacole' icebox is a cheap and efficient method for storing small quantities of cooked food in summer in particular. A cubical icebox of side 30 cm has a thickness of 5.0 cm. If 4.0 kg of ice is put in the box, estimate the amount of ice remaining after 6 h. The outside temperature is 45 °C, and co-efficient of thermal conductivity of thermacole is 0.01 J s^{-1} m^{-1} K^{-1}. [Heat of fusion of water = 335 × 10^3 J kg^{-1}]

Sol^n:

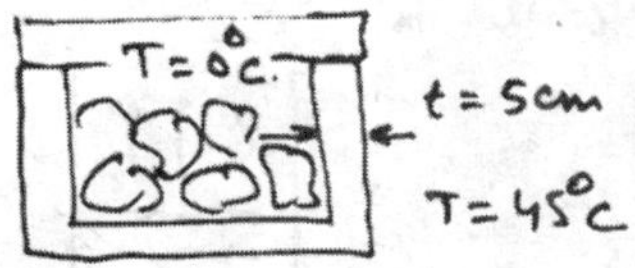

Area through which heat is Conducted, is given as

$$A = 6 \times (30)^2 = 5400 \times 10^{-4}\ m^2$$

Amount of heat Conducted = heat used in melting the ice.

$$\frac{kA\Delta T}{t} \times 6 \times 3600 = m_i L_f$$

$$\Rightarrow m_i = \frac{kA\Delta T \times 6 \times 3600}{t \times L_f}$$

mass of ice melted

$$= \frac{0.01 \times 0.54 \times 45 \times 6 \times 3600}{0.05 \times 335 \times 10^3}$$

$$= 0.313\ kg.$$

Mass of ice remaining in ice box = 4.0 − 0.313 = 3.687 kg ≃ 3.7 kg Ans

Web Reference at www.physicsgalaxy.com

Video Sol. : Class 11th NCERT Solutions | **Sec. -** Heat & Thermodynamics | **Topic -** Thermal Properties of Matter

Theory Reference. : Grade - 11 & 12 | **Sec. -** Heat & Thermodynamics | **Topic -** Heat Transfer

Video Solution

- A brass boiler has a base area of 0.15 m^2 and thickness 1.0 cm. It boils water at the rate of 6.0 kg/min when placed on a gas stove. Estimate the temperature of the part of the flame in contact with the boiler. Thermal conductivity of brass = 109 J s^{-1} m^{-1} K^{-1}; Heat of vaporisation of water = 2256 × 10^3 J kg^{-1}.

Sol^n: Rate of heat Conduction from flame to water is

$$\frac{dQ}{dt} = \frac{kA(T-100)}{\omega}$$

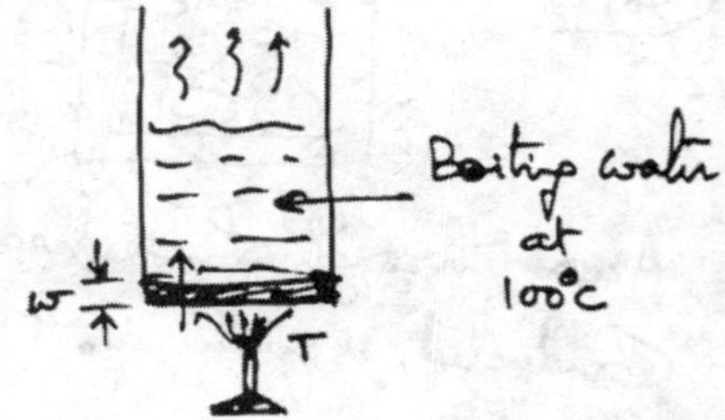

if m_ω is mass of water evaporating/second

⇒ we use

$$\frac{dQ}{dt} = \frac{kA(T-100)}{\omega} = m_\omega \cdot L_v$$

$$T-100 = \frac{(6.0/60) \times 2256 \times 10^3 \times 0.01}{109 \times 0.15} = 137.98°C$$

⇒ flame temp $T = 137.98 + 100 = 237.98 \simeq 238°C$ Ans

- Explain why :

(a) a body with large reflectivity is a poor emitter

(b) a brass tumbler feels much colder than a wooden tray on a chilly day

(c) an optical pyrometer (for measuring high temperatures) calibrated for an ideal black body radiation gives too low a value for the temperature of a red hot iron piece in the open, but gives a correct value for the temperature when the same piece is in the furnace

(d) the earth without its atmosphere would be inhospitably cold

(e) heating systems based on circulation of steam are more efficient in warming a building than those based on circulation of hot water

Sol^n (a) By kirchhoff's law good absorbers are good emitters,

for radiation falling on a body surface, we use

$a + r + t = 1.$

⇒ for low a, its e will also be low.

(b) Due to high Conductivity of brass, when we touch it, quickly heat is conducted from our body to brass & it gives a cold feeling due to sudden loss of heat. wood has low conductivity.

(c) T = Reading high temp body

in a furnace body at high temp behaves like a black body

$E_R = \sigma T^4$

but in open space due to low temp & emissivity of body

$E_R' = e\sigma(T^4 - T_0^4)$

$\Rightarrow E_R' < E_R$

Sol^n: (d) Earth atmosphere acts as an envelope & traps heat inside to keep it warm.
& this is becaus atmospheric gases behave like poor conductor of heat through which low conduction take place.

(e) steam has excess latent heat compared to hot water. So due high capacity of heat retention steam based heating systems are more efficient.

- A body cools from 80 °C to 50 °C in 5 minutes. Calculate the time it takes to cool from 60 °C to 30 °C. The temperature of the surroundings is 20 °C.

Sol[n]: We use avg form of Newton's law of cooling

$$\frac{T_2 - T_1}{\delta t} = k\left(\frac{T_2 + T_1}{2} - T_S\right)$$

In first case $\frac{80-50}{5} = k\left(\frac{80+50}{2} - 20\right)$ — (1)

In second case $\frac{60-30}{t_1} = k\left(\frac{60+30}{2} - 20\right)$ — (2)

$\frac{(1)}{(2)} \Rightarrow \frac{t_1}{5} = \frac{45}{25} \Rightarrow t_1 = 9 \text{ min}$ Ans.

Chapter 12

Thermodynamics

QR Code of Link to the Video Lectures of Theory of this chapter Thermodynamics at 'Physics Galaxy' web portal

QR Code of Link to the NCERT textbook Video Solutions of unsolved exercises at the end of each chapter in sequence of this chapter at 'Physics Galaxy' web portal

- A geyser heats water flowing at the rate of 3.0 litres per minute from 27 °C to 77 °C. If the geyser operates on a gas burner, what is the rate of consumption of the fuel if its heat of combustion is 4.0×10^4 J/g ?

Sol^n: Heat required per min is

$$\Delta Q = ms\,\Delta T$$

$$= 3 \times 4.2 \times 10^3 \times (77-27) = 63 \times 10^4 \text{ J/min}$$

If m gm fuel is being consumed per min, we have

$$m \times 4 \times 10^4 = 63 \times 10^4$$

$$m = \frac{63}{4} \text{ gm/min}$$

$$= 15.75 \text{ gm/min} \quad \text{Ans.}$$

- What amount of heat must be supplied to 2.0×10^{-2} kg of nitrogen (at room temperature) to raise its temperature by 45 °C at constant pressure ? (Molecular mass of N_2 = 28; R = 8.3 J mol^{-1} K^{-1}).

Sol^n: At Constant pressure, heat required to raise the temp of a gas is given as

$$\Delta Q = nC_p \Delta T$$

(for a diatomic gas $C_p = \frac{7}{2}R$)

$$\Delta Q = \left(\frac{m}{M}\right)\left(\frac{7}{2}R\right)\Delta T$$

$$= \frac{2 \times 10^{-2}}{28 \times 10^{-3}} \times \frac{7}{2} \times 8.31 \times 45 \simeq 934 J \text{ Ans.}$$

- Explain why

(a) Two bodies at different temperatures T_1 and T_2 if brought in thermal contact do not necessarily settle to the mean temperature $(T_1 + T_2)/2$

(b) The coolant in a chemical or a nuclear plant (i.e., the liquid used to prevent the different parts of a plant from getting too hot) should have high specific heat

(c) Air pressure in a car tyre increases during driving

(d) The climate of a harbour town is more temperate than that of a town in a desert at the same latitude

Sol^n: (a) $T_1 > T_2$

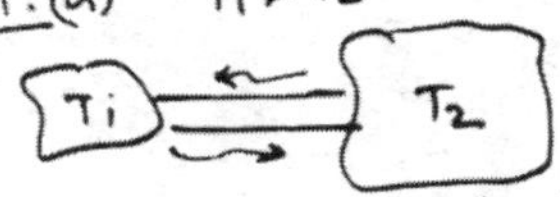

If T_{eq} is the final equilibrium temp then we use

$$m_1 s_1 (T_1 - T_e) = m_2 s_2 (T_e - T_2)$$

$$T_e = \frac{T_1 + T_2}{2} \text{ only if } m_1 s_1 = m_2 s_2$$

(b) with high value of specific heat, coolant can extract more heat from machinary for a given temp difference

$$\Delta Q_{abs}\uparrow = m s\uparrow \Delta T$$

(c) During driving, due to friction temp of tyre increases & we use

$$P\uparrow \propto T\uparrow$$

as $V_{tyre} \to$ Const.

(d) A desert is open & in a harbour town humidity is high which traps more heat as it is enveloping the town so temp is higher.

- A cylinder with a movable piston contains 3 moles of hydrogen at standard temperature and pressure. The walls of the cylinder are made of a heat insulator, and the piston is insulated by having a pile of sand on it. By what factor does the pressure of the gas increase if the gas is compressed to half its original volume ?

Sol^n: As cylinder & piston are insulated ⇒ this compression is an adiabatic process.

for an adiabatic process we use

$$P_1V_1^{\gamma} = P_2V_2^{\gamma}$$

here $V_2 = \frac{V_1}{2}$ ⇒ $P_1V_1^{\gamma} = P_2\left(\frac{V_1}{2}\right)^{\gamma}$

$$\Rightarrow \frac{P_2}{P_1} = (2)^{\gamma}$$

for H_2 (diatomic gas) we use $\gamma = 1.4$ ⇒ $\frac{P_2}{P_1} = (2)^{1.4} = 2.64$ Ans.

- In changing the state of a gas adiabatically from an equilibrium state *A* to another equilibrium state *B*, an amount of work equal to 22.3 J is done on the system. If the gas is taken from state *A* to *B* via a process in which the net heat absorbed by the system is 9.35 cal, how much is the net work done by the system in the latter case ? (Take 1 cal = 4.19 J)

Sol^n: change in internal energy from state A to B is $\Delta U = +22.3\,J$

$U_B - U_A = 22.3\,J$

↑ remain same in all processes.

in second case, given that heat supplied to system is $\Delta Q = 9.35 \times 4.19 = \underline{39.18\,J}$

By first law of thermodynamics, we have $\Delta Q = \Delta U + W$

$\Rightarrow W = \Delta Q - \Delta U = 39.18\,J - 22.3\,J$

$= 16.9\,J$ Ans.

- Two cylinders *A* and *B* of equal capacity are connected to each other via a stopcock. A contains a gas at standard temperature and pressure. *B* is completely evacuated. The entire system is thermally insulated. The stopcock is suddenly opened. Answer the following :

(a) What is the final pressure of the gas in *A* and *B* ?

(b) What is the change in internal energy of the gas ?

(c) What is the change in the temperature of the gas ?

(d) Do the intermediate states of the system (before settling to the final equilibrium state) lie on its *P-V-T* surface ?

Sol^n: (a) When stopcock is opened "free expansion" of gas takes place & in free exp we use for constant T $\Rightarrow$ $P_1V_1 = P_2V_2$

$$1(V) = P_2(2V) \Rightarrow P_2 = \tfrac{1}{2} = 0.5\text{atm} \quad \text{Ans}$$

(b) For free expansion we know $\Delta U = 0$ Ans

(c) For free expansion T = Const $\Rightarrow \Delta T = 0$ Ans

(d) No as free expansion a very quick process so intermediate states do not obey gas law.

- A steam engine delivers 5.4×10^8 J of work per minute and services 3.6×10^9 J of heat per minute from its boiler. What is the efficiency of the engine? How much heat is wasted per minute?

Sol: Efficiency of a heat engine is given as

$$\eta = \frac{\text{work done}}{\text{heat input}} \times 100\,\%.$$

$$= \frac{5.4\times10^8}{3.6\times10^9}\times100 = \frac{3}{20}\times100 = 15\%. \text{ Ans.}$$

Heat wasted $\Delta E_{loss} = Q - W$

$$= 3.6\times10^9 - 5.4\times10^8 \text{ J/min}$$

$$= 3.06\times10^8 \text{ J/min} \sim 3.1\times10^8 \text{ J/min Ans}$$

- An electric heater supplies heat to a system at a rate of 100 W. If system performs work at a rate of 75 joules per second. At what rate is the internal energy increasing?

Sol^n By First law of Thermodynamics, we have

$$\Delta Q = \Delta U + W$$

$$\Delta U = \Delta Q - W$$

per unit time FLT →

$$\Delta U = 100 - 75 = 25\,W \text{ Ans.}$$

- A thermodynamic system is taken from an original state to an intermediate state by the linear process shown in figure. Its volume is then reduced to the original value from *E* to *F* by an isobaric process. Calculate the total work done by the gas from *D* to *E* to *F*

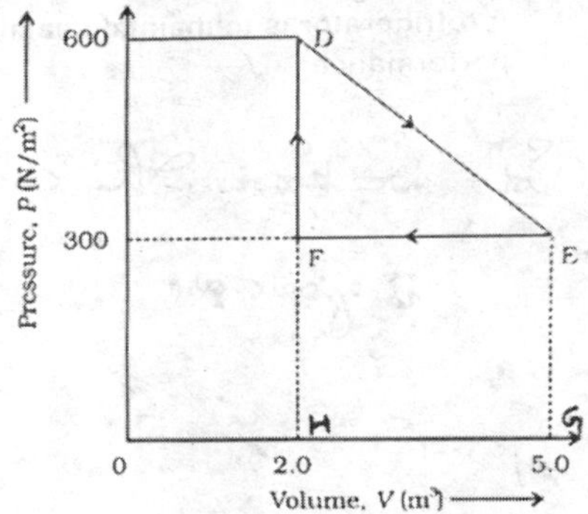

Solⁿ: Work done → area under P-V curve.

$W_{DE} = +$ area DEGHFD

$W_{EF} = -$ area EGHFE

$W_{D\,to\,E\,to\,F} = W_{DE} + W_{EF} = +$ area of triangle DEFD

$= \frac{1}{2} \times 300 \times 3 = 450\,J$ Ans.

- **A refrigerator is to maintain eatables kept inside at 9°C. If room temperature is 36°C, calculate the coefficient of performance.**

Sol: We know the coefficient of performance of a refrigerator is given as-

$$K = \frac{T_2}{T_1 - T_2}$$

here $T_2 = 273 + 9 = 282\,K$

& $T_1 = 273 + 36 = 309\,K$

$$\Rightarrow \quad K = \frac{282}{309 - 282} = \frac{282}{27} = 10.4 \text{ Ans.}$$

Chapter 13

Kinetic Theory

QR Code of Link to the Video Lectures
of Theory of this chapter Kinetic Theory
at 'Physics Galaxy' web portal

QR Code of Link to the NCERT textbook Video Solutions
of unsolved exercises at the end of each chapter in sequence
of this chapter at 'Physics Galaxy' web portal

- Estimate the fraction of molecular volume to the actual volume occupied by oxygen gas at STP. Take the diameter of an oxygen molecule to be 3 Å.

Sol^n: Volume occupied by one Oxygen molecule is $V_1 = \frac{4}{3}\pi r^3$

$$r_0 = 3/2 = 1.5\,\text{Å}$$

actual volume of space occupied by one molecule in its gaseous motion

$$V_s = \frac{22.4\times10^{-3}}{6.023\times10^{23}}\ m^3$$

1 mole → 22.4 litre
$22.4\times10^{-3}\,m^3$
↓
N_A

⇒ fraction of molecular volume to gaseous volume by Oxygen gas at STP is given as

$$\frac{V_1}{V_s} = \frac{4/3\times3.14\times(1.5\times10^{-10})^3}{22.4\times10^{-3}}\times6.023\times10^{23}$$

$$= 3.8\times10^{-4}\ \text{Ans.}$$

- **Molar volume is the volume occupied by 1 mol of any (ideal) gas at standard temperature and pressure (STP : 1 atmospheric pressure, 0 °C). Show that it is 22.4 litres.**

Solⁿ: By Gas Law, we have

$$PV = nRT$$

$$\Rightarrow \quad V = \frac{nRT}{P}$$

$$= \frac{1 \times 8.314 \times 273.15}{1.013 \times 10^5}$$

$$= 0.0224\ m^3 = 22.4 \text{ litre. Ans}$$

Video Solution

- Figure shows plot of PV/T versus P for 1.00×10^{-3} kg of oxygen gas at two different temperatures.

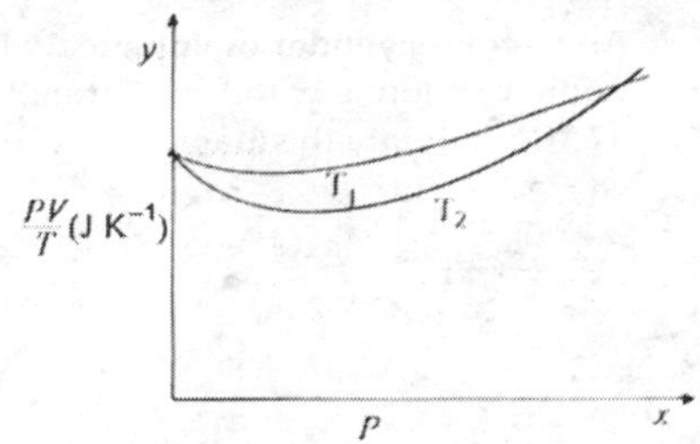

(a) What does the dotted plot signify?

(b) Which is true: $T_1 > T_2$ or $T_1 < T_2$?

(c) What is the value of PV/T where the curves meet on the y-axis?

(d) If we obtained similar plots for 1.00×10^{-3} kg of hydrogen, would we get the same value of PV/T at the point where the curves meet on the y-axis? If not, what mass of hydrogen yields the same value of PV/T (for low pressurehigh temperature region of the plot) ? (Molecular mass of H_2 = 2.02 u, of O_2 = 32.0 u, R = 8.31 J mol⁻¹ K⁻¹).

Solⁿ: (a) The dotted plot signified $\frac{PV}{T}$ = Constant by gas law

$PV = nRT$

$\frac{PV}{T} = nR \rightarrow$ Const.

This signifies ideal gas behaviour of O_2 gas.

(b) As curve of temp T_1 is more close to dotted curve

$\Rightarrow T_1 > T_2$

as at higher temp gas more behave like ideal.

(c) By gas law

$\frac{PV}{T} = nR$

$= \left(\frac{1 \times 10^{-3}}{32 \times 10^{-3}}\right) \times 8.314$

$= 0.26$ J/K Ans.

(d) For H_2 it will not be same due to different no of moles

So if m mass of H_2 yields same value of PV/T

$\Rightarrow m = n \times M$

$= \frac{1}{32} \times 2 \times 10^{-3}$

$= 6.3 \times 10^{-5}$ kg Ans.

- An oxygen cylinder of volume 30 litres has an initial gauge pressure of 15 atm and a temperature of 27 °C. After some oxygen is withdrawn from the cylinder, the gauge pressure drops to 11 atm and its temperature drops to 17 °C. Estimate the mass of oxygen taken out of the cylinder ($R = 8.31$ J mol^{-1} K^{-1}, molecular mass of $O_2 = 32$ *u*).

Sol^n: By gas law no of moles in cylinder

initially $n_i = \frac{P_1V_1}{RT_1} = \frac{(15+1)\times 1.013\times 10^5 \times 30\times 10^{-3}}{8.31\times(27+273.15)} = 19.48$ mol

finally $n_f = \frac{P_2V_2}{RT_2} = \frac{(11+1)\times 1.013\times 10^5\times 30\times 10^{-3}}{8.31\times(17+273.15)} = 15.12$ mol

no of moles leaked out are $\Delta n = n_i - n_f$

$= 19.48 - 15.12 = 4.36$ mol.

mass of O_2 leaked / taken out is $\Delta m = \Delta n \times M = 4.36\times 32\times 10^{-3}$

$= 0.1396$ kg $\simeq 0.14$ kg Ans

Video Solution

- An air bubble of volume 1.0 cm³ rises from the bottom of a lake 40 m deep at a temperature of 12 °C. To what volume does it grow when it reaches the surface, which is at a temperature of 35 °C ?

<u>Solⁿ</u>: Given that at a depth h

$$P_1 = P_{atm} + h\rho g = 1.013\times10^{5} + 40\times10^{3}\times9.8$$
$$= 4.93\times10^{5}\ Pa$$

$$V_1 = 10^{-6}\ m^3$$

$$T_1 = 273.15 + 12 = 285.15\ K.$$

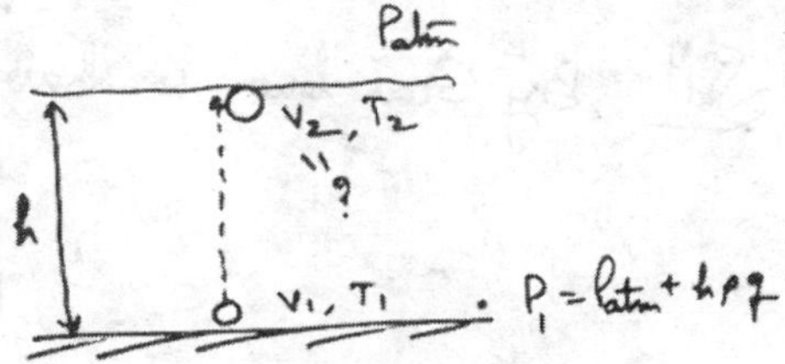

At the surface of lake

$$P_2 = P_{atm} = 1.013\times10^{5}\ Pa$$

$$V_2 = ?$$

$$T_2 = 273.15 + 35 = 308.15\ K.$$

→ By gas law for air moles in the bubble, we use

$$\frac{P_1V_1}{T_1} = \frac{P_2V_2}{T_2}$$

$$\Rightarrow V_2 = \frac{P_1V_1}{T_1}\times\frac{T_2}{P_2} = \frac{(4.93\times10^{5})(10^{-6})(308.15)}{285.15\times1.013\times10^{5}}$$

$$= 5.26\times10^{-6}\ m^3$$

$$\sim 5.3\ cm^3 \quad \underline{Ans.}$$

Web Reference at www.physicsgalaxy.com

Video Sol. : Class 11th NCERT Solutions | **Sec. -** Heat & Thermodynamics **| Topic -** Kinetic Theory

Theory Reference : Grade - 11 & 12 | **Sec. -** Heat & Thermodynamics **| Topic -** Kinetic Theory of Gases

Video Solution

- Estimate the total number of air molecules (inclusive of oxygen, nitrogen, water vapour and other constituents) in a room of capacity 25.0 m^3 at a temperature of 27 °C and 1 atm pressure.

Sol^n: By Gas law we have

$$PV = nRT$$

$$PV = \frac{N}{N_{AV}} \cdot RT = NkT \quad \text{(Boltzmann's Const } k = \frac{R}{N_{AV}})$$

$\Rightarrow$ no. of air molecules in room are

$$N = \frac{PV}{kT} = \frac{1.013 \times 10^{5} \times 25}{1.38 \times 10^{-23} \times (27 + 273.15)}$$

$$= 6.11 \times 10^{26} \text{ molecules Ans.}$$

- Estimate the average thermal energy of a helium atom at (i) room temperature (27 °C), (ii) the temperature on the surface of the Sun (6000 K), (iii) the temperature of 10 million kelvin (the typical core temperature in the case of a star).

Sol^n. Average thermal energy of a monoatomic gas molecule is given as-

$$E_{av} = \frac{f}{2}kT$$

here $f = 3 \Rightarrow E_{av} = \frac{3}{2}kT$

(i) $T = 27 + 273.15 = 300.15\ K \Rightarrow E_{av} = \frac{3}{2} \times 1.38 \times 10^{-23} \times 300.15 = 6.21 \times 10^{-21}\ J$ Ans

(ii) $T = 6000\ K \Rightarrow E_{av} = \frac{3}{2} \times 1.38 \times 10^{-23} \times 6000 = 1.241 \times 10^{-19}\ J$ Ans.

(iii) $T = 10^7\ K \Rightarrow E_{av} = \frac{3}{2} \times 1.38 \times 10^{-23} \times 10^{7} = 2.07 \times 10^{-16}\ J$ Ans.

- **Three vessels of equal capacity have gases at the same temperature and pressure. The first vessel contains neon (monatomic), the second contains chlorine (diatomic), and the third contains uranium hexafluoride (polyatomic). Do the vessels contain equal number of respective molecules ? Is the root mean square speed of molecules the same in the three cases? If not, in which case is v_{rms} the largest ?**

Solⁿ: By Avogadro's hypothesis → at same temp & pressure for equal volumes all gases have same no of molecules.

YES all 3 vessels have same no of molecules.

& rms speed of gas molecules $v_{rms} = \sqrt{\frac{3RT}{M}}$

$$\Rightarrow v_{rms} \propto \frac{1}{\sqrt{M}}$$

thus for the 3 vessels v_{rms} are different & for neon M is least so its v_{rms} is largest. Ans

Video Solution

- **At what temperature is the root mean square speed of an atom in an argon gas cylinder equal to the rms speed of a helium gas atom at – 20 °C ? (atomic mass of Ar = 39.9 u, of He = 4.0 *u*).**

Solⁿ: rms speed of an atom $v_{rms} = \sqrt{\dfrac{3RT}{M}}$

here we use

$$v_{rms\,Ar} = v_{rms\,He\ at\ -20^\circ C}$$

$$\sqrt{\dfrac{3RT}{M_{Ar}}} = \sqrt{\dfrac{3RT_{He}}{M_{He}}}$$

$$\Rightarrow \quad T = T_{He}\left(\dfrac{M_{Ar}}{M_{He}}\right) = (273.15 - 20)\left(\dfrac{39.9}{4}\right)$$

$$= 253.15 \times \dfrac{39.9}{4}$$

$$= 2523.67\ K \sim 2.52 \times 10^3\ K$$

Ans.

- **Estimate the mean free path and collision frequency of a nitrogen molecule in a cylinder containing nitrogen at 2.0 atm and temperature 17 °C. Take the radius of a nitrogen molecule to be roughly 1.0 Å. Compare the collision time with the time the molecule moves freely between two successive collisions (Molecular mass of N_2 = 28.0 *u*).**

Sol^n: Mean free path is given as

$$\lambda = \frac{1}{\sqrt{2}\times \pi n' d^2}$$

d → diameter; n' → molecular density (per m^3)

By gas law, we have $PV = NkT$

$$\Rightarrow P = \left(\frac{N}{V}\right)kT$$

$$\Rightarrow n' = \frac{P}{kT}$$

$$\Rightarrow \lambda = \frac{1}{1.414\times 3.14\times(2\times10^{-10})^2}\times\frac{1.38\times10^{-23}\times(273.15+17)}{2\times1.013\times10^5}$$

$$= 1.1\times10^{-7}\,m$$

λ (distance between successive collisions)

Collision freq $\nu_c = \frac{v_{rms}}{\lambda} = \frac{1}{\lambda}\sqrt{\frac{3RT}{M}}$

$$= \frac{1}{1.1\times10^{-7}}\cdot\sqrt{\frac{3\times8.314\times290.15}{28\times10^{-3}}}$$

$$= \frac{1}{1.1\times10^{-7}}\times 508.3\,m/s$$

$$= 5.1\times10^{9}\,sec^{-1}$$

⇒ approx particles/atoms remain in contact for a time (Collision time)

$$t_c = \frac{d}{v_{rms}} = \frac{2\times10^{-10}}{508.3} = 4\times10^{-13}\,sec$$

Time between two successive collisions

$$t_\lambda = \frac{\lambda}{v_{rms}} = \frac{1.1\times10^{-7}}{508.3} = 2\times10^{-10}\,s \approx 500\,t_c$$

- A metre long narrow bore held horizontally (and closed at one end) contains a 76 cm long mercury thread, which traps a 15 cm column of air. What happens if the tube is held vertically with the open end at the bottom ?

Sol^n:

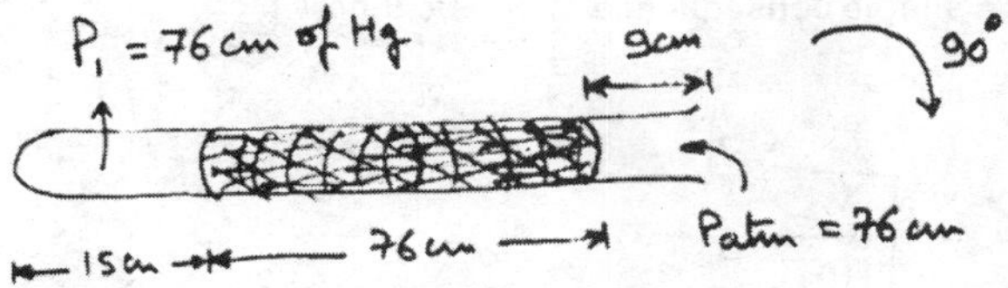

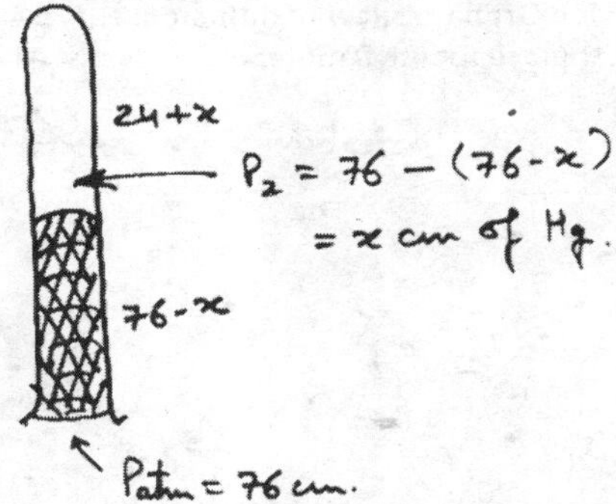

By Gas laws, we have $\frac{P_1V_1}{T_1} = \frac{P_2V_2}{T_2}$

as $T_1 = T_2 \Rightarrow P_1V_1 = P_2V_2$

$$76 \times 15 = x \times (24 + x)$$

$$\Rightarrow x^2 + 24x - 1140 = 0$$

$$\Rightarrow x = \frac{-24 \pm \sqrt{(24)^2 + 4 \times 1140}}{2} = 23.8 \text{ cm or } -47.8 \text{ cm} \ (\times)$$

final length of air column left in tube is $24 + 23.8 = \underline{47.8 \text{ cm}}$

- From a certain apparatus, the diffusion rate of hydrogen has an average value of 28.7 $cm^3 s^{-1}$. The diffusion of another gas under the same conditions is measured to have an average rate of 7.2 $cm^3 s^{-1}$. Identify the gas.

[Hint : Use Graham's law of diffusion: $R_1 / R_2 = (M_2 / M_1)^{1/2}$, where R_1, R_2 are diffusion rates of gases 1 and 2, and M_1 and M_2 their respective molecular masses. The law is a simple consequence of kinetic theory.]

Sol^n: By Graham's law, we have

$$\frac{R_1}{R_2} = \sqrt{\frac{M_2}{M_1}}$$

$$\Rightarrow \quad R_2 = R_1 \sqrt{\frac{M_1}{M_2}}$$

$$\Rightarrow \quad M_2 = M_1 \left(\frac{R_1}{R_2}\right)^2$$

$$= 2\left(\frac{28.7}{7.2}\right)^2 = 32.09 \sim 32$$

$\Rightarrow$ unknown gas here is O_2 Ans.

Video Solution

- A gas in equilibrium has uniform density and pressure throughout its volume. This is strictly true only if there are no external influences. A gas column under gravity, for example, does not have uniform density (and pressure). As you might expect, its density decreases with height. The precise dependence is given by the so-called law of atmospheres

  $$n_2 = n_1 \exp\,[-mg\,(h_2 - h_1)\,/\,k_B T\,]$$

  where n_2, n_1 refer to number density at heights h_2 and h_1 respectively. Use this relation to derive the equation for sedimentation equilibrium of a suspension in a liquid column:

  $$n_2 = n_1 \exp\,[-mg\,N_A\,(\rho - \rho')\,(h_2 - h_1)\,/\,(\rho RT)]$$

  where ρ is the density of the suspended particle, and ρ′ that of surrounding medium. [N_A is Avogadro's number, and R the universal gas constant.]

[Hint : Use Archimedes principle to find the apparent weight of the suspended particle.]

Sol^n: In a liquid column the apparent wt of a submerged particle is given

as $W_{app} = W\left(1 - \frac{\rho_l}{\rho_s}\right) = mg\left(1 - \frac{\rho'}{\rho}\right)$

we also use $k_B = \frac{R}{N_A}$

$\Rightarrow$ from law of atmospheres $n_2 = n_1\, e^{-W_{app}(h_2 - h_1)/(R/N_A)T}$

$n_2 = n_1\, e^{-mg N_A(\rho - \rho')/\rho RT}$ Hence proved

- Given below are densities of some solids and liquids. Give rough estimates of the size of their atoms :

Substance	Atomic Mass (u)	Density (10^3 Kg m^{-3})
Carbon (diamond)	12.01	2.22
Gold	197.00	19.32
Nitrogen (liquid)	14.01	1.00
Lithium	6.94	0.53
Fluorine (liquid)	19.00	1.14

[Hint : Assume the atoms to be 'tightly packed' in a solid or liquid phase, and use the known value of Avogadro's number. You should, however, not take the actual numbers you obtain for various atomic sizes too literally. Because of the crudeness of the tight packing approximation, the results only indicate that atomic sizes are in the range of a few A].

Sol^n: for an atom if its radius is r, then volume of one mole of atoms is given as

$$V = \frac{4}{3}\pi r^3 . N_{AV}$$

we use $M = V\rho \Rightarrow M = \frac{4}{3}\pi r^3 N_{AV} \rho$

$$\Rightarrow r = \left(\frac{3M}{4\pi \rho N_{AV}}\right)^{1/3}$$

Carbon (D) → $r = 1.29 \text{ Å}$

Gold → $r = 1.59 \text{ Å}$

liq N_2 → $r = 1.77 \text{ Å}$

Lithium → $r = 1.73 \text{ Å}$

liq F_2 → $r = 1.88 \text{ Å}$ Ans.

Video Solution

Chapter 14

Oscillations

QR Code of Link to the Video Lectures of Theory of this chapter Oscillations at 'Physics Galaxy' web portal

QR Code of Link to the NCERT textbook Video Solutions of unsolved exercises at the end of each chapter in sequence of this chapter at 'Physics Galaxy' web portal

- Which of the following examples represent periodic motion?

(a) A swimmer completing one (return) trip from one bank of a river to the other and back

(b) A freely suspended bar magnet displaced from its N-S direction and released

(c) A hydrogen molecule rotating about its centre of mass

(d) An arrow released from a bow.

Sol^n: (a)

Not a periodic

(b)

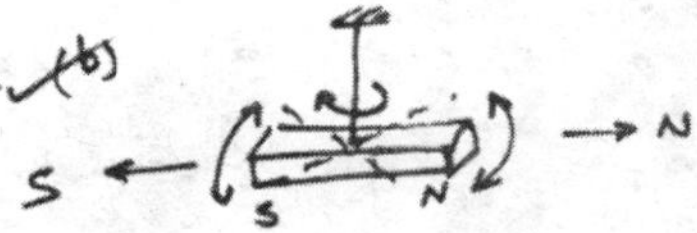

✓ periodic

(c)

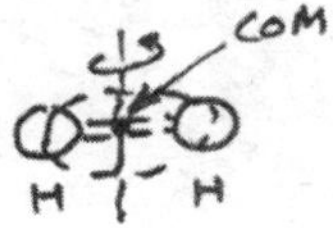

✓ periodic

(d)

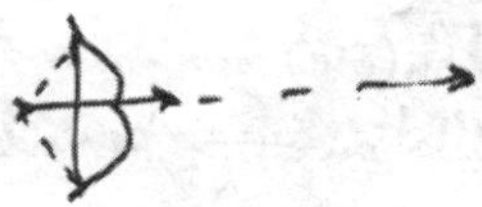

Not a periodic

- **Which of the following examples represent (nearly) simple harmonic motion and which represent periodic but not simple harmonic motion?**

(a) **the rotation of earth about its axis**

(b) **motion of an oscillating mercury column in a *U*-tube**

(c) **motion of a ball bearing inside a smooth curved bowl, when released from a point slightly above the lower most point**

(d) **general vibrations of a polyatomic molecule about its equilibrium position**

Sol^n: (a)  → Periodic NOT SHM.

(b)  → SHM ✓

(c) 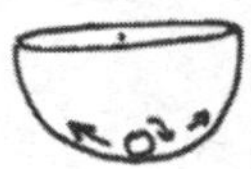 → for small amplitude it is SHM

(d) A Polyatomic molecule has several degrees of freedom (osc) → its motion is a superposition of several oscillation → periodic NOT SHM.

Video Solution

- **Figure depicts four *x- t* plots for linear motion of a particle. Which of the plots represent periodic motion? What is the period of motion (in case of periodic motion) ?**

(a)

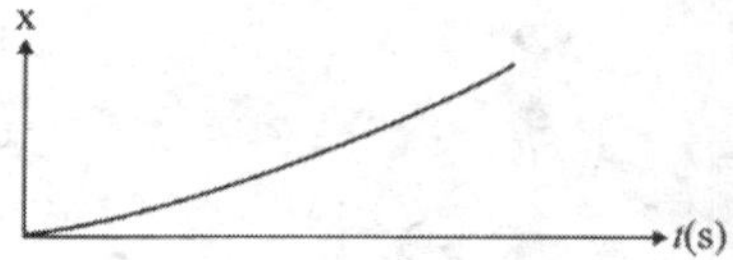

(b)

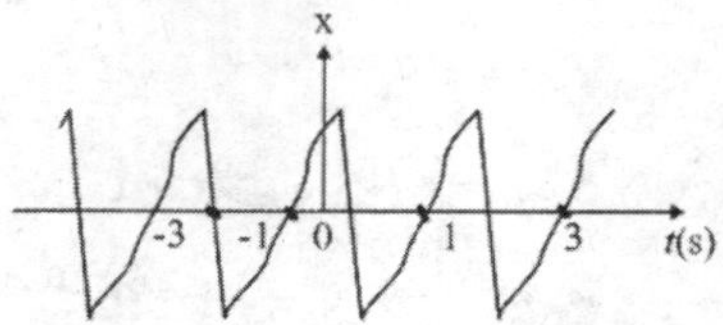

(c)

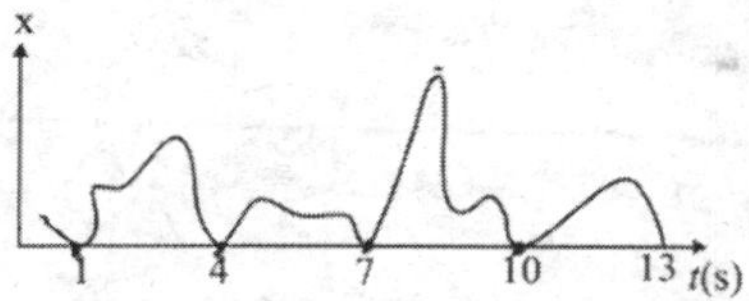

(d)

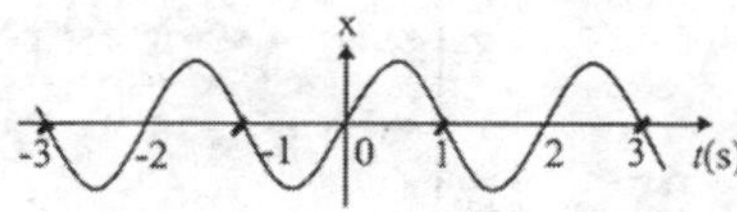

Sol:

Solⁿ: (a) → Not periodic

(b) → curve is repetitive
⇒ periodic motion
$T = 2$ sec

(c) → curve is not repetitive
⇒ Not periodic

(d) → curve is repetitive
⇒ periodic motion
$T = 2$ sec.

- **Which of the following functions of time represent (a) simple harmonic, (b) periodic but not simple harmonic, and (c) non-periodic motion? Give period for each case of periodic motion (ω is any positive constant):**

(a) $\sin \omega t - \cos \omega t$ (b) $\sin^3 \omega t$ (c) $3 \cos (\pi/4 - 2\omega t)$ (d) $\cos \omega t + \cos 3\omega t + \cos 5\omega t$

(e) $\exp(-\omega t^2)$ (f) $1 + \omega t + \omega^2 t^2$

Sol^n: (a) $\sin \omega t - \cos \omega t$

$\Rightarrow y = \sqrt{2}\left(\frac{1}{\sqrt{2}} \sin \omega t - \frac{1}{\sqrt{2}} \cos \omega t\right)$

$= \sqrt{2} \sin(\omega t - \pi/4)$

eq^n of SHM ✓

time period $T = \frac{2\pi}{\omega}$

(b) $y = \sin^3 \omega t$

$\Rightarrow y = \frac{1}{4}(3 \sin \omega t - \sin 3\omega t)$

the period of both SHMs getting superposed is $T_1 = \frac{2\pi}{\omega}$; $T_2 = \frac{2\pi}{3\omega}$

Here $T_1 = 3T_2 \Rightarrow T_1$ is the time period of motion

$\Rightarrow$ Periodic but Not SHM

(c) $y = 3\cos(\pi/4 - 2\omega t) = 3\cos(2\omega t - \pi/4)$

this is an eq^n of SHM

with time period $T = \frac{2\pi}{2\omega} = \pi/\omega$.

(d) $y = \cos \omega t + \cos 3\omega t + \cos 5\omega t$

$T_1 = \frac{2\pi}{\omega}$ $T_2 = \frac{2\pi}{3\omega} = T_1/3$ $T_3 = \frac{2\pi}{5\omega} = T_1/5$

with period $T_1 = \frac{2\pi}{\omega}$ the motion is periodic but Not SHM.

(e) $y = e^{-\omega t^2}$

As it is a decreasing function it is Nonperiodic.

(f) $y = 1 + \omega t + \omega^2 t^2$ | This is an increasing function hence Nonperiodic.

Video Solution

- A particle is in linear simple harmonic motion between two points, *A* and *B*, 10 cm apart. Take the direction from *A* to *B* as the positive direction and give the signs of velocity, acceleration and force on the particle when it is

(a) at the end *A*,
(b) at the end *B*,
(c) at the mid-point of *AB* going towards *A*,
(d) at 2 cm away from *B* going towards *A*,
(e) at 3 cm away from *A* going towards *B*, and
(f) at 4 cm away from *B* going towards *A*

Sol[n]:

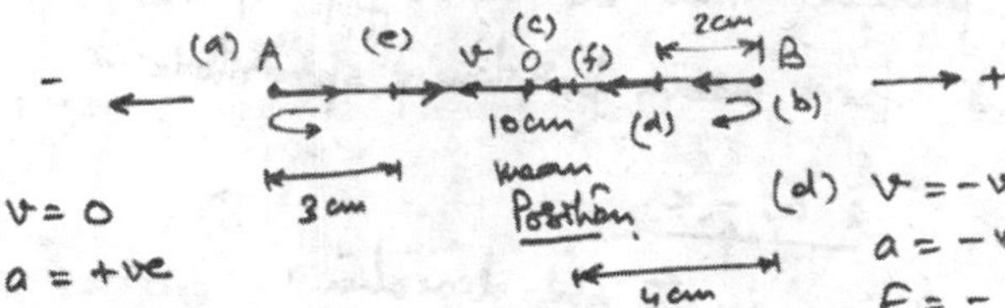

(a) At end A $v = 0$, $a = +ve$, $F = +ve$.

(b) At end B $v = 0$, $a = -ve$, $F = -ve$

(c) At mid point of AB $v = -ve$, $a = 0$, $F = 0$

(d) $v = -ve$, $a = -ve$, $F = -ve$

(e) $v = +ve$, $a = +ve$, $F = +ve$

(f) $v = -ve$, $a = -ve$, $F = -ve$. Ans.

- **Which of the following relationships between the acceleration a and the displacement x of a particle involve simple harmonic motion?**

(a) $a = 0.7x$ (b) $a = -200x^2$ (c) $a = -10x$ (d) $a = 100x^3$

Sol^n: For SHM, acc^n of particle must be directly proportional to its displacement from mean position & opposite to it.

$\Rightarrow$ $a \propto -x$. (− denotes opp direction)

hence only in option (c) the function represents SHM.

- **The motion of a particle executing simple harmonic motion is described by the displacement function, $x(t) = A\cos(\omega t + \phi)$. If the initial ($t = 0$) position of the particle is 1 cm and its initial velocity is ω cm/s, what are its amplitude and initial phase angle ? The angular frequency of the particle is $\pi\ s^{-1}$. If instead of the cosine function, we choose the sine function to describe the SHM : $x = B\sin(\omega t + \alpha)$, what are the amplitude and initial phase of the particle with the above initial conditions.**

Sol^n: $x = A\cos(\omega t + \phi)$

at $t = 0$, $x = 1$ cm $\Rightarrow$ $1 = A\cos\phi$ — (1)

velocity of particle

$$v = \frac{dx}{dt} = -A\omega\sin(\omega t + \phi)$$

at $t = 0$; $v = \omega$ cm/s

$\Rightarrow$ $\omega = -A\omega\sin(\phi) \Rightarrow -1 = A\sin\phi$ — (2)

$(1)^2 + (2)^2 \Rightarrow 2 = A^2$
$\Rightarrow A = \sqrt{2}$ cm Ans

$\frac{(2)}{(1)} \Rightarrow -1 = \tan\phi$
$\Rightarrow \phi = \tan^{-1}(-1) = 7\pi/4$ Ans

$\rightarrow$ if we use sine function

$x = A\sin(\omega t + \phi)$

at $t = 0$ $x = 1$ cm $\Rightarrow 1 = A\sin\phi$ — (3)

at $t = 0$ $v = \omega$ cm/s $\Rightarrow v = \frac{dx}{dt} = A\omega\cos(\omega t + \phi)$

$\Rightarrow \omega = A\omega\cos\phi \Rightarrow 1 = A\cos\phi$ — (4)

Here $(3)^2 + (4)^2 \Rightarrow 2 = A^2 \Rightarrow A = \sqrt{2}$ cm

$\frac{(3)}{(4)} \Rightarrow 1 = \tan\phi \Rightarrow \phi = \pi/4$ Ans

- **A spring balance has a scale that reads from 0 to 50 kg. The length of the scale is 20 cm. A body suspended from this balance, when displaced and released, oscillates with a period of 0.6 s. What is the weight of the body ?**

Solⁿ At 50kg wt scale gets displaced by 20cm.

If k be the force constant of spring, we use

$$mg = kx$$

$$\Rightarrow \quad k = \frac{mg}{x} = \frac{50 \times 9.8}{0.2} = 2450 \text{ N/m}$$

for spring oscillation $T = 2\pi\sqrt{\frac{m}{k}}$

$$\Rightarrow \quad m = \frac{T^2 k}{4\pi^2} = \frac{(0.6)^2 \times 2450}{4 \times (3.14)^2} = 22.36 \text{ kg.}$$

weight of body $= mg = 22.36 \times 9.8 = 219.13 \text{ N}$ Ans.

- A spring having with a spring constant 1200 N m^{-1} is mounted on a horizontal table as shown in figure. A mass of 3 kg is attached to the free end of the spring. The mass is then pulled sideways to a distance of 2.0 cm and released. Determine (i) the frequency of oscillations, (ii) maximum acceleration of the mass, and (iii) the maximum speed of the mass.

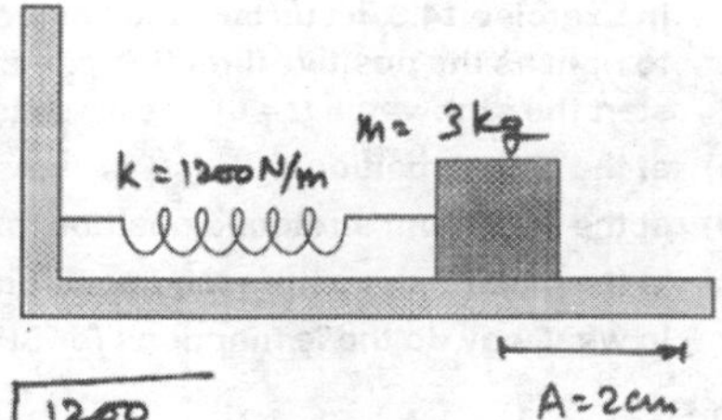

Solⁿ: (i) frequency of oscillations of a spring block system $n = \frac{1}{2\pi}\sqrt{\frac{K}{m}} = \frac{1}{2 \times 3.14} \times \sqrt{\frac{1200}{3}} = 3.2\ Hz$ Ans

(ii) maximum acceleration $|a_{max}| = \omega^2 A$

$= (2\pi n)^2 A = 4 \times (3.14)^2 \times (3.2)^2 \times 0.02$

$= 8.0\ m/s^2$ Ans.

(iii) maximum speed $|v_{max}| = \omega A$

$= (2\pi n) A = 2 \times 3.14 \times 3.2 \times 0.02 = 0.4\ m/s$ Ans.

- In Exercise 14.9, let us take the position of mass when the spring is unstreched as $x = 0$, and the direction from left to right as the positive direction of x-axis. Give x as a function of time t for the oscillating mass if at the moment we start the stopwatch ($t = 0$), the mass is

(a) at the mean position,

(b) at the maximum stretched position, and

(c) at the maximum compressed position.

In what way do these functions for SHM differ from each other, in frequency, in amplitude or the initial phase?

Sol^n: Angular freq $\omega = 2\pi n = 2 \times 3.14 \times 3.2 = 20$ rad/s

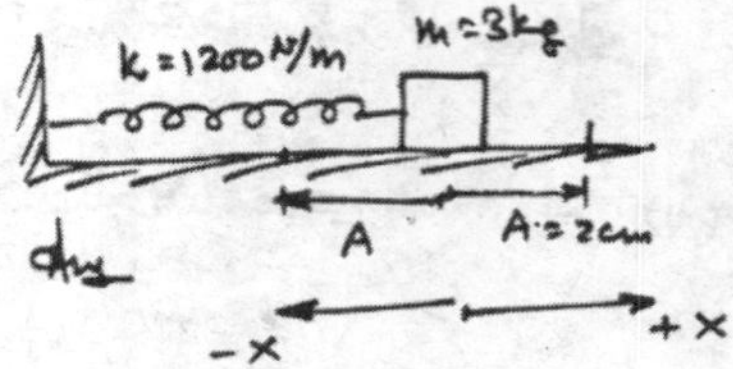

(a) if at $t=0$, m is at mean position ($\phi = 0$)

$\Rightarrow$ SHM eq^n $x = A\sin(\omega t + \phi) = 2\sin(20t)$ cm Ans

(b) at $t=0$, m is at rightmost position ($\phi = \pi/2$)

$\Rightarrow$ SHM eq^n $x = A\sin(\omega t + \phi) = 2\cos(20t)$ cm Ans

(c) At $t=0$, m is at leftmost position ($\phi = -\pi/2$)

$\Rightarrow$ SHM eq^n $x = A\sin(\omega t + \phi) = -2\cos(20t)$ cm Ans.

Video Solution

- Figures correspond to two circular motions. The radius of the circle, the period of revolution, the initial position, and the sense of revolution (i.e. clockwise or anti-clockwise) are indicated on each figure. Obtain the corresponding simple harmonic motions of the *x*-projection of the radius vector of the revolving particle *P*, in each case.

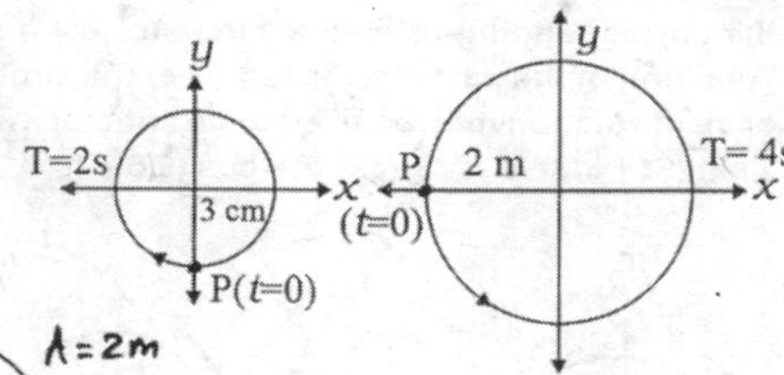

Sol[n]:

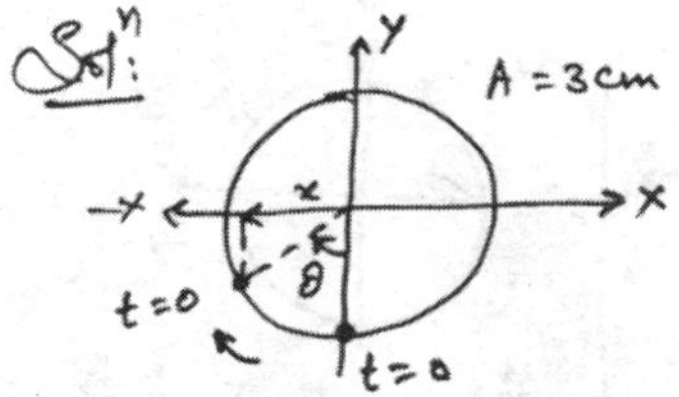

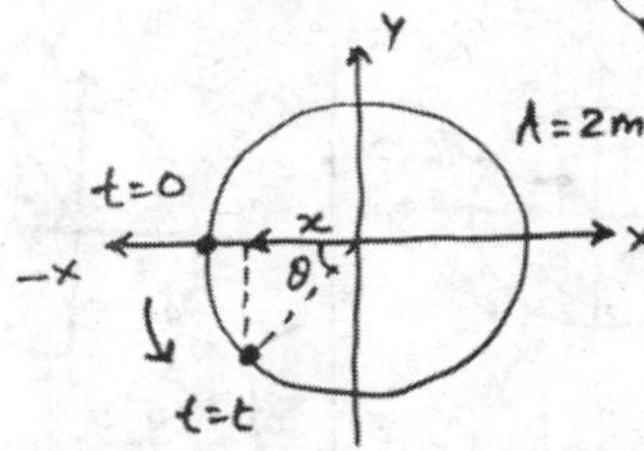

$T = 2s$

$\omega = \frac{2\pi}{T} = \frac{2\pi}{2} = \pi$ rad/s

$\theta = \omega t$

$\Rightarrow -x = A\sin\omega t$

$x = 3\sin\pi t$ cm

Ans.

$\theta = \omega t$

where $\omega = \frac{2\pi}{T} = \frac{2\pi}{4} = \frac{\pi}{2}$ rad/s

$-x = A\cos\theta$

$x = -2\cos(\frac{\pi}{2}t)$ m Ans.

- **Plot the corresponding reference circle for each of the following simple harmonic motions. Indicate the initial ($t = 0$) position of the particle, the radius of the circle, and the angular speed of the rotating particle. For simplicity, the sense of rotation may be fixed to be anticlockwise in every case: (x is in cm and t is in s).**

(a) $x = -2 \sin (3t + \pi/3)$ (b) $x = \cos (\pi/6 - t)$ (c) $x = 3 \sin (2\pi t + \pi/4)$ (d) $x = 2 \cos \pi t$

Sol^n:

(a)

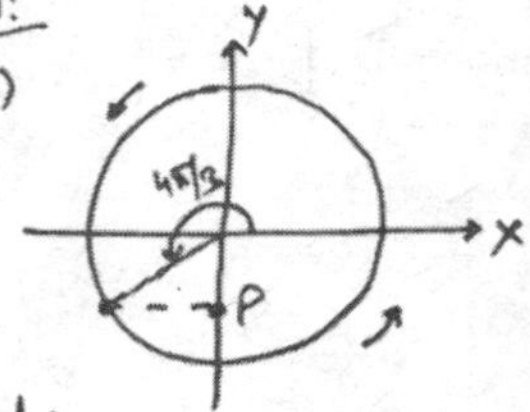

at $t=0$

$x = -2\sin(\pi/3)$

$x_{t=0} = -\sqrt{3}$ cm.

$A = 2$ cm

$\omega = 3$ rad/s Ans.

(b)

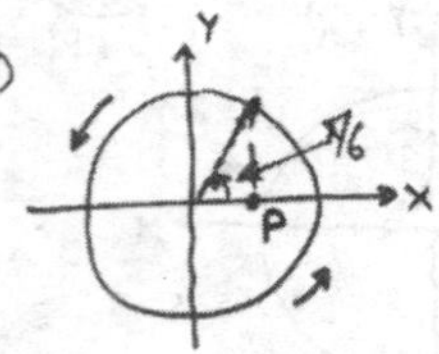

at $t=0$

$x = \cos(\pi/6) = 0.5$

$A = 1$ cm

$\omega = 1$ rad/s Ans

(c)

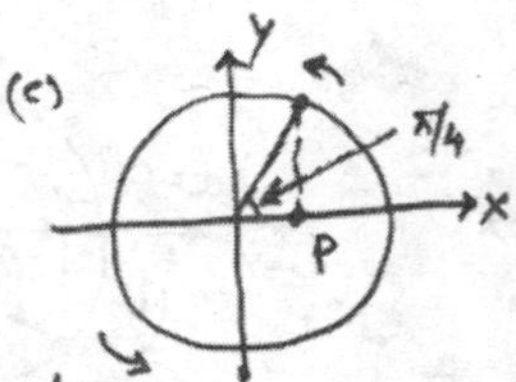

at $t=0$

$x = 3\sin(\pi/4)$

$x = 3/\sqrt{2}$ cm

$A = 3$ cm

$\omega = 2\pi$ rad/s Ans.

(d)

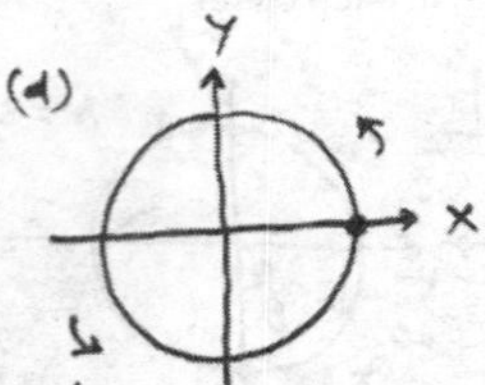

at $t=0$

$x = 2$ cm

$A = 2$ cm

$\omega = \pi$ rad/s Ans.

- Figure (a) shows a spring of force constant k clamped rigidly at one end and a mass m attached to its free end. A force $\vec{F}$ applied at the free end stretches the spring. Figure (b) shows the same spring with both ends free and attached to a mass m at either end. Each end of the spring in figure (b) is stretched by the same force $\vec{F}$.

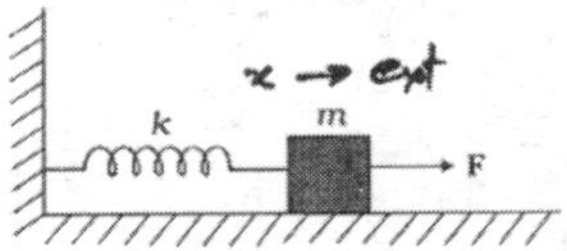

(a)

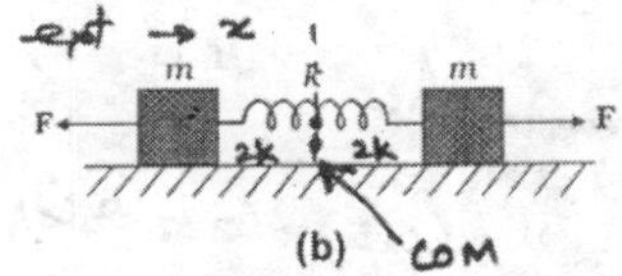

(b)

(a) What is the maximum extension of the spring in the two cases ?

(b) If the mass in figure (a) and the two masses in figure (b) are released, what is the period of oscillation in each case?

Sol^n: (a) At equilibrium position

in figure (a) $F = kx \Rightarrow x = \frac{F}{k}$ Ans

in figure (b) $F = kx$ for both masses

$\Rightarrow x = F/k$ Ans

(b) In figure-(a) the period of spring-block system, we know is given as

$$T = 2\pi\sqrt{\frac{m}{k}} \text{ Ans}$$

In fig-(b), on releasing both masses oscillate with their COM fixed as no external force is present $\Rightarrow$ $T = 2\pi\sqrt{\frac{m}{2k}}$ Ans

- **The piston in the cylinder head of a locomotive has a stroke (twice the amplitude) of 1.0 m. If the piston moves with simple harmonic motion with an angular frequency of 200 rad/min, what is its maximum speed ?**

Sol^n: The maximum speed in SHM is given as

$$|v_{max}| = A\omega$$

$$= (0.5) \times (200 \text{ rad/min})$$

$$= 100 \text{ m/min} \quad \text{Ans.}$$

Video Solution

- The acceleration due to gravity on the surface of moon is 1.7 m s^{-2}. What is the time period of a simple pendulum on the surface of moon if its time period on the surface of earth is 3.5 s ? (*g* on the surface of earth is 9.8 m s^{-2})

Sol^n: The time period of oscillations of a simple pendulum is given as $T = 2\pi\sqrt{\frac{l}{g}}$

If T_e & T_m are the time periods on earth & moon surface respectively then we use

$$\frac{T_m}{T_e} = \sqrt{\frac{g_e}{g_m}}$$

$$\Rightarrow T_m = \sqrt{\frac{g_e}{g_m}} \times T_e = \sqrt{\frac{9.8}{1.7}} \times 3.5 = 8.4\,s \text{ Ans.}$$

Web Reference at www.physicsgalaxy.com

Video Sol. : Class 11th NCERT Solutions | **Sec. -** Oscillation & Waves | **Topic -** Oscillations

Theory Reference : Grade - 11 & 12 | Sec. - Oscillation & Waves | **Topic -** Simple Harmonic Motion

Video Solution

- **Answer the following questions :**

(a) Time period of a particle in SHM depends on the force constant k and mass m of the particle: $T = 2\pi\sqrt{\frac{m}{k}}$. A simple pendulum executes SHM approximately. Why then is the time period of a pendulum independent of the mass of the pendulum?

(b) The motion of a simple pendulum is approximately simple harmonic for small angle oscillations. For larger angles of oscillation, a more involved analysis shows that T is greater than $2\pi\sqrt{\frac{l}{g}}$. Think of a qualitative argument to appreciate this result

(c) A man with a wristwatch on his hand falls from the top of a tower. Does the watch give correct time during the free fall ?

(d) What is the frequency of oscillation of a simple pendulum mounted in a cabin that is freely falling under gravity ?

Solⁿ(a)

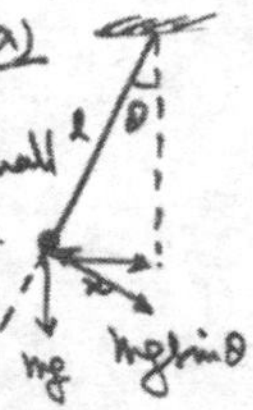

θ → Small

$\theta = \frac{x}{l}$

$\omega = \sqrt{\frac{g}{l}}$

Restoring force

$F_R = -mg\sin\theta$

$F_R = -mg\theta$

$F_R = -\left(\frac{mg}{l}\right)x$

$F_R = -kx$

here $k = \frac{mg}{l}$

$\Rightarrow k \propto m$

For a simple pendulum as $k \propto m$

$T = 2\pi\sqrt{\frac{m}{k}}$ is independent of mass.

(b) As restoring force

$F_R = -mg\sin\theta$

$\sin\theta < \theta \Rightarrow \omega < \sqrt{\frac{g}{l}}$

$\Rightarrow T = \frac{2\pi}{\omega}$

here $T > 2\pi\sqrt{\frac{l}{g}}$ if θ is Not Small.

(c) Yes as wrist watch works on spring osc so its osc frequency is independent of g

(d) for a simple pendulum, osc freq is $n = \frac{1}{2\pi}\sqrt{g/l}$ & in free fall we consider

$g_{eff} = 0 \Rightarrow n = 0$ Ans

- **A simple pendulum of length l and having a bob of mass *M* is suspended in a car. The car is moving on a circular track of radius *R* with a uniform speed *v*. If the pendulum makes small oscillations in a radial direction about its equilibrium position, what will be its time period ?**

Sol^n:

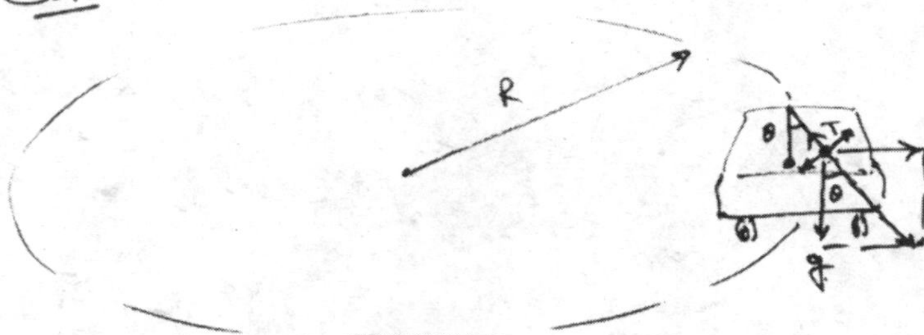

$a_{cf} = \frac{v^2}{R}$

eq^m position is given as

$\theta = \tan^{-1}\left(\frac{v^2}{Rg}\right)$

$\theta = \tan^{-1}\left(\frac{a_{cf}}{g}\right)$

$g_{eff} = \sqrt{g^2 + a_{cf}^2}$

$g_{eff} = \sqrt{g^2 + \frac{v^4}{R^2}}$

About new mean position of simple pendulum in the reference frame of car, its time period is given as

$$T = 2\pi\sqrt{\frac{l}{g_{eff}}} = 2\pi\sqrt{\frac{l}{\sqrt{g^2 + v^4/R^2}}} \quad \text{Ans.}$$

- A cylindrical piece of cork of density ρ of base area A and height h floats in a liquid of density ρ_l. The cork is depressed slightly and then released. Show that the cork oscillates up and down simple harmonically with a period

$$T = 2\pi\sqrt{\frac{h\rho}{\rho_l g}}$$

where ρ is the density of cork. (Ignore damping due to viscosity of the liquid).

Solⁿ:

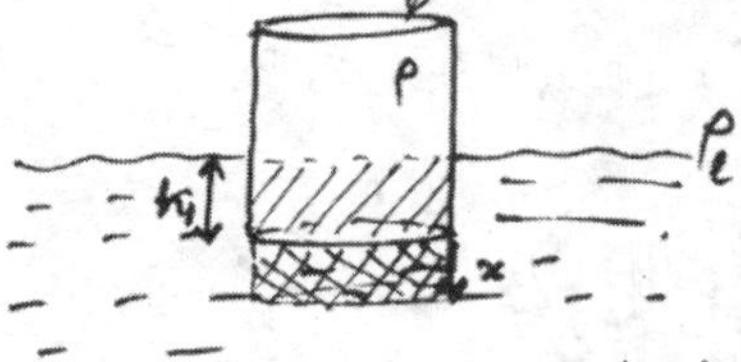

At equilibrium if cork is floating with a submerged depth h_1, we use

$$(\underbrace{\rho A h}_{m})g = (\rho_l A h_1)g$$

$$\Rightarrow h_1 = \frac{\rho h}{\rho_l}$$

after depressed by x, net upward restoring force on cork is due to excess buoyant force, given as

$$F_R = -(xA\rho_l)g$$

$$a = \frac{F_R}{m} = \left(-\frac{A\rho_l g}{m}\right)x$$

$$\Rightarrow a \propto -x$$

As $a \propto -x$

$\Rightarrow$ the cork is executing SHM. Now we compare its acceleration with

$$a = -\omega^2 x$$

we get

$$\omega = \sqrt{\frac{A\rho_l g}{m}}$$

$$\Rightarrow \omega = \sqrt{\frac{A\rho_l g}{A\rho h}} = \sqrt{\frac{\rho_l g}{\rho h}}$$

$$\Rightarrow T = \frac{2\pi}{\omega} = 2\pi\sqrt{\frac{\rho h}{\rho_l g}}$$

- **One end of a *U*-tube containing mercury is connected to a suction pump and the other end to atmosphere. A small pressure difference is maintained between the two columns. Show that, when the suction pump is removed, the column of mercury in the *U*-tube executes simple harmonic motion.**

<u>Sol</u>

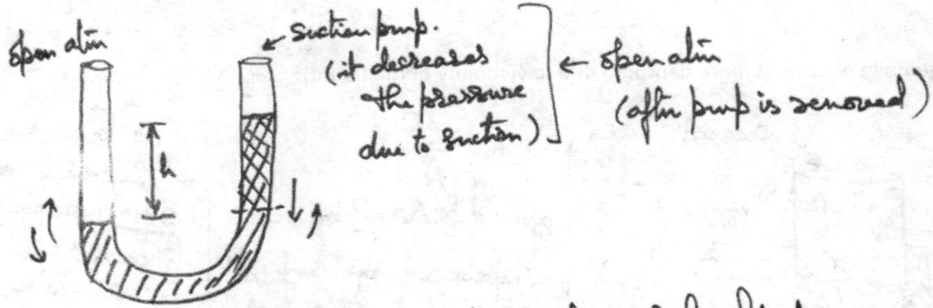

The restoring force on Hg is due to a column of height h

and $F_R \propto h$.

$\Rightarrow$ it will execute <u>SHM.</u>

- An air chamber of volume *V* has a neck area of cross section *a* into which a ball of mass *m* just fits and can move up and down without any friction (figure). Show that when the ball is pressed down a little and released, it executes SHM. Obtain an expression for the time period of oscillations assuming pressure-volume variations of air to be isothermal [see figure].

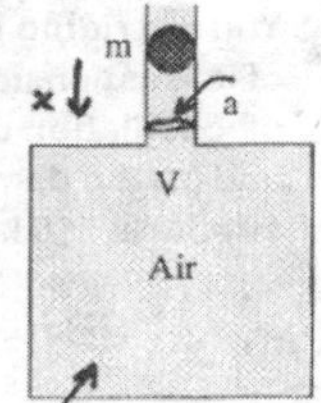

$P+\Delta P$ ← excess pressure

Sol^n: On pressing the ball by x, the volume of chamber decreases by $\Delta V = ax$ due to which if the pressure of chamber increases by ΔP, we use

$PV = $ Constant (under isothermal conditions)

$\Rightarrow P\Delta V + V\Delta P = 0$

$\Rightarrow Pax = -V\Delta P$

$\Rightarrow \Delta P = -\frac{Pa}{V}\cdot x$

Thus ball will move up due to the restoring force given as

$\rightarrow f_R = \Delta P a = -\frac{Pa^2}{V}x$

acceleration of ball

$a = \frac{f_R}{m} = -\frac{Pa^2}{mV}\cdot x$

As $a \propto -x$

$\Rightarrow$ ball is executing SHM.

$\rightarrow$ Compare with $a = -\omega^2 x$ we get

$\omega = \sqrt{\frac{Pa^2}{mV}}$

$\Rightarrow T = \frac{2\pi}{\omega} = 2\pi\sqrt{\frac{mV}{Pa^2}}$ Ans

for isothermal bulk mod we use

$B = P \Rightarrow T = 2\pi\sqrt{\frac{mV}{Ba^2}}$

- You are riding in an automobile of mass 3000 kg. Assuming that you are examining the oscillation characteristics of its suspension system. The suspension sags 15 cm when the entire automobile is placed on it. Also, the amplitude of oscillation decreases by 50% during one complete oscillation. Estimate the values of (a) the spring constant *k* and (b) the damping constant *b* for the spring and shock absorber system of one wheel, assuming that each wheel supports 750 kg.

Sol^n: At equilibrium of automobile at each wheel spring,

(a) we use

$$kx = mg$$

$$k = \frac{mg}{x} = \frac{750 \times 9.8}{0.15} = 4.9 \times 10^4 \text{ N/m} \sim 5 \times 10^4 \text{ N/m Ans}$$

(b) For damping situation we use $A = A_0 e^{-bt/2m}$

time period of oscillation

$$T = 2\pi\sqrt{\frac{m}{4k}} = 2 \times 3.14 \times \sqrt{\frac{3000}{4 \times 5 \times 10^4}}$$

four wheels

$$= 0.769 \text{ s}$$

→ After $t = T$ we use $A = A_0/2$

→ we use $\frac{A_0}{2} = A_0 e^{-bT/2m}$

$$\Rightarrow b = \frac{2m\ln(2)}{T} = \frac{2 \times 750 \times 0.693}{0.769}$$

$$= 1351 \text{ kg/s Ans.}$$

Video Solution

- Show that for a particle in linear SHM the average kinetic energy over a period of oscillation equals the average potential energy over the same period.

Solⁿ: During SHM the KE and PE of a particle varies with time & its function is given as-

$$K_t = \frac{1}{2} m\omega^2 A^2 \cos^2 \omega t \quad \& \quad P_t = \frac{1}{2} m\omega^2 A^2 \sin^2 \omega t$$

$$\langle K_t \rangle = \frac{1}{2} m\omega^2 A^2 \langle \cos^2 \omega t \rangle = \frac{1}{2} m\omega^2 A^2 (1/2) = \frac{1}{4} m\omega^2 A^2$$

$$\langle P_t \rangle = \frac{1}{2} m\omega^2 A^2 \langle \sin^2 \omega t \rangle = \frac{1}{2} m\omega^2 A^2 \left(\frac{1}{2}\right) = \frac{1}{4} m\omega^2 A^2$$

$$\langle K_t \rangle = \langle P_t \rangle = \frac{1}{4} m\omega^2 A^2 = \frac{1}{2}(TE)$$

- **A circular disc of mass 10 kg is suspended by a wire attached to its centre. The wire is twisted by rotating the disc and released. The period of torsional oscillations is found to be 1.5 s. The radius of the disc is 15 cm. Determine the torsional spring constant of the wire. (Torsional spring constant α is defined by the relation $J = -\alpha\,\theta$, where J is the restoring couple and θ the angle of twist).**

Soln: For a Torsional Pendulum, oscillation period is given as

$$T = 2\pi\sqrt{\frac{I}{C}} \Rightarrow C = \frac{4\pi^2 I}{T^2}$$

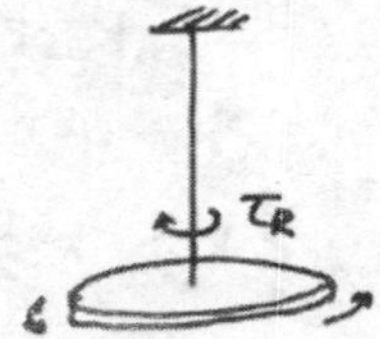

Moment of inertia of disc

$$I = \frac{1}{2}mR^2 = \frac{1}{2}\times 10\times(0.15)^2$$

$$= 0.1125 \text{ kg-m}^2$$

$$\Rightarrow C = \frac{4\times(3.14)^2\times 0.1125}{(1.5)^2}$$

$$\Rightarrow C = 1.972 \text{ N-m/rad}$$

Ans.

- A body describes simple harmonic motion with an amplitude of 5 cm and a period of 0.2 s. Find the acceleration and velocity of the body when the displacement is (a) 5 cm (b) 3 cm (c) 0 cm.

Solⁿ: For a given SHM, the accⁿ and velocity of particle are given as

$$a = -\omega^2 x$$

$$\& \quad v = \omega\sqrt{A^2 - x^2}$$

(a) $x = 5$ cm.

$$a = -\left(\frac{2\pi}{0.2}\right)^2 \cdot 0.05$$

$$= -5\pi^2 \text{ m/s}^2 \text{ Ans}$$

$$v = \left(\frac{2\pi}{0.2}\right)\sqrt{(0.05)^2 - (0.05)^2}$$

$$= 0 \text{ m/s Ans}$$

(b) $x = 3$ cm.

$$a = -\left(\frac{2\pi}{0.2}\right)^2 \times (0.03)$$

$$= -3\pi^2 \text{ m/s}^2 \text{ Ans.}$$

$$v = \left(\frac{2\pi}{0.2}\right)\sqrt{(0.05)^2 - (0.03)^2}$$

$$= 0.4\pi \text{ m/s Ans}$$

(c) $x = 0$ cm.

$$a = 0 \text{ m/s}^2$$

$$v = \omega A$$

$$= \left(\frac{2\pi}{0.2}\right) \times 0.05$$

$$= 0.5\pi \text{ m/s Ans.}$$

- A mass attached to a spring is free to oscillate, with angular velocity ω, in a horizontal plane without friction or damping. It is pulled to a distance x_0 and pushed towards the centre with a velocity v_0 at time $t = 0$. Determine the amplitude of the resulting oscillations in terms of the parameters ω, x_0 and v_0.

[Hint : Start with the equation $x = a\cos(\omega t + \theta)$ and note that the initial velocity is negative.]

Sol^n: As velocity of particle in SHM is given as-

$$v = \omega\sqrt{A^2 - x^2}$$

at a position x from mean position.

here we use at $x = x_0$, $v = v_0$ so we have

$$v_0 = \omega\sqrt{A^2 - x_0^2}$$

$$\Rightarrow \quad A = \sqrt{x_0^2 + \frac{v_0^2}{\omega^2}} \quad \text{Ans.}$$

Video Solution

Chapter 15

Waves

QR Code of Link to the Video Lectures
of Theory of this chapter Waves
at 'Physics Galaxy' web portal

QR Code of Link to the NCERT textbook Video Solutions
of unsolved exercises at the end of each chapter in sequence
of this chapter at 'Physics Galaxy' web portal

- **A string of mass 2.50 kg is under a tension of 200 N. The length of the stretched string is 20.0 m. If the transverse jerk is struck at one end of the string, how long does the disturbance take to reach the other end?**

Sol^n: Wave speed in stretched string is given as

(linear mass density of string $\mu = \frac{m}{l}$)

$$v = \sqrt{\frac{T}{\mu}} = \sqrt{\frac{200}{2.5/20}} = 40 \text{ m/s.}$$

time taken by jerk to the length of string is

$$t = \frac{l}{v} = \frac{20}{40} = 0.5 \text{ s} \quad \text{Ans.}$$

- **A stone dropped from the top of a tower of height 300 m high splashes into the water of a pond near the base of the tower. When is the splash heard at the top given that the speed of sound in air is 340 m s^{-1}? (g = 9.8 m s^{-2})**

Solⁿ:

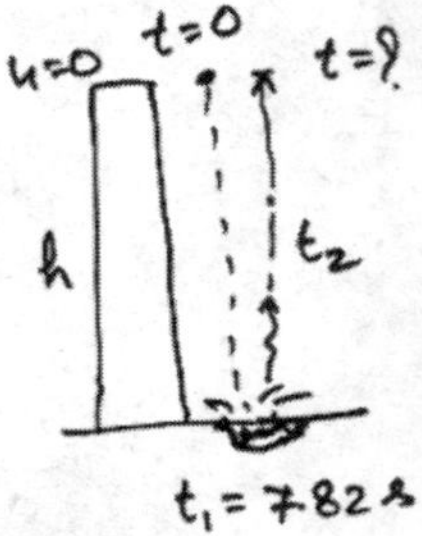

time taken by stone in its fall into pond is say t_1

$$\Rightarrow \quad h = \frac{1}{2} g t_1^2 \Rightarrow t_1 = \sqrt{\frac{2h}{g}} = \sqrt{\frac{2 \times 300}{9.8}} = 7.82\,s$$

time taken by sound from pond to the top of tower is

$$t_2 = \frac{h}{v} = \frac{300}{340} = 0.88\,s$$

Total time $T = t_1 + t_2 = 7.82 + 0.88 = 8.7\,s$ Ans.

Video Solution

- **A steel wire has a length of 12.0 m and a mass of 2.10 kg. What should be the tension in the wire so that speed of a transverse wave on the wire equals the speed of sound in dry air at 20°C = 343 m s⁻¹.**

Solⁿ: speed of transverse wave in a stretched wire is given as –

$$v = \sqrt{\frac{T}{\mu}} = v_{sound}$$

here $\mu = \frac{m}{l}$ linear mass density of wire

$$\Rightarrow \quad T = \mu v_{sound}^2 = \frac{m v_{sound}^2}{l}$$

$$= \frac{2.10 \times (343)^2}{12.0} = 2.06 \times 10^4 \text{ N} \quad \text{Ans.}$$

- Use the formula $v = \sqrt{\frac{\gamma p}{\rho}}$ to explain why the speed of sound in air

(a) is independent of pressure, (b) increases with temperature, (c) increases with humidity.

Sol^n: by Gas law we have $PV = \left(\frac{m}{M}\right)RT$

(a)

$\Rightarrow P = \rho \frac{RT}{M}$

$\Rightarrow \frac{P}{\rho} = \frac{RT}{M}$

here if $T \to$ Constant $\Rightarrow \frac{P}{\rho} \to$ Constant

At Constant temp P/ρ is Const thus speed of sound is independent of pressure.

(b) As $v = \sqrt{\frac{\gamma P}{\rho}} = \sqrt{\frac{\gamma RT}{M}}$

$\Rightarrow v \propto \sqrt{T}$

As $T \uparrow \Rightarrow v \uparrow$

(c) As $v = \sqrt{\frac{\gamma P}{\rho}}$

$\Rightarrow v \propto \frac{1}{\sqrt{\rho}}$

with humidity, ρ decreases $\Rightarrow v \uparrow$

because $M_{H_2O} = 18$ & $M_{air} \sim 29$

Video Solution

- You have learnt that a travelling wave in one dimension is represented by a function $y = f(x, t)$ where x and t must appear in the combination $x - vt$ or $x + vt$, i.e. $y = f(x \pm vt)$. Is the converse true? Examine if the following functions for y can possibly represent a travelling wave :

(a) $(x - vt)^2$ (b) $\log[(x + vt)/x_0]$ (c) $1/(x + vt)$

Sol^n: (a) $y = (x - vt)^2$

at $x = 0$ & $t = 0 \rightarrow y = 0$

but as x increases or at a specific x as t increases y increases continuously thus it is an unbound expression which cannot represent a physical wave.

within limits of x & t it can represent a wave.

(b) $y = \log\left[\frac{x + vt}{x_0}\right]$

at $x = 0$ & $t = 0$

$y = \log(0) \rightarrow \infty$

here as displacement is not finite this cannot represent a wave.

(c) $y = \frac{1}{x + vt}$

at $x = 0$ & $t = 0$

$y = \frac{1}{0} \rightarrow \infty$

here also the function cannot represent a wave.

(*) The converse is NOT True all functions containing $x \pm vt$ cannot represent a wave.

- A bat emits ultrasonic sound of frequency 1000 kHz in air. If the sound meets a water surface, what is the wavelength of (a) the reflected sound, (b) the transmitted sound? Speed of sound in air is 340 m s^{-1} and in water 1486 m s^{-1}.

Sol^n: wavelength of sound in air is given as

$$\lambda_{air} = \frac{v}{n} = \frac{340}{10^6} = 3.4 \times 10^{-4}\ m$$

(a) after reflection in air sound wavelength remain same at 3.4×10^{-4} m. Ans.

(b) after transmission in water, sound wavelength is given as

$$\lambda_w = \frac{v_w}{n} = \frac{1486}{10^6} = 1.486 \times 10^{-3}\ m \text{ Ans.}$$

$n \longrightarrow$ constant in all media

Video Solution

- **A hospital uses an ultrasonic scanner to locate tumours in a tissue. What is the wavelength of sound in the tissue in which the speed of sound is 1.7 km s^{-1}? The operating frequency of the scanner is 4.2 MHz.**

Solⁿ: wavelength of sound in tissue is given as

$$\lambda = \frac{v}{n}$$

$$= \frac{1.7 \times 10^{3}}{4.2 \times 10^{6}} = 4.1 \times 10^{-4} \text{ m Ans.}$$

- **A transverse harmonic wave on a string is described by**

  $$y(x, t) = 3.0 \sin (36\, t + 0.018\, x + \pi/4)$$

  where x and y are in cm and t in s. The positive direction of x is from left to right.

(a) Is this a travelling wave or a stationary wave ?

If it is travelling, what are the speed and direction of its propagation ?

(b) What are its amplitude and frequency ?

(c) What is the initial phase at the origin ?

(d) What is the least distance between two successive crests in the wave ?

Sol^n General eq^n of a travelling wave is $y = A \sin(\omega t + kx + \phi)$ so the given function is representing a travelling wave.

Comparison with general eq^n, we get

$A = 3.0\,cm$

$\omega = 36$ rad/s

$k = 0.018\,cm^{-1}$

$\phi = \pi/4$

(a) wave speed $v = \frac{\omega}{k}$

$\Rightarrow v = \frac{36}{0.018} = 2000$ cm/s

$= 20$ m/s Ans.

wave is travelling in $-x$ direction $\Rightarrow$ right to left

(b) $A = 3.0$ cm.

$n = \frac{\omega}{2\pi}$

$= \frac{36}{2 \times 3.14} = 5.73\,Hz$

Ans

(c) $\phi = \pi/4$ Ans.

(d) distance between two successive crests is wavelength $\lambda = \frac{v}{n}$

$\Rightarrow \lambda = 20/5.73 = 3.49\,m$ Ans.

Video Solution

- **For the wave described in Exercise 15.8, plot the displacement (*y*) versus (*t*) graphs for *x* = 0, 2 and 4 cm. What are the shapes of these graphs? In which aspects does the oscillatory motion in travelling wave differ from one point to another: amplitude, frequency or phase ?**

Sol^n: $y(x,t) = 3.0\sin(36t + 0.018x + \pi/4)$

at $x = 0$ & $t = 0$ ⇒ $y = 3.0\sin(\pi/4) = \frac{3.0}{\sqrt{2}} = 2.12$ cm

at $x = 2$ cm

& $t = 0$ ⇒ $y = 3.0\sin(0.036 + \pi/4)$

$= 2.19$ cm

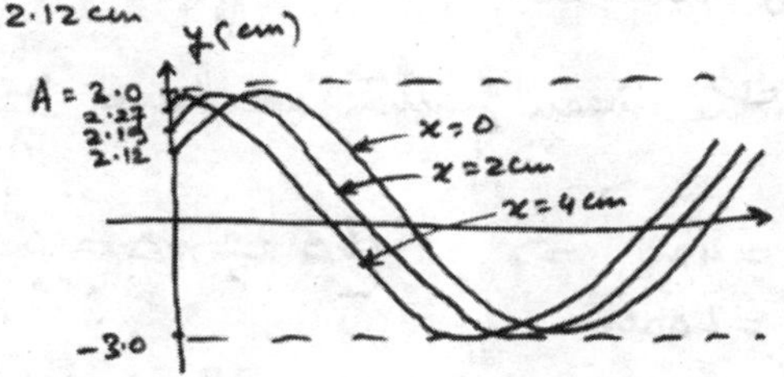

at $x = 4$cm

& $t = 0$ ⇒ $y = 3.0\sin(0.072 + \pi/4)$

$= 2.27$ cm.

All oscillatory motion have same amplitude & frequency but have different initial phases Ans

- For the travelling harmonic wave
  $y(x, t) = 2.0 \cos 2\pi (10t - 0.0080\, x + 0.35)$
  where x and y are in cm and t in s. Calculate the phase difference between oscillatory motion of two points separated by a distance of

(a) 4 m, (b) 0.5 m, (c) $\lambda/2$, (d) $3\lambda/4$

Sol: We know that phase difference $= \frac{2\pi}{\lambda} \times$ path difference

from the given function we have $\frac{2\pi}{\lambda} = 2\pi \times 0.0080 = 0.016\pi\ cm^{-1}$

(a) $\Delta = 4m = 400 cm \Rightarrow \phi = \frac{2\pi}{\lambda} \times \Delta = 0.016\pi \times 400 = 6.4\pi$ rad Ans.

(b) $\Delta = 0.5m = 50 cm \Rightarrow \phi = \frac{2\pi}{\lambda} \times \Delta = 0.016\pi \times 50 = 0.8\pi$ rad Ans.

(c) $\Delta = \lambda/2 \Rightarrow \phi = \frac{2\pi}{\lambda} \times \Delta = \frac{2\pi}{\lambda} \times \lambda/2 = \pi$ rad Ans

(d) $\Delta = 3\lambda/4 \Rightarrow \phi = \frac{2\pi}{\lambda} \times \Delta = \frac{2\pi}{\lambda} \times 3\lambda/4 = \frac{3\pi}{2}$ rad $= \pi/2$ rad Ans (opp phase)

Video Solution

- **The transverse displacement of a string (clamped at its both ends) is given by**

$$y(x, t) = 0.06 \sin\left(\frac{2\pi}{3}x\right) \cos(120\,\pi t)$$

where x and y are in m and t in s. The length of the string is 1.5 m and its mass is 3.0×10^{-2} kg. Answer the following :

(a) Does the function represent a travelling wave or a stationary wave?

(b) Interpret the wave as a superposition of two waves travelling in opposite directions. What is the wavelength, frequency, and speed of each wave ?

(c) Determine the tension in the string

Sol^n (a) For a clamped string sustained oscillations exist in stationary waves only.

(b) We compare the given expression with the std expression of s/w derived in basic theory videos → $y = 2A \sin kx \cos \omega t$

here we get

$2A = 0.06$

$A = 0.03\,m$

$k = \frac{2\pi}{3} = \frac{2\pi}{\lambda}$

$\Rightarrow \lambda = 3m.$

$\omega = 120\pi = 2\pi n$

$\Rightarrow n = 60\,Hz$

Ans.

(c) wave speed in string is given as

$v = \sqrt{\frac{T}{\mu}}$

$\Rightarrow T = \mu v^2 = \frac{m}{l} v^2 = \frac{3.0 \times 10^{-2} \times (180)^2}{1.5}$

$= 648\,N$ Ans.

- (i) For the wave on a string described in Exercise 15.11, do all the points on the string oscillate with the same (a) frequency, (b) phase, (c) amplitude? Explain your answers.

  (ii) What is the amplitude of a point 0.375 m away from one end?

Sol^n (i) $y(x,t) = 0.06 \sin\left(\frac{2\pi}{3}x\right) \cos(120\pi t)$

$R = 0.06 \sin\left(\frac{2\pi}{3}x\right)$

$\lambda = 3m.$

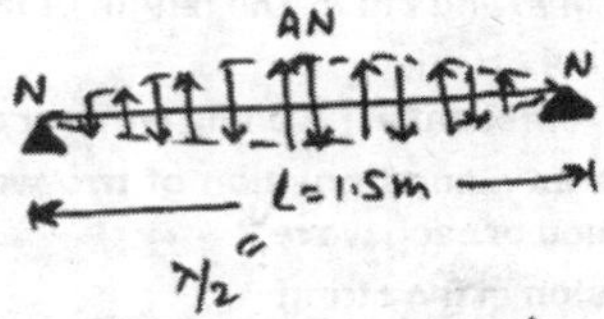

As all particles are between two successive nodes of a S/w, these all will oscillate in same phase & same frequency but different amplitudes.

(ii) In the given S/w, particle amplitude is given as

$$R = 0.06 \sin\left(\frac{2\pi}{3}x\right) = 0.06 \sin\left(\frac{2\pi}{3} \times 0.375\right)$$

($0.375 = 3/8$)

$$= 0.06 \sin\left(\frac{2\pi}{3} \times \frac{3}{8}\right) = 0.06 \sin(\pi/4)$$

$$= 0.042 \text{ m } \textbf{Ans.}$$

Video Solution

- **Given below are some functions of x and t to represent the displacement (transverse or longitudinal) of an elastic wave. State which of these represent (i) a travelling wave, (ii) a stationary wave or (iii) none at all:**

(a) $y = 2\cos(3x)\sin(10t)$

(b) $y = 2\sqrt{x - vt}$

(c) $y = 3\sin(5x - 0.5t) + 4\cos(5x - 0.5t)$

(d) $y = \cos x \sin t + \cos 2x \sin 2t$

Sol^n: (a) std eq^n of a S/W → $y = 2A\cos kx \sin\omega t$. → stationary wave

(b) $y = 2\sqrt{x - vt}$ → y is unbound so this cannot represent any Physical wave

(c) $y = y_1 + y_2$, where $y_1 \to A\sin(kx - \omega t)$ and $y_2 \to A'\cos(kx - \omega t)$] superposition of two travelling wave (resulting wave)

(d) $y = \cos x \sin t + \cos 2x \sin 2t$, where $\cos x \sin t \to$ S/W - 1 and $\cos 2x \sin 2t \to$ S/W - 2] superposition of two stationary wave.

- **A wire stretched between two rigid supports vibrates in its fundamental mode with a frequency of 45 Hz. The mass of the wire is 3.5×10^{-2} kg and its linear mass density is 4.0×10^{-2} kg m^{-1}. What is (a) the speed of a transverse wave on the string, and (b) the tension in the string?**

Sol^n: linear mass density $\mu = \frac{m}{l}$.

$$\Rightarrow \quad l = \frac{m}{\mu} = \frac{3.5 \times 10^{-2}}{4.0 \times 10^{-2}}\ \text{m} = 0.875\ \text{m}.$$

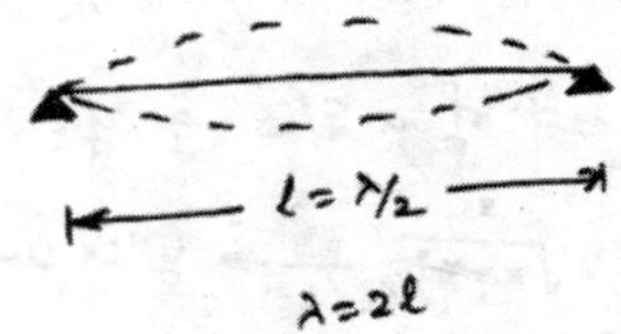

(a) speed of wave on the string

$$v = n\lambda = 45 \times 2 \times 0.875 = 78.75\ \text{m/s}. \quad \text{Ans.}$$

(b) Wave speed on a stretched string is given as

$$v = \sqrt{\frac{T}{\mu}} \Rightarrow T = \mu v^2 = 4.0 \times 10^{-2} \times (78.75)^2$$

$$= 248.06\ \text{N} \quad \text{Ans.}$$

Video Solution

- **A metre-long tube open at one end, with a movable piston at the other end, shows resonance with a fixed frequency source (a tuning fork of frequency 340 Hz) when the tube length is 25.5 cm or 79.3 cm. Estimate the speed of sound in air at the temperature of the experiment. The edge effects may be neglected.**

Sol^n:

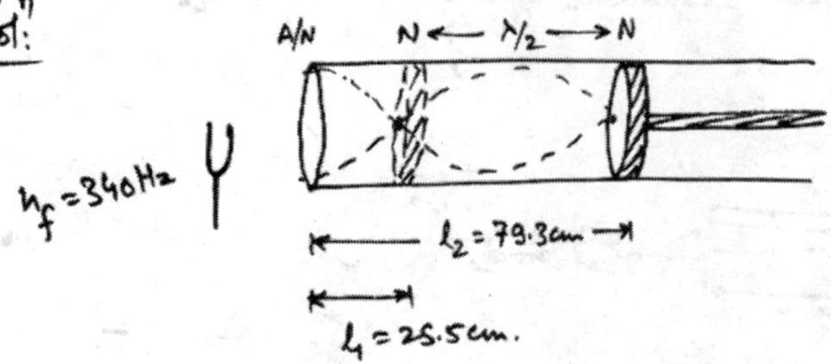

for first & second resonance lengths l_1 & l_2, we use

$$l_2 - l_1 = \lambda/2$$

$$\Rightarrow \lambda = 2(l_2 - l_1)$$

speed of sound $v = n\lambda$

$$= 340 \times [2(0.793 - 0.255)]$$

$$= 365.84 \text{ m/s} \quad \text{Ans.}$$

- A steel rod 100 cm long is clamped at its middle. The fundamental frequency of longitudinal vibrations of the rod are given to be 2.53 kHz. What is the speed of sound in steel?

Sol^n: Displacement curve of longitudinal oscillations of a clamped rod is given as

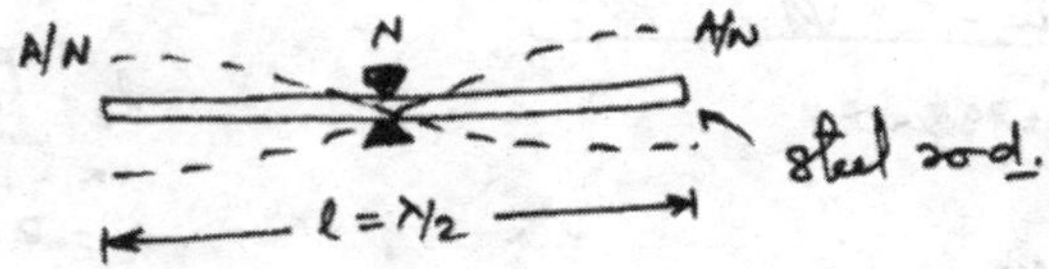

$\Rightarrow \lambda = 2l$

Speed of sound in steel $v = n\lambda$

$= 2.53 \times 10^3 \times 2 \times 1 = 5.06 \times 10^3$ m/s

$= 5.06$ km/s Ans.

Video Solution

- A pipe 20 cm long is closed at one end. Which harmonic mode of the pipe is resonantly excited by a 430 Hz source? Will the same source be in resonance with the pipe if both ends are open? (speed of sound in air is 340 m s^{-1})

Solⁿ for closed pipe fundamental oscillation frequency is given as

$$n_0 = \frac{v}{4l} = \frac{340}{4 \times 0.2} = 425\,Hz$$

Not exactly but approx. the pipe will resonate in its fundamental mode only.

For open pipe, the fundamental frequency is

$$n_0 = \frac{v}{2l} = \frac{340}{2 \times 0.2} = 850\,Hz$$

$\Rightarrow$ No oscillations can be sustained in open pipe. No resonance.

- Two sitar strings *A* and *B* playing the note '*Ga*' are slightly out of tune and produce beats of frequency 6 Hz. The tension in the string *A* is slightly reduced and the beat frequency is found to reduce to 3 Hz. If the original frequency of *A* is 324 Hz, what is the frequency of *B*?

Solⁿ: As we have $n_A = 324\text{ Hz}$

& if freq of fork B is n_B

$\Rightarrow n_B = 324 \pm 6\text{ Hz}$

& $n_B = 330\text{ Hz}$ or 318 Hz

On reducing tension in string A, frequency of A decreases

$\Rightarrow$ after reducing tension in A, $n'_A < 324\text{ Hz}$

Thus n_B cannot be 330 Hz, it must be 318 Hz so that $n'_A - n_B = 3\text{ Hz}$ finally

Ans.

Video Solution

- **Explain why (or how):**

(a) in a sound wave, a displacement node is a pressure antinode and vice versa,

(b) bats can ascertain distances, directions, nature, and sizes of the obstacles without any "eyes",

(c) a violin note and sitar note may have the same frequency, yet we can distinguish between the two notes,

(d) solids can support both longitudinal and transverse waves, but only longitudinal waves can propagate in gases, and

(e) the shape of a pulse gets distorted during propagation in a dispersive medium

Sol^n (a) At a displacement Node Pressure variation with time is maximum & at displacement Antinode the pressure variation is least.
→ Pressure Antinode
Pressure Node.

(b) Bats emit ultrasonic waves in their surr.

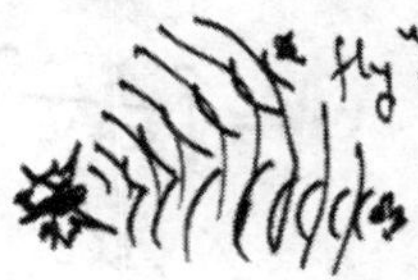

Due to reflected wave dir and intensity it is able to perceive the Nature of obstacle

(c) because of quality of sound. & this includes the type of waveform and no of overtones present in a specific Sound.

(d) Transverse waves require Shear strain in the medium thats why in gases Transverse wave cannot propagate.

(e) A pulse is a superposition of different wavelength waves thats why it gets distorted in medium where speed (solid)

- **A train, standing at the outer signal of a railway station blows a whistle of frequency 400 Hz in still air. (i) What is the frequency of the whistle for a platform observer when the train (a) approaches the platform with a speed of 10 m s^{-1}, (b) recedes from the platform with a speed of 10 m s^{-1}? (ii) What is the speed of sound in each case ? The speed of sound in still air can be taken as 340 m s^{-1}.**

Soln: (i)(a)

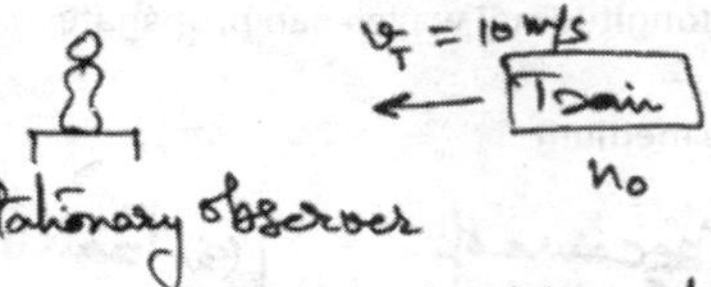

By Doppler's Effect, the apparent frequency heard by observer is

$$n_{ap} = \left[\frac{c}{c - v_T}\right] \cdot n_0$$

$$= \frac{340}{340 - 10} \times 400 = 412.12 \text{ Hz}$$

Ans.

(i)(b)

By Doppler's Effect, we use

$$n_{ap} = \left[\frac{c}{c + v_T}\right] n_0$$

$$= \frac{340}{340 + 10} \times 400 = 388.57 \text{ Hz}$$

Ans.

(ii) Speed of sound remain same in all cases at 340 m/s.

- A train, standing in a station-yard, blows a whistle of frequency 400 Hz in still air. The wind starts blowing in the direction from the yard to the station with a speed of 10 m s^{-1}. What are the frequency, wavelength, and speed of sound for an observer standing on the station's platform? Is the situation exactly identical to the case when the air is still and the observer runs towards the yard at a speed of 10 m s^{-1}? The speed of sound in still air can be taken as 340 m s^{-1}.

Sol.: In first case

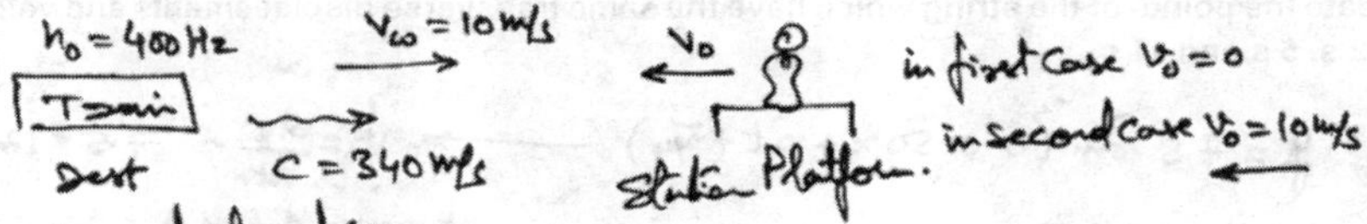

for observer effective sound speed is

$$v_{sound} = C + v_\omega = 340 + 10 = 350 \text{ m/s}$$

As freq never changes so here freq remain same as there is no relative motion between source & observer

$$n_{ap} = n_0 = 400 \text{ Hz}$$

Sound wavelength $\lambda = \frac{v_{sound}}{n_0} = \frac{350}{400} = 0.875$ m. Ans.

In second case, $v_{sound} = 340$ m/s as $v_w = 0$

$$n_{app} = n_0 \cdot \left(\frac{C + v_0}{C}\right) = 400 \times \frac{340+10}{340} = 411.76 \text{ Hz}$$

Sound wavelength $\lambda = \frac{c}{n_0} = \frac{340}{400} = 0.85$ m. Ans

- A travelling harmonic wave on a string is described by

  $y(x, t) = 7.5 \sin(0.0050x + 12t + \pi/4)$

(a) what are the displacement and velocity of oscillation of a point at $x = 1$ cm, and $t = 1$ s? Is this velocity equal to the velocity of wave propagation?

(b) Locate the points of the string which have the same transverse displacements and velocity as the $x = 1$ cm point at $t = 2$ s, 5 s and 11 s.

Sol(a) $y = 7.5 \sin(0.0050x + 12t + \pi/4) \longrightarrow v = \frac{dy}{dt} = 7.5 \times 12 \cos(0.0050x + 12t + \pi/4)$

at $x = 1$ cm & $t = 1$ s

$y = 7.5 \sin(0.0050 \times 1 + 12 \times 1 + \pi/4)$

$= 1.663$ cm Ans.

at $x = 1$ cm & $t = 1$ s

$v = 7.5 \times 12 \cos(0.005 \times 1 + 12 \times 1 + \pi/4)$

$= 87.75$ cm/s Ans

velocity of propagation $v = \frac{\omega}{k} = \frac{12}{0.005} = 2400$ cm/s $= 24$ m/s. (No.)

(b) All particles oscillating in same phase have same displacements all the time

Same phase particles are separated by distance $N\lambda$, $N \in I$. $\Rightarrow$ here $\lambda = \frac{2\pi}{0.005} = 1256$ cm $= 12.56$ m.

Video Solution

- A narrow sound pulse (for example, a short pip by a whistle) is sent across a medium. (a) Does the pulse have a definite (i) frequency, (ii) wavelength, (iii) speed of propagation? (b) If the pulse rate is 1 after every 20 s, (that is the whistle is blown for a split of second after every 20 s), is the frequency of the note produced by the whistle equal to 1/20 or 0.05 Hz ?

Sol[n] (a) In a non dispersive medium the pulse travel at a fixed speed.

But it does not have a definite frequency & wavelength.

(b) Here $1/20$ Hz is the frequency of repetition of pulse not that of the 'note' produced.

- **One end of a long string of linear mass density 8.0×10^{-3} kg m^{-1} is connected to an electrically driven tuning fork of frequency 256 Hz. The other end passes over a pulley and is tied to a pan containing a mass of 90 kg. The pulley end absorbs all the incoming energy so that reflected waves at this end have negligible amplitude. At $t = 0$, the left end (fork end) of the string $x = 0$ has zero transverse displacement ($y = 0$) and is moving along positive y-direction. The amplitude of the wave is 5.0 cm. Write down the transverse displacement y as function of x and t that describes the wave on the string.**

Sol^n:

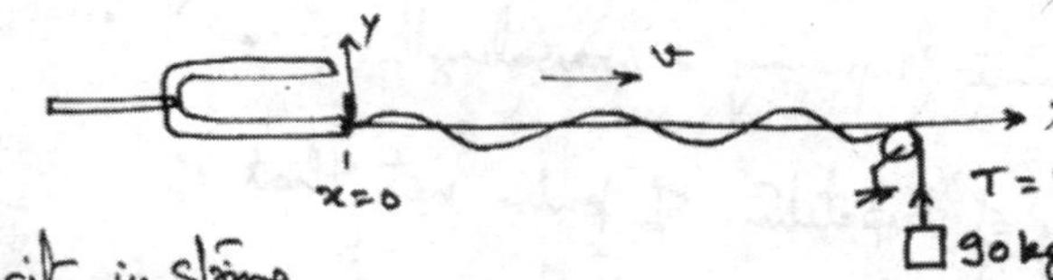

$T = mg = 90 \times 9.8 = 882 N$

wave velocity in string

$$v = \sqrt{\frac{T}{\mu}} = \sqrt{\frac{882}{8.0 \times 10^{-3}}} = 332 \text{ m/s}$$

here $\omega = 2\pi n = 2\pi(256) = 1607.6$ rad/s

$\simeq 1.61 \times 10^3$ rad/s

and $k = \frac{2\pi}{\lambda} = \frac{\omega}{v} = \frac{1.61 \times 10^3}{332} = 4.84 \text{ m}^{-1}$

Equation of traveling simple harmonic wave in string is given as

$$y = A \sin(\omega t - kx) \Rightarrow y = 0.05 \sin(1.61 \times 10^3 t - 4.84x) \text{ Ans.}$$

$\phi = 0$ as $y = 0$ at $x = 0, t = 0$

Video Solution

Web Reference at www.physicsgalaxy.com

Video Sol. : Class 11th NCERT Solutions | **Sec. -** Oscillation & Waves | **Topic -** Waves

Theory Reference : Grade - 11 & 12 | **Sec. -** Oscillation & Waves | **Topic -** Stationary Waves and Beats

- **A SONAR system fixed in a submarine operates at a frequency 40.0 kHz. An enemy submarine moves towards the SONAR with a speed of 360 km h^{-1}. What is the frequency of sound reflected by the submarine ? Take the speed of sound in water to be 1450 m s^{-1}.**

Sol^n: speed of sound in water $c = 1450$ m/s

speed of enemy sub $v_s = 360 \text{ km/hr} \times \frac{5}{18} = 100$ m/s

received freq n_R

freq of reflected sound received back at SONAR.

By Doppler's Effect

$$n_R = n_0\left(\frac{c+v_s}{c}\right)$$

apparent freq received at SONAR is

$$n_{ap} = n_R\left(\frac{c}{c-v_s}\right)$$

$$n_{ap} = n_0\left(\frac{c+v_s}{c}\right)\left(\frac{c}{c-v_s}\right)$$

$$= 40\times10^3\left(\frac{1450+100}{1450-100}\right)$$

$$= 45.93\times10^3 \text{ Hz} = 45.93 \text{ kHz}$$ Ans

Web Reference at www.physicsgalaxy.com

Video Sol. : Class 11th NCERT Solutions | **Sec. -** Oscillation & Waves | **Topic -** Waves

Theory Reference : Grade - 11 & 12 | **Sec. -** Oscillation & Waves | **Topic -** Doppler's Effect

Video Solution

- **Earthquakes generate sound waves inside the earth. Unlike a gas, the earth can experience both transverse (*S*) and longitudinal (*P*) sound waves. Typically the speed of *S* wave is about 4.0 km s^{-1}, and that of *P* wave is 8.0 km s^{-1}. A seismograph records *P* and *S* waves from an earthquake. The first *P* wave arrives 4 min before the first *S* wave. Assuming the waves travel in straight line, at what distance does the earthquake occur ?**

Sol^n: If from the location of seismograph earthquake occured at a distance l

$\Rightarrow$ if time taken by S & P waves are t_s and t_p we use

$$t_s - t_p = 4 \text{ min} = 240 \text{ s} \quad \Rightarrow t_p = 240 \text{ s}$$

we also use $\quad l = v_s t_s = v_p t_p$

$$4 t_s = 8 t_p$$

$$t_s = 2 t_p$$

$$\Rightarrow \quad l = v_p t_p = 8 \times 10^3 \times 240 = 1920 \times 10^3 \text{ m} = \underline{1920 \text{ km}}. \text{ Ans}$$

- **A bat is flitting about in a cave, navigating via ultrasonic beeps. Assume that the sound emission frequency of the bat is 40 kHz. During one fast swoop directly toward a flat wall surface, the bat is moving at 0.03 times the speed of sound in air. What frequency does the bat hear reflected off the wall ?**

Sol^n: velocity of bat is $v_B = 0.03c$

$c \rightarrow$ speed of sound.

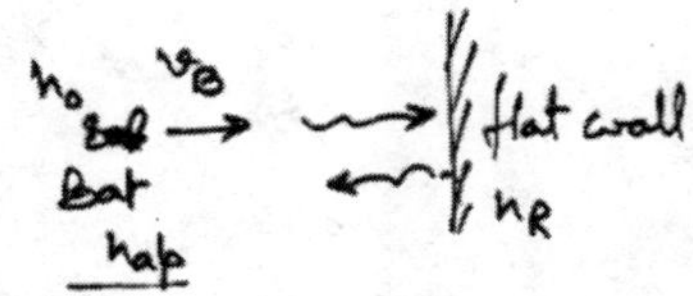

By Doppler's Effect, the frequency received by wall is

$$n_R = n_0\left(\frac{c}{c-v_B}\right)$$

The frequency of sound reflected by wall which is received by bat is given as

$$n_{app} = n_R\left(\frac{c+v_B}{c}\right) = n_0\left(\frac{c+v_B}{c-v_B}\right) = 40\times10^3\left(\frac{1.03}{0.97}\right) = 42.47\ \text{kHz}$$

Ans.